#4649

Australia through the Looking-Glass

Australia through the Looking-Glass

CHILDREN'S FICTION 1830–1980

Brenda Niall

assisted by
Frances O'Neill

MELBOURNE UNIVERSITY PRESS

First published 1984
First paperback edition 1987
Printed in Australia by
Globe Press Pty Ltd, Brunswick, Victoria, for
Melbourne University Press, Carlton, Victoria 3053
U.S.A. and Canada: International Specialized Book Services, Inc.,
P.O. Box 1632, Beaverton, OR 97075
United Kingdom, Europe, Middle East, Africa:
HB Sales
Littleton House, Littleton Road, Ashford, Middlesex,
England TW15 1UQ

National Library of Australia Cataloguing-in-Publication entry

Niall, Brenda, 1930–
    Australia through the looking-glass: children's fiction
    1830–1980.

    Bibliography.
    Includes index.
    ISBN 0 522 84356 5.

    1. Children's stories, Australian — History and criticism.
    2. Australia in literature. I. O'Neill, Frances. II Title.

A823'.009'3294

Contents

Illustrations

Foreword

A full account of one hundred and fifty years of Australian children's novels would demand not only a much larger volume than this, but one quite different in kind. This is not a history—nor even a short history—of fiction written for children in this country. H. M. Saxby's two-volume *History of Australian Children's Literature* (1969-71) is the detailed, inclusive work which allows later writers like myself to choose a particular focus of interest. As its title suggests, *Australia through the Looking-Glass* concentrates on perceptions of Australian life in books for children. It looks at the growth of a national tradition from British beginnings and considers some of the reasons why certain modes of writing flourished in Australia while others barely survived transplantation.

The books discussed here were chosen for their representative qualities. They include some minor works and exclude some well-known ones. Readers who miss a favourite book of their childhood should not assume that it has been slighted or forgotten. In considering the ways in which the material of Australian life invited or challenged literary assimilation, it was sometimes as useful to look at the failures as at the successes; hence, for example, the space—disproportionate in terms of literary merit—given to the school story, or to some early attempts at fantasy.

The decision to exclude books whose interest was primarily pictorial was made easier by the publication in 1982 of Marcie Muir's *History of Australian Childrens Book Illustration*. Such artists as Ida Rentoul Outhwaite, to whom I have only briefly referred, are given their due recognition by Mrs Muir; it is a pleasure to refer readers to her book.

In describing the principles of selection for *Australia through the Looking-Glass* I should like to acknowledge an important debt to Marcie Muir's *Bibliography of Australian Children's Books* (1970-76). Without Mrs Muir's essential scholarly work of identifying Australian authorship and content in some thousands of children's books, my own task would have been immeasurably harder. The wide reading list, from which I chose about 275 representative texts, was in turn based mainly on the Muir bibliography. All serious historical study of Australian children's books must begin with this work; it would be impossible to over-estimate its value. I thank Mrs Muir also for her interest in the present work.

The selection of texts for discussion and the organization of this book was a shared responsibility. I acknowledge with gratitude the skill and judgement of Frances O'Neill and I thank the Australian Research Grants Committee for making possible her appointment as research assistant for this project. I have been fortunate in the interest and encouragement of my family, friends and colleagues. Among those who solved particular problems I am especially grateful to Mr John Arnold, Miss Juliana Bayfield, Miss Lorraine Bullock, Mrs Kay Cole, Mrs Elisabeth Culican, Mr David Elder, Mr Frank Eyre, Dr Geoffrey Hiller, Dr Douglas Muecke, Mr Terence O'Neill, Dr Enid Neal, Miss Brenda Rush, Mrs Isabel Russell and Dr Chris Worth. A number of authors of Australian children's novels responded with patience and generosity to a questionnaire about their work. The members of staff at the Monash University Library have been unfailingly helpful as have those at the Baillieu Library, University of Melbourne; the La Trobe Library, State Library of Victoria; the Mitchell Library, State Library of New South Wales; the State Library of South Australia, the National Library and the Fryer Memorial Library of Australian Literature, University of Queensland. I thank Mrs Sheila Wilson, Mrs Doreen Dougherty and Mrs Berna Tyndall for their care and skill in preparing the typescript. The resources of the English Department at Monash University have been essential to this project and I am grateful to Professor David Bradley and Professor Clive Probyn for making them available.

Brenda Niall

May 1984

Acknowledgements

For permission to reproduce illustrations and to quote from unpublished material I am indebted to the following:

Angus & Robertson, Sydney, for the illustration by G. W. Lambert from Louise Mack's *Girls Together*, on p. 173; for the illustration by Norman Lindsay from *The Magic Pudding*, on p. 204; for the illustration by May Gibbs from *Snugglepot and Cuddlepie*, on p. 199; for the illustrations by Margaret Horder from Joan Phipson's *The Family Conspiracy*, on p. 226; from Joan Phipson's *Threat to the Barkers*, on p. 229; and from Patricia Wrightson's *The Rocks of Honey*, on p. 308; and for Jennifer Tuckwell's illustration from Ivan Southall's *To the Wild Sky*, on p. 241; Angus & Robertson, the estate of the late James Devaney and the Mitchell Library, State Library of New South Wales, for correspondence between Devaney and Angus & Robertson.

The Bodley Head, London, for the illustration by Rex Backhaus-Smith from K. Langloh Parker's *Australian Legendary Tales*, on p. 214;

Collins, London, for the jacket design by Jillian Willett from Lilith Norman's *Climb a Lonely Hill*, on p. 246;

André Deutsch, London, for the illustration by Robert Hales from Reginald Ottley's *Rain Comes to Yamboorah*, on p. 238;

Mrs Margaret Harriss (Margaret Paice) for the illustration from *Run to the Mountains*, on p. 287;

Hutchinson Books, London, for the illustration by Jean Elder from Rosalind Miller's *The Adventures of Margery Pym*, on p. 186, the illustration by Margaret Horder from Patricia Wrightson's '*I Own the Racecourse!*', on p. 278, and the illustration by Noela Young from Patricia Wrightson's *An Older Kind of Magic*, on p. 310;

Oxford University Press for the cover by Cyrus Cuneo from Joseph Bowes's *Comrades*, on p. 140; for the illustrations by Geraldine Spence from Nan Chauncy's *Devils' Hill*, on p. 220, and from Eleanor Spence's *The Green Laurel*, on p. 255; for the illustration by Nikki Jones from Margaret Balderson's *A Dog Called George*, on p. 260; for the illustration by William Papas from H. F. Brinsmead's *Beat of the City*, on p. 276;

for the illustration by Doreen Roberts from Eleanor Spence's *Jamberoo Road*, on p. 297;

Mrs Genevieve Rees (Genevieve Melrose) for the illustration from Mavis Thorpe Clark's *The Min-Min*, on p. 265;

Ward Lock, London, for the illustrations by A. J. Johnson from Ethel Turner's *Seven Little Australians*, on p. 85, from *The Family at Misrule*, on p. 83, and from Ella Chaffey's *The Youngsters of Murray Home*, on p. 100; for the illustrations by J. Macfarlane from Lilian Turner's *The Perry Girls*, on p. 105; from Ethel Turner's *Mother's Little Girl*, on p. 90; from Mary Grant Bruce's *Captain Jim*, on p. 122, *Glen Eyre*, on p. 127, and *Dick*, on p. 156; and Lillian Pyke's *A Prince at School*, on p. 161; for the illustration by Victor Prout from Vera Dwyer's *With Beating Wings*, on p. 109; for the illustration by J. F. Campbell from Mary Grant Bruce's *Captain Jim* (1952 edition), on p. 123; for the illustration by J. Dewar Mills from Lillian Pyke's *Sheila the Prefect*, on p. 178; and for extracts from Ward Lock correspondence.

Mrs Edwina Williams (Edwina Bell) for the illustration from Valerie Thompson's *Rough Road South*, on p. 300.

Some of the material in Chapters One and Two was published in a different form in an article in *This Australia* (vol. 2, no. 1, Summer 1982). I thank Greenhouse Publications and Sally Milner for permission to republish this material and for lending some of the art work prepared for the magazine article.

Introduction

'I wonder if I shall fall right *through* the earth! How funny it'll seem to come out among the people that walk with their heads downwards! The antipathies, I think—'(She was rather glad there *was* no one listening, this time, as it didn't sound at all the right word)—'but I shall have to ask them what the name of the country is, you know. Please Ma'am, is this New Zealand? Or Australia? ... And what an ignorant little girl she'll think me for asking! No, it'll never do to ask: perhaps I shall see it written up somewhere.'

Alice in Wonderland

This study of Australian children's fiction begins with versions of Antipodean life scarcely less bizarre than Alice's fantasy of a land upside down at the bottom of the world where people walk as though on the ceiling. Even there, Alice expects signposts and the exchange of civilities. The expectation of strangeness and the unconscious assumption of likenesses between Old World and New World were combined in a body of fiction which today, understandably, is almost forgotten. The child's map of Australia, drawn by armchair travellers from the 1830s onwards, is sometimes quaint and colourful, but so misleadingly ill-drawn as to seem hardly worth the trouble of unrolling it. Only a few reflections of early Australian life in children's books are known or valued today; these came from the settlers and travellers who wrote from their own experience. Australian children's fiction, it may be argued, does not properly begin until the 1890s, when local writers displaced the hastily-scribbling travellers and the stay-at-home romancers.

In this study the early colonial novels have their place not as curiosities, but as antecedents. I am as much concerned with Australia in children's books as with Australian children's books; the one preceded and influenced the other. The colonial tales may have little literary merit, but they have the intrinsic interest of showing how the new land was perceived by British writers, and what lessons it offered, in a consciously didactic age, for schoolroom and nursery reading. For the greater part of the nineteenth century the literary perspective from which Australian scenes were created was predominantly that of the outsider. Even the

1

insiders' narratives–those written from direct and detailed colonial experience–were presented mainly for outsiders: the children ten thousand miles away who were their first and most substantial readership. So long as London was the principal place of publication, as it was for much of the twentieth century and all of the nineteenth century, the British child had to be taken into account. As the colonial population grew, the Australian juvenile readership became more important, but it did not necessarily demand, or get, stories of Australian life. A child in Sydney or Melbourne might well prefer *Tom Brown's Schooldays* (1857) to an 1850s tale of the goldfields. *Cole's Funny Picture Book* (1876), a major event in colonial publishing history, would be central to any study of Australian children's reading. It is outside the scope of this survey, which is confined to novels written for a juvenile audience, with Australian settings and characters. The view from Britain, therefore, is the appropriate starting point for a study of the transition of British literary modes and characters into an Australian tradition of children's literature.

The way others see us is part of our perception of ourselves. Thus the stereotypes of colonial romances, for adults as well as for children, helped to shape an Australian sense of self. Young Anzacs of life and legend may be found in early colonial novels as the lean sun-bronzed, adaptable bushmen who made the ideal settlers. The nature of the new land demanded self-reliance, physical strength and energy from its pioneers; and even long after Australia became a nation of city dwellers, the image of the outback hero remained, confirmed in fiction and celebrated in nostalgic films to the present day. The hero's antithesis, the over-civilized 'new chum' who is either toughened or defeated by his Australian experience, appears in many colonial novels: British authors created him, and Australian authors drew him again and again before turning him into that degenerate native product, 'the cousin from Sydney'.

Until the 1890s, outback settings and characters predominated in juvenile fiction. British and Australian writers used the distinctively new material of colonial life within the flourishing nineteenth century genre of the adventure story. It was natural that they should do so. Australian life offered blacks, bushrangers and gold-seekers to divert the British boy. Yet the colonial adventure stories vary more in treatment than has been recognized by critics who see only an Antipodean Wild West. I have distinguished four main ways of approach. The settlers' novels, described in Chapter 1, are characterized by moral earnestness and a commitment to emigration. They balance the need for an exciting story against their *raison d'être*: to help to make more room in an overcrowded Britain. To dwell on the dangers of the new country might make lively reading, but it was more important for the writers of the settlers' novels to have British boys saving their passage money. By contrast, the adventure story could make the most of colonial perils, with any number of unpleasant tests for a young hero. A shipwreck on the way out might well make him an orphan; and if a family voyage happened to be uneventful, there were many ways of losing parents in the colonies without resorting to natural causes. Although the native animals were more remarkable for their odd shapes and habits than for their menace, there were plenty of satisfactory poisonous snakes. Floods and bushfires and hostile Aborigines, convicts, bushrangers, and rascals at the goldfields offered plenty of choice for an adventure story. Many writers used the whole package. A third group of novels is distinguished by its religious impulse. The power of prayer and the need to read the Bible could be shown most dramatically in a strange land, away from church, clergy and habits of family piety. In many of the productions of the Religious Tract Society, Australia is a mission field, and the happy ending comes, not with the finding of a nugget, but with the building of a church or chapel in the wilderness, and the conversion of at least one Aborigine.

The last and smallest group of nineteenth century stories is the semi-documentary, in which authentic settlers' or travellers' experiences are presented in anecdotal form, with a thin thread of fiction to unite them. Although the boundaries between these four groups are not clearly defined, and certain events and characters may find their way into any one of them, the tone of the ending usually shows the author's primary interest. Satisfaction in having made a new start in life is the settlers' ending, and it almost always takes place in Australia. Adventurers and pilgrims are free to go home to England if they wish, having found fortune or salvation. The semi-documentary or diary seldom has the sense of an ending; it just stops.

The common element in these pioneering novels is their emphasis on the qualities which most sharply differentiate Australian from British life. The desire to be distinctively Australian remained. But during the 1890s, in the domestic novels of Ethel Turner and her successors, images of city and suburban life emerged. There was surprise as well as pleasure in the response of Australian children to finding familiar places and circumstances in fictional form; and many adults, looking back, have recorded the special importance of Ethel Turner's *Seven Little Australians* (1894) among the books of their childhood.

It should be emphasized here that the move in the 1890s from the epic to the domestic style, with the discovery of everyday Australia by local writers, did·not mean a break with British publishing. Angus and Robertson of Sydney, the first major Australian publishing house, was founded in 1888. Its list of juvenile fiction includes many of the best and most important titles, from Louise Mack's *Teens* (1897), to Norman Lindsay's *The Magic Pudding* (1918), the work of May Gibbs, and more recently that of Ivan Southall. But Ward Lock of London published *Seven Little Australians* and most of the later Turner novels; the firm's representative in Melbourne, William Steele, promoted Ethel Turner as 'the Louisa Alcott of Australia', and with equal energy and enthusiasm fostered Mary Grant Bruce's Billabong series, which began in 1910. Steele's role in establishing Ward Lock's large, successful Australian juvenile list is described in Part Two of this book. The persistence as well as the value of the British connection may be seen in a much later period. The renaissance in Australian children's books after World War II deserves a volume to itself, and I have only briefly discussed its main directions in Part Three. Any history of this period will undoubtedly stress the importance of Frank Eyre, the manager of Oxford University Press's Australian branch from 1950 to 1975. Eyre, the author of *Twentieth-Century Children's Books, 1900-1950* (1952),[1] had a double influence. During the 1950s and 1960s he built up the Oxford list with the work of Nan Chauncy, H. F. Brinsmead, Eleanor Spence and others. To find new and talented Australian writers was only one part of Eyre's achievement. In the early post-war years, when Australian confidence in the local product needed strengthening, the combination of Eyre's enthusiasm and prestige and the Oxford imprint was invaluable. The advantages of this British connection far outweighed the disadvantages of having most of the Oxford Australian children's books, as late as the 1970s, still printed and published in England. It must have been inconvenient for Oxford's Melbourne branch that whenever a Chauncy, Brinsmead or Spence novel won the Australian Children's Book of the Year award a telegram had to go to London, doubling the print run and ordering an immediate shipment to fulfil Australian demands. One anomaly in a time of transition for Oxford authors in Australia was that the Australian sales of their novels counted as 'overseas', and drew only half the royalty paid on their British sales.[2] That arrangement was changed in 1979, but it is worth recording as an example of the complex Anglo-Australian publishing relationship. The British market remained important. Such post-war developments as the founding of the Australian Children's

Book Council, the Children's Book of the Year awards, and the growth of school and municipal children's libraries in the years of 'baby-boom' and large-scale immigration, did not mean that Australian publishers could ignore overseas markets. United States sales have become an essential part of the success of a number of contemporary writers, including Ivan Southall and Joan Phipson.

Today there is little indication that Australian children's writers feel any external pressure to use local settings or to stress distinctively national qualities in their characters. The determination to find the exotic in Australian life has never been stronger than it was in the nineteenth century; no one used local colour more lavishly than the untravelled author of *The Kangaroo Hunters* (1859), an English lady with an encyclopaedia. As the settlers became more at home in their country they could take it for granted, as they do today. And yet there is a sense in which the landscape, vast, empty, indifferent, still dominates contemporary fiction. Nineteenth century fictional children were left to themselves or lost in the Australian bush. Their modern counterparts, in the work of such writers as Southall or Phipson, are lost too; for these authors the landscape is a place of psychological as well as physical ordeal. An uneasy relationship with the land has, I believe, made the writing of fantasy especially difficult. Patricia Wrightson's novels show its problems and possibilities, with *The Nargun and the Stars* (1973) a turning-point in Australian children's literature for its evocation of authentic bush magic. The past, too, eludes most Australian writers, and for the same reason: the sense that the land has a history from which they are excluded. Ruth Park's *Playing Beatie Bow* (1980), the first historical novel of real distinction, unites past and present within the context of European settlement. The Aboriginal past, which a number of writers for children have attempted to reach, is still elusive. To say that the attempt should not be made by white Australians would be to deny imaginative possibilities and to recommend a literary separatism which, logically extended, would limit everyone to writing autobiographies. Nevertheless, the first success will probably come from within the tradition.

The development of children's literature is a small part of Australia's cultural history, but because of the vigilance with which children's books are monitored, they may reflect their society's values with special clarity. The French social historian, Paul Hazard, said in a much-quoted phrase that pre-war England 'could be reconstructed from its children's books'.[3] A confident, pragmatic acceptance of things as they are, a sense of imperial mission, a belief in England's absolute superiority to other

nations, a lack of logic and a delight in nonsense were the qualities
Hazard discerned from his 1930s perspective. In looking at a large number of Australian children's books, with a time-span of a century and
a half, I kept Hazard's claim in mind. What could be deduced about
Australian society from the children's books of this period? The following chapters will give their evidence, but a few general comments can
be made here. Predictably, in a new country, the sense of nationhood
is asserted rather than assumed. The relationship with the land is a constant preoccupation, and a troubling one. Although most Australians
live in coastal cities, they cannot, it seems, forget the vast inner spaces
of the continent. Our writers create contrasting images of the outback;
and whether it is paradise or purgatory, dream or nightmare, it is still
'the real Australia'. The nineteenth century view from Britain of Australia as the land of prosperity and material success was well-founded.
One national dream, now gone, may be found in comic form in Norman Lindsay's *The Magic Pudding*: a vision of endless ease and pleasure
with all needs supplied by the everlasting Puddin'. Such confidence is
hard to find in contemporary writing, which by its nostalgic backward
glances at an older pastoral Australia, or its dispirited view of the new
society, reveals the fear that the luck of the Lucky Country may not
last much longer.

PART ONE
1830–1890

1

The Young Settlers

One of the first to see the value of Australia as a setting for a children's story was the author of *Alfred Dudley or The Australian Settlers* (1830). This novel, published anonymously, is attributed to Mrs Sarah Porter, the sister of the economist David Ricardo. Written 'for the amusement of youthful readers', the narrative combines entertainment with the clearly defined purpose of encouraging emigration. Information about the colony fills out the account of the fortunes of a young hero whose moral and material success is never in doubt. The author assures her readers' parents that they may rely on the accuracy of 'whatever is found in these pages relating to the natural history of Australia and the manners and characters of its native inhabitants'. As authority she cites the 'kind communication' of Robert Dawson, author of *The Present State of Australia*.[1] The novel presents the colony as a land of opportunity and defines the qualities of the model settler in its central character.

The opening pages of *Alfred Dudley* enact the stock situation, repeated with slight variations in novels of Australia for most of the nineteenth century: the sudden loss of fortune which makes emigration a necessity. This is the Micawber theme; it embodies the belief that those who have failed financially in England will prosper in Australia. The Dudley family must leave their 'elegant and commodious mansion', because Mr Dudley, too trusting, has been swindled by his business partner. After a short stay in France, for cheap living, Mr Dudley decides to migrate to Australia, having been given 'a brilliant account' of the colony. Alfred is to accompany him, and the females of the family to wait behind until father and son have established themselves. Temptation comes with a bribe from a rich uncle who threatens to withdraw the large fortune reserved for Alfred, because to have an heir settled in Botany Bay would disgrace him. Without hesitating, Alfred decides to go with his father. It is true, he admits, that Botany Bay has unpleasant associations. But 'I can be as virtuous and free in Australia as if it were not contaminated by vice and misery'. As for the inheritance, it cannot deflect him from his duty.

The voyage out is uneventful. Alfred and his father make friends with a family of their own social class, and are reassured that Australia will not mean isolation from genteel companionship. In Sydney they are a little dismayed. Although they find some 'respectable society', Alfred is 'occasionally shocked at the sight of a native in a state of intoxication'. He also sees, 'with the most painful feelings', convicts working in chains. But given the choice of employing convicts or Aborigines the Dudleys unhesitatingly choose the latter. Unlike the heroes of later settlers' novels, they are on good terms with the Aborigines almost from the first. The mutual good will is partly due to one of Alfred's characteristic acts of kindness. In a scene which prefigures one from *Little Lord Fauntleroy* (1886) he comes to the aid of an Aboriginal woman who is limping painfully and carrying a crying child. Alfred dismounts, lifts mother and child on to his horse, and walks cheerfully beside them all the way to their camp. If Alfred is apparently forgetful of race and class, the author is not: the incident works to show that a true gentleman extends his chivalry to all.

Alfred's action is rewarded; he acquires an Aboriginal servant, Mickie, who rescues him when he is lost in the bush, and thereafter is devoted to the interests of the Dudleys. The contrast with convict labour is underlined. The Dudleys praise the Aborigines for 'the inoffensive manners and kind-hearted dispositions [which] attract us greatly in preference to the convicts with whom otherwise we should be obliged to be surrounded'. When an ignorant white man speaks of Mickie as 'vermin', Alfred rebukes him, and reflects 'how much superior in the scale of being was the kind-hearted Mickie to [that] brutal wretch . . .'. The 'brutal wretch' is a convict; and the incident suggests the establishment of a social structure rather like that of the Dudleys' English village. The blacks are the equivalents of the deserving poor and the convicts are the undeserving, for whom society has no place.

As the Dudleys prosper in Australia, they create for themselves an environment as like as possible to that of England. The 'mansion' they build is named Dudley Park after the lost family seat; and its gardens are planned to make Mrs Dudley and the girls feel at home. Letters to England describe Australian flowers as 'more showy and various' than English ones but less sweetly scented, just as the birds are beautiful and bright, but not so musical. There is nothing here to offend an English audience. The effect is to make readers conscious that Australia has much to offer and that its birds and flowers may be enjoyed once it is conceded that they lack the true English tone. By the time the family is reunited Alfred has proved his worth as a settler. Cheerful, buoyant and adaptable, he not only learns to cook and sew and mend the holes in his stockings, but finds time to keep up his Latin and Greek. Mr Dudley's lament that his brilliant promising son is caught in 'colonial drudgery' gives Alfred the chance to assert the optimistic fervour of the young settler. The novel gives the weight of the argument to Alfred. It also endorses his decision to stay in Australia when the rich uncle, relenting, leaves his vast wealth to the 'Botany Bay nephew' after all. But when Alfred is free to go back to England, he looks at what has been built up in Australia and sees it as 'a little Paradise' which he will not relinquish. 'Here will I distribute my undesired wealth', he announces; '. . . my power of doing good may be more certain than in an old and over-populated country'.

The final chapter of *Alfred Dudley* is an ingenious solution to the problem of choice between the Old and the New World. The 'little paradise' in Australia is extended to take in the best of English village life. Alfred makes a voyage home and returns with a Noah's Ark of villagers, chosen from the 'respectable poor' of the Dudleys' old estate. All except the 'idle and vicious' are invited to the Dudley Park of New South Wales, where Alfred gives out small tracts of land and enough money for each family to make a start. The civilizing process is almost complete when Mrs Dudley and the girls arrive to take possession of their New World garden. Finally, Alfred imports the old vicar from their village, builds a church for him, and establishes beside it a school 'in which the white and black children [are] without any distinction, admitted'.

The author of *Alfred Dudley* shows little detailed knowledge of Australian life. There is not much close observation of landscape, nor are Alfred and his father shown at work, except in the most general way. The speech of Mickie and the other Aborigines is Old Plantation style, borrowed from writings about the American South: Alfred is Mickie's 'Massa'.

Alfred Dudley, then, is no documentary. As a guide to the young emigrant it would offer no practical instructions, except the general ones of the need for hard work, thrift, energy and adaptability. To avoid the society of convicts and to be kind to the Aborigines are moral imperatives. It is clear that Australia can be colonized successfully, and that the best of English life can be reproduced there. The design is completed when everyone moves into his proper place, with Alfred as the Young Squire, presiding over his Australian 'village', complete with vicar, church, school, and deserving poor. The main differences between this world and the English life Alfred rejects are that the former tenants own their own land, and their children learn to read and write and pray, side by side with the children of the Aborigines.

Frank Layton: an Australian Tale (1865) has almost the same structure and moral tone as *Alfred Dudley*. The same need—money—takes the young hero to Australia in both novels, where the same virtues of industry and piety ensure his success. There is a difference in class. Frank Layton is the son of a gentleman farmer: Alfred Dudley belongs to the squirearchy. Yet if the two heroes offer more or less the same model to their readers, the colonial experience of the later novel is better documented and morally more complex. Its author, George Sargent, had many more settlers' and travellers' tales of Australia on which to base his novel. For him the question of the Aborigines could not be so easily solved as for the author of *Alfred Dudley*. And, writing in the 1860s, he had the new topic of gold to work into his fiction.

Frank Layton, published by the Religious Tract Society, raises several problems of conscience. In dealing with the Aboriginal question it draws on a pamphlet, also published by the Religious Tract Society, which had described European settlement in Australia as 'almost an unmitigated evil to the black population'.[2] This pamphlet challenged the comfortable belief that white settlers had merely displaced the Aborigines, causing them to retreat some distance into the interior. Pointing out that each tribe had its own hunting ground, the writer described the disruption of social patterns:

> As the country became occupied with the flocks and herds of the settlers, the kangaroos, emus and other wild animals fled away or were destroyed; and thus deprived of one principal means of subsistence the natives have been largely thinned by famine, hardship and misery. But the diseases communicated by contact with Europeans, and the intemperance learned from them, have formed a far more influential cause of decay.

In *Frank Layton*, this view of the destructive effect of white settle-

The discovery of the lost traveller
From *Frank Layton*

ment is put forward by the heroine, Mercy Matson, who becomes Frank's wife. She does not wish to live elsewhere, she says, but her pleasure in the beauty of the new country can never be complete, because of her sense of the injustice done to its people. Against Mercy's belief, others argue that in an overcrowded world the vast spaces of Australia cannot be left to a few hundred thousand Aborigines. The debate is not resolved, but the best hope offered is the example of one settler who employs black workers 'to the exclusion of men of his own complexion', pays them well, and offers them, with their wives and children, a Christian education.

Apart from Mercy's debate with the other settlers (interrupted by a bushfire), the race question in *Frank Layton* is developed through an Aboriginal stockman, Dick Brown, and Abraham, an American Negro prospector. The latter is one of the most admirable men on the goldfields, and Dick Brown—unlike most Aborigines in fiction of this period—is intelligent and brave. He also speaks English correctly: Sargent resists working up comic effects through pidgin.

The children who read *Frank Layton* would have been offered some lessons in race relations. They would also have been invited to shudder at the squalor and depravity of the goldfields. Sargent gives a lurid account of Melbourne, 'a Babel or a Bedlam' as he describes it, in the days of gold-fever:

In dens of nine feet square, in the stifling heat of an Australian summer–half devoured by fleas of the most ferocious character, crawled over by myriads of disgusting cockroaches, blinded by clouds of mosquitoes, and menaced by bold and angry rats–men, women and children sweltered together by the dozen . . .

Such conditions are shown as the direct result of greed: the wish to be rich without working for it. The gold-seekers are all, finally, disillusioned. A few come away with profits, but the author makes them suffer for it. The best thing to do, as the novel clearly shows, is to ignore the goldfields as Frank Layton does and get on with the work of cultivating the land.

When Frank takes his first job as a stockman he sets a good example by washing all the dirty blankets in the men's hut, and by planting vegetables outside it. As a fictional hero he is dull: brave enough when challenges come, but too prudent for most readers. His friend Percy Effingham seems to have been designed to show up Frank's solid worth. Percy tries the goldfields, gets into difficulties, and learns by experience the evils of drink and gambling. By the end of the novel he is a reformed character, but he is still not pioneer material. He sails for England. Percy Effingham for the Old World, and Frank Layton and his wife Mercy for the New World–the author's choice of names shows his priorities. What the new country needs is Frank's honesty and hard work, with Mercy's spiritual vision. It is no place for a Percy Effingham. Like the hero and heroine in this novel, the villains, Chauker (Choker?) and McWeevil, are labelled rather than characterized. The author's strength is in the descriptions of flood and bushfire, shanty-town and goldfields. Sargent probably did not visit Australia but he used his sources well to give a persuasive and detailed visual impression of the time and place of his novel.

Frank Layton ends, like *Alfred Dudley*, with an account of the building of a church in the bush, and the hero's acknowledgement of the providence that led him to Australia. An author's postscript adds a warning that the colony, especially its large towns, offers temptation as well as opportunity, and that only the morally and physically fit should think of emigrating. Similar values and preoccupations, as well as the stock situations of colonial life used in *Frank Layton*, appear also in the work of Sargent's contemporary, W. H. G. Kingston. *The Gilpins and Their Fortunes*, published in 1865–the same year as *Frank Layton*–makes a useful comparison. Sargent is more concerned with ideas; Kingston tells a better story. Frank Layton, as hero, is left behind while the author denounces gold-fever or examines attitudes towards the Aborigines. The Gilpin boys are cardboard cut-outs, certainly, but Kingston gives some liveliness to their colonial adventures. The plot fits the Gilpins, more or less, while in *Frank Layton* the hero is too often passive, irrelevant or apparently forgotten. The social historian will find Sargent's the more interesting work, but English children in 1865 would have voted for *The Gilpins*, and the professionalism of its author.

For W. H. G. Kingston, Australia was only one of the many distant lands to which he despatched his young British hero. There is no evidence that he ever visited the country himself: indeed he would scarcely have had time. Between 1851 and 1884 he wrote over one hundred adventure stories. He edited the *Colonial Magazine* from 1849 to 1852, and was the honorary secretary of the Colonization Society. His manual for the young emigrant was distributed by the Society for the Propagation of Christian Knowledge during the 1850s; and his boys' books translated the manual's precepts into fictional form.

'You were not born into this world for the purpose of amusing yourselves', the readers of *Kingston's Magazine for Boys* were told.[3] Nevertheless, Kingston's novels combined moral instruction with entertainment. One wonders whether his heroes would have been allowed to read their own stories; probably not. Except on Sundays, when they read the Bible, they never stop working. Seven Kingston novels of Australian settlement, published between 1865 and 1884, have in common the conviction that 'the lot of all people, high and low, rich and poor, is to labour'. Some of his heroes know this from the first page: all of them learn it. Most were written for boys, but girls too could profit from them.

Kingston's *Milicent Courtenay's Diary* (1873) is about the making of a colonial girl. It is unusual among his novels in taking a feminine viewpoint and looking at the domestic aspects of emigration. Sixteen-year-old Milicent, the narrator, is about to follow her sister Helen into the life of a young lady of fashion in London when the family fortunes collapse. Major Courtenay inexplicably fails to return from a voyage to India, Mrs Courtenay dies, and the two girls, with a younger brother and sister to support, must become governesses or go to Australia where their rich friends, the Radlands, offer all four a home. Albert, a wastrel older brother, has followed his father's example and disappeared. The going is not as rough as in most Kingston novels. Although the voyage out has its hazards, Milicent's cabin is 'fresh and neat and pretty', with pink chintz curtains. Sydney is bypassed after a ladylike shudder at its 'tatooed [sic] New Zealanders, and wild-looking stock-men', and the Radlands' station shows the Courtenay girls how civilization may be maintained in the bush. Milicent at first finds the landscape gloomy, but soon learns to 'gaze with delight' at its sunlit plains and to enjoy the bright evenings when, she says, 'we can frequently read a small print by the light of the moon'. The Courtenays also discover that pioneer skills may be combined with drawing-room accomplishments. The Radland girls, 'capital horse-women', who go out mustering the cattle with their father are 'perfectly feminine . . . a little freckled [but] not sunburnt'. They read, sing and sketch, and look forward to having a piano sent to the station; but they can also cook, milk cows, and make butter. With this example, Milly and Helen Courtenay quickly adapt themselves to the new life. Since the Radlands are so prosperous, there are few occasions for pioneer endurance; the station has already been transformed from a wilderness into 'a smiling paradise'.

What remains to be done is seen as women's work rather than men's: to keep up Christian morals and genteel manners in the new land. Sundays at the station are strictly observed, with Mr Radland reading prayers for his employees and neighbours. Milicent notes that colonial appearances are an unreliable guide to class differences: among those who come to the Sunday services are

> several men, who, although their beards were long and bushy, and they wore shooting coats and cabbage hats . . . by the tone of their voices and by their manners, were gentlemen. Others, both men and women, were of the lower order. Though . . . even better dressed, they kept aloof from the rest.

However, the Radlands speak to everyone 'in a friendly way'. One of the concerns of such families as the Radlands is to encourage temperance societies throughout the colony, so that the bullock drivers will not spend all their wages on drink in Sydney. Milicent and Rose Radland find their special mission among black children on the station. They open a little school, in which their first success is to get one 'bright little fellow' to spell 'sheep'. Milicent describes the children as 'engaging, active, intelligent little creatures' and is disappointed that they do not stay long enough to master reading and writing. She thinks the blacks 'a much finer race of people than they are often represented to be' and reports some success in getting them to adopt the manners and customs of white people. A few of the black workmen 'dress in shirts and trousers, putting on hats and jackets on Sundays as a mark of respect to the day, although they may very imperfectly comprehend even the simplest truths of Christianity'.

It is clear from this novel that, like *Alfred Dudley*'s author, Kingston believes the Aborigines can be assimilated into a station class structure very like that of an English village. They have 'immortal souls' and so are entitled to pastoral care, which, in the absence of church and clergy, will come from the gentry. It is consistent with the moral tone of this novel that Milicent should disapprove of the goldfields. Her comments on the diggings stress the physical and moral dangers, with drunkenness, sickness and beggary as the most likely fate of the gold-seekers. But the novel is not primarily one of religious conversion. The nearest Kingston comes to a redemption theme is in the ordeals of the missing Courtenay men—both conveniently guided to Australia. Major Courtenay turns up as a mysterious, melancholy hutkeeper who, still incognito, teachers his daughters to make damper, and impresses them with the evidence of culture (including a flute) in his bush hut. His identity is revealed after he has rescued his own son, Ranald, lost in the bush. The other missing Courtenay, Albert, saves Milicent and Rose from a fire. Albert and his father, having endured physical hardships and shown penitence, have earned their reinstatement in the family; and Albert is even rewarded with marriage to Rose Radland. Milicent marries Rose's brother and they all settle down in New South Wales.

Milicent Courtenay's Diary presents an optimistic picture of life in the colony; it seems calculated to attract the young migrant with its promise of sure rewards for hard work. Its advantages are summed up by one new arrival: 'From all I have seen and heard of the country, I like it amazingly, and if it has its drawbacks, the three girls at all events are sure to get husbands, and the boys to find employment, neither of which objects are over easy of attainment in England'. The novel's ending bears this out, with husbands and jobs all round. It is a great deal better than staying in England to be governesses.

By choosing a female narrator in *Milicent Courtenay's Diary*, Kingston limited the action to whatever was appropriate for his heroine. His other novels of Australian life are for and about boys. They do, however, follow the same basic pattern in which a needy English family combines faith and good works to find a modest fortune in Australia. The Kingston hero prospers, but not too easily; he makes money, but not too much. Although he usually comes from an upper middle-class family, he has no hesitation in working side by side with men who might have been his father's tenants; indeed the lower-class characters often protect and instruct him in his new life. Kingston's commitment to the work ethic did not quite transcend his sense of class, but it did help to form a hero who would readily adapt himself to colonial society.

The Kingston novels are not tales of Empire in the tradition later established by G. A. Henty. Their impulse comes more from the mid-

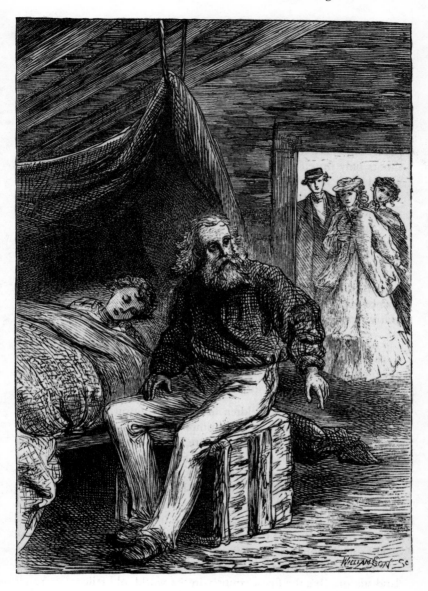

Finding a father
Illustration by Williamson from *Milicent Courtenay's Diary*

nineteenth century concern to solve Britain's problems of over-population than from dreams of imperial glory. They are common-sense, practical narratives, in which the hero does not invite danger for its own sake. It is not surprising that while Kingston took Australia as the setting for seven novels, Henty, almost as prolific, used it only once. The Henty hero flourishes in warfare, willing to die for the Brit-ish flag, or to kill for it. Africa or India gave more scope for that sort of thing than Australia, where the Aborigines were too few and too poorly organized to make a respectable literary war. The Kingston hero shoots only in self-defence. In his encounters with the Aborigines he would much rather produce the Bible than the rifle.

All but one of the Kingston novels move from England to Australia so that the reader may identify with the newcomers' discovery of the new country. The exception is *The Young Berringtons* (1880), which seems better calculated to appeal to Australian than to English readers, since its 'cornstalk' characters so consistently triumph over the 'new chums'. This novel opens with the Queensland members of the Ber-rington family waiting for their English cousins and assessing the chances that they will be 'fine gentlemen' and 'proper' young ladies. Harry Berrington predicts:

> ... I don't think I shall be able to help laughing when I see the exquisite Mr Hector and his brother Reginald attempting to round up cattle, riding after stray horses, or milking cows ... but we shall have rare fun with the girls if they have got any life in them.

Since there are eight children in each Berrington family, Kingston could have avoided a too easy triumph for the home side. But apart from Reginald who, though exquisite, is also 'game', the newcomers are unimpressive. The girls do *not* have much life in them. They 'shriek' at the slightest alarm, dress elaborately, and guard their English com-plexions with sunshades as well as wide-brimmed hats. Kingston under-lines the contrast with their Queensland counterparts who are fearless about snakes, dress plainly, are good at riding, shooting and milking, and 'do not mind a few freckles'. The unluckiest of the English cousins is Hector, described as 'bored' and 'disdainful'. He resists his cousins' attempts to reform him, announced on his first evening at the Queens-land station: 'It's the finest country in the world, old fellow ... You'll learn to like it in time. So cheer up, we'll soon make a man of you'.

With sixteen Berrington children at his disposal, Kingston could have killed off one or two. It is indicative of his cheerful picture of colonial life that all survive. There are no illnesses, and the one 'lost child' episode is soon over, with very little fuss. The children are scarcely seen as individuals; they are grouped, with the tough resourceful Queenslanders contrasted with their timid, languid English cousins. The emphasis is on an ideal way of life, and on 'making a man' of Hector. The clash of values anticipates such later Australian novels as those of Mary Grant Bruce for whom the 'new chum' comes to the bush from Melbourne or Sydney to endure the same ordeals as Hector Berrington:

> 'You don't expect me to milk cows?' said Hector, as they walked along.
> 'Indeed I do, if you are to have milk for breakfast; it is what young hands like you and the girls are most suited for.'
> 'I am older than you are,' exclaimed Hector, looking indignantly at Harry.
> 'Older in years, but younger in this country. Why, my little brother Rob is of more use than you'll be for months to come, if you don't look sharp about it.'

Hector's inferiority is made more apparent by displays of physical courage from his cousins, and by their ostentatious refusal to boast. The laconic Queenslanders always get the advantage. 'Oh! it's nothing! [Paul] said, trying to laugh. 'A black fellow's spear merely grazed my side . . .'.

After months of this sort of thing, as well as being chased by a cow and falling down a wombat hole, it is no wonder Hector still wants to go home. Kingston's illustrator reinforces the failure to be assimilated by giving Hector a bowler hat to contrast with the shady cabbage-trees worn by his cousins. It is hard to say what brings about his reform: somehow he survives, and in the last chapters, his cheeks are 'well-browned' and his general air 'infinitely more manly and fit for work'.

The Young Berringtons is no different from the earlier Kingston novels in its insistence on the need to be 'fit for work'. It is, however, of particular interest in its use of contrasting national stereotypes. Published by Cassell, the first English firm to establish an Australian branch,[4] it may have been commissioned with some local sales in mind. It is less a didactic novel for future emigrants than a congratulatory exercise for the children of those who had left Britain, perhaps with Kingston's emigrants' manual in their pockets, during the 1850s and 1860s.

Kingston's work owed a good deal to Captain Frederick Marryat's *Mr Midshipman Easy* (1836). Jack Easy's adventures on land and sea are in the eighteenth century picaresque style, but his courage, honesty and instinctive sense of an Englishman's natural superiority to men of all other races and nationalities make him the forerunner of many

A new chum's ordeal
From *The Young Berringtons*

young Victorians abroad in nineteenth century juvenile fiction. The main difference between the Marryat and Kingston heroes is that the latter are less exuberant, and more conscious of themselves as Christians than as gentlemen, though they are usually both. Jack Easy, as his name suggests, does less work and has more fun than the industrious, devout heroes of Marryat's successors.

Marryat did not set any of his novels in Australia, but his daughter Emilia Marryat Norris and his niece Augusta Marryat did. Emilia Norris's *The Early Start in Life* (1867), like Kingston's work, continues the line from *Alfred Dudley* in the novel of settlement. It is worth examining in some detail for its treatment of such matters as the emigrants' duties and opportunities, the Aborigines, gold, religion and the work ethic.

It is often hard to be sure that an adventure story of this period is intended for children. Marryat's *Mr Midshipman Easy* clearly was not: the celebrated excuse of Jack Easy's nurse for her illegitimate child ('only a very little one') suggests that the novel got into Victorian schoolrooms by mistake. There is no mistaking Emilia Marryat Norris's audience. She addresses her readers directly: 'You may think, little people, . . . that were you to . . . go to Australia . . . you could easily turn your hand to anything . . . but if you are not useful at home, you would be no more use than the fire-logs there'.

Her emigrant family consists of the very useful Alexander Stirling, who is eighteen, his equally hard-working sister Maggie, fourteen-year-old Hugh, an idler, and the youngest, Archie. The novel begins in the late 1840s. It has an approving word for Governor Macquarie, and for John Macarthur because he saw how the land could be used. Governor Bligh is dismissed as a bully. The author omits the usual account of the voyage from England, saying only that the Stirlings' experiences were like everyone else's. Their view of Sydney is like Alfred Dudley's; Alexander and Maggie are repelled by its dirty, unpaved streets, and by its people – 'sailors, blacks, New Zealanders and Jews'. Hugh, the unreliable member of the group, finds bad company in Sydney; he goes to the playhouse, drinks brandy, smokes cigars which make him sick, and gets into a scuffle for which he is arrested. After this the family makes its way to the country for more wholesome adventures, and plenty of hard work.

Maggie Stirling's adaptation to colonial life is described in more detail than Alexander's, presumably because Mrs Norris was more interested in household matters than in the outdoors. Readers would have learned how to keep food safe from sugar ants by standing the kitchen-table legs in water and how to cook almost anything. Like Augusta Marryat's emigrant children, the Stirlings do not fuss about their diet. Parrots are quite acceptable, and so is a possum. Hugh shoots and roasts a dingo, and pronounces it 'capital'. They are not, however, so hard-pressed for food as Augusta Marryat's hero John Lambert who saves himself from starvation when lost in the bush by killing his horse Mazeppa, and eating it 'raw, like a cannibal. But do not let us talk about it; it is too disgusting'. The Marryat heroes are certainly practical, but one begins to wonder if they are genuine English gentlemen; the horse episode really goes too far.

Maggie Stirling worries sometimes about being unladylike. The author describes her as 'very pretty', but has reservations about a colonial girl's complexion: 'her face was still brown from living so constantly in the open air'. Her brother says she is worth half a dozen men; and in emergencies she shows physical courage and endurance. Her main role in the novel is to make a civilized home and to keep up religious practices. The feminine influence is expressed in her producing a clean tablecloth when the Stirlings first pitch their tents in the bush, and in her wish for a garden. Although she says, 'there is scarcely anything prettier than a bed of carrots or onions', she manages to have flowers as well. When water is short, she puts the vegetables first.

With the Aborigines, who frighten the Stirlings' servant, Hannah, Maggie is fearless. Hannah thinks they are devils; Maggie knows better: 'I believe it is an Australian native ... Don't be foolish, nursey; it is no more the devil than you are'. Emilia Marryat seems not quite to have decided how to present the Aborigines in her novel. In one episode they are a genuine threat; they attack the house and kill a friend of the Stirlings. In a macabre act of 'retributive justice', the Aboriginal leader is killed in turn, and his bones left 'bleaching in the sun for long afterwards, for the dingoes and the vultures to turn over'. On the other hand, Maggie clearly has the author's endorsement when she says of the first Aborigine to come to the house: 'As if the poor fellow has not a right to come and see what we are doing. After all, it is his own land that we have taken possession of ... We are not better than thieves; and I am sure he must look upon us as such'. The idea of the white settlers as thieves is not followed up. The Stirlings' only initiative is to take in and Christianize one Aboriginal whom they call Monkey; he is 'good-natured', but 'a dreadful coward'.

The discovery of gold is a moral issue on which the author seems more sure of herself. The feckless Hugh sets off, by way of 'filthy, promiscuous' Melbourne (the cities get a bad report in this novel) to the diggings. Some good comes of his foolishness, but only because the hardships of the diggings bring physical collapse and fever. Hugh is near death when he recalls his Christian precepts, and repents. 'I shall never dig gold again if I can help it', he says.

The chapter called 'Christmas Day in the Bush', a set piece in this novel as in many other stories of Australian life, shows British customs assimilated in a new tradition. The Stirlings see the incongruity of making mince pies in summer, but it is a duty as well as a celebration to do so. The scene is cheerful, even idyllic, with a 'bright blue sky' and 'warm sun' when they go to pray on Christmas morning beside the grave of the friend who was killed by the Aborigines. The 'rustic cross' on the grave, round which 'twined a native creeper' stresses the integration of Christianity in the new land, as does the Stirlings' choosing a gum tree on which to hang their Christmas presents. The novel ends with the Stirlings thanking God for having brought them to Australia and given them 'every earthly blessing'. It is in fact an earthly paradise, and the final tableau is one of Australia's 'glorious sunsets' over a peaceful pastoral landscape.

Augusta Marryat, for whom Port Augusta was named, wrote from first-hand knowledge. The wife of a governor of South Australia, she lived here from 1848 to 1861. Her novel, *The Young Lamberts* (1878), has much in common with Emilia Marryat Norris's work. Again, audience and purpose are clearly defined. Dedicating the story to 'The Boys of England', the author says she writes to amuse but hopes to teach her readers that 'a life of work is more honorable and happy than one of idleness'.

In spite of this rather daunting remark, Augusta Marryat aims at liveliness in narrative and characterization. Her twelve-year-old hero George Lambert is announced as 'not the most perfect example of decorum'; and although hard work in Australia does him good, he never becomes one. In the opening chapter, entitled, as nearly all these settlers' novels might be, 'A Reverse of Fortune', George appears almost to bring about the family's difficulties. Complaining to his older brother John, that 'it's a horrid bore having nothing to do', he makes three wishes: 'I wish I could go for a sailor ... I wish we were not so rich ... I wish you and I had to make our own living. I'd catch fish for dinner every day'. As in the traditional fairy story, George gets his wishes. His father enters, white-faced, to announce that the Lamberts are 'beggars', dispossessed of house and fortune. George should feel repentant; instead he is delighted, and goes off cheerfully to Australia with Mr Lambert and John to make a new start.

The arrival in Sydney contrasts with most other novels of this kind in its enthusiasm for a 'staid and beautiful' city. Perhaps this was vice-regal tact. It suits the settlers' tale better to contrast city ugliness and vice with country wholesomeness and beauty. The Lamberts make their way to the country, giving the author plenty of scope for how-to-do-it information, like a detailed recipe for rabbit stew, and instructions for making the fire for billy tea.

The Lamberts take misfortunes calmly. When George nearly drowns, there are no tears, or prayers of thankfulness: only a rebuke for his being a nuisance and the comment that the boy has 'no more head than an empty pumpkin'. Mr Lambert dies; again the tone is matter-of-fact. The boys get on with their work, which, the author says, is the best antidote for grief. They establish a farm and begin to plant a garden for their mother who is still in England. George learns to cook and make beds. He announces, perhaps defensively: 'I don't feel like a molly-coddle . . . When things must be done, I think the manliest way is to do them without any nonsense'. Both boys become remarkably useful. With a neighbour's tuition they learn to milk, to make candles, to wash and mend their own clothes, to keep pigs and fowls. There are detailed accounts of how they plant potatoes, and a set of instructions on the art of stuffing birds—the latter, apparently, a special study of the author's.

Augusta Marryat's interest in the Aborigines does not take her beyond the almost obligatory domestication of one child, little Susannah: 'a useful girl she is too'. The version of Aboriginal speech in the novel is American plantation style. Comparing this novel with Emilia Marryat Norris's work, one would be likely to guess that Augusta was the one who stayed at home; her time in Australia does not show for much.

In spite of all the emphasis on emigrant skills which places this novel with the settlers' tales rather than adventure stories, the ending is a return to England where the family fortunes are as suddenly restored as they were lost. John is relieved but George regrets giving up the farm they have established with such difficulty. Unlike the close of Emilia Marryat Norris's novel with its vision of a new country, this one ends with a new George, matured by his colonial experience.

W. H. Timperley's perspective in *Bush Luck* (1892) is bifocal: English and Australian. As the superintendent of Rottnest Island, Western Australia, he had first-hand local knowledge, but in choosing the familiar 'voyage out' framework he followed the pattern of the settlers' novels already described. His hero, Hugh Thornley, is the usual penniless English boy who seeks his fortune in Australia; and the novel ends with a summing up of the risks and rewards of colonial life. Although *Bush Luck* was published in 1892 its action belongs to the 1870s, and it is embellished by many anecdotes of much earlier pioneering days. Timperley was writing in a genre which was almost worked out; by the 1890s the settlers' tale had to move north or to become an historical novel if it was to keep any exotic flavour.

The opening chapter of *Bush Luck* is an odd reversal of the set piece, used in *Alfred Dudley* and in many of its successors, in which a little England is established in the new country. Instead of the cultivated English garden in the colonial wilderness it presents a microcosm of Australia in an Old World setting. This is a rough bush hut, built in the grounds of an English country house by the hero's rich uncle, a former pioneer. Here, leaving his servants to their own devices, Uncle Tom goes for long periods of nostalgic retreat. Dressed in moleskin trousers and red woollen shirt, and smoking a short black pipe, he invites his bewildered nephew to join him for some damper and a mutton chop. They share billy tea in a kind of initiation ceremony, with Uncle Tom watching Hugh for signs of pioneering promise. Hugh passes the tests and is despatched to Australia with just as much money as his uncle thinks is good for him. The bizarre opening scene in Uncle Tom's model hut is the most original note in *Bush Luck*. It is counterpointed, after Hugh's arrival in Western Australia, by his first glimpse of England transplanted to the New World:

> . . . we passed through a large iron gate, rattled along between an avenue of trees, and pulled up in front of a long, low cottage, the verandah of which was covered with real English roses, and then a soft, sweet English voice gave us a pleasant greeting, and again I asked myself if I were in a dream, or [if] I had crossed that huge waste of waters to inhale the perfume of English roses, and hear a voice which recalled happy memories of the old home far away?

To move from Kingston and the Marryats to Timperley is to feel a drop in the temperature of moral earnestness. It is worth noting that although *Bush Luck* was published by the Religious Tract Society, the title pages of later editions had the Boy's Own Paper imprint. The name of the Religious Tract Society in these editions appeared only in the small print at the end of the book among the advertisements for series such as the 'Brave Deeds' Books or 'The Boys' Library of Adventure and Heroism'.

Bush Luck puts its emphasis on Hugh Thornley as good settler, but it has a little more adventure for its own sake and considerably less religious fervour than earlier settlers' novels. Since the setting is Western Australia in the 1870s, gold is not an issue. On the Aborigines the author has an each-way bet. There are 'friendly' tribes and 'savage' ones. Some Aborigines are dirty and repulsive but others are brave and handsome. The dramatic needs of the novel seem to determine which kind of black man will leap from behind a gum tree to threaten or to rescue the young hero. Timperley has no impulse to convert; indeed, unlike Kingston and Sargent, he seems not to believe the Aborigines capable of understanding Christian doctrine. There is sympathy but no comfort for an Aboriginal woman who has lost her child:

> 'Mine boy dead!, mine boy dead!' she wailed forth, with such an outburst of grief that I found my own tears beginning to flow . . . the usual words of comfort would have been worse than useless; for how could I tell the poor old savage of a brighter future beyond the skies, and a joyful meeting in a world to come? 'Mine boy dead' was the sum total of her belief. Dead now, and for ever and ever.

Like the submerging of the Religious Tract Society in the *Boys' Own Paper*, this episode in *Bush Luck* shows the erosion of Christian missionary confidence. Without any strong religious impulse in his dealings with Aborigines the Timperley hero has less sense of obligation. When Hugh Thornley kills one of them in self-defence he is horrified: 'In the sight of God and man', he says, 'I believe I'm innocent of that man's blood; but the horror of having killed a human being is with me, for all that; and I can't shake it off'. This reaction, however, seems mainly intended to show Hugh's admirable but unusual sensitivity. Mr Munro, Hugh's benign employer and friend, sees the incident differently. He tells Hugh that 'you must not kill a savage except in defending yourself or one of your party . . . They are British subjects under the protection of British law; and although we have taken their country, we are not allowed, except in self-defence, to take their lives'. Reading this sentence today one looks for authorial irony in Mr Munro's words, but there is nothing in the novel to suggest that it is intended. Where writers like Sargent and Kingston had seen the Aborigines as God's creatures, they are now British subjects. Frank Layton would have said some prayers for the dead Aborigine. Hugh Thornley masters his instinctive remorse and, to clear himself of legal blame, writes a report for the Colonial Secretary. The good settler, though still a Christian, is no longer a missionary, but a citizen of the Empire with legal rather than spiritual obligations.

In this shift of moral emphasis, as well as in the fact that Hugh

Thornley settles in an already established district, *Bush Luck* marks a turning point. Stories of emigration would continue but the perspective was changing. The days of armchair travellers were virtually over. Books set in Australia were more likely to come from writers with first-hand knowledge than from professionals like Kingston or Henty who manufactured Australian tales (or African or Canadian ones) from a stock plot filled from the reference book stock-pot. As Australia became better known there was less need or excuse for loading a narrative with guide-book information. And, although the penniless English boy making good in the New World could still be the centre of interest, he could not be represented, as Alfred Dudley had been, as a founder of a new social order. By the 1890s he was a 'new chum', and he had to acquire skills which were the birthright of the children of earlier settlers. There was a move away from the idea of adapting English values to Australian conditions towards that of the hero's *becoming* an Australian.

By the 1890s, too, several English publishing houses had set up Australian agencies. A double readership could be assumed. Books which would appeal to English and Australian children alike began to take the place of the 'young England abroad' novel. The viewpoint Kingston used in his later novel, *The Young Berringtons*, with English boys proving themselves to their Australian cousins, became increasingly popular. It persisted in various forms for many years, with the 'cousin from England' becoming the 'cousin from town'. In both the early and the late forms of this kind of novel is the assumption that the real Australia is the bush. That is where initiation takes place. Whether the hero (or anti-hero) comes from London or from Sydney, his ordeal is much the same, and he will need the same qualities of independence, industry and resourcefulness to become a worthy Australian bushman.

2

Adventures Unlimited

With their direct appeal to the young emigrant, their theme of difficulties overcome and their happy endings in Australia, the settlers' novels form a distinct and easily defined category of their own. A second grouping of colonial stories shows more diversity. To call them adventure stories is not satisfactorily to define them, since there is little written for children which is not in some sense an adventure, but it does suggest their common emphasis on strange and exciting events. These novels offer differing mixtures of fact and fancy, of the possible and impossible, and are alike mainly in their use of Australia as a place where things happen. Their heroes need not have the humdrum qualities demanded of the ideal settler; they will encounter all kinds of dangers and privations, but no one will ask them to grow vegetables. These adventure stories of nineteenth century Australia include a few authentic travellers' tales, but most are second-hand. The characters matter less than the narrative; in general they exist to keep it moving. Touches of local colour may be applied in a slapdash way that gives a minimum guarantee of reliability, or painstakingly applied with a large debt to the encyclopaedia.

Two novels of the 1850s by stay-at-home Englishwomen make their appeal not only to the reader's sense of excitement but to the commitment of parents and teachers to the importance of facts. Mrs Sarah Lee's *Adventures in Australia* (1851) and Mrs Anne Bowman's *The Kangaroo Hunters* (1859) are in the Robinson Crusoe tradition. Both begin with a shipwreck and go on until the whole Australian continent has been explored for all its dangers and strange discoveries. Neither has much to offer in human interest. Mrs Lee's hero, Captain John Spence, journeys across Australia from the north-west coast, where his ship is wrecked, to the east from which he embarks for India and a return to Army duties. He is accompanied by his faithful dog, his horse and his talking parrot, Charlie. The parrot seems to be Mrs Lee's main concession to a juvenile audience. Along the way Captain Spence finds an Aboriginal Man Friday, a companion so devoted that he refuses to be left behind in Sydney and goes cheerfully to India, presumably to join the Army as Spence's batman-servant. The emphasis of the novel is on the powers of endurance, observation and adaptability which keep Spence from starving or losing himself in the Australian desert. Mrs Lee proceeds on the assumption of the Victorian schoolroom that information is good in itself. Accordingly her readers are offered a large assortment of facts about Australian plants, birds and animals. Some of these might be useful to future castaways but they are not assembled with that in mind. Unlike the bread-and-butter, how-to-do-it tone of the settlers' tales, *Adventures in Australia* invites a sense of wonder at the variety of the natural world. Because of Mrs Lee's disdain for plot and character and her relentless categorization of Australian plant and

The wreck
The frontispiece by J. S. Prout from *Adventures in Australia*

animal life, it would have been hard for most readers to go all the way with Captain Spence.

Mrs Anne Bowman must have called her novel *The Kangaroo Hunters* because it made a good title. It could just as easily be *The Emu Hunters* or *The Wombat Hunters*. The shipwrecked Mayburn family, who like Captain Spence cross Australia from west coast to east, hunt, kill and eat almost anything they see on their long walk to civilization. Adventure and instruction are ingeniously combined in the story of the Mayburns' ordeal. The children's quickly-acquired hunting skills are supplemented by their clergyman father's scholarly knowledge of Australian wildlife. While he describes with leisurely precision the quaint habits of a wombat or an emu, his sturdy sons go after it with knives, spears or bows and arrows. 'Doubtless this creature is the *Phascolomys ursinus*', Mr Mayburn remarks contemplatively, before the animal is removed to be cooked and carved for dinner.

In the preface to her novel, Mrs Bowman made it clear that she was writing romance, not a catalogue of facts, and that she believed the imagination needed exercise. She wrote for 'the weary schoolboy, who relieves his mind after arithmetical calculations and pages of syntax, by fanciful adventures amidst scenes of novelty and peril . . .'. Such stories, which 'do not profess to be true, though they are composed of truths', would neither mislead the judgement nor corrupt the taste of young readers, since their end was the contemplation of 'the marvellous works of creation'. Mrs Bowman had reason to insist on the rights of the imagination. There is nothing plausible about the survival of the ill-equipped Mayburn party. Led by vague, indolent Mr Mayburn, it includes four children and three servants, two convicts and an Aboriginal woman and her little girl. Although most of the company narrowly escape death, and all are constantly threatened by hostile Aborigines, Mr Mayburn is so absorbed in the novelties he observes that he can say, 'This is truly a tour of pleasure, my children, and I care not how long I linger on the flowery road'. Their wanderings on the 'flowery road' across the Australian continent take fifteen months and more than four hundred closely-printed pages. The last two chapters bring them back to white society. The Mayburns walk into the pages of a quite different kind of novel when they arrive at Daisy Grange, the New South Wales property of their friends, the Deveralls. Like Alfred Dudley, Mr Deverall wants to complete his little settlement with a clergyman; the church is already built and waiting. Mr Mayburn agrees happily to fill the gap, and asks that his children be allowed to stay too: 'Teach them to be useful and happy as you are; and allow

An attack by a wild bull
Plate engraved by Dalziel after Harrison Weir from *The Kangaroo Hunters*

us to form part of your new colony'. The novel closes on a note of harmony, with the Aboriginal child, Nakinna, already converted to Christianity, ready to go to school on the Daisy Grange estate with the white children, and 'be a little English girl in all but complexion'.

Weighed down by facts and pseudo-facts, the narratives of Mrs Lee and Mrs Bowman move slowly. They have neither the authority of first-hand experience nor the confidence of the natural story-teller. These assets are combined in the work of Richard Rowe who spent several years in Australia during the 1850s, worked as a journalist with the *Sydney Morning Herald*, and later wrote of colonial life for children under the pseudonym of 'Edward Howe'. In welcome contrast with the Gradgrinders of information Rowe's work is engagingly informal, varied in mood and incident, and obviously written to please. *The Boy in the Bush* (1869) and *Roughing It in Van Diemen's Land* (1880) are family adventure stories, written in the first person in a style which at its best has the sound of a story-teller's voice speaking directly to an audience of children.

The Boy in the Bush, first published as a serial in *Good Words*, recounts a number of episodes in the lives of the Lawsons of Wonga-Wonga, New South Wales. Each chapter is a more or less self-contained story, told by the Lawsons' English friend, Mr Edward Howe. Howe interprets the Australian boys, Sydney and Harry Lawson, for their northern hemisphere contemporaries. His relaxed, conversational tone is a useful means of reducing disbelief in the Lawsons' crowded days. All the colonial set pieces are described. The Lawson boys are besieged by bushrangers and Aborigines; they survive a flood and a bushfire, they search for a lost child, visit the goldfields, and save their mother from almost certain death by snake-bite. Fortunately, the author varies the dramatic temperature, and does not allow a sense of character to be overwhelmed by the sequence of events. In the bushranger episode the mood of suspense breaks into comedy:

> Next morning, just as day was breaking, Warrigal and his two mates, with crape masks on, rode up to Wonga-Wonga. I don't know which were the bigger cowards, those three great fellows going to bully a lady and a boy, or the half-dozen and more of great fellows about the place who they knew would let them do it. They made as little noise as they could, but the dogs began to bark, and woke Sydney. When he woke, however, Warrigal had got his little window open, and was covering him with his pistol. Sydney put out his hand for his revolver, and though Warrigal shouted 'Throw up your hands, boy, or I'll shoot you through the head,' he jumped out

A visit to the goldfields
From *The Boy in the Bush*

of bed and fired. He missed Warrigal, and Warrigal missed him . . .
Miss Smith [the governess] went into hysterics, and Gertrude and
her sisters couldn't help looking as white as their night-dresses,
though they tried hard to show Miss Smith how much braver native
girls were than English . . . Mrs Lawson had fired off her blunder-
buss, but it had only broken two panes of the parlour-window, and
riddled the verandah-posts; so Wonga-Wonga was at the bushrangers' mercy . . . Then they marched Mrs. Lawson, and Miss Smith,
and Sydney, and his sisters, and Mr. and Mrs. Jones, and Ki Li, into
the keeping-room, and sat down to breakfast, with pistols in their
belts, and pistols laid, like knives and forks, on the table. The bushrangers tried to be funny, and pressed Mrs. Lawson and the other
ladies to make themselves at home and take a good meal. One of
the robbers was going to kiss Miss Smith, but Sydney, pinioned as
he was, ran at him, and butted him like a ram. He was going to
strike Sydney, but Gertrude ran between them, calling out, 'Oh, you
great coward!' and Warrigal felt ashamed, and told the man to sit
down. 'We call him Politeful Bill,' Warrigal remarked in apology;
'but he ain't much used to ladies' serciety.'

Rowe's portrait of a bashful bushranger in this early chapter is balanced
in a later one by that of a 'greedy, savage brute' called Hook-handed
Bill who enjoys 'ripping up' his victims with the sharp hook which
replaces his lost right hand. In both stories Rowe undermines the myth
of the gallant outlaw of the Australian bush. For an encounter with
the Lawson children, the bungling Warrigal provides just enough suspense, and his defeat is plausible. The boys do not meet Hook-handed
Bill; a figure of 'the old convict times', he survives only in the memory
of an earlier generation of settlers.

The perspective of *The Boy in the Bush* is that of the experienced
traveller, not the settler. As Howe, the author presents with a touch
of irony the tendency of the 'cornstalk' boys to glorify the ways of the
new country at the expense of the old:

'. . . Father talks about England sometimes, but I'm sure he likes the
colony twenty times better. Houses everywhere, and all the little bush
you've got left cut up into paddocks! *I* wouldn't live in England if
you paid me for it. You brag about your horses, but they can't run
against ours, when they do come out. I wonder they live out the voyage, from the way I've heard you coddle them. Look at *our* horses—*they*
don't want corn and cloths, just as if they were babies . . .'

Harry was always very fond of 'cracking up the colony', but he was especially inclined to do so that forenoon, having had his temper somewhat irritated (although he protested that he was as cool as a water-melon) by the hot wind that had been blowing for three days.

The amused tone in this passage is one example of the way in which *The Boy in the Bush* differs from the settlers' novels already described. Harry's boastfulness about colonial ways and his denigration of new chums as 'a set of stuck-up milk-sops' are put in perspective by the narrator. Edward Howe does not sound like a milk-sop, and he does not hesitate to comment, with some comic exaggeration, on the less attractive aspects of Australian life:

[The flies] buzzed about one's head like swarming bees, they covered one's back like a shirt of mail, at meal-times they made the chops and steaks look as black as if they had been smothered in magnified peppercorns. It *was* hot then. The mercury stood at a good bit over 100° in the shade: it was almost impossible to find out what it stood at in the sun without getting a sunstroke. At every corner poor dogs were lying with their tongues out askew, panting like high-pressure steamboats just about to blow up.

The narrator distances himself from the colonial boys further and more seriously when he discusses their attitude towards the Aborigines. He sees savagery on both sides, white and black, but he reminds the reader that the Aborigines were the first to be injured, when their hunting grounds were taken from them. There is a sharp edge of irony in his account of the double standard of morality among the settlers. Reflecting that there is 'a terrible amount of the tiger in human nature', he shows how easily families like the Lawsons become accustomed to killing:

When blood has once been tasted, so to speak, in savage earnest, 'civilization' peels off like nose-skin in the tropics, and 'Christian' men, and even boys, are ready–eager–to shed blood like water . . . when the white women hear of what the black fellows have done or tried to do to their darlings, they are very apt to frame excuses for the white atrocities which they dimly guess at when they kneel beside their beds at night to give God thanks for their darlings' return to districts in which it is possible to go to a 'real church' and 'regular services' every Sunday.

In the scene in which the Lawson boys decide that it is right to shoot blacks but not to poison them ('We'll fight fair. I'll have no strychnine used', says Sydney), the author raises a moral question which he cannot resolve within the framework of his novel. Sydney and Harry are presented as likeable boys who do wrong without fully understanding it. Since they cannot be enlightened without changing their whole way of life, the author leaves them in ignorance. It is an uncomfortable conclusion. The young readers for whom Rowe seems to have written are not allowed to give final approval to the heroes whose dangers they have shared.

There are similar difficulties in Rowe's *Roughing It in Van Diemen's Land* (1880), but they are less obtrusive because the novel is set in the comparatively remote past. The hero takes part in the 'Black War' of 1830 in Van Diemen's Land, and moves to the new Port Phillip settlement with John Batman's party. There are some satirical comments on Batman's treaty with the Aborigines who 'of course, according to Batman's account, were quite delighted . . . to part with their land to so amiable a white-skinned fellow-countryman'. But it all happened a long time ago, before the appearance of 'that magnificent mushroom', the city of Melbourne; the narrator does not make his readers uneasy with moral problems as he did in *The Boy in the Bush*. As L. P. Hartley says, 'The past is a foreign country: they do things differently there'. What would be disturbing in a contemporary story is softened by the lapse of time. The reader is often reminded that the events are those of another era and invited to smile at its primitive ways:

> I do not know whether mensuration is taught at your school, or, if so, whether you learn it. Supposing that to be the case, I think you would prefer the system in vogue in Tasmania, in Frank's young days, to that employed by English surveyors. The Tasmanian land-measurers tied a string to a dog's tail, and when he stopped, they said he had gone a mile. Thousands of acres were measured in that way in those primitive times: and some years later, indeed, Tasmanian professional people behaved in a manner which would have made their contemporary English co-professionals stare. For instance, the manager of one bank used to trundle a wheelbarrow every morning to another bank for cash – just as if he had come for gravel.

Richard Rowe's stories of Australian adventure do not depend for their excitement on any clash between virtue and villainy. His young heroes are seen at their bravest and best when they confront the forces of nature. As I have shown in discussing *The Boy in the Bush* Rowe was uncomfortable about white attitudes towards Aborigines; and he despised convicts and bushrangers too much to allow any one of them the status of a genuine adversary. In saying that Hook-handed Bill lacked the 'redeeming qualities' which 'a certain set of story-tellers' was fond of attributing to bushrangers, Rowe dissociated himself from a fast-growing literary industry. Wronged convicts and gentlemanly bushrangers abound in the adventure stories of the 1870s and 1880s. They provide the central figures in two striking and successful adult novels of this period: Marcus Clarke's romance of the convict system, *His Natural Life*, which appeared in serial form in 1870-72, and Rolf Boldrewood's bushranger story, *Robbery Under Arms*, serialized in 1882-83. Clarke's hero, Rufus Dawes, continued a well-established literary tradition which includes Sydney Carton in *A Tale of Two Cities* and the Count of Monte Cristo. Boldrewood's gallant bushranger, Captain Starlight, is a new version of that romantic figure, the highwayman. Already outmoded in Britain and obviously unsuited to the railway age he could ride again in the Australian wilds. The call to 'Bail up!', less courtly than 'Stand and deliver!', reflected the rough vigour of the new country. Although both *His Natural Life* and *Robbery Under Arms* are novels of the past, the period they describe was still within living memory at the time of their publication. They combine documentary detail with melodramatic characterization and plot contrivance, making Australia a land of authenticated romance. No juvenile novel rivalled the work of Clarke and Boldrewood, but there were many in the late nineteenth century with similar plots and backgrounds. The confrontation between man and nature in the Australian bush took second place in such novels to a less impersonal warfare, with some larger-than-life-sized heroes and all kinds of villainy.

It was less trouble to write about the clash of virtue and wickedness against an Australian backdrop than to make the setting part of the action. Richard Rowe's novels reflect his own observations; Mrs Lee and Mrs Bowman were inaccurate but industrious compilers of information. When human conflict moved into the foreground, Australia was often suggested only by the flimsiest of stage properties. In *Edward Bertram or The Emigrant Heir* (1882) the prolific English writer, Grace Stebbings, used the convict period for a story of persecuted virtue in which some popular images of Australian life serve as a decorative motif. The young hero, neglected at home and bullied at school, embarks for Australia as a stowaway on a convict ship. Poorly equipped for the voyage, the boy nearly starves to death in the hold; he has eaten his last asset, his Latin verse book, before the sailors discover him. Once revived, Edward Bertram wins the heart of nearly everyone on the ship. Public school experience proves useful; as a fag for senior boys he has already learned to cook and sew. His concern for the condition of the convicts ('crowded worse than my uncle's pigsties') arouses their affection; they find his 'bright face and frank honest look as good as a sea-breeze'. Innocence survives in *Edward Bertram*; and after some years in outback Australia 'a fine, strong, sunburnt lad of twenty' is reclaimed by a penitent uncle. Meanwhile the former school bully, Robinson, has been sent down from Oxford and exiled to hide his disgrace in the Australian bush, where eventually he dies alone and miserable, without the last-minute repentance which frequently softens the final chapter of a Victorian novel.

Grace Stebbings's novel is a very faint echo of *His Natural Life*. It uses the convict-ship scenes, as Clarke does, to contrast innocent hopeful childhood with degradation and despair. Both novels have a missing heir theme; both have an irredeemable, sadistic villain. The young readers of *Edward Bertram* are, however, spared the horrors of the convict system which Clarke documented so fully. The 1830s colonial setting, as Grace Stebbings presents it, is sketchy and unconvincing; it exists only to provide dangers for the hero and punishment for his enemy. And, as the celebrated Tichbourne case demonstrated during the 1860s and 1870s, Australia was a likely place to look for a missing heir.

Captain Kangaroo (1889), by J. Evelyn, is a melodrama like *Edward Bertram*, but with more vigorous action. Its opening scenes take place at an English public school during the 1820s, when a friendship is established between Will Norton, the orphan heir of a rich, cruel uncle, and Ned Holderness, the son of a kindly, moderately prosperous squire. Holidays with the Holderness family provide a softening influence on rebellious Will. Winnie, the squire's daughter, gives the boy his first Bible as a birthday present. Soon there is a reversal of fortunes for both boys. Ned's father loses his money and the family has to emigrate to Australia. Will's wicked uncle torments the boy into an uncontrollable rage: a fatal blow is struck and Will is charged with murder. Because of the uncle's reputation for cruelty and Will's youth, the death sentence is commuted to transportation for life.

Ten years later in Australia the Holderness family have become model settlers. They have been told that Will died in prison, and Winnie still prays for him. Will, embittered by the mistaken belief that his only friends rejected him, escapes and takes to bushranging as 'Captain Kangaroo' whom colonial gossip describes as 'awfully handsome and the very devil himself'. Notable for his courtesy to women and children, he saves Ned's fiancée from his own gang, guiding her to safety with the words: 'Try to think as little harm of me as you can'.

As Captain Kangaroo, Will is presented as sympathetically as morality allows, considering his criminal record. Once he finds out that Ned did not, after all, desert him in prison, he is ready for a redemptive death, with Winnie at his side. 'Goodbye and God bless you', he says, clasping the Bible he has been carrying for ten years. Of course he has to die, but Will and Winnie are given the momentary happy ending of melodrama. The moral emphasis here is quite different from that of the settlers' novel, *Frank Layton*, in which reliable Frank remains the author's favorite, with his unsteady friend Percy used as an example of weakness to contrast with Frank's calm strength. In spite of the Bible, which is less important here for itself than as a symbol of Winnie's love, *Captain Kangaroo* is a romance, celebrating individual will, in the aptly christened hero, and rebelliousness rather than order and duty.

As a wholeheartedly romantic literary creation, it would be hard to outdo Alfred St Johnston's bushranger hero, Starlight, of *In Quest of Gold* (1885). He is not, like Captain Kangaroo, merely wilful and misguided. He is more like the character in a Thurber story who announces that 'we all have our faults and mine is being wicked'. Apart from being wicked ('guilty', the author breathlessly sums up, 'of every crime and cruelty that a man who was absolutely without heart or conscience could cram into a lifetime'), Starlight is perfectly delightful. He is handsome, brave and charming, with a 'silver voice' and 'a bright melodious laugh'. No woman can resist him and he knows it: 'he therefore never neglected his appearance and was always becomingly dressed'. As leader of a gang he commands absolute loyalty; his men, fascinated by his 'fiendish ... unblushing iniquity', lose all sense of right and wrong in his service. This fallen angel of a bushranger retains only one touch of virtue. Starlight loves his mother. 'Dare to mention her name again, and, as I live, I'll strangle you', he says to some presumptuous underling. There is no repentance, no redemptive death-bed gesture from Starlight. Cornered in a wild and rocky place, he takes 'one tremendous leap' on his beautiful grey horse and vanishes for ever.

Boldrewood's *Robbery Under Arms* began to appear in serial form only two years after Ned Kelly's execution. In portraying their bushrangers as upper-class adventurers, the authors of *Captain Kangaroo* and *In Quest of Gold* followed literature rather than life, with Boldrewood's idealized Starlight as their model. E. B. Kennedy, the author of *Blacks and Bushrangers* (1889) took a different line. He makes an indirect satirical comment on the literary tradition in which he was writing, and deflates the sentimentality of books like *Captain Kangaroo*. But if he refuses to allow heroic status to his bushranger, the uncouth ironclad Magan, Kennedy tilts the balance of the novel back to romance in the portrayal of the noble black chief, Drummoora. *Blacks and Bushrangers* opens in England, where the young gypsy hero, Mat Stanley, is befriended by a former 'wool king' of Australia. The ex-squatter, now known as 'Squire' Bell, retains enough of his colonial democratic spirit to let Mat loose in his library where the boy reads two books about Australia. 'I know 'em pretty nigh by heart', Mat says. Perhaps one of them was *Robbery Under Arms*. It is surely no coincidence that when Mat is falsely accused of poaching, the place is Boldre Wood. Although he manages to outrun the law, Mat has to emigrate to Australia to avoid being convicted. Among his few possessions on the voyage he takes the copy of *Robinson Crusoe* given to him by Annie Bell, the squire's daughter. Annie chose better than she knew. Mat and his brother Tim, who accompanies him to Australia, become young Crusoes in north-west Queensland, the sole survivors when their ship is wrecked.

After a short time alone, in which Mat's hunting skills prove useful, the boys are captured by Aborigines, kindly treated, and eventually assimilated into the tribe. Kennedy's portrait of Aboriginal life is a compromise between the requirements of the adventure story, which needs its villains, and an evident admiration for tribal skills and loyalties. From a rival tribe, the Tingura, he provides adversaries who besiege Mat's friendly hosts, the Waigonda. The boys have a gun, retrieved from the shipwreck, but see it as a matter of honour not to exploit the white man's superior weapon. So long as there is a fair fight they hold their fire, but when the Tingura break the rules, Mat puts them to flight with one shot. At the end of the novel, when the boys return to civilization, they reward the chief, Drummoora, with *one* rifle, exacting a promise that it will be used only to shoot game.

Kennedy divided his novel into two more or less equal parts, according to his title. The 'Blacks' section takes up six years of the lives of Mat and Tim. This allows plenty of time for Squire Bell to become bored with English country life and to return to Australia. In New South Wales, blacks meet bushrangers when Annie Bell is kidnapped by Magan's brutal gang and Mat goes to the rescue with his friend Drummoora. The chief, more observant than Mat, discovers that Magan is almost bullet-proof: he warns Mat to aim low, since only the bushranger's legs have no 'iron skin'. Bushranger Magan, an obvious and unflattering version of Ned Kelly, collapses and dies with horrible oaths, cursing Mat and the 'nigger' Drummoora, as he contemptuously calls the chief.

Kennedy's treatment of the bushranger episode, taken with the 'Boldre Wood' clue, indicates a conscious purpose to ridicule the myths of Ned Kelly and Captain Starlight. Yet *Blacks and Bushrangers* is not an anti-romance. Mat's years with the Aborigines are in the heroic mode; so is his profession of brotherhood with Drummoora, a noble savage whose dignity and strength are emphasized throughout the novel. Their parting is a matter for emotion, on both sides:

> When the white men turned their faces homewards the chief and his whole tribe accompanied them as far as the boundaries of the Waigonda country ... when Mat turned round for a last wave of the hand he saw his old chief ... seated on a stone, the attitude of despair. The tears rose in [Mat's] eyes as he witnessed this spectacle, which [his companion], observing, said soothingly,—
> 'Never mind, old man, you might see them again, some day.' 'Yes, in heaven, I hope,' responded our forester in a choking voice, as he turned his face southwards.

The way south is back to well-established white settlement in New South Wales. Romance and adventure, Kennedy seems to say, belong in the as-yet-unclaimed land in the far North. With some regrets Mat settles for a squatter's life and marriage to Annie Bell whose memory he has cherished along with her copy of *Robinson Crusoe*. This confirms the colony's comparative freedom from class distinction: here, Mat's gypsy birth bothers no one except Annie's snobbish, ill-bred mother. In the final chapters, Kennedy introduces a possible rival for Annie's hand in a foppish new-chum, the Honourable Lionel Fulrake. Given the novel's literary allusiveness, Fulrake may be intended to evoke the famous Tom Wildrake whose exploits in India and Australia were celebrated in the periodical *Boys of England* during the 1880s.[1] Lionel Fulrake's affected manner and apparently frail physique are deceptive: he is a first-class boxer who might even have defeated sturdy Mat. But no such contest takes place. Kennedy sends Lionel back to England without involving him in the central plot: his main function seems to be to subvert the literary convention of the effete new-chum as thoroughly as mean-spirited Magan undermines the idea of chivalry among the bushrangers.

The story of Mat the Squatter-Gypsy is uneven in tone and awkwardly constructed, with an anti-climactic ending. As with most adventure stories of this kind, its characterization is a matter of simple outlines and labels: sturdy Mat, bluff Squire Bell, brave, gentle Annie. Its narrative lacks the professionalism of Henty or Stables, but is more convincing in local detail.

The cover design of *Blacks and Bushrangers*

An account of Australian adventure fiction in this period is incomplete without Jack Harkaway, the universal traveller of Bracebridge Hemyng's endless and mindless series. Like his contemporary Ned Nimble, Jack went everywhere: he went among the Chinese and the Cubans, to Greece, to America and, comparatively late in life, to Australia to deal with the bushranger problem. *Jack Harkaway and His Son's Adventures in Australia* makes everything already described in this chapter look like sober realism. The Harkaways' task in Australia is to get rid of a gang of convict-bushrangers led by proud, reckless Captain Morgan and his wife, Fighting Sue. On the way to their High Noon with Morgan, the Harkaways, accompanied by their faithful Aboriginal servants, Sunday and Monday, sample Australian life. Young Jack mounts a dangerous wild colt and subdues it by the novel and surely unsporting method of breaking a bottle of champagne on its head. There is a complex turn of the plot involving a treacherous former school friend of the older Jack who gets lost in the desert and emerges only to be hanged by the impetuous Captain Morgan. Jack arrives a little late but manages to cut him down, forgive everything, and witness his edifying death. Then it is time to deal with Morgan and the gang, all of whom are quickly disposed of, except for Fighting Sue, the Queen of the Bushrangers, who presents a problem until she decides to shoot herself rather than be captured. This saves the Harkaways the embarrassment of choosing between chivalry and prudence; with a 'Hurrah for old England!' they set sail again, leaving Australia a cleaner, better place.

3

Pilgrims' Progress

It would be hard to find a children's novel of nineteenth century England in which Christianity had no place, but some are more singlemindedly devotional than others. The Sunday-school teacher whose main aim was to bring the Bible, the means of salvation, to poor and illiterate children, had first to teach these children to read. Hence, a very large number of books produced with the double aim of fostering literacy and piety came from such publishers as the Religious Tract Society and the Society for the Propagation of Christian Knowledge. Tales for Sunday-school consumption naturally stressed the duty to take the gospel to foreign lands. The young settlers whose chronicles I have already described seldom forgot to pack a Bible, but it was not their main purpose, in going to Australia, to save souls. For the novel of salvation, however, Australia offered some useful situations. Aborigines were there to be enlightened, and convicts to be brought to repentance. Moreover, the hardships of the colony gave a new fictional means of testing the faith and fortitude of a young hero or heroine.

In the early period of colonial settlement, the writers who chose Australia as a backdrop for a juvenile story were more often drawn to themes of migration or adventure than to the purely moral tale. Until the goldfields brought an obvious source of spiritual conflict, there was nothing from England or Australia to compare in religious fervour with *Allan le Jeune Déporté à Botany-Bay* (1836), by E. Fouinet. The French author, with no commitment to the cause of emigration, and no knowledge of the colony to tether his inventiveness, fixed his mind on sin and its consequences, and let the material world take whatever shape was most convenient. Although I have restricted this study to fiction written in English, it is hard to resist making an exception of *Allan le Jeune Déporté*. Not only does it offer a useful comparison with *Alfred Dudley* as an 1830s novel, it also shows, more singlemindedly and absurdly than any English example, Australia as a place for punishment and redemption.

The story begins in a Welsh parsonage in the late eighteenth century. Allan is an idle, turbulent younger son, disobedient, and jealous of his well-behaved elder brother. He robs the poor-box, finds evil companions and is eventually sentenced to ten years' transportation. New South Wales, where Allan labours as an assigned servant, is a landscape of parable which exists to demonstrate the moral order. The bush must be cleared so that the sun may fertilize the soil; so men's hearts must be cleared of vicious tangled thoughts. Because the trees of New South Wales frequently grow in straight lines, a cunning axeman who fells one of them can bring down the rest. Even so, one wicked fellow ruins another, who in turn . . . The Aborigines (sometimes called 'Indiens') deserve to be driven off the land because they did not carry out God's wish that it should be cultivated. Allan does not learn these lessons fast enough. Reverting to old habits, he steals a compass and sets off impetuously to the North-West in the hope of somehow reaching Wales. But there are the cannibal 'Indiens', the 'coula' bear of the Blue Mountains and other menaces. Supplies of coconuts, bananas, figs, plums, acacia gum and eucalyptus manna, plentiful at first, run out. Allan loses his compass, walks in a circle, falls ill, repents of his sins, is captured and about to be roasted, escapes, and is found by his brother who has spent the intervening years of the story in getting himself ordained as a minister in order to be useful in crises such as this one.

Together again, the brothers build a house on the exact model of the Welsh parsonage of their childhood; they work hard and prosper. Allan sends back the money he stole from the poor-box just in time; his father (whose heart suffered from the shame of the theft) has been living on only to deliver a death-bed 'I forgive him'. The elder brother then brings the widowed mother to Australia to join Allan who meanwhile has been busy civilizing whatever comes his way: Aborigines, convicts, edible native plants. From old north Wales to New South Wales the family comes full circle to domestic unity and piety. The readers who make the journey through 320 closely-printed pages cannot miss the central lesson of filial duty. A disobedient son will almost certainly kill at least one of his parents; and nothing is more certain to bring on a father's heart attack than a son who robs a poor-box.

There is a resemblance to *Alfred Dudley* in *Allan le Jeune Déporté* in the idea of reproducing an Old World pattern of living in the colony. But there are obvious differences. *Alfred Dudley* is about rebuilding a fortune, and *Allan le Jeune Déporté* concentrates on the remaking of a soul. Although both are family stories, the English one shows a strong interest in the colony's future, with Alfred and his sisters as its model settlers. The household of *Allan le Jeune Déporté* exists only to point out the risks of disobeying parents. No marriages are forecast for Allan and his brother; indeed there are no available females. Sex is so unmentionable that the only woman in the novel is Allan's mother. (There were sisters, who died.) The supremacy of the mother (a frail, negligible figure in *Alfred Dudley*) may suggest a difference between French and English family patterns. At any rate the narrow focus of *Allan le Jeune Déporté* allows no distraction from the moral. To obey one's parents is almost the same as obeying God and it seems to be more important. By contrast, in the English and Australian moral tales I shall discuss in this chapter, there are at least as many delinquent parents as children, and part of the child's spiritual ordeal may be to resist the temptation to obey.

One of the most popular English writers of evangelical novels, Hesba Stretton (author of *Jessica's First Prayer*) used a colonial motif in *Enoch Roden's Training* (1865). This is the story of two brothers from a West Midland town: industrious Enoch and wastrel Titus. Titus runs away to sea, leaving Enoch to support the family which includes two adopted sisters. In a Melbourne hospital, apparently dying of fever, Titus repents having abandoned his family and his religious practices. Recovery follows repentance; and in a denouement which reflects the nineteenth century status of Australia as a missing persons' bureau, Titus finds the rich uncle of the two girls whom Enoch is toiling to support. The Roden family is rewarded with passages to prosperity in Australia when the newly-found uncle adopts them all. It may seem unfair that delinquent Titus brings this about, but the author's characterization of him as the Prodigal Son places it in its Biblical context.

Hesba Stretton's Melbourne is not a place but an idea: a suitably degraded setting for the prodigal's repentance. No doubt contemporary accounts of the effect of 'gold fever' on the colony influenced the author's choice of city. One might expect some more detailed observation in a locally-produced moral tale, *The Fernythorpe Choristers*, by 'Europa' (1876). Yet, in spite of its Melbourne imprint, this novel could have come from any English village. Dedicated to 'The Boys of All Saints, St Kilda', this slight didactic story concerns half a dozen members of the church choir. Jack Thomson ('a better boy never walked up the aisle') is framed for stealing by another chorister, Dan Robins, who envies Jack's popularity. Dan repents after Jack saves him from drowning, and makes a public confession which is the beginning of regeneration. Besides Dan's conversion, the author offers the exemplary death-bed of little Dick Forester, who dies on Christmas Day 1865, after a long illness which is the direct result of an illicit boating expedition. There is a disapproving reference to colonial beer-drinking, but almost nothing else to mark *The Fernythorpe Choristers* as an Australian story. It is notable only for its extreme dullness, and would not be mentioned here except to make the point that an insider's story of Melbourne in the 1860s could be even less revealing of local scenes and manners than the second-hand accounts provided by London authors.

Frank Oldfield (1877), by T. P. Wilson, won the Band of Hope's prize for 'the best tale illustrative of temperance in its relation to the young'. Its sub-title, 'Lost and Found', refers partly to the two central characters: Frank, 'lost' through intemperance, and Jacob 'found' by God in becoming a total abstainer. The lost and found motif is also worked out in the wanderings of the two young men in Australia at the time of the gold rushes. Frank, the much-indulged, gifted and handsome son of rich parents, loses everything (fortune, fiancée, health and, finally, reason) in spite of the dogged attempts of Jacob, his young servant, to save him from drunkenness. Jacob, a collier's son, who 'never knew the wholesome stimulant of a sober father's smile', runs away from home when his parents forbid him to pledge himself to total abstinence. Both young men are shown as victims of their parents' attitudes to drink. Lady Oldfield wants Frank to conform to the pattern of upper-class society, and to drink 'like a gentleman'. Jacob's mother drives her son from home because he insists on signing the pledge; then, in drunken despair, she hangs herself.

The Australian settings of the central chapters of the novel are not in themselves of much importance. The colony serves as a place of moral testing for Frank and Jacob, where, away from family ties, they can affirm or deny the influences of their upbringing. The scenes in Adelaide and in the countryside stress the natural beauty of Australia, but the all-pervasive temperance theme leaves little room for accounts

of everyday life. There is no enthusiasm for the diggings; easy money
is a moral danger. The Aborigines play no part in the action, but the
author's attitude towards them is made clear in one scene, outside
Adelaide, in which Frank and two companions see a bedraggled group
on the road:

> 'Poor creatures!', exclaimed Hubert; 'what miserable specimens
> of humanity; indeed, they hardly look human at all.'
> 'Ah,' said his uncle, 'there are some who are only too glad to declare
> that these poor creatures are only brutes, that they have no souls. I've
> heard a man say he'd as soon shoot a native as a dingo . . .'
> 'But *you* don't think so, dear uncle?'
> 'Think so! no indeed. Their intellects are sharp enough in some
> things. Yes, it is very easy to take from them their lands, their kanga-
> roo, and their emu, and then talk about their having no souls, just
> to excuse ourselves from doing anything for them in return. Why,
> those very men who will talk the most disparagingly of them, do
> not hesitate to make use of them; ay, and trust them too. They will
> employ them as shepherds, and even as mounted policemen.'

In this passage the author affirms what seems to be the orthodox
evangelical position towards the Aborigines. But, since the plot
demands that Frank and Jacob return to England and confront their
families, this question is not explored, and the common themes of the
settlers' novel, concerning the colony's future, are left alone.

The moral triumph in *Frank Oldfield* belongs to the working-class
boy, Jacob. This, and the general tone of the novel, suggests that the
author was writing for a working-class audience who would–or
should–be satisfied when Jacob, back in England, works contentedly
as an itinerant knife-grinder, distributing temperance tracts, until marriage and an equally lowly job bring complete fulfilment.

A similar insistence on fulfilment through hard work and religious
faith may be seen in *The Children in the Scrub* (1878), by Sophia Tandy.
Subtitled 'A Story of Tasmania', this novel claims that its central incident, in which three children are lost in the bush for five days, is based
on fact. The familiar colonial literary theme of the lost child is used
here as a story of conversion. As in *Frank Oldfield*, there are weak or
delinquent parents. Joe, a farm labourer on a property near Launceston,
has been 'weaned' from drink by his employer, but his wife Jane remains
in a different kind of moral danger. She dislikes her three youngest children's religious beliefs, complains of their 'canting talk' and says: 'I
won't have any young Methodists about me'. The children pray for

her, which annoys her even more. She thinks of the Aborigines as 'heathens', little realizing, the author says, that 'her own soul was in a worse position than theirs', since she has had the opportunity of listening to the Gospel. Jane's devout, cheerful neighbour, Bessie, says that the settlers in Tasmania should have given the Aborigines religion, and not taken their land from them. The author does not share the comparative hopefulness of the settlers' novels described above. Perhaps the Tasmanian setting accounts for the pessimistic verdict: that violence had bred violence, and must lead to 'the total extermination of the Aborigines'.

Jane's three devout children, Janie, Ned and Tom, lost in the bush for five days, pray for rescue. The ordeal brings a change of heart to their mother: she too begins to pray. So does their older brother Richard, an unattractive character who enjoys kangaroo-hunting (seen by the younger children as 'needless cruelty') and is determined to be rich.

When Richard's unaccustomed prayers are answered and he finds the lost children, he and his mother resolve to live by the Gospel. The family is now united in belief. Richard says he will turn his energy to better causes. 'You know I like work . . . my *first* piece of work will be to build a church in the bush on the very spot where I found you, under the shadow of the hollow white-gum tree.' As in the ending of *Frank Oldfield*, the uniting of the work ethic with a sense of Christian mission provides the happy ending.

The narrative viewpoint of *The Children in the Scrub* assumes an English audience. Australian seasons, the author explains, are unlike 'ours'. The ideal emigrant, Bessie, is praised for making 'a little English home' in Tasmania. Nevertheless, the choice of so essentially Australian an incident as the bush search for lost children makes this novel of conversion a little stronger in local flavour than its predecessors. Unlike *Enoch Roden's Training* and *Frank Oldfield* it is set wholly in Australia, and unlike *The Fernythorpe Choristers* its central theme is directly related to the setting.

In *Florence Godfrey's Faith: A Story of Australian Life* (1882) several of the motifs of conversion already described come together in a substantial and reasonably entertaining novel. The author, Emma Pitman, finds in colonial experience material ready-made for illustrating three parables: the Sower, the Prodigal Son and the Good Shepherd. The moral pattern shows very plainly, but, within the conventions of this genre, it succeeds better than most. The reader gains some sense of Australia as a place of real sheep as well as emblematic ones; and the principal Prodigal Son (a convict turned bushranger) is seen as a practical bushman before repentance reduces him to an abstraction.

The story begins in Manchester in 1863 where the Godfrey family faces the familiar choice between ruin and emigration. Mr Godfrey's is one of the many jobs in the cotton manufacturing industry lost because the American Civil War has left the mills idle. He accepts unemployment cheerfully because the war is 'to let the oppressed go free, to set the slaves at liberty' on Southern cotton plantations. Having a little money and some knowledge of farming he believes he can succeed in Australia, and his wife, after initially 'shrinking in true womanly fashion' from the prospect of leaving home, accepts his decision. The heroine of the novel, their daughter Florence, does not want to go, but is persuaded by her Sunday-school teacher to see Australia as an opportunity: 'We are not transplanted from one country to another without an ultimate purpose of good in it. You, unaided and alone, may, under God's direction, be a minister of good to many a one far from his native country and the means of grace'.

Florence's sense of mission becomes the central theme of the novel. She organizes Sunday prayers and gives her own sermon, choosing for the first meeting in the Australian bush the parable of the sower. One by one the members of her congregation begin to see that the material gains of the colony have distracted them from spiritual matters. The isolation of the settlers is soon broken down by regular Sunday prayer-meetings. When the two small children of one of the hutkeepers are lost in the bush, the search party depends as much on faith as on bushcraft. As in *The Children in the Scrub* the lost child incident is the means of conversion for one of the parents. Finally Florence's group of bush converts aquires a minister under whose direction a 'fair-sized iron chapel' is built.

> On a Sunday morning the little community was early astir, and the one little bell . . . struck out a cheerful 'ding-dong' note, which seemed to put a great gulf between the life of the Sabbath and that of yesterday. All in that little community went to the chapel, even down to the babies and dogs. Anybody but a backwoods missionary would have been nervous at the infantile interruptions, and a ritualistic dandy would have considered the presence of the sheep-dogs a pollution. Not so Mr Marsden.

By now Florence's missionary work is over. She is allowed the happy ending which English readers would probably have chosen: to marry and return to England. Before she goes, Mrs Godfrey underlines the

A letter from home
Illustration by Paul Hardy from *Florence Godfrey's Faith*

book's message to its Sunday-school audience by admitting her own dependence on Florence's spiritual strength. 'My own child was my mother in the faith' , she says humbly. Rather inadequately Florence replies that a younger daughter, Mabel ('growing up quite a thoughtful girl') can take her place. Parents need children: the author makes that clear.

Although Florence's Antipodean mission-field is a novelty, the missionary heroine was already familiar in English juvenile fiction. Charlotte Yonge's Etheldred May, with her project for a new parish church, is a forerunner of Florence Godfrey, and a much more engaging character. *Florence Godfrey's Faith* lacks the humour of *The Daisy Chain* (1856) with its admission that Etheldred's enthusiasm is not all that is needed in the cure of souls. Florence is meek, persistent, dedicated and totally uninteresting. Fortunately the author manages narrative and background better than characterization. Her images of Australian life do not suggest much detailed knowledge or research, but she does make an effective contrast between the dispiriting scenes of poverty and unemployment in a Manchester winter and the raw energy of the colony, with its haphazard settlements and its bright sunshine.

Most of the juvenile novels of Australian life have bush settings with Melbourne and Sydney seen as places of spiritual risk. The ideal of village life as the safe retreat from England's industrialized cities is translated into colonial terms with the making of genial little townships like Florence Godfrey's Burntie Glen. One of the few novels to use an urban background, Alexander Fraser's *Daddy Crips' Waifs* (1886), reinforces the city–country moral contrast. The main figure in this long and improbable chronicle is Daddy Crips, the saintly shoemaker of the Rocks district of Sydney. An ex-convict of good family, Daddy has stayed on in this shady neighbourhood to expiate his past by helping others. He has two main protégés, Frank and Rose, both of whom have some mystery of name or birth to unravel before they can marry. Frank also needs money; he goes on a long voyage to New Zealand to prove his steadiness, but on the ship proves his heroism instead when he takes command after the ship's captain is murdered during a mutiny. Meanwhile in Sydney Daddy Crips discovers Rose's parentage. She is a missing heiress, the daughter of a notorious drunkard, now dead, from whom she inherits a property at Parramatta.

Frank spends a long time in New Zealand, where he becomes involved in a Maori tribe's rebellion and converts its chieftain to Christianity. Rose, who cannot enjoy her inheritance while Frank is missing, stays with Daddy Crips at the Rocks, helping with his waifs. They take care of a delirious 'Mr Jones' who has one lucid moment in which he reveals himself as Frank's wicked uncle, before he loses his reason for ever. Frank returns to find his name and property restored: he and Rose then marry.

The plot of *Daddy Crips' Waifs* has a great many more complications than this summary suggests. In tone, however, it is a simple enough moral tale with a strong temperance message. The image of Australia is principally that of a place where people get lost. Daddy Crips is fully occupied in rescuing demented waifs of various kinds and extracting from them the secrets essential to someone else's happiness. As for Daddy, virtue is its own reward.

During the 1870s and 1880s the Australian-born Robert Richardson produced a series of short novels for children in which a moral crisis is central. Although Richardson takes some trouble to interpret the Australian scene for English readers, spelling out the differences in climate and custom between the two hemispheres, his main interest is not setting but character. This may be seen in a comparison between two ostensibly very different narratives, *The Cold Shoulder, or A Half-Year at Craiglea* (1876) and *Black Harry, or Lost in the Bush* (1877). Both are stories of persecuted virtue and both might aptly have been sub-titled 'Misunderstood'. *The Cold Shoulder*, set in a Sydney boarding-school, has a pattern of events familiar to any reader of the English public school story of this period. Its hero is a shabbily-dressed newcomer who has to prove his worth against the prejudice and snobbishness of his form-mates:

> 'There's a new fellow in our form ... He's the queerest figure I've seen at Craiglea for some time. He looks as if he'd just come out of a national school, which perhaps he has; wears Blücher boots; clothes that, I'll be bound, were either bought ready-made or done at home; and the most splendid broad, turned-down collars that fellows used to wear years ago.'
>
> 'What's his name? and who is he?' asked George.
>
> 'His name's Freeling—Christian, Philip. As to who he is, I haven't tried to find out. I believe he comes somewhere from the country, and he looks it.'
>
> 'He may be none the worse for that,' said Alan Kell rather quickly.
>
> 'Oh, I beg your pardon, old chap,' answered Fred. 'I forgot you were born in the bush; but you've lived so much in Sydney, you know, that one couldn't tell.'

Philip, the newcomer to Craiglea, is not only shabby, but clever. A promising classical scholar, he soon wins the approval of his form-master and the hostility of the acknowledged leader of the school, Frank Laidley. In failing to use his influence against those who give the awk-

DADDY CRIPS' WAIFS.

A Tale of Australasian Life and Adventure.

BY

ALEXANDER A. FRASER.

THE RELIGIOUS TRACT SOCIETY,
56 PATERNOSTER ROW, 65 ST. PAUL'S CHURCHYARD,
AND 164 PICCADILLY.

The title page from *Daddy Crips' Waifs*

ward country boy 'the cold shoulder', Frank shows his moral weakness; he cannot bear to come second to Philip in construing Virgil and, like most of the Craiglea boys, he sets great store on appearances. In Richardson's moral scheme Philip represents Humility and Frank is Pride:

> Frank was inclined to be particular about his person and attire. He was a handsome boy, with dark brown eyes and hair, and a warm tinge of dark red in his complexion. His graceful young figure showed to advantage the well-fitting jacket, of the latest cut, and made of the finest Tweed. His collar and neck-scarf, fastened with a small gold pin, were always faultlessly clean, except when occasionally disarranged in the heat of out-door sport.

Something in that description—probably the wholesome warmth of complexion—signals to the reader that Frank is not beyond redemption. It is not the portrait of a cad. All he needs is the shock of discovering how he and the other boys have misjudged Philip; and this comes about when Frank's chum George is bitten by a snake. Philip has a pen-knife and knows exactly what to do; he risks his own life in sucking the poison from the wound. The novel ends with all the Craiglea boys thoroughly ashamed of having failed to see true worth in ill-cut clothes. It is a vindication not only of Philip's bush upbringing, but of his Christian acceptance of suffering:

> With a simple sincerity, and out of a grateful and undoubting heart, [Philip] thanked his Father in Heaven for His guidance in the events of the past week, for the opportunity that had been given him of turning the dislike, contempt, and indifference of his schoolfellows for himself into kind feelings and gratitude.

Richardson wrote several other school stories which have special interest in being the earliest Australian exercises in the genre established in England by *Tom Brown's Schooldays* (1857). They differ, inevitably, from their English models. The schools are small and homely, with none of the sense of tradition which gives the fictional dramas of Rugby or Harrow their emotional intensity. Sydney in the 1870s could not stage the 'Big Match' nor give the scholarship examination its full sense of Oxbridge achievement. The headmaster of Craiglea is not a remote awe-inspiring figure; there are only three or four masters, and the school itself sounds more like a large suburban house than an institution. Richardson's Grange House, the New South Wales boarding-school in *A Perilous Errand* (1876), has an atmosphere of cheerful family life:

> We were just twenty in number at Grange House. That was as many

pupils as Mr Cecil—the Reverend Henry Barclay Cecil, M.A., was his name and title in full—cared to take. Mrs Cecil and he tried to make us comfortable, though we weren't pampered or coddled either . . . We were a happy lot on the whole. We fell out and squabbled occasionally, of course; but being only twenty in number, Mr Cecil had us pretty well in command, and much quarrelling among his pupils was a thing which he could never have put up with.

In effect, Richardson's school stories differ very little from his novels of family life. Home and school provide a context for testing moral worth. *Black Harry* is *The Cold Shoulder* reworked in a domestic setting, with the misunderstood outsider an Aboriginal servant. The narrator, a fourteen-year-old schoolboy, Jack Mailer, resents his little sister's affection for Black Harry. Anna Mailer is a delicate nine-year-old whose role is to play Little Eva to Black Harry's devoted Uncle Tom. Jack is jealous. 'The thought that a half-civilised black-fellow, as I chose to regard him, should supplant me in any way in my sister's regard was a bitter and galling one, and I took no pains to conceal . . . my dislike and ill-will.' Harry patiently endures a campaign of petty persecution, in which Jack knocks down his carefully-built woodheap and destroys his gifts to Anna. It takes the ordeal of being lost in the bush to bring Jack to prayer and repentance. After a few days with nothing to eat except a little parrot, raw or cooked, and some parrots' blood to drink, he is rescued by the magnanimous Harry. He asks Harry to forgive him. 'Say no more 'bout it, Massa Jack', Harry replies. 'You and me be berry good friends all along now.'

Robert Richardson specializes in finding strength and virtue in unlikely places. The arrogant hero of *The Boys of Willoughby School* (1877) disobeys the headmaster's edict against swimming; he gets cramp and is saved from drowning by the despised French master, Monsieur Flavelle. The pattern is the same as that of *The Cold Shoulder*, or *Black Harry*: a spiritual turning-point comes with the seeking of forgiveness. All these novels would have made suitable Sunday-school prizes. The narratives are competently organized, with enough suspense and local colour to make acceptable entertainments. Not all Richardson's stories have Australian settings, but for his purposes Australian life was useful in placing a few comparatively new hazards on the pilgrim's path.

4

Documentaries and Diaries

Among all the colonial children's books discussed here, *A Mother's Offering to her Children* deserves special attention for several reasons. It was published in Sydney in 1841, and therefore is not only one of the earliest juvenile works about Australia, but the first local production. Its author, Charlotte Barton, wrote as 'A Lady Long Resident in New South Wales', a cumbersome title which advertised the book's factual reliability. Unlike the armchair travellers who wrote from secondary sources, or the visitors who made the most of a brief experience of Australian life, Charlotte Barton could claim to know the colony to which she had come in 1827 to be governess to the children of Hannibal Macarthur. Within a few months of her arrival she married James Atkinson, a friend of the Macarthurs, whom she had met on the voyage out. After little more than six years of marriage, Charlotte was left a widow with four small children. She married again, but her second husband, George Barton, was found to be insane, and had to be kept under restraint.[1] Thus, at the time of writing *A Mother's Offering* Charlotte Barton was again alone, bringing up her four children, whose names and ages correspond closely with the four Saville children of her book.

For a personal narrative, Charlotte Barton's experiences in Australia sound full of promising material; and the title of her book suggests domestic drama. However, the form of *A Mother's Offering* is severely educational. What the mother offers is information, and it comes in the question-and-answer form of the Victorian schoolroom text. On shipwrecks, sea-shells, birds and beetles, iron-mines and Aborigines,

Mrs Saville has a formidable stock of facts and anecdotes, for which her children plead each evening. The mother sews and talks: the children practise sketching, and ask questions. The chapters often end with an exemplary show of gratitude for the evening's entertainment:

> *Lucy*: I shall like shells better than ever, Mamma, now I find there are such pretty little histories about them.
> *Mrs S.*: When I meet with a little work on Conchology (as the study of shells is called) suited to your understanding, I will purchase it for you.
> *Lucy*: Good, kind Mamma.

Charlotte Barton makes no attempt to characterize the children or to give the reader much sense of the domestic setting and background. Only in the last chapter, 'Anecdotes of the Aborigines of New South Wales', does she involve the young Savilles in a narrative from their everyday life. Here they match their mother's stories of Aboriginal customs with observations of their own. Clara Saville describes a walk with her nurse in the paddock where she found the 'burnt bones, ashes and hair' of an Aboriginal child, killed by its mother because it was 'too much trouble to rear'. Emma, her younger sister, makes her contribution: 'Billy the black man killed one of his little babies'. Mrs Saville, still calmly sewing, assents: 'Yes, he took it by its feet and dashed its brains against a tree'. She proceeds then to tell the children a more detailed and brutal story of Aboriginal motherhood:

> I remember a tall woman, quite a stranger, coming with a black infant, of less than a month old. It was so ugly, and covered with long hair, as not to look like anything human: but worse than all, the poor little creature had been terribly burned, by the mother putting it too near the fire; and falling asleep. From the ankle to the hip, on one side, it was nearly burned to the bone. It had been done some days ... I therefore had it dressed with lard spread on rags: soon after, I heard the bandages were off. The negligent mother had left it; and one of their hungry dogs, attracted by the smell of the lard, had torn off the rags; and dragged them away; notwithstanding they had been tied on carefully. They were replaced; but the cruel mother appeared quite indifferent to the sufferings of her tender babe. About a week after, I understood it was dead: probably made away with.

This appalling anecdote (which the Saville children receive impassively) invites comparison with the famous incident in *The Fairchild*

Family (1818) in which Mr Fairchild takes his children to see a murderer dangling from a gibbet, so as to show them the consequences of quarrelling. There are no concessions, in Mrs Sherwood's book or in Mrs Barton's, to nursery sensibilities: material which in a later period of the nineteenth century would have been censored was apparently then considered suitable for children. There is, however, an important difference. The Fairchilds' grisly excursion makes a moral point: to frighten the children into peaceable habits. The Savilles are not getting a lesson in motherhood. The story of the murdered child comes through as an example of the 'otherness' of the Aborigine. It is just one more of the curious and interesting 'facts' offered by Mrs Saville to her children, deriving value, so the author claims in the preface, from 'the *truth* of the subjects narrated'. She does not suggest that readers would enjoy it; and since the main narrative interest comes from the evocation of horror, that is probably just as well.

The genre in which Charlotte Barton chose to write should not be judged by the standards of fiction. *A Mother's Offering* is not a failed novel but a collection of facts and anecdotes within a fictional framework. Nevertheless, it is interesting to compare it with an English contemporary, Catherine Sinclair's *Holiday House* (1839), to see how much, in kind and in quality, writing for children might vary at this period. In the characterization of plausibly imperfect children, Catherine Sinclair was ahead of her time. Her protest, in the Preface to *Holiday House*, against those juvenile works which 'stuff the memory, like a cricket-ball, with well-known facts and ready-made opinions' might not have applied to *A Mother's Offering* which has at least the merit of exploring strange new regions. But in a decade of innovations in children's writing which produced Harriet Martineau's *The Crofton Boys* (1841), and Captain Marryat's *Masterman Ready* (1841-42) and *The Children of the New Forest* (1847), Charlotte Barton chose a form with limited imaginative possibilities. The question-and-answer formula leaves the Saville children totally undifferentiated, passive and porous as blotting paper to absorb the relentless flow of maternal instruction.

Australia had to wait until the 1890s for its equivalent of *Holiday House* in domestic comedy and realism. The semi-documentary mode could, however, be given some degree of authentic life. William Howitt's mid-century travelogue, *A Boy's Adventures in the Wilds of Australia* (1854), uses a boy's first-person narrative to give informality and a certain gusto to his stories of colonial life. Herbert, the young hero, keeps a notebook—an 'amusing diary' as he calls it—to take back to England. At its best, *A Boy's Adventures* gives the sound of the spoken rather than the written word, and the sense of one boy talking

to others. The informal style ('But what I was going to say was . . .')
of Herbert's narrative is engaging: so is his delight in the details of
camping-out at the goldfields:

> . . . we do things in style; when we camp, we set down a pair of
> tressels, place on them a piece of stringy bark for a table, and sit
> there with plates, and tea-cups, and glass tumblers at our meals,
> much to the astonishment of the diggers. We are first-rate! And
> what a jolly life it is!

The tea-cups and the glass tumblers point to a well-organized party
of travellers. Herbert, his father, his brother Alfred, his cousin Harry,
and Mr B. the painter are not adventurers or castaways but purposeful
observers of colonial life. Their attitude to gold-seeking is sceptical. The
price of fruit and vegetables is so high in Melbourne, they say, that
farmers turned prospectors might just as well go home and dig their
own gardens. Herbert's cheerful common-sense perspective and the
absence of any major disaster for the travellers might have made this
book too low-key for readers accustomed to more colourful tales from
Australia. Howitt's remedy is to let the harsher side of bush life show
through in tales told to Herbert and his companions. One of these is
the story of Stockman Still, a melancholy exile through whom Howitt
conveys the loneliness of the outback. He also makes room for a lesson
in temperance when Herbert hears about Stockman Still's resolution
before coming to the colony:

> 'I will bury myself in the woods of the Antipodes, far from men
> and from temptation; and, as God hears me, I vow never, never again
> to touch any spirituous liquors. Tea, the great beverage of the Aus-
> tralian Bush, shall be my strongest potion.'

Melancholy anecdotes or comic ones; it is all the same to Herbert.
He enjoys everything. His notebook records the pleasures of discovering new birds and animals and he often exclaims 'What a glorious time
we have had!' He shows only a mild interest in the Aborigines. There
is no evangelical fervour for their conversion; indeed some of the observations are surprisingly off-hand. Speaking of Aboriginal women, Herbert says that they 'show no want of natural affection for their children
in general, though they do kill and eat them occasionally . . .' The difficulty of carrying children and 'household stuff' on their wanderings
is given as the reason for such killings, and Herbert leaves it at that.
Howitt has none of Charlotte Barton's ghoulish relish in stories of
cannibalism. He remains the interested traveller, reporting what he sees

A hunting adventure
Illustration by William Harvey from *A Boy's Adventures in the Wilds of Australia*

and hears, and not inclined to temper Herbert's pleasure—or his readers'—by complex moral issues. The book ends with the party turning towards England and home, and Herbert's predicting a time when 'all this idyllic strange country' will appear 'as but a pleasant dream'.

Louisa Meredith's *Tasmanian Friends and Foes, Feathered, Furred and Finned* (1880) combines family chronicle and natural history. Part of the book is made up of a series of letters to a cousin in England from Lina Merton, the eldest daughter of a Tasmanian farmer. Like Herbert's notebook in *A Boy's Adventures*, Lina's letters are an attempt to give freshness and immediacy to a great deal of very detailed information about Australian birds and animals. Before posting her letters, Lina reads them aloud to the rest of her family. The comments of parents and younger brothers and sister work to some extent in breaking up the large blocks of descriptive writing. So, too, do Lina's anecdotes about family pets, which show the author's concern to reach a juvenile audience:

> We had a tame [kangaroo], a good while ago, that used to hop after us everywhere, even upstairs, and if you had seen him coming down in a hurry, with his long tail and long legs slipping and sprawling as he came scuttering down, you would have felt certain he must tumble over head-first; but he shuffled along all right, finishing off with a leap over the two or three lowest stairs, and a grand scamper round the hall and parlour, as if in delight at his clever performance.

The impression of a girl's voice talking directly and informally to an audience of equals is not consistently maintained, but Lina's letters work better than many similar authorial strategies of this period. They are placed within a larger fictional framework in which the everyday life of the Merton family is described. Although two of the set pieces of colonial adventure—a flood, and a search for lost children—are included, the general effect of Louisa Meredith's book is of a sedate, well-established way of life with pioneering hardships comfortably remote, and England a matter of family legend. The Merton children, Tasmanian-born, are sympathetic but surprised when the sight of a ring-barked forest in a snowfall brings tears to their mother's eyes with its reminder of an English winter scene. They enjoy hearing reminiscences of earlier, pioneering days from both parents, but for them such stories are almost as exotic as for English children.

Writing in old age, Louisa Meredith was able to draw on her memories of Tasmania in the 1840s, and on those of her husband, to give a double focus on colonial experience. The present-day children—Lina, her brothers and sister—are sheltered; they experience none of the ordeals which their father recalls from the early days. But, because the Mertons are not especially prosperous, they keep the pioneering virtues of thrift and hard work. For contrast, some rich friends, the Bexleys, are given a moral lesson when Lina goes to stay with them. Discovering that Lina, like a true colonial girl, is a competent cook, Mr Bexley is disgusted that his daughters spend their time on 'rubbishy fancy-work'. With a twenty-pound wager on her success, he puts Lina to work for a day in his kitchen to produce 'just a plain farm-house dinner' of kangaroo-tail soup, turkey, mutton and some rabbits, followed by pastries, creams and custards. When she wins the bet for him he puts an end to his wife's ambition to make young ladies of fashion out of his daughters:

> '. . . Lucy, and the young ones too, *shall* know how to cook, and to do true woman's work, or, by George, they shall learn nothing else. A parcel of trash and vanity—that's what they learn now, like the rest of the girls. A smattering of languages—not one thoroughly understood. A tasteless squalling and strumming, in the name of music, that, though they're my own daughters, sets my teeth on edge. I don't believe one of them can make herself a frock, or me a shirt . . .'

There is a good deal more domestic interest in this book than the title suggests. *Tasmanian Friends and Foes, Feathered, Furred and Finned* is in some ways a misnomer but it does declare the author's priorities. The three strands of the book—the doings of the Merton children, their father's experience in retrospect, and Lina's letters—are united by a con-servation theme. Evil is typified by the 'greedy Vandalism' which destroys Tasmanian fern-tree valleys or by the 'thoughtless cruel and atrocious habit' of killing birds or animals for sport. The author's moral plan shows clearly when the 'lost in the bush' episode is made to follow indirectly from young Harry Bexley's enthusiasm for kangaroo-hunting. His father questions him angrily: 'And do you mean to say that, for the brutal pleasure of chasing that kangaroo, *you deserted your trust*, and left those poor children by themselves . . ?' The children's uncle says that neither he nor their father would ever 'wantonly' fire a shot; although of course they kill animals for food. Mrs Merton does not allow the children to 'seek out' pets and domesticate them for their own pleasure; they may adopt only animals which could not survive without them.

In general hostile towards the Aborigines, Louisa Meredith adds to

the score against them the charge that they often kill kangaroos without any need of them for food. She is scornful too about British upper-
class rituals of hunting and shooting. So pervasive is her concern for
the preservation of wild life that she risks her moral lesson with repeti-

The cover design of *Tasmanian Friends and Foes*

tiveness, and makes the Merton children at times sound self-righteous. However, the sympathy and accuracy of observation shown in the author's illustrations redress the balance. Her sketches of kangaroos, bandicoots and emus are consistent with her beliefs, since they are not anthropomorphized or domesticated into self-conscious cuteness.

Tasmanian Friends and Foes, a large, handsome and expensive volume, with full-page colour plates as well as black-and-white sketches, is a considerable advance on *A Boy's Adventures* in its presentation of Australian material. The similarities in the use of a first person narrative in a comparatively unsensational style, interwoven with stories from a more romantic past, help to distinguish their differences. With all the limitations of Herbert's naïve vision, *A Boy's Adventures* is a panorama of Australian life in which readers are shown typical scenes and representative figures. Louisa Meredith's book is structurally clumsy: three books in one, awkwardly put together. It does, however, give a sense of ordinary life in a particular region and community which was not available to Howitt the traveller. Perhaps for the first time there is a sense of a 'usable past', in the pioneer tradition of Mr Merton's childhood memories. And, though the Merton children are sketchily drawn, differentiated by age and sex rather than by personality, the author has some ear for dialogue, so that interchanges between children and parents escape the mechanical note of *A Mother's Offering*. If Louisa Meredith had been as interested in children as in birds and animals, she might have written the first Australian children's novel of domestic life. Instead, she produced the most enterprising of the documentaries.

PART TWO
1890–1950

5

The 1890s: Transition

In the last decade of the nineteenth century the children's books set in Australia were still, more often than not, written from a British perspective, published in the United Kingdom, and dependent for their readership mainly on British children. As the colonies' population grew, the balance began gradually to shift. British writers of adventure stories lost interest when Australia became more settled and suburban. The far North for a time replaced New South Wales as a place of fictional adventure, but it was obvious, at the turn of the century, that the frontiers of romantic enterprise were receding fast. That did not mean, of course, that stories of adventure or settlement vanished overnight, but they were no longer dominant. There were other ways of writing about Australia for children, and an increasing number of local authors ready to make use of their own experience by writing in the domestic mode.

It would be too simple to say that the Australian child came indoors in the fiction of the 1890s because, before the 1890s, there were almost no child-like characters in the children's books of Australia. The nature of the adventure story or the settlers' tale demanded young adults engaged in what were essentially adult activities. The appeal of these books was not that of recognizing mirror images, but of seeing figures, larger than life-size, on whom readers might, in imagination at least, model themselves. The books concentrated on event, not character, so that the hero was usually a representative figure rather than an individual. He was much more often seen working than playing. His satisfactions were in endurance and achievement; and although achievement could be spiritual as well as physical there was little inner conflict. Fun, quarrelling, childish mistakes had no place in his life. Such simple outlines of 'pattern' heroes or heroines are not, of course, found only in the stories of outdoor adventure and settlement with which writers about Australian life were most concerned. Characters so pure as to be abstractions may be seen in English and American domestic settings throughout the nineteenth century. It was part of the writer's task to provide models for emulation. Critics who see the history of children's books as a steady progress towards modern psychological insight often mistake what Victorian writers were trying to do. Lack of understanding of the nature of childhood and sheer literary incompetence account for many of the uninteresting, over-simplified characters in nineteenth century children's books. But anyone who thinks the Victorians generally incapable of understanding children should remember *Jane Eyre* and *David Copperfield*. Perhaps if Brontë and Dickens had writing for children, they would have chosen as protagonists saintly Helen Burns and child-woman Agnes Wickfield instead of self-willed Jane and egotistical little David. Fortunately, they were not. These adult novels of the 1840s, read by children as well as their parents, may have had some influence in showing how, without moral confusion, the juvenile novel could deal with the difficulties of flawed or divided characters. Whether or not this is so, the mid-century brought to children's fiction a new kind of heroine, in Ethel May of *The Daisy Chain*. Plain, awkward, clever, not especially lovable, Ethel is no more an exemplary heroine than the young Jane Eyre. She is also, recognizably, a child.

The move towards an imitation of childhood rather than an idealization of it was taking place in English and American juvenile novels at a time when Australian fictional children were still playing their adult roles. In the 1880s, however, there were the first signs of a change. Benjamin Farjeon's *The Golden Land* (1886) has exactly the same basic situation as *Alfred Dudley* or any of the mid-century settlers' novels. It takes a penniless English family, of a father and five young children, to Australia to join a rich uncle at his station property, Golden Bush. The uncle's invitation strikes a familiar note when he writes about the opportunities of the colony:

> There is no reason why [the boys] should not be thriving and prosperous men, and as for your little girl—well, she will be able to make herself useful, too ... I can promise you one thing— opportunity, which you don't often meet with in the old country.

On my vast cattle station, and in this free land, your boys will grow to be *men*; they will not be cooped up; they will have room to breathe. They are not to come out with an idea that they are going to be fine gentlemen; they are to come with the view of doing manly work. We will soon discover what they are fit for . . .

That sounds like Kingston in *The Young Berringtons* and, reading the passage in isolation, one would expect the novel to show how the young Spencers prove themselves in 'manly work'. Yet *The Golden Land* does nothing of the kind. Even though its author had travelled in Australia and New Zealand, he makes little use of local colour and gives no hints for young settlers. More than half the book is taken up with the decision to emigrate and the children's feelings about leaving England. When Mr Spencer calls a family council to discuss Uncle William's invitation, the dialogue has less to do with the decision than with conveying a sense of everyday family relationships:

'Then we shall have a meeting when you come home, papa,' said Harry.

'Yes, Harry, and each shall give his vote on the subject.'

'Splendid!' cried Irving. 'Girls don't vote—mind that, Eleanor.'

'They do, they do!' exclaimed the damsel, standing up in defence of woman's rights.

'They don't, they don't', said Irving, inclined to teaze. 'Didn't you hear papa say that each shall give *his* vote on the subject? Now, as you are a her, where do you come in, I should like to know?'

'Papa,' said Eleanor, earnestly, 'am I not to have a vote?'

'Yes, my dear', said Mr. Spencer, smoothing her hair. 'You must have a vote. Irving is only teazing you.'

'I dare say,' remarked Harry, 'when you are a big woman you will be able to go into parliament if you care to.'

'My!' exclaimed Eleanor, her eyes growing very large. 'I wonder where *is* parliament, and what I should do if I got there?'

'Upset everything,' said Irving.

As this inconsequential exchange suggests, Farjeon's subject is family life, with emigration providing a thin thread of a plot. The children's arguments, fantasies and games take precedence over the account of their travels. The perspective is deliberately naïve, and Farjeon would certainly have claimed to be writing about realistically observed children. The book might well have been based on stories told by Farjeon to his own children, among whom the future author Eleanor Farjeon (of *The Little Bookroom*) provided the model for Eleanor Spencer.

Throughout the novel, the mood is conversational and the pace deliberately slow. By lingering over the details of the decision, packing, sea voyage and land-travel to Golden Bush on the Murray River, Farjeon holds back the appearance of rich Uncle William until the last chapter. Within the narrative, a number of fanciful stories told to the children about Australian life delay the moment of arrival, and mildly satirize the colonial tradition of tall tales.

In *The Golden Land* for the first time children move into the foreground of an Australian story without losing their childish qualities. In *Tom's Nugget* (1888) J. F. Hodgetts holds on to the stage properties of the earlier adventure stories but gives the leading part to a precocious eight-year-old with an extraordinary record of life-saving and gold-finding. By making a small boy the main agent of all the rescues and discoveries in this tale of the goldfields, the author changes the tone of the adventure story to make comedy prevail over suspense. All the good Tom does is more or less by accident. When the family fortunes are low, his mother ill, and his father making no progress at the diggings, Tom does *not* set out to find gold. He is much more interested in seeing a kangaroo or a platypus. Idly throwing stones by the river at 'Bendiggerat', near his father's mining claim, Tom picks up 'a nugget of gold as big as an egg, weighing about a pound', and almost immediately loses it by throwing it at a platypus. Retrieving this first nugget, he finds a far more valuable one—the largest ever seen on the diggings. News of his luck brings on the scene the notorious bushranger Captain Galton, who steals the nugget. Galton is captured, through Tom's quick-wittedness, escapes, and is recaptured, again because Tom is more observant than anyone else. While the adults exclaim at Tom's courage, the child is shown to be unaffected by his triumphs, and intent only on finding the curious animal which he calls 'horny-floflinxus' for ornithorhynchus.

The description of Tom and his friend Billy searching for the platypus shows some of the ways in which the children's stories of Australia at this time differ from their predecessors:

> There was no sign of the animal, however hard Tom pecked at the bank or Billy dug into the sand. At last our hero, tired and hungry, threw down his pick, exclaiming—
> 'Beastly country this is! You never find what you want. In England, now, if you want frogs or anything, you know where to look and how to find them. Perhaps, after all, there are no horny-floflinxuses at all! Disappointing, isn't it?'

An illustration by Gordon Browne from *The Golden Land*

'You have no right to growl, considering you have the finest nugget ever found.'

'You shut up about the nugget! It was a fluke, I tell you, and has brought me nothing but bother.'

The colloquial language ('beastly', 'bother', 'fluke'), Tom's attempt to pronounce ornithorhynchus, and the companionable rudeness with which the two boys address one another, all show Hodgetts' attempt at a realistic portrait of childhood. The platypus is not there to be scientifically categorized, as it was in such mid-century stories as *The Kangaroo Hunters*. Its quaint appearance and habits are less important than Tom's fascination with them: the focus of the story is on the observing child, not what he observes. The illustrator Gordon Browne has cooperated with the mood of the book by making the confrontation between Tom and the bushranger anything but alarming; the latter looks heavy and stupid, no threat to the small alert figure of the child.

The effect of *Tom's Nugget* depends on the reader's willingness to suspend disbelief about Tom's accidental achievements and to tolerate the archness of tone of much of the narrative. In his exchanges with adults, Tom's habit of artless questioning is used so as to leave him with a moral advantage he is too innocent to understand. When, for example, he scores a point in cross-examining a soldier about the morality of killing, Tom is made to say with no intention of sarcasm: 'Funny people are, ain't they? ... Mr Forbes has a medal like one of yours for saving the life of a man who was drowning, and you have half a dozen for killing people! Funny, isn't it?'

It seems unlikely that any reader today would respond to Tom with the delighted admiration and amusement he draws in the novel for his incessant, innocent questioning. Naïve charm is not easy to achieve, and J. F. Hodgetts lacks the necessary literary tact. His novel has some historical interest for its portrayal of Melbourne as 'Canvastown' in the 1850s; and, like *The Golden Land*, it marks a transitional stage in juvenile stories of Australia. The stock characters and situations, the goldseekers and bushrangers, remain, but the hero has shrunk to child-size, a Little Lord Fauntleroy of the Antipodes.

Eleanor Stredder's novel, *Archie's Find* (1890), brings a boy and a nugget together again. As a fictional hero Archie has some negative virtues. He is neither universally loved nor preposterously lucky, as Tom is. His creator does not extract laborious humour from his mispronunciations of the language or his misconceptions of the adult world. And yet one could hardly say that Archie is lifelike. He is the colourless central character in a tangled plot which begins with his discovery of gold in a neighbour's property and ends with his acceptance of the difficult tenth commandment: Thou shalt not covet thy neighbour's goods. This is even less satisfying than Tom's tedious accumulation of gold, legacies and good opinions. Archie's mother is pleased that her son gives up his find with good grace to someone who needs it more than

Tom confronts the bushranger
Illustration by Gordon Browne from *Tom's Nugget*

he does, but her quiet satisfaction is an anti-climax after the promise of gold in a secret cave. The setting, on a farm near Melbourne, and some sense of community among a set of Australian families, may be said to mark a further stage of domestication in colonial children's stories, but that is almost all that can be said for *Archie's Find*. It is perhaps worth adding that its perspective and implied audience are clearly English, and that its presentation of Australian life is vague and flattering, with emphasis on the richness of the land:

> The ground was undulating and varied. Golden fields of corn flourished on the uplands, and the waste places in the less fertile valleys were bright with patches of banksia. Some of the fields were hedged with flowering gorse, and others were railed in with strong, rough fences of wood; but that wood was mahogany–a wood which we reserve for chairs and tables, but the Australian settler thinks little of it. He uses cedars for floor-boards and window-frames, and brings logs of sweet-scented myrtles, which grow to the size of trees in this favoured land.

For Eleanor Stredder, as for Farjeon and Hodgetts, Australia was still the golden land even though its romantic possibilities were scaled down to a child's perspective. More matter-of-fact versions appear in two auto-biographical works, both published in 1892. Mrs Hughes' *My Childhood in Australia* and Ellen Campbell's *An Australian Childhood* are alike in the reminiscent grandmotherly tone in which they address their readers. Both look back with nostalgic enjoyment to the scenes and events of rural family life in mid-century Australia. Plotless and anecdotal, these books draw their charm from the ease and naturalness of the narrative voice. Nothing heroic was demanded from either of the colonial girls whose early memories are captured here. They recall the minor domestic comedies of a secure and relatively prosperous way of life in the outback. Because they were period pieces at the time of their publication, the Campbell and the Hughes 'childhoods' are doubly illuminating. The facts as presented are, no doubt, faithful enough to experience in the 1850s. The perspective, looking back from the 1890s to recreate a younger self, reveals something of the mood of the later period, and its attitude to childhood. Mrs Campbell, for example, presents herself as 'Nellie', a sturdy little bush girl who spends most of her time out of doors. Inventive, thoughtless and courageous, Nellie is usually in trouble of some kind but her enterprises are all, in the end, matters for laughter, with her parents' justifiable anger always tempered by amusement. There is no moral disapproval for Nellie. Disobedience, which in many stories

ARCHIE'S FIND

A Story of Australian Life

BY
E. STREDDER

THE EAGLE. page 15

The title page of *Archie's Find*

for children leads to disaster, repentance and moral regeneration, is accepted here as a matter of course, as the tone of this passage indicates:

> I paid surreptitious visits to the blackfellows' camp across the creek, and to the barn.
>
> We were forbidden to haunt the former place, the society of lubras and picaninnies not being considered edifying by the authorities; but who could consider orders when a pair of young possums was in the question, and what were gum-trees for, if not to dodge behind, or fleet legs, unless to elude 'grown-ups.'

Nellie, Ellen Campbell's self-portrait, appears again in fictional form in *Twin Pickles* (1898) as Grace Templeton. There is virtually no difference between Nellie and Grace, but in *Twin Pickles* the author takes advantage of the freedom of fiction to give her narrative a more satisfying shape. As the title indicates, this novel celebrates mischievous children. The adventures of Grace and her brother Ted on a country property in New South Wales are presented in a deliberately anti-heroic style. Like Ethel Turner, in whose *Seven Little Australians* (1894) the authentic spirit of Australian childhood was seen as 'joyousness and rebellion and mischief', Ellen Campbell writes in conscious reaction against the literary tradition of angelic children. She stresses the normal unruly state of Grace and Ted by contrasting them with the heroes and heroines of the books they read. Their attempts to reform themselves according to the model of 'Little Comfort', in one of Grace's favourite books, has different motives but the same effect as the Woolcots' plan of good behaviour in *Seven Little Australians*. 'Little Comfort', Grace says, got her name because

> she was so good and kind to everybody, and did such lots of things to help. The things she did always came just right, and everyone praised her for doing them. She used to teach little children in Sunday-schools, and Ted and I wished very much that we could keep a little Sunday-school, and teach little children to be good . . . There was one little child on the place. He was our gardener's son, and we thought we would begin a Sunday-school on him, but when we went to his mother . . . she was not at all nice about it.
>
> She said: 'Hadn't you best learn the way first yourselves, Miss Grace?'
>
> So we could not keep a school, but we used to read a great deal about 'Little Comfort', and all she used to do . . . She used to get up early, and do all the house-work, and help her mother with sewing and all sorts of things. Her mother was a widow and used to

lean on her, that was another advantage she had over us. Our mother wasn't a widow, never seemed to want to lean on us, and there never seemed to be any house-work to do.

When their parents go away for a day, Grace and Ted decide that 'Little Comfort' would not miss such an opportunity to do good. Their attempt to tidy their father's study, and his reaction to it, cure them of 'Little Comfort' and literary models, for, as Ted says: 'If we are officious, interfering mischievous brats [their father's words], then 'Little Comfort' was one too, and I'll never read another line of that book, never.'

Grace's point of view, in her first-person narrative, works far better for comedy than Hodgetts' self-consciously whimsical presentation of childhood in *Tom's Nugget*. And where Tom is intended to be both endearingly childish and exceptionally resourceful, Grace and Ted are allowed to be ordinary. Their only chance for heroism comes when they mistakenly believe the house to be surrounded by bushrangers: they scream for help and hide: 'It's bushrangers,' sobbed Ted from under the table. 'The verandah's full of them, and there are more at the back. Come under the table, Mother, before they fire and kill you.'

Apart from Ethel Turner's work, which will be discussed in the next chapter, Ellen Campbell's two books are the most engaging portraits of childhood from the 1890s period, with *Twin Pickles* having the advantage over the autobiography for its well-managed comic perspective and a better narrative structure.

The move in the 1890s towards domestic realism did not mean the disappearance of the outdoor adventure story. It did mean, however, that the young adventurers were more likely to be seen in the context of their everyday family life, and that their enterprises dwindled from the almost impossible to the mildly improbable. The events of *The White Kangaroo* by E. Davenport Cleland (1890) take place in the school holidays of two boys, home for the summer on a South Australian cattle station. Neither fourteen-year-old Ralph nor his cousin Ernest, who is thirteen, is represented as any more than average in ability or courage. They are not even expected to be particularly useful. Ralph's father, Mr Everdale, welcomes them home genially with an invitation to enjoy themselves: '. . . you two must make as much noise as ever you can, and get into all the scrapes possible to enliven us'. Ralph and Ernest have a pillow fight on their first night at home, forget to brush their hair in the morning, and play good-humoured practical jokes on the station hands. There is a good deal more detail given about everyday station life than is characteristic of earlier adventure stories.

The Everdale family is seen at meals, and at family prayers, with the piano wheeled into the dining room and all the servants assembled. There is talk of the drought, and the need to save water: 'If we don't use too much soap', the boys say, 'it will do for the dogs to drink afterwards, so it won't be wasted'. When Ralph and Ernest go mustering with Mr Everdale, they are only moderately competent. Adventure comes to them mainly through their own carelessness: tempted to chase the famous white kangaroo they lose their way, forget to tether their

The frontispiece of *The White Kangaroo*

horses and try to walk home. Lost in the bush without food they feel the need of the kind of hero they have read about: in fiction 'there was generally some wonderful fellow . . . who knew everything, a kind of cyclopaedia on two legs'. Ralph says he will write to the papers about their own experience: Ernest suggests 'Boys in the Bush' as a title. 'Or the "Innocents in the Interior",' added Ralph. By stressing the contrast between fiction and real life, with direct reference to Richard Rowe's adventure story of 1872, the author of *The White Kangaroo* satirizes the convention in which he is writing. Ralph and Ernest are kidnapped by 'wild blacks', and held for a short but very uncomfortable time. When they manage to escape, their lack of bushcraft tells; they are near starvation when Mr Everdale finds them. In courage and cheerfulness the boys perform well, but, since they brought their ordeal on themselves, it amounts to a maturing experience rather than a creditable enterprise. One of the incidental lessons of the kidnapping episode is to find the Aborigines not worth any missionary efforts: '. . . even the short time during which the boys had been with them was sufficient to show how very degraded a nation they were.' Ernest's ideas of Christianizing them are discarded. Mr Everdale sums up: '. . . I do not see what can be done for them, except that we must treat them kindly, and not render their life any more miserable than it is. They have no religion, and therefore no hope.'

The White Kangaroo is in part a tall tale but one with medium-sized boys in it. Ralph and Ernest have to rely on Mr Everdale and his stockmen to rescue and return them to the safety of the homestead. The adventure is enclosed in what is essentially a family story, and the author shows some sense of the probable in his portrayal of the boys. The subtitle, 'A Tale of Colonial Life Founded on Fact', is given credence by what seems an accurate representation of station routine and a contemporary setting. Hodgetts, Mrs Hughes and Ellen Campbell look back to the 1850s. Eleanor Stredder's uncertain grasp of Australian life makes *Archie's Find* hard to date, but its references to the diggings and 'ticket of leave men' suggest an early period. Time past, then, or the remote place, several hundred miles north of Adelaide, in which *The White Kangaroo* is set, give these 1890s books a touch of romance, tempered by a growing realism in the depiction of children.

6

Ethel Turner: Domestic Interiors

During the 1890s it became increasingly clear that the sturdy boy-settler and his reliable, home-making sister were out of fashion in tales of Australia. This was the decade of little pickles, little rebels, little larrikins and—instead of young Anglo-Australians—little Australians. It was the decade of Ethel Turner. She united the nationalistic spirit of the period with a talent for drawing lifelike and likeable children, none of them models of good behaviour, against a background of suburban Sydney. She filled in the child's map of Australia, for the first time, to show city streets, shops, theatres, schools, factories and warehouses, so that Sydney was no longer a landing-place, a point of departure for bush adventure but a place for ordinary families with white-collar wage-earning fathers.

Ethel Turner, who came to Australia in 1880,[1] at the age of eight with her mother, sister and stepsister, recalled in her autobiographical novel, *Three Little Maids* (1900), her first shock of disappointment on landing at Sydney to find it 'merely a city' like those left behind in England, with none of the exotic sights her reading had led her to expect:

> No chocolate-coloured beings, clad in bright, scanty garments, darted down to a yellow beach and pushed off in strange boats to welcome their ship; no kangaroos leapt back into the thick forests near the water's edge startled at their approach . . . Nowhere lay a field dug into holes, the greenness of its grass showing up brilliantly the careless heaps of sparkling nuggets.

But, as her life and her novels show, Ethel Turner was happy to leave unexplored the myths and realities of the Australian bush. Most of her books are set in the Sydney she knew, with the outback seen occasionally: a place of dust, heat, flies and, generally, boredom. The illustrators commissioned by her London publishers must have found the Turner novels surprisingly easy work; for the most part they had only to draw domestic interiors like those of any English story, with never a kangaroo in sight. Only the ring-barked gum tree which kills Judy Woolcot in *Seven Little Australians* (1894) placed small figures in a threatening bush landscape.

In refusing to use the boomerang and bushranger formula Ethel Turner brought her work much closer to the experience of most Australian children, and thereby ran the risk of making it too commonplace for the British readers on whom her sales might be expected to depend. A combination of talent and timing helped her solve the common problem of colonial fiction with its necessarily divided audience, and its dependence on British publishers. It is illuminating to consider Ethel Turner's success in the 1890s against the comparative failure of Catherine Helen Spence whose *Clara Morison* (1854), a competent low-key adult novel of domestic life in Adelaide, could compete neither with its great contemporaries in British social fiction nor with the Anglo-Australian writers of romance. In the 1850s an Australian novel in the style of Mrs Gaskell looked colourless beside Kingsley's *Geoffry Hamlyn* (1859). Catherine Spence saw the difficulties in these terms: 'If stories are excessively Australian they lose the sympathies of the bulk of the public. If they are mildly Australian the work is thought to lack distinctiveness'.[2] She was only half right. The 'excessively Australian' did better than the 'mildly Australian'. *Clara Morison* has had its belated recognition in recent years, but it is easy to see why it won so little attention a century ago. The Australian reader who wanted domestic realism looked to Britain; and the British reader looked to Australia only for romance.

Ethel Turner, coming later to the literary scene, was more fortunate than Catherine Spence in the size and disposition of her local readership. As the colonies moved towards Federation there was not only a numerically larger audience but one with more confidence in the local literary product. It is relevant that Ethel Turner was seen as one of the *Bulletin* school and she drew on the literary nationalism of the 1890s.[3] This might well have made her 'excessively Australian' for a writer of children's books, whose sales depended not only on the children's pleasure but on the scrutiny of parents and teachers. The achievement of Ethel Turner was to be distinctively Australian within the mode of domestic realism, and to please adults and children in both hemispheres. At times her 'Australianism' came into conflict with her publishers' sense of propriety and profit: such conflicts make a fascinating study in Anglo-Australian literary relations. Because of the questions raised in these disputes and because *Seven Little Australians*, still in print nearly a century after first publication, affirms her lasting talent, the Turner history deserves close examination.

Ethel Turner accomplished a double revolution. She took Australian fictional children away from the station homesteads and goldfields of earlier novels. More important, she developed a new literary type in her heroes and heroines, in whom the models from her own reading in English and American juvenile fiction were reshaped and given a sense of authentic life as Australian children, unselfconsciously distinctive in idiom and outlook.

As I have suggested, the 1890s—in fiction at least—favoured the naughty child. The authors of the period, having themselves been given an early diet of heavily didactive works, rejected the saintly, sickly little Erics or little Evas in favour of little imps and scapegraces. These, of course, could be equally tedious, equally sentimental. The naughty child was not necessarily any more interesting than the good child. The only advantage might be that he could be given a happy ending, by reforming himself and growing up. The good child could make progress only by dying. But since many readers liked crying over a death-bed scene it is impossible to say that the maturing of Louisa Alcott's imperfect heroine Jo March was more satisfying than the death of Jo's perfect little sister Beth. Jo's growing-up is, in fact, the end of everything that defined her personality: a kind of death, for which the author will not allow any tears.

Ethel Turner's first fictional children appeared in the *Parthenon*, a Sydney monthly magazine of which she and her sister Lilian were joint founders, owners and editors. They also wrote nearly all of it (including the Letters to the Editor) and Ethel's share included the Children's Page. Here, in 1889, when she was seventeen, she published the serial, 'A Dreadful Pickle'. It was followed in 1890 by 'Bobbie', the story of a tomboy (revised as *Miss Bobbie*, 1897), and by 'That Young Rebel' in 1891. Ethel Turner did not take these stories very seriously. She and her sister had larger literary ambitions which may be seen in the unconsciously comic 'adult' serials they wrote for the *Parthenon*. The casualness with which the children's serials were written, and the sense of a local audience for whom Sydney settings were appropriate, were advantages of which the author was not then aware. These early fictional children—pickle, tomboy and rebel—went through a series of escapades which showed narrative inventiveness and a comic sense, but not much originality in characterization. The inventiveness, indeed, sometimes wore thin, as may be seen in one of Ethel Turner's diary entries: '. . . Night wrote Young Rebel, Chapter XIV—a chapter on smoking. Taffie has done every possible and impossible naughty thing, I don't know how to keep him going to the end of the year'.

Somehow she did keep 'That Young Rebel' going; and this story seems to have been the first she submitted for publication in book form. Ward Lock, a London publisher with an office in Melbourne, rejected it in March 1892. Their verdict, summarized by Ethel Turner, was 'a good story . . . but it doesn't pay them to publish local things'. Late in the following year she sent *Seven Little Australians* to Ward Lock. This time she had an immediate acceptance, a request for a sequel and Ward Lock's official welcome to 'the Louisa Alcott of Australia'.

The Alcott label was predictable: surely the choice of Woolcot for the Australian fictional family name invites the comparison. So does the story itself, with its contrasting pair of sisters. Meg and Judy Woolcot parallel Meg and Jo March in a number of ways. The older sisters are both pretty, slightly vain and worldly, impatient with the family's genteel poverty, almost ready for love and marriage, and finally guaranteed as good wives in the making. Jo and Judy take the rebel role; they are quick-tempered, clever, strong-willed and disdainful of the ladylike ways they associate with growing up. Other resemblances might easily be noted in a fuller analysis. Yet the Australian story gives no sense of being second-hand.

Ethel Turner gave her family story an Australian idiom and setting; and with an irascible father and an ineffectual stepmother, made the Woolcot children more or less self-sufficient in a style which flattered the national sense of independence and freedom from convention. She extended the family, and thereby the range of her readers, by giving Meg and Judy two brothers, a very young sister, and a baby stepbrother, 'the General'. These provide comedy and carefully subdued pathos. Sometimes, as Ward Lock's Melbourne manager, William Steele, seems to have thought, they risk the self-consciously whimsical note of *Helen's Babies*, a best-seller of 1876, whose appalling archness shows the dangers of writing about very small children. Nell Woolcot follows Amy March quite closely, but the fourth March sister, saintly Beth, has disappeared. And yet Ethel Turner managed to have the death-bed scene so popular in Victorian fiction. This is done with a difference because it is not the good child who dies, but the imperfect, difficult Judy, who,

The schoolroom at Misrule
Illustration by A. J. Johnson from *The Family at Misrule*

like Jo March, does not want to grow up, but unlike Jo, does not have
to. 'Killed Judy to slow music', Ethel Turner noted irreverently in her
diary, but she was delighted when William Steele (self-described as 'a
man of 40, tough as businessmen go') confessed to being deeply moved
by the death scene. So were many contemporary readers: the death of
Judy was a recitation piece, in the manner of a Dickens reading, in Australian literary meetings as late as 1925. Twentieth century readers habitually dismiss all death scenes in Victorian children's fiction as sentimental, but those who re-read *Seven Little Australians* in the context
of nineteenth century literature should concede that Ethel Turner was
unusual in knowing when to stop. She does not transform the dying
child: Judy will not accept death easily, nor is Meg made instinctively
capable of consoling her with the traditional hymn or prayer. What
makes the scene moving is the children's struggle to meet the demands
of Judy's death, with an uncertain faith and no adult protection against
their own fear.

In *Three Little Maids* Ethel Turner described her own imaginative
life when, just too old to play with dolls, she constructed stories to
match the faces on the pack of cards with which she and her sisters
played 'beggar my neighbour'. Dolly Conway, the future author of *The*

Sins of Six, who is Ethel Turner's fictional counterpart, takes the Queen of Spades as her heroine:

> she saw in her a dark little girl with flashing eyes and a propensity for getting into terrible mischief, and then dying with pious words of exhortation on her lips and all her weeping relatives around her bed. She was a unique mixture of Topsy and Eva, and Dolly named her Judy.

That 'unique mixture of Topsy and Eva' suggests something of Ethel Turner's method of characterization. Where the Victorians had tended to divide their heroines—fair or dark, angel or vampire, in adult fiction—and to make similar simplifications in children's books, the Turner novels allow for some degree of complexity and inner contradiction. They depend less on plot than on small, everyday incidents which illuminate character in family relationships. Ethel Turner was never again to create a group so convincing in its family life as the Woolcot children in *Seven Little Australians* and *The Family at Misrule*, but she did establish a line of heroines (Brigid in the *Cub* series, Jennifer J., Nicola Silver) of whom readers would ask, not the question 'what will happen to her?', but 'what will she do?' Her heroines are often gifted, in art, literature, music, acting. Some have to choose between marriage and a career; they always choose marriage but the decision is not automatically made even though the moral pattern is clear.

Such heroines, and some heroes, co-exist in the Turner novels with the small children from whom the author's main comic effects are derived. It makes, sometimes, for an awkward mixture which reflects the author's wish to write about children for adults and her publisher's determination to keep her within the juvenile range. In *The Little Larrikin* (1896) the main plot is Ethel Turner's semi-autobiographical story of a girl whose ambitions as a painter conflict with her love for a young Sydney barrister. The parallels with Ethel Turner's own life are obvious, especially in the discovery of the heroine, Linley Middleton, that she can only paint children, and that her adult portraits are grotesquely bad. Whether Ethel Turner knew it or not the wooden hero and heroine in her novel demonstrate this point rather too well. Understanding the limits of her talent, Linley refuses a chance to study in Rome, marries the barrister, and stays at home in Sydney. The 'little larrikin' of the title is incidental to all this. Except that he is the hero's youngest brother and one of the financial obstacles to marriage, Lol has no part to play except comic diversion. He does not bring the lovers together, as in the *Helen's Babies* formula. He exists in his private, lawless world, a Sydney street urchin from a shabby-genteel family, self-absorbed and more or less selfish. A little rebel with an Australian vocabulary and a larrikin 'push' of his own, Lol is interesting mainly as an attempt to draw a portrait of a specifically Australian child. He is neither clean, polite, chivalrous nor particularly truthful; his portrait, clearly, is intended to comment on the literary stereotype of those innocent children who shame a corrupt adult world into moral awakening.

In *The Little Larrikin* and in *Seven Little Australians* Ethel Turner asserts a relationship between children's qualities and the new country to which they belong. Not one of the seven Woolcot children was 'really good', because 'Australian children never are'. English children, Ethel Turner conceded with evident irony, might be models of virtue. Since she did not know any such prodigies, she would write of what she did know: the ordinary Australian family. Her commitment to realism was thus clearly stated in her first novel. Her early literary strategy was to reflect the actual, not the ideal: to use the looking-glass, not the lamp. With *Seven Little Australians* and its sequel *The Family at Misrule* (1895) she moved beyond the stereotype of the 'little pickles' of her *Parthenon* stories to show character and family relationships with some degree of complexity. A chapter heading in the first novel, 'Bunty in the Light of a Hero', is illuminating. Having created Bunty Woolcot

Nursery tea
Illustration by A. J. Johnson from *Seven Little Australians*

in deliberately anti-heroic terms, as greedy, lazy, timid and untruthful, Ethel Turner gives him a chance to show courage in the family conspiracy to keep Judy's escape from boarding school a secret from Captain Woolcot. Given Bunty's fear of his father, his efforts to keep Judy hidden and fed are heroic; but his collapse into abject tears and recriminations against his brother and sisters ('Twasn't me, twasn't my fault—hit the others some') shows the author's refusal of quick character changes.

Ethel Turner's world is not, of course, a moral wilderness. Bunty's lapses are seen with contempt by Pip and Judy who affirm the family code of honour. But the reader is likely to feel that they expect too much from Bunty: they fail in sympathy and perceptiveness as much as he fails in courage. Thus, implicitly, the author asserts her system of values, refusing a monopoly of wisdom and virtue to any of the children, or to their parents, but giving her readers their moral bearings in the whole pattern of family relationships. Here, again, she differs from Louisa Alcott. The March girls have their infallible, devoted 'Marmee' to guide them, and an idealized father, away at the Civil War but an influence none the less. The Woolcot children are not orphans, but they might as well be. They apply their own rough justice to one another; their collective judgement works as a kind of Children's Court without a magistrate.

Perhaps it was this sense of anarchy in the Turner world that prompted an English reviewer's solemn rebuke: 'We gather from the pages of [Seven Little Australians] that Antipodean boys and girls are brought up rather too much on the lines of American children to leave much room for grace, modesty and reverence in their composition'.[4]

The Woolcots, according to this reviewer, might perhaps profit from the freedom of their upbringing and become fine men and women, but they were in danger of developing 'the wrong way' into the larrikin type. Was it in response to this warning that Ethel Turner wrote The Little Larrikin, in which Lol Carruthers ends as he began—with no 'grace, modesty or reverence' achieved or even promised?

With The Little Larrikin Ethel Turner came for the first time into serious disagreement with her publishers. William Steele liked to see himself as the godfather of Seven Little Australians, and he delighted in that novel's success. It was natural that he should want a larger international audience for its successors, and that British sales and good opinions should be more important to him than any others. He had reason to be pleased with Ethel Turner's local reception, with Seven Little Australians sold out in Sydney within weeks of its publication.

In Britain, however, sales were pleasing, but not outstanding: the London office reported to Steele that 800 copies were sold in the first three months of publication. To make the book better known, Ward Lock's London manager sent out complimentary copies to well-known children. By such means, polite letters of congratulation were extracted from Prince Alexander of Battenburg and the Duchess of Albany. This campaign suggests Ward Lock's priorities and Ethel Turner's problem in writing for a British publisher and a geographically divided audience.

In 1895 William Steele, having read *The Little Larrikin* in manuscript and disliking its Australian flavour, did his best to remove Ethel Turner from Sydney and remodel her work for English tastes. He was uneasy about the language and setting of *The Little Larrikin*, with its accounts of 'the push'; and he had his solution: the young author should go to England:

> ... a little English experience would help to (excuse me so putting it) correct the free and easy, somewhat rowdy associations due to atmosphere, climate, environment and the influence of The Bulletin ... To ensure your complete success, the English people must be reckoned with and that is why I advocate your staying for a time in their midst.

Ethel Turner rejected Steele's advice, not because she was satisfied with local fame, but because she was to be married early in 1896. She had been engaged for more than four years to Herbert Curlewis, a young Sydney barrister whose fictional counterpart is Roger Carruthers, the oldest brother and guardian of the 'little larrikin'. In suggesting that she postpone her marriage, take her manuscript to England, and rewrite it in more refined surroundings, Steele was asserting control over a good deal more than a literary career. A revised version of *The Little Larrikin*, without its assertive Australianism, was, ostensibly, what Steele asked for. But, since the novel dramatizes its author's private dilemma, in a heroine who must choose between art and love, a revised *Little Larrikin* might have had its ending changed, and Carruthers–Curlewis, in fact as well as fiction, rejected for the sake of a career. Linley, the fictional heroine, lets art take its chance. Ethel Turner's diary for this period shows that she put marriage first, but was confident that she could have fame as well.

Steele had to give up the idea of an Anglicized Ethel Turner. He did, however, continue to send advice about what she might safely give her public. One recurring problem was her use of Australian slang. In 1901 a Dunedin bookseller complained to Ward Lock about the language of *The Camp at Wandinong* (1898). This book had so shocked a customer that he tore it up 'leaf by leaf', burned it and banned Ethel Turner's books from his house for ever. Steele and his successor, Charles Bligh, also enforced the prohibitions, common for children's writers anywhere, on matters of morality and decorum. Twice in her career at least Ward Lock censored a Turner novel on a matter of sexual morality. A young man in love with an unattainable married woman, in *The Little Larrikin*, had to take his yearning elsewhere, to an equally unattainable single woman. Years later, in *Nicola Silver* (1924) a reference to the first marriage, followed by divorce, of the heroine's father was deleted by a Ward Lock editor because 'marital unfaithfulness and divorce . . . by general consent are absolutely banned in books for the young'. Such episodes illustrate Ethel Turner's difficulty in keeping within the limits of propriety prescribed for children's fiction. She did not want to write Sunday-school prize novels, yet, as her publishers often reminded her, the Sunday-school market was large and profitable. She would have liked to move into adult fiction, but she knew that her best writing was about children. She proposed, then, to write about children for adults. Ward Lock dissuaded her, telling her in 1904 that she would lose her public ('your sales would drop to tens, where it is now thousands') if she chose this course. Although she gave in and continued to write for the juvenile market, most of her books after *The Family at Misrule* tackle adult themes. If she was not to be allowed to write about children for adults, she would write about adults for children, choosing plots and situations in which small children might be witnesses, or older ones play major roles, in what were essentially adult problems. This truce between literary ambition and financial sense had the accidental result of broadening the territory of the Australian children's novel. Ethel Turner's work would not bring a blush to the cheek of the Young Person, but it did deal with adult emotions and social and moral problems. She refused to fulfil the expectations of those who wanted more and more about the Woolcot children. After *The Family at Misrule* she wrote a tepid sequel, *Little Mother Meg* (1902), about marriage, money and motherhood and then gave up the Woolcot family until Ward Lock extracted her last book, *Judy and Punch*, from her in 1928 with a frankly commercial challenge to match Mary Grant Bruce's Billabong series with another Misrule book.

The difference between early and later Turner novels is partly one of perspective. If Ethel Turner had rewritten *Seven Little Australians* ten years later, the heroine would probably not have been Judy but the bewildered young stepmother, Esther. A 1904 novel, *Mother's Little*

Girl, exemplifies the author's changing interest. The child of the title ('a vulgar, namby-pamby title', Ethel Turner wrote angrily when her own choice, *The Gift Impossible*, was rejected by the publishers) is given very little of the author's attention. The story is that of two sisters, one rich and childless, and the other poor and the mother of six. The rich woman adopts her sister's baby: she offers opportunity for this child, and a better chance of survival for the other five; and she pleads her own need to be a mother since wealth and indolence are making her selfish. The redemptive value of a child is widely accepted in juvenile fiction, but Ethel Turner does not fully endorse it here, perhaps because to buy one is not right. The rich, adoptive mother spoils the child, who has too many possessions and no one to play with. It is made clear that she would be happier in a Sydney suburban cottage with her brothers and sisters. Ethel Turner cheats a little by quickly raising the real parents' income from near-destitution to the shabby but comfortable level she thought best for developing character. The novel ends with the rich sister's renunciation, and the spoiled five-year-old's delighted entry into a new world of playmates, porridge and plain brown pinafores.

Mother's Little Girl is mostly soap opera, with little of the domestic realism and comedy of Ethel Turner's best work. The social philosophy implicit in all her novels is spelled out here at times in sermon style. She believed in home ownership as the basis of family life, and she defined a home as neither mansion nor inner city flat, but a roomy suburban weatherboard house, not too tidy, with half an acre of land. The house to which 'mother's little girl' is restored is a guarantee of good family life; it is 'one more home, one more asset for Australia. Here would grow up a little band of citizens, endowed with responsibilities and love of property, striking far deeper roots into the soil than would the plants, shifted hither and thither continuously'. Ethel Turner recommended large families—six or seven children—as a school for character; there is not much hope, and very little fun, for an only child, rich or poor. Her characteristic family pattern is matriarchal. Fathers are usually defective in some way: remote and harsh, dead, weak or ineffectual, but that does not matter so long as the mother is in control. In *Mother's Little Girl*, the two husbands are alike in leaving all decisions to their wives: in giving away a baby or in adopting one, the father's role is determined by his income.

Mother's Little Girl, with its debate on motherhood and the rights of the child to her natural parents, reads like a thesis novel. Yet for all its apparent artificiality, it had its basis in the author's experience.

'She wants to buy—my baby!'
Illustration by J. Macfarlane from *Mother's Little Girl*

According to Turner family legend, a rich uncle who made roll-top desks in Coventry offered Mrs Turner a thousand pounds for Ethel whom he promised to bring up in England 'like a little Queen'.[5] The novel (in which the adoption price is only a hundred pounds) affirms not only the worth of the natural mother but the moral challenge of growing up in a Sydney suburb on a small income, as Ethel Turner did.

Nearly all the Turner novels and short stories are set in Sydney. Although they often reflect the struggles of families just on the lower-middle-class edge of poverty, they always give a happy ending in which a small adjustment in income brings the security which is far better than riches. Sunshine, suburban comfort, space and informality, a view of the Harbour, and, for some, the chance to develop a creative talent, are the best gifts Ethel Turner could bestow on her fictional children. Within this pattern, and no other, she endorses Australian life. Her version of the 'settlers' novel', *Three Little Maids*, deflates the idea of Australia as a land of quickly-won wealth in a pastoral setting. In this novel the immigrant family of three Conway girls and their widowed mother endure 'two breathless terrible summers' in a country town before retreating to Sydney where Mrs Conway keeps a boarding-house for a time, and then marries a doctor. At the time of writing *Three Little Maids* Ethel Turner was reading *Geoffry Hamlyn*; her depiction of rural Australia is perhaps a conscious reply to Kingsley's celebration of 'a new heaven, a new earth' in the outback. She did not solve the Conways' problems by giving them a squatter stepfather. Even if the novel had not been autobiographical, it would never have occurred to her to find a happy ending away from the city. Sydney is the middle way between 'the pitiless London streets' the Conways leave behind and the 'parched and panting' Moondi-Moondi of their first two years in Australia. It combines the best of both worlds: outdoor freedom and a feminine refinement, which is the European heritage transplanted to a Sydney garden. It is a women's world but, within the limits of firm but gentle feminine control, masculine Philistinism is allowed to express the energy and confidence of the new nation.

When one of the young stepbrothers, added to the Conway family by their mother's Australian marriage, is given a European Grand Tour by his rich grandfather, his letters home make an obvious appeal to the local pride of Australian readers:

> Well, then we went to another place, I forget the name—oh,
> Florence, I think. Didn't think much of it, but it's not quite so

tumble-down as the what's-it's-name town. Oh, I didn't tell you about the river at the other place. Old Olly had spouted about it—the Tiber it's called—all the way in the train, and I really thought I was going to see something at last ... I give you my word I thought he was having a lark with me. The dirtiest, miserablest bit of a river you ever saw. I didn't want to catch typhoid, so I held my nose and turned around to see if he was holding his. But he wasn't. He was blowing it hard and crying.Yes, by Shimminy. I told him he just ought to see our Hawkesbury.

Well, about Florence. It's got a lot of buildings and things in it, and some of them look rather nice; they're higher too than the buildings in Sydney ... there was one of the waiters, a real good sort, going to a place five miles off to see some races, so you bet we went too. But the horses were as smashed-up as the buildings are—not a goer in the lot—so it wasn't much fun. Australia could put them up to a thing or two on racing, my word.

In the travels of Alf, an early version of the Ocker, the obvious comic point is the boy's insularity and lack of aesthetic sense. Yet Ethel Turner is not interested in correcting his vision. Any healthy Australian boy, she implies, would see Europe as Alf does. She sends him home with his nationalist pride intact, and through the words of an aunt who helps him run away from the rich grandfather, endorses the values of Australia, home and poverty:

This is no place for you, here with a soured old man and a sourer old maid; you would have grown to far healthier manhood across the sea in that merry family that I have never let you talk about just as much as you wanted ... go back to them and be poor and happy, and grow up in the healthy atmosphere of 'give and take' instead of our most wretched one of 'keep'.

It would be hard to find a Turner novel in which the economic motif is missing. More than most writers Ethel Turner recorded the price of things, adding up pounds, shillings and pence while she weighed the morality of possession. A taste for luxury and a Puritan conscience make many of the moral conflicts in her work. She described herself as 'always ... more than a bit of a socialist', and her concern with social justice is more or less explicit in all her work. She could write an exhilarating shopping scene, as she did in *Nicola Silver*, when the neglected, badly-dressed Nicola is suddenly let loose in a Sydney shop with thirty-five pounds to spend. Part of the pleasure is in the limitation to an exact amount and the sense of an experience of beauty earned through years of privation, which will never come again. The Turner heroines have the aesthetic sense their creator thought proper for girls, but not for boys like Alf, in the passage quoted above, or for the young men in her later novels whose social conscience gives the conventional love story a source of conflict.

A typical Turner debate may be found in this scene from *The Cub* (1915) the first book in a war trilogy. Brigid Lindsay, the heroine of the series, is English-born, with a social-climbing mother whose small income makes it a matter of anxious effort to keep up appearances. The 'Cub', John Calthrop, is Australian, the son of an immensely wealthy pastoralist family. Here, he shows Brigid the Calthrops' newly redecorated Sydney mansion:

'This is the music-room,' said the Cub, displaying a white and gold apartment. 'You notice those busts of the music Johnnies over there?'

'Beethoven—Wagner!' cried Brigid, absolutely horrified at him.

'Make you a present of their names,' said the Cub; 'only know they're made of Carrara marble, and cost fifty each, and heaven knows how much more for shipping and customs, for we carted them back with us from Rome.'

'Don't be such a perfect Goth,' said Brigid, 'you make me positively ill. They are most exquisite . . . and think who they are!'

'Music Johnnies,' said the Cub, 'never did a thing in their lives to make the world better. Just tum-tummed on the piano.' . . .

'To attack music!' said Brigid. 'To attack Beethoven . . . Why, music is the divinest, most uplifting thing in the world, you stupid boy!'

'Then why doesn't it ever uplift some one?' said the Cub.

'There's enough of it, God knows! Opera-houses and concert-halls thick all over the world; tremendous stars with tremendous salaries; audiences, covered with diamonds and dress clothes, tumbling over each other to get seats, and what happens?' . . .

'The crowded audience with the tears wet on its face gathers itself up and tucks itself into its motor-car and drives home. Have you ever driven home, near midnight, Brigid, along the Embankment, in London, or through the Paris streets, or the streets in Milan?'

'Yes,' said Brigid.

'Have you forgotten those poor wretches, those lonely devils of men and women on the seats and in doorways or getting moved on?'

'No, I haven't forgotten,' Brigid said in a low voice. 'But it's just no good remembering. It only makes one unhappy for nothing.'

'Like music,' said the Cub. 'You take it from me, young woman, if this music of yours *was* any good, those audiences wouldn't drive home and see and forget.'

In scenes like this, and in the debates about the war in the *Cub* series, Ethel Turner moved well away from the irresponsible pleasures of Misrule. Her temperance novel, *St. Tom and the Dragon* (1918), and its sequel, *King Anne* (1921), re-worked the dispute between Brigid and the Cub over moral and aesthetic values. In *King Anne* the feminine viewpoint is justified by the argument that slum clearance (the hero's project) is all very well, but the new cottages need to be pretty as well as clean.

Ethel Turner's audience must have found her fiction disconcertingly varied. A single volume of short stories, *The Stolen Voyage* (1907), for example, contained comic nursery escapades as well as the skilful, understated ironic study of suburban culture-shock, 'A Broken Siesta'. Sometimes, to please her publishers, she wrote what she called a 'young story', in which the central character is a small child, and the adult problems there for childish goodness to resolve. *Flower o' the Pine* (1914) fits this prescription; it is the closest to a Pollyanna story Ethel Turner ever came. *John of Daunt* (1916) is a war novel like the *Cub* series, but from a child's perspective. The plea for tolerance for the German people, made seriously in *The Cub*, is repeated in *John of Daunt* through the comedy of a Sydney eight-year-old hero's patriotic attempt to poison a neighbour's dachshund. In all these novels Ethel Turner's commitment to the war is clear. She was sure enough of its justice to campaign for conscription in 1916, but her fiction presents with sympathy those who, like the Cub, are at first unwilling to fight.

In her willingness to look at moral ambiguities, Ethel Turner was unusual among juvenile writers of her time. She has no villains (even the millionaire whisky manufacturer of *St. Tom and the Dragon* is merely misguided) and her heroes and heroines are seldom perfect. The variety of her literary career, in which she moved from nursery farce to moral crusade, has some continuity in her lasting commitment to psychological realism, her rejection of types or ideal characters. There are plenty of sermons in her novels but no single character is made to carry the full burden of authorial approval.

Ethel Turner brought Australian children's fiction into the mainstream of Anglo-American domestic realism. She drew on her own childhood reading, especially the work of Charlotte Yonge and Louisa Alcott, as well as that of her older contemporary, Frances Hodgson Burnett. There are differences as well as resemblances. Lack of religious fervour separates Turner from Yonge and Alcott; only in *The Wonder-Child* (1901), published by the Religious Tract Society, is there anything like a crisis of religious belief. The larrikin qualities of her fictional children are a flat contradiction of the idealization which produced Burnett's *Little Lord Fauntleroy* (1886) and *A Little Princess* (1888). There is an affinity between the Turner novels and those of E. Nesbit in their sense of the separateness of the child from the adult world. What distinguishes them is the dimension of fantasy in Nesbit's work which Turner does not share. Both Turner and Nesbit published in the *Windsor Magazine* in the 1890s. Although this juxtaposition shows Turner taking her place among English writers, it was not done without some degree of Anglo-Australian tension. It was in the *Windsor Magazine* that Ethel Turner scored one of her early victories over William Steele. He objected to her story, 'A Champion in Ankle-Straps', because it mentioned the *Bulletin* with evident approval. Could she not set the same story in England, Steele asked, and have *Punch* take the *Bulletin*'s place? Ward Lock, the owners of the *Windsor Magazine*, strongly objected to her mentioning the Sydney journal because of its frequent, disrespectful references to the Royal Family. Ethel Turner refused to alter the story; and British readers of the *Windsor Magazine* had to puzzle over some uncompromisingly local references to the Red Page and Sydney politics. 'A Champion in Ankle-Straps' is a feeble sentimental anecdote, but its appearance in the English monthly in 1896 with all its Australianisms uncensored is evidence of Ethel Turner's achievement: a reputation strong enough to sell even a mediocre story of Sydney suburban life. Eight years later, Ward Lock's London manager, G. E. Lock, conceded not only that 'their Australian character' was essential to the Turner stories, but that their Australian sales were more important than the traditional 'home' market. The revolution brought about by the children of Misrule was thereby confirmed.

7

The Turner Circle

When Ward Lock agreed to publish *Seven Little Australians*, William Steele wanted to place it in an established series of gift books designed for family reading. He wrote to Ethel Turner with this proposal: 'I should recommend you to issue your tale in a pretty picture cover at 1/- in the Lily series ... where you would be in excellent company'.[1] The company would have been international: the Lily titles included *Little Women, Uncle Tom's Cabin, The Wide, Wide World, What Katy Did, Ben Hur* and *Ministering Children*. Ward Lock advertised them as 'admirable Volumes for School Prizes and Presents to Young Ladies'; and assured prospective buyers that 'no author whose name is not a guarantee of the real worth and purity of his or her work, or whose book has not been subjected to a rigid examination, is admitted into "The Lily Series"'. Ethel Turner resisted: she disliked the appearance of the Lily series, and asked for something distinctive and aesthetically pleasing. Steele did not press his point. When *Seven Little Australians* appeared it delighted its author 'in an art green cover with Judy running across it, a quaint little gilt figure in top corner, and Bunty eating bread and butter at back—Lovely altogether, beautiful type and thick paper'.[2] At half a crown, it had the elegance and individuality which the uniform cheap format of the Lily books could not provide. *The Family at Misrule* was an equally handsome production. Yet what seemed to be a Turner victory became one for Ward Lock. In 1896 Ella Chaffey's *The Youngsters of Murray Home* was published in the same format as the Turner novels, and illustrated by A. J. Johnson, who had drawn the Woolcot children for the earlier volumes. In a letter which seems designed to soothe Ethel Turner with a little flattery as well as to announce a new publishing venture, Steele wrote of his satisfaction with *The Youngsters of Murray Home*:

> I do not look for any great success, as compared with your own books for Mrs Chaffey's for there is not the same literary ability, but I hope it will have a nice sale and build up our Australian Gift Book series.[3]

Thus, having refused to join a series, Ethel Turner found that a series had joined her. From that point, Ward Lock steadily increased its Australian juvenile list, building on the Turner success, and for the next fifty years selling Ethel Turner's novels in uniform format with those of her sister Lilian, Mary Grant Bruce, Lillian Pyke, Vera Dwyer, and others, including her daughter Jean Curlewis. The green or red and gilt of the 1890s volumes changed; the small line-drawings of A. J. Johnson were replaced by the full-page illustration of J. Macfarlane. But, whatever their format, the Turner novels published by Ward Lock (all but six of the author's thirty-five volumes of fiction) remained indistinguishable in appearance from the others in Ward Lock's Australian list: 'as alike as tins of jam', as Ethel Turner complained.

Seven Little Australians had an influence well beyond expectations. It gave Ward Lock the impetus for an Australian publishing programme, and it seems likely that it encouraged Angus and Robertson to produce its first children's book in 1897: *Teens* by Louise Mack. In 1888 at Sydney Girls' High School Louise Mack and Ethel Turner had edited rival school magazines; it was appropriate that *Teens* should not go to Ward Lock but continue the authors' rivalry with another publisher. The Australian Ward Lock volumes varied more than their uniform appearance might suggest, but a very large number of them were influenced by their founding author. Some aspiring young Sydney women writers, including Vera Dwyer, even described themselves in 1913 as 'Ethel Turner's girls'.[4] They wrote for the 'flapper' market, following the model of Ethel Turner's later work with some romantic interest and a Sydney family setting.

Ward Lock's first choice to follow the Turner books, *The Youngsters of Murray Home*, was thought by reviewers to be an imitation of the Misrule stories but, according to William Steele, most of it was written in 1890.[5] Without the success of the Turner novels it probably would have remained unpublished. It is a mild—and 'mildly Australian'— family chronicle of six children whose everyday life in a country district on the Murray River supplies an entertainment, indoors or outdoors, for every chapter. The children are carefully disposed as to age and temperament to give a satisfying range of action. There is the almost obligatory model oldest sister, thirteen-year-old Olga whose fair hair and 'sweet kind expression' contrasts with dark, scowling Hubert, two years younger. Two 'mischief-loving mites', Ralph and Katrina (Rat and Kat) come next; then the youngest two, Bertram and Dollie, to provide quaint nursery mishaps and mispronunciations, or to be the victims of family games that go too far. Dollie's role, for example, includes being bitten by what she mistakenly calls 'a dear likka baby snake' which Kat has thoughtlessly hidden in the nursery. Since all the men are away at the time of this accident, Hubert must ride 'as he had never ridden before' to fetch the doctor. Mrs Chaffey's treatment of this incident is typical of her approach to her material. Although all the elements of a big dramatic scene are there, in the guilty sister, the brother's heroic ride, the mother's agonizing vigil, and the pathos of the child at the point of death, the author keeps calm. Kat is soothed and forgiven by her mother even before the doctor arrives. There is very little suspense about the child's recovery, and the whole incident is over in a few pages. The chapter ends unemotionally with the father's returning home to hear the story. No comments are recorded, no reproaches, no prayers of thankfulness. Mr Olsen simply goes off to the nursery to look for the snake:

> He discovered it curled up in a corner under the chest of drawers where it had first taken refuge, and a smart blow from the stick with which he had armed himself quickly rendered it harmless for ever after.

As with the snake incident, so with all the other adventures of the Olsen children. Marooned for several days on an island in the Murray River, they are not especially anxious. Only Olga is afraid; she calms herself with prayers until 'at last a peaceful drowsiness stole over the child's senses, and before she even knew she was sleepy, good, faithful Ollie was asleep!'

The Youngsters of Murray Home has been praised for its realism and its restraint. Its picture of Australian country life does give a sense of authenticity; clearly, Mrs Chaffey wrote from her own experience. The Olsen children are not idealized. The accounts of their experience – a travelling circus, a fishing expedition, Christmas Day, a party with fireworks – are convincingly detailed. As a period piece, this novel has a certain charm, but in spite of the present vogue for the 1890s and some recent critics' praise, no one has as yet reprinted it. Why does

Seven Little Australians remain in print, with recent translations into television and musical comedy form, while *The Youngsters of Murray Home* survives only in collections of rare books? Perhaps its neglect has something to do with Mrs Chaffey's tone and viewpoint. Her characters are well-observed but always from a distance, and often in a voice of adult complacency. By comparison Ellen Campbell's *Twin Pickles*, with its first-person narrative, is much more engaging: its comic irony does not deflate the emotions of the child's world. Mrs Chaffey too often asserts a false comradeship with her audience. The last few paragraphs of her novel may illustrate this point:

> Could we but look ahead a few months, we should be pleased to see Hub, a tall school-boy in a glazed hat, much more devoted to his books than of yore, and exhibiting a mild enthusiasm for cricket very different from his former passionate devotion to the gun, which hangs in his room on the wall, unused but still loved. And we should find Rat, already thinner and longer, as good-natured and as mischievous as ever, dividing his affections equally between his football on the one hand, and a familiar friend of his own age and sex, a little boy rejoicing in the name of Sammy Grunt, on the other . . .

That note of Olympian condescension indicates an author not quite at home with her audience. Moreover, although restraint may be a literary asset, there are times in *The Youngsters of Murray Home* when one feels, not the author's tact, but the want of anything much to restrain. Mrs Chaffey's novel is a pastoral idyll of childhood, more likely to appeal to adults than to children. Nothing seriously threatens the serenity of Murray Home. The Olsen parents—a 'grave and dignified papa' and a strong, loving and sympathetic mother—guarantee happy endings for all misadventures. The children have the energy and freedom of young colonials but within a framework of order quite different from Ethel Turner's Misrule. The Murray Home servants, cook, nurse and governess, directed by Mrs Olsen, provide a reliable structure for the children's lives, safe but not restrictive. Mrs Chaffey describes an ideal combination of order and freedom, in which a traditional way of life is harmoniously adapted to the New World:

> The kitchen, with the servants' quarters, at Murray Home, was separated from the main building by a broad, covered passage. The house itself was a large stone edifice, comfortable, roomy, and cool, except in the hottest weather, when no place was cool. A wide verandah ran the whole way round it, and on the east side, in one corner of a pleasant green lawn, stood a large round summer-house, the

Illustration by A. J. Johnson from *The Youngsters of Murray Home*

walls and roof of which were entirely formed of ever-green creepers: the English ivy and semi-tropic passion-vine mingling their contrasting greens as they grew freely, according to their own sweet will.

Ella Chaffey's perspective on Australian life was that of an observant newcomer. The wife of Charles Chaffey, one of the three Canadian brothers who pioneered irrigation in Australia, she came to the Murray River district of Renmark early in 1889 and there brought up her children. Her responsiveness to the distinctive experience of 'growing up Australian' is one of the strengths of her writing. It may, however, be a corresponding limitation that she wrote of something quite different from her own northern hemisphere childhood. Ellen Campbell knew how it felt to be a bush child; the heroine of *Twin Pickles* is her younger self. Ella Chaffey's book, with its maternal viewpoint, lacks the sharpness and the special authority of memory.

Ward Lock's next addition to its list of Australian writers for children was the very prolific Lilian Turner, who, like her sister Ethel, had more serious ambitions in fiction than a place in a juvenile series. She started promisingly with *The Lights of Sydney* (1896) which won first prize in 1894 in an open competition organized by Cassell, a London publisher with a branch office in Melbourne. Thereafter, Lilian's career was a depressing contrast with her sister's success. She wrote fashion and social notes for the *Australian Town and Country Journal*, to which Ethel contributed a weekly Children's Page. In 1895 the *Journal* made retrenchments, dismissing Lilian but keeping Ethel. 'I have £1 a week still', Ethel said. 'Poor Lil has nothing from it but she says she doesn't care, it was a fearful nuisance to do . . .'[6]

Eventually Lilian Turner made her compromise. She settled down to write 'flapper novels' for Ward Lock, year after year, from 1902 to 1931. She seldom tried to write for young children. *An Australian Lassie* (1903), an early exception to her rule, shows that she was right to make it. In this novel she attempted a child-centred story and a very young heroine: Betty Bruce, a Sydney ten-year-old who tries to save the family fortunes by an appeal to her rich grandfather. The plot is conventional in all but its refusal of a happy ending. Betty fails to soften her grandfather's heart. The novel ends with the child's new understanding of the value of poverty and independence, and a grudging recognition from the grandfather of the courage with which she had confronted him. The reversal of a well-worn formula might have worked, but the presentation of wilful Betty is as sentimental as that of her angelic literary model, the archetypal grandfather-softener Little Lord Fauntleroy.

A sequel to *An Australian Lassie*, *Betty the Scribe* (1906), is unusual among sequels in being better than its predecessor. The change in perspective, from Betty at ten to Betty at seventeen, suited Lilian Turner. Instead of the artificial conflict with her grandfather, the heroine is caught between her vocation as a writer and her duty as her father's housekeeper and substitute mother to six young brothers and sisters. *Betty the Scribe* makes a useful point of comparison between the Turner sisters. In 1922 Ethel reworked the situation of *Betty the Scribe* in *Jennifer J.*, giving a similarly talented girl the main responsibility for a vague, ineffectual journalist father and a large family of brothers and sisters. Betty's mother has died (or, as Lilian Turner euphemistically puts it, 'slipped away'). Jennifer's mother is more culpable: tired of the domestic role, she has left Sydney for two years in Oxford to resume studying for the degree she gave up in order to marry. Both novels, then, raise the same questions about the woman's traditional role. Ethel Turner resolved them by asserting the prior claims of marriage and motherhood: Jennifer's mother fails at Oxford, but not before she realizes that her true fulfilment is in her family. Jennifer is left in adolescence at the end of the novel, but it is clear that growing up means marriage, with a career either given up or firmly subordinated. Family life in *Jennifer J.* has more compensations than in *Betty the Scribe*. Jennifer's brothers and sisters are tiresome but affectionate; Betty's family relationships are dominated by jealousy, resentment and selfish indifference. When rescue comes, with the return of a spoiled older sister, Betty leaves home to live alone in a rented room in Sydney. The last page shows Betty at nineteen, with her first book accepted for publication, defiantly and unconvincingly refusing the love of the young man who wants to work and wait for her:

> It was hateful to be a woman—she simply *wouldn't* be a woman.
> 'Good-bye', she repeated, moving hurriedly from the table, not even shaking hands ... When she reached home she feverishly put on the shortest dress her wardrobe held and let her hair down her back, and tied it with a piece of pink ribbon.
> It was her way of indignantly insisting to Fate that she refused to be a woman.

Of course the author knows better: refusal is impossible. It is characteristic of Lilian Turner that love and marriage are wholeheartedly endorsed only for the beautiful, domesticated secondary heroines. For the plain, awkward talented sister, growing up is a defeat.

Betty Bruce is Lilian Turner's version of Jo March: she resembles Jo in temperament and aspirations, but lacks her resilient good humour.

When she wrote *Betty the Scribe*, Lilian Turner was thirty-six, married, a mother, and comparatively poor—poor, at least compared with her younger sister Ethel, and much less successful as a writer. It seems likely that some of the emotional energy of this novel is derived from Lilian's sense of disappointment. Juvenile fiction could not contain so unacceptable an emotion as a mother's anger; transferred to a seventeen-year-old sister it was forgivable. The household from which Betty escapes is uniformly depressing; and the family relationships generally unrewarding:

> She looked into the dining room.
>
> It was the end of the week with the table-cloth, as with them all. A few dying violets drooped weary heads in the four vases; the silver had lost the smile it had worn not quite a week ago; Mary, in her haste, had put on uncleaned knives—she often did; the bread board was dingy, the cruets neglected . . .
>
> In the hall her father's voice reached her, pleasant as usual, but with a tired note in it.
>
> 'Betty, my dear,' he cried, 'can't you stop baby crying? We can hardly hear each other speak.'
>
> 'Where's that lazy little wretch of a Nancy?' said Betty aloud stormily; 'she's of no use to anyone . . .'
>
> 'You heard me!' said Betty, 'you needn't pretend you didn't. Here, take baby somewhere—out in the paddock, if you like, and get her to sleep.'
>
> But Nancy was in provocative mood.
>
> 'Sha'n't,' she said.
>
> 'Do as I tell you, instantly,' said Betty.
>
> 'Won't,' said Nancy . . .
>
> The next second Betty had dealt her a sounding smack on one cheek and left the room, not daring to trust herself to stay longer.

Among Lilian Turner's many later novels, a few are of particular thematic interest. *Three New Chum Girls* (1910) presents an English immigrant family, fatherless, and unrealistic in their expectations of Australian life, who settle on forty acres of uncleared land in New South Wales. Australian outback life in the Turner version has little to recommend it. Heat, drought and poverty almost defeat even the most optimistic of the new chum girls, the patient, domesticated Peggy. Their brother Tom is selfish and inconsiderate. The second sister,

Honora, rebels against Tom's automatic headship of their household; her inheritance, she says, has gone into the land, and an exact share of the forty acres should be hers to farm. Describing herself as a 'Woman's Righter', Honora insists that she has as much endurance and 'grit' as her brother and declares her independence: 'It's our right, individually. I'm not going to let Tom work my plot and then tell some girl he can't marry her because he has sisters to support.' 'But,' said Peggy, 'you'll work for Tom at home . . . Won't you sew for Tom and cook for Tom, and keep the fireside bright and homely for Tom?'

Although this passage seems to give Honora the best of the argument (an impression strengthened by Tom's boorishness) Lilian Turner makes Peggy's the only workable viewpoint. Honora collapses, unequal to physical labour on her share of the farm; nursed through a severe illness by Peggy she comes to see the value of the womanly role. There is some vague hope that Tom will improve but Lilian Turner does not do much to make this convincing. Peggy's marriage gives a happy ending, but one which leaves Honora's future unresolved.

The confused but impassioned feminist feeling of *Three New Chum Girls* is muted in *Paradise and the Perrys* (1908) and *The Perry Girls* (1909). The issues here are more practical. How can three suddenly impoverished girls make a living for themselves and their mother? Mrs Perry is an unusually helpless lady who takes six months to learn how to make a sago pudding, or a blancmange without lumps in it. In the Perry novels Lilian Turner moves into the territory of genteel survival: careers are not in question. Teaching, typewriters and teashops are the temporary solutions before rescue through marriage. 'Paradise' is the Perry girls' teashop; it gives them more independence than its alternatives but it does not easily accommodate Theo, the family misfit, who is not good at cooking, and is too plain and shy to please the customers as a waitress.

1914 brought Lilian Turner a new theme and her heroines a new occupation. Like Ethel Turner's Cub series, her novel, *War's Heart Throbs* (1915), shows war's beneficial effects on women. They stop thinking of clothes and parties and start knitting. The novel's worldly heroine Cynthia says, after her transformation: 'I only care for England'. It is not only women who are changed for the better; the whole nation finds its soul. 'Australia, the child, has grown to manhood in a moment. Australia is now a patriot with his heart on fire!'

Lilian Turner's patriotism did not differentiate, as Ethel Turner's did, between individual Germans and the military policy of their country. The dedication of her heroines goes well beyond the demands of the

The glory box
Illustration by J. Macfarlane from *The Perry Girls*

Red Cross knitting group. One of them, strolling with a friend in a Sydney street, remarks confidingly: 'I say, don't you hate the Germans and the Vaterland? I'm so glad now I learned French . . .'. This is overheard by a passing German: 'Mein Gott!' he exclaims, 'You dirty little Australian. You take not the name of the Vaterland upon your Bretish lips'. It takes more than that to intimidate an Australian girl. Grasping the 'burly foreigner' by the wrist she calls imperiously, 'Police! Intern this German!' The police are too slow; the German escapes and the girls are inconsolable. 'Oh, why did I let him go! I'd love to have got even one German interned—as my contribution. Oh, how I wish I were a man!'

A comparison between *War's Heart Throbs* and *The Cub*, published in the same year, is all to Ethel Turner's advantage but it shows the basic similarities of the sisters' fictional worlds. Both present the same view of frivolous girlhood redeemed by wartime dedication. Both assert Australia's link with Britain in the same terms: little Mother England, in need of rescue, creating Australian manhood overnight. This wartime pattern is a variation on a common Turner theme of redemptive feminine influence. Men in this matriarchal world can be strong only if women make them so. The melodramatic tendencies of the sisters are balanced in Ethel's work by some degree of psychological subtlety, and a well-developed comic sense. Lilian's work is humourless. Some of her earlier books bring a querulous energy to family problems and feminist issues, but her post-war novels have unlikely plots and lifeless characters. Ward Lock, who published twenty of her twenty-two books, never gave Lilian even the second place in their listing of 'popular Australian writers'. In 1915 she was ranked fourth on Ward Lock's Australasian letterhead, after Ethel, Mary Grant Bruce and the New Zealand writer, Isabel Maud Peacocke. Her work is of interest today mainly as a reflection of popular attitudes. Under financial pressure she wrote too much for too long; and a slight but genuine talent worked itself into mediocrity. As her more fortunate sister often exclaimed in a diary entry 'Poor Lil!'

Whether they liked it or not, most Australian writers of girls' books in the early twentieth century were defined in the terms established by Ethel and Lilian Turner. Mary Grant Bruce, Ward Lock's second major discovery, defined herself in opposition. Her Billabong series, which I shall discuss in detail in Chapter 8, was in many ways a contrast and a challenge to the Turner style. By 1910, when the first Bruce novel was published, Ethel Turner had lost interest in writing children's books: like Lilian, she wrote mainly for what the *Bulletin* described as the readership of 'girls . . . fluttering a brief and tremulous gown at the

meeting of the calf and ankle'. Mary Grant Bruce wrote for boys as well
as girls, and by avoiding the emotional problems of growing up, kept
within the territory of the children's book. Her active, outdoor heroine,
Norah Linton, never goes through the flapper stage; there is no fluttering or trembling of any kind at Billabong, nor any of the artistic or
romantic aspirations which characterize the Turner world.

The influence of the Turners may be seen most clearly in the career of
Vera Dwyer, who joined the Ward Lock list in 1913. As a child Vera
Dwyer won prizes in the short story competitions organized by Ethel
Turner as editor of the *Australian Town and Country Journal*'s Children's Page. Her first novel, *With Beating Wings*, written when she was
only seventeen, was publicized as a Turner discovery. It has the Sydney
suburban setting, the family conflicts and the problems of genteel poverty with which readers of the Turner novels were thoroughly at home.
It also has a number of the mannerisms which, though not exclusive to
the Turners, immediately recall both Ethel and Lilian. The opening
chapter, with its direct and deliberately informal address to the reader, is
one example of a pervasive influence:

> Gwen was quite a small person. If you had stood her against the
> wall to be measured, I don't believe—even had you refrained from
> flattening her hair down very much with the Dictionary, and merci-
> fully pretended not to know she was standing on tip-toe—I don't
> believe you could have made her more than five feet two, the odd
> inches being for her own gratification, and not at all a scrupulously
> exact statement of facts.

Measured against the Misrule nursery wall, Meg Woolcot, too, gains
'an unlawful inch' until her hair is flattened with a book. Yet it is not so
much correspondences in details of this kind that suggest Vera Dwyer's
literary model as the tone of the passage. In establishing a confiding
relationship between writer and reader it echoes the first chapter of *Seven
Little Australians*.

The plots of the Dwyer novels are closer to Lilian Turner's than to
Ethel's in their concentration on the frustrations of talented girls
repressed by poverty or parents. The faulty parent is usually a father: in
girl's fiction of this kind, mothers may defect by dying, but domestic
tyranny almost always comes from an unfeeling father. The 'beating
wings' of Vera Dwyer's first novel are those of the two heroines, Gwen
and Pat Pemelby. Both are unusually gifted—one as a writer, the other
as a violinist—but systematically thwarted by harsh, snobbish Mr
Pemelby, a disgruntled schoolmaster at a Sydney grammar school.

When he loses his job, Pat makes a small but acceptably ladylike living as a music teacher, but Gwen is forbidden to work in a Sydney publishing office.

Vera Dwyer had a weakness for a big scene, but no skill in relating it to the characterization of the novel. Mr Pemelby speaks with the violent possessiveness of a Barrett of Wimpole Street when Gwen defies him, yet he is nowhere shown to have the attachment to his daughter which could produce a scene of this kind:

> 'I am going to town now' [Gwen said]. 'I don't want to disobey you, but I must.'
> She was moving away, but he jumped up, caught her round the waist, and forced her into a chair, as the mother and Pat entered, with scared faces and fast-beating hearts . . .
> 'You will stay at home!' he hissed. 'You will stay at home, do you hear?'
> He, too, was breathless and excited, and as she looked up at his pale, furious face, and blazing eyes, a comprehensive sense of his power swept over her, and she covered her face with her hands.
> 'Oh, you are so strong – so strong – so strong!' she moaned.
> 'I am strong by right of ownership. You are mine, do you hear? Mine! I swear to you that I will uphold my authority over you at any cost. I will wring obedience out of you as long as I live!'

After this rhetorical overkill, it is an anti-climax to find that when Gwen manages 'another burst of defiance', takes the next ferry to Sydney and accepts the office job, she comes home to nothing worse than her father's refusal to speak to her: in the circumstances, no great loss.

A later Dwyer novel, *The Kayles of Bushy Lodge* (1922), uses the same mixture of feminine talent and frustration, but depicts a slightly more plausible father. Mr. Kayle is a widower who practises dentistry in a dispirited way which attracts few patients. His daughter Shirley, a gifted violinist, is also the family housekeeper; with three brothers and two sisters who take no interest in domestic matters, she is as oppressed as Lilian Turner's heroine in *Betty the Scribe*. Unhappiness in this novel, as in Lilian Turner's, is summed up in a tea-stained table-cloth:

> Shirley's glance swept the table. It had been carelessly laid for seven, five of whom had already dined – the dishes and cutlery they had used were still uncleared from the five places.
> There was some cold corned beef under a wire cover upon the table, there was bread and there was butter, and also there was

'I would like to see the editor . . .'
Illustration by Victor Prout from *With Beating Wings*

jam—at the bottom of a sticky-rimmed dish. Table decorations were conspicuously absent, the cloth was a little tea-stained, and at the place where the youngest usually sat three large drops of yesterday's gravy, stiff and dry now, were an additional offence to a fastidious eye.

A good deal more of this sort of thing causes Shirley to have a nervous breakdown. Her younger sister, who fortunately has no artistic talent, discovers home-making as her true vocation, and takes over. The novel, which is set in wartime Sydney, ends with Shirley's engagement to the young Anzac who once inconsiderately walked across her newly-polished floor in muddy boots, thereby contributing to her breakdown.

Vera Dwyer's fiction, like much of Lilian Turner's, seems to move outside the juvenile range, not in quality, but in its concern with house-keeping problems. The recurring figure of the heroine awaiting rescue from the tyranny of fathers or floor-polish must have appealed to women as well as to girls between school and marriage. It is formula fiction for which the *Bulletin*'s dismissive label, 'flapperature', is not necessarily the right one. These novels do, of course, observe the proprieties of the Young Person's reading. The harsh fathers quarrel with their daughters, not their wives. Presumably open marital discord was as unacceptable a theme as divorce, which, as Ward Lock reminded Ethel Turner in 1924, was a forbidden topic.

In a survey of Australian 'flapperature' in 1915, the *Bulletin* prescribed Vera Dwyer's *A War of Girls* for seventeen-year-old girls, for whom it had 'just enough young love to please'. An 'unsophisticated and unexacting reader of 20' would enjoy Lilian Turner's *War's Heart Throbs*. Ethel Turner's *The Cub*, which could 'seduce even the hardened heart of the adult' was thought to transcend its category; it was literature.[7] The difference was in the psychological insight with which the characters were portrayed. The *Bulletin*'s gradation of merit according to appropriate age group misses the point. There is more for children in *The Cub* than in either *War's Heart Throbs* or *A War of Girls*, and yet it is quite true that it touches adult emotions. Vera Dwyer's portrayal of family relationships in *With Beating Wings* would require, in a reader of seventeen or seventy, a simple-mindedness which has nothing to do with youth. Most of Vera Dwyer's novels and some of Lilian Turner's fitted the juvenile gift book format of Ward Lock's Australian list only in being guaranteed innocuous.

Ethel Turner's daughter, Jean Curlewis, joined the Ward Lock list in 1921 with her first novel, *The Ship That Never Set Sail*. In format it matched the other Ward Lock juvenile novels of that year, which included Ethel Turner's *King Anne*. In style, however, it seemed to take a new direction. Jean Curlewis did not share her mother's interest in family life, nor her gift for comedy. *The Ship That Never Set Sail* fits with difficulty into the flapper mode. Its three successors, *Drowning Maze* (1922), *Beach Beyond* (1923) and *The Dawn Man* (1924) must have disconcerted Ward Lock's traditional readership. In form they are boys' adventure stories with a general debt to Stevenson and Buchan. They have little to do with the themes of love and marriage: women and children play minor roles in novels which depend on action and suspense, and on the sense of place which was Jean Curlewis's strength. No wonder they sold poorly: they were not at all what was expected from Ethel Turner's daughter and the Ward Lock format. It was not that outdoor adventure was unwelcome. Mary Grant Bruce, Ethel Turner's only successful rival, had already proved that. But, compared with the cheerful simplicity of the Billabong novels, Jean Curlewis's work is introspective and at times self-consciously literary, without the moral certainties the adventure story demands.

Jean Curlewis died in 1930, aged thirty-one. It is hard to guess what her literary career might have been, but she would almost certainly have had to move into adult fiction, leaving behind the girl readers whose expectations she could not fulfil. *The Ship That Never Set Sail* is a far more interesting novel than any of the imitation Turners produced by Vera Dwyer and others. Its successors, too, have strong individual qualities. There can be no doubt of Jean Curlewis's talent, but there were disadvantages in being Ethel Turner's heiress.

The Ship That Never Set Sail, a semi-autobiographical novel, does much to explain the personal and literary predicament of Jean Curlewis. Its heroine, Brenda Paling, appears first as a gifted fourteen-year-old, the much-indulged daughter of a distinguished Sydney academic and his charming, intelligent wife. The girl grows up in a harbourside suburb, seeking in imagination something different from the civilized, serene world of her family. She reads Stevenson and Masefield and the *Boy's Own Paper*, disdains her own 'dresden china' prettiness and remodels herself in fantasy as an appropriate heroine of outdoor adventure: 'tall, well-knit, strongly-built, with sun-browned skin and eyes like grey steel'. (That sounds like Norah Linton, Mary Grant Bruce's heroine, except for the chilly 'steel'.) The central theme in all Brenda's fantasies is that of escape by pirate ship, cargo ship—any ship that sails beyond Sydney Harbour, into the unknown. Jean Curlewis presents the inner world of Brenda Paling with more sympathy than irony. Even though the novel shows that Brenda must enter the adult feminine world, the author does not give much more than a formal assent to the relinquishing of childish dreams.

At eighteen, Brenda falls in love with an idealistic young man who plans to be Prime Minister of Australia and to reawaken 'the spirit of honour, of service, of *esprit de corps*, of personal responsibility—the spirit that animated the nation in war time, but that died in peace time . . .'. The last section of the novel shows this vague idealism yielding to circumstance. The young man, Jimmy Stevenson, learns that the best way to achieve social justice is to accept his rich uncle's offer of a partnership in a Sydney retail store: to make money and use its power for good. Brenda learns not to despise the 'haberdashery' on which the Stevenson fortune is built. She writes:

> . . . I now think that Jimmy is quite right to love his office, and all the things that he is going to do in life now seem to me infinitely more glorious than ever—than even a square-topsailed three-masted schooner, breaking out her canvas in the morning sun just outside Sydney Heads, which until last year was always my standard of perfect glory and beauty.

The Ship That Never Set Sail was written in the year of Jean Curlewis's engagement to a young Sydney medical student, Leo Charlton. Although it does not take quite the same form as Ethel Turner's autobiographical account of her choice between 'love and fame' in *The Little Larrikin*, it makes essentially the same decision. Imagination yields to reality: love and work are better than dreams. The ships of Brenda Paling's fantasy world are the symbolic equivalent of whatever aspirations Jean Curlewis gave up. Marriage and the writing of juvenile novels for Ward Lock meant making the same choice her mother had made. *The Ship That Never Set Sail* is the only Curlewis novel to deal with the recurring Turner theme of the woman's role. As the novel's rueful title suggests, the matter was settled. The choice of the worthy suitor with the family business instead of an adventurous rival who offers Brenda a world of experience outside Australia is a traditional ending in its affirmation of solid worth. As a metaphor for Jean Curlewis the writer, it may have an added significance. To join the family business, surely, was to write for Ward Lock's gift book series, like her mother and her aunt Lilian. Ethel Turner had protested about Ward Lock's 'tins of jam'. Her daughter may have seen their products as 'haberdashery'.

The next three Curlewis novels share with *The Ship That Never Set Sail* the theme of aspiration defeated by everyday life. *Drowning Maze* takes an idea familiar to readers of John Buchan or G. K. Chesterton: that if life does not offer adventure it is necessary to create it. In this novel the frail schoolboy son of a famous explorer fakes a conspiracy, and challenges two bored sixth-formers to accompany him into its illusory dangers. Humphrey ('Humpty-Dumpty') King's society for providing adventures brings Ruritanian romance to the Sydney resorts of Palm Beach and Newport. The manufactured adventure turns into a real one, in which the explorer's son succeeds in matching his father in courage and ingenuity. The interest of the story is in the coming together of the worlds of imagination and reality. The 'real' adventure is a stylized affair of stolen Crown jewels and secret formulas, with the deliberate incongruity of a beautiful, exotic Grand Duchess taking a bus from Newport to Sydney. The mixture of realism and romance does not quite work, but there are some good moments of suspense and comedy. In the boy who is sure of his father's love but wants his respect as an equal, it is easy to see something of the author's relationship with her celebrated mother.

Jean Curlewis's best novel is *Beach Beyond*. It is the only one for which she found a story to fit her theme. Again, there is a frail hero whose strength is his capacity to enact his dreams. Having inherited nine million pounds from an American uncle, David Hartley decides to use it to build a new world on a Pacific island. For its founding fathers, he kidnaps a small group of Sydney's most distinguished and creative men, who have conveniently isolated themselves, with their wives and children, at a remote beach resort where they spend their summers in primitive simplicity. Believing that the simple life chosen by rich people on holiday can be perpetuated in an island Utopia, Hartley plans his Noah's Ark:

'I . . . decided that this Ark of wise men and healthy women and children should sail away to some new land and found a model State . . . where life should be as simple and happy as at Beach Beyond . . . When it was established, we should open the gates, and all those who were tired of the mistakes of the old world could come in . . .

The dream fails. Hartley cannot launch his Ark at gunpoint, and he concedes defeat. The author allows the anti-Utopians to win the argument: '. . . the only place for a decent man to build his Utopia is fair in the heart of factories and smoke and grime and muddle'. The conclusion is the same as Ethel Turner's in her anti-Utopian novel of 1909, *Fugitives from Fortune*: that the true reformer begins at home. There are two important differences in Jean Curlewis's treatment of the theme. The Turner novel was a family story, in which the millionaire's Ark foundered on the individualism of his children; it ends happily in a compromise which satisfies everyone. The Curlewis story is in a quite different style, with the narrative interest drawn from the fear and suspense of the besieged community at Beach Beyond. Except for the idealistic motives of David Hartley, it works like any other story of a master-mind outwitted by his victims. Hartley does not accept failure. He has no time for the gradual reform, beginning in Sydney factories, which his captives see as the best way to reshape the world. Knowing that he will soon die from tuberculosis, he refuses to go back to Sydney:

> 'I'm too tired,' he said fretfully. 'You don't know how tired I am. I did my best and I can't begin again. I'll give you my money and you can build your Utopia and live in it. But I shall go to my own and live there always—beyond Beach Beyond. It's quite close—in five minutes I shall have arrived.'

With this, he walks into the surf to drown.

As a novel of ideas within an adventure story framework, *Beach Beyond* is intelligent and persuasive. Yet it is not hard to see why, like the earlier Curlewis novels, it was a commercial failure. An adventure novel in which the villain turns into the hero could please an adolescent readership well enough, but an ending in pathos and defeat is emotionally unsatisfying. The genre in which Jean Curlewis was writing thrives on the moral absolutes she refused.

Like *The Ship That Never Set Sail*, *Beach Beyond* has biographical interest. Jean Curlewis died of tuberculosis in 1930 after a long illness. After *Beach Beyond* she wrote only one more novel, *The Dawn Man*, another adventure story centred round an idealist's defeat. Whether or not she could have predicted her own death when she wrote of David Hartley's, the pattern of failure can be traced in all her fiction. The talented daughter of one of Australia's most successful writers could not have been satisfied with four juvenile novels, none of which had a second edition, published in the series within which her mother's work continued to flourish. Ethel Turner's *King Anne, Jennifer J.* and *Nicola Silver*, written in the same period as her daughter's work, all made handsome profits with many printings. In joining the 'family business', Jean Curlewis went into direct competition with the unbeatable Ethel. Like Lilian Turner before her, she failed,in spite of a narrative gift and a sense of place which is beyond either of the Turners. The theme of aspiration and defeat, central to her fiction, did not appeal to readers accustomed to her mother's buoyant spirits; and the Ward Lock format made comparisons inevitable.

8

Mary Grant Bruce and the Outdoor Family

In the early twentieth century in Australia several distinct modes of writing for children may be discerned. Ethel Turner and her disciples continued to write within the framework of domestic realism; their novels depended for success on skill and subtlety in characterization. At their best, the Turner novels created for children a world of feeling in which anger and tears, change and growth and death were given their place. Imitation Turners produced similar situations of domestic comedy or drama but missed the feeling of the originals. In direct contrast with the domestic style were the stories of outdoor adventure and exploration in which such writers as Alexander Macdonald and Joseph Bowes developed the pioneering chronicles of early Australia well beyond the limits of probability. Such novels depended on narrative interest, suspense and an exotic setting. Characterization was unimportant; heroes and villains were usually simple antitheses of virtue and vice, the embodiments of a young reader's fantasies of power.

Between the world of feeling and the world of action, between the domestic interiors of Sydney suburbia and the wilds of northern Australia, it would seem hard to find a middle ground. Mary Grant Bruce did just that. She moved the fictional Australian family into a bush setting which retained just enough pioneering dangers to give a satisfying balance of romance and realism. Her central characters in the Billabong series—Jim and Norah Linton and Wally Meadows—are kept within the range of childhood, yet they have the bush skills which make them the equals at least of the Billabong stockmen and boundary riders. The Bruce novels are the inheritors of the colonial tradition of settlers' tales from *Alfred Dudley* onwards. Norah Linton is the heiress of a century of settlement in Australia: a colonial girl in courage and strength, she is completely at home in an outback setting which is by now thoroughly domesticated. Because her squatter father, David Linton, is well-established and prosperous, Norah has the pleasures of a country childhood as well as its responsibilities. The Billabong stories owe much of their appeal to the skill with which Mary Grant Bruce blended the family story and the outback romance. They evoke nationalist feeling too by showing the Lintons' way of life as a distinctively Australian development from the best British traditions.

Mary Grant Bruce was Ethel Turner's almost exact contemporary; she published with Ward Lock in William Steele's Australian gift book series, and her output of thirty-eight volumes almost equalled the Turner total of forty-four. Yet a comparison between these two immensely popular writers shows as many differences as similarities. They present the classic Australian alternative of 'Sydney or the Bush', with Ethel Turner's ideal family setting a harbourside suburb and Mary Grant Bruce's the self-contained world of a remote cattle-station. The Turner family pattern is matriarchal, with mothers and daughters as the centre of value and gently-wielded power. The Bruce family is patriarchal; the characteristic Bruce heroine must prove her worth in an outdoor masculine world and also provide a refining feminine note by knitting socks and playing the piano for the men. Ethel Turner's literary background is the English domestic novel. Mary Grant Bruce, who wrote for boys as well as girls, drew on the nineteenth century adventure story of the kind I have discussed in Part One. In an autobiographical essay she described her childhood reading: '. . . when I was eight I was steeped in Kingston, Marryat [and] Ballantyne . . . Penny dreadfuls, too; my limited pocket money was spent recklessly on all the 'Jack Harkaway' series . . .'[1] It is likely that her reading of Kingston included his novels of Australian life; his novel of 1880, *The Young Berringtons*, has a pattern of action and character strikingly similar to that of her Billabong novels.

In sales and popular affection Mary Grant Bruce rivalled and perhaps surpassed Ethel Turner. Although no single Bruce novel matched the success of *Seven Little Australians*, with its stage, film and television versions, its numerous reprints, and translations into many European languages, it is probably safe to claim for the fifteen Billabong books a total readership larger than that of any fifteen Turner novels. Mary Grant Bruce had the advantage usually won by writers willing to keep a series going. Yet her achievement cannot be dismissed as simply one of formula fiction: one needs to ask what it was in the formula that held at least two generations of readers, from 1910 to the late 1940s, and gave Billabong a place in the national mythology.

Mary Grant Bruce was born in 1878 in Sale, Victoria, where her father, Eyre Lewis Bruce was a government land agent.[2] Her maternal grandfather, William Whittakers, had a cattle-station on the La Trobe River where the Bruce children spent holidays. In part, the Whittakers property, Fernhill, gave a model for Billabong. The perspective of the country-town girl for whom, in childhood, station life had an element of wish-fulfilment, helped to give Billabong its idyllic quality. But Norah is not a self-portrait. For the fictional heroine Billabong is total contentment, and boarding-school a barely-endurable interruption of the perfect outdoor life. Her creator, by contrast, was ambitious; she read widely and had early academic success at the Sale Ladies' High School. At sixteen she qualified for matriculation, and within the next three years she won the Shakespeare Society's annual essay prize three times. Her parents would have liked her to marry and live in the country, as her older sister did. Instead she left home to make a career in Melbourne journalism.

The first step towards becoming a professional writer of juvenile fiction came with the editorship of the children's page of the *Leader*, a weekly paper published by the Melbourne *Age*, mainly for country readers. As the *Leader*'s 'Cinderella', Mary Grant Bruce began to write stories for children, to set competitions, and to publish a column of her readers' letters. There is a close parallel here with Ethel Turner's early work. Both women gained a sense of audience from the Australian children for whom their first stories were written, matter-of-factly, as part of the job both were paid to do. The *Leader*'s country readership as well as Mary Grant Bruce's own background helped to determine the kind of stories she would write.

Her first serial, 'Ragamuffins', appeared in 1901-2 in the 600-word instalments which must have encouraged an economical prose style and the use of simple, clearly defined characters. As the title suggests, this story fits the fashion of the period in its celebration of naughty children. Kitty Ross and her brothers in 'Ragamuffins' differ from Ethel Turner's young rebels and little pickles of the 1890s mainly in their background: a country-town day-school and a small farm. The next Bruce serial, 'The Adventures of Timothy' (published in 1912 as *Timothy in Bushland*) was an attempt at fantasy on the model of Ethel Pedley's *Dot and the Kangaroo* (1899), but with a basis in everyday country life. In 1904-5 'The Interlopers' (published as *Gray's Hollow* in 1914) showed the beginnings of a distinctive Bruce style. It affirms the moral value of country life, as well as its pleasures, by a direct contrast with the triviality, boredom and unwholesomeness of an urban upbringing. The country children who read *Gray's Hollow* must have been flattered to discover how much they could teach their city cousins. This novel follows the same pattern as the new-chum story of the nineteenth century, with the cousins from town replacing the English newcomers who develop muscle and moral fibre in learning Australian ways.

The setting is a Victorian country town. The children who provide the standard against which their city cousins are measured are twelve-year-old Madge Gray and her three brothers. All are characterized as straightforward, fearless, loyal and thoroughly at home in any outdoor activity. Their cousins from Sydney are pale and languid with limp handshakes and exquisite clothes: they dislike games and despise country simplicity. One by one, they are reformed. The youngest, a spoiled seven-year-old, gives in easily, captivated by the genuine warmth of the Grays' family life. His sister Thelma has to be cured of vanity and 'sneaky ways': this comes about when she cheats at school, and finds herself despised by the country girls to whom she has felt superior. The headmistress sighs over Thelma:

> The little girl seemed to have had little or no training about matters which were all-important to the teacher. Honour, straightforwardness, fair dealing, were scarcely more than names to Thelma. Smartness, acuteness, were of infinitely more importance. It was not that she was naturally bad. But she had been brought up in an unhappy school—left to servants, encouraged to deceive and impose on her parents.

Thelma's moral reform goes with a physical transformation. She becomes brown and active, and discards her elegant Sydney clothes for the plain cotton dresses worn by her cousin.

It is interesting that, while Mary Grant Bruce chose the cheating incident as the means towards the city girl's self-discovery, the test for her older brother is one of physical courage. Too vain to admit that he is no horseman, Horace is nearly killed when he rides his uncle's thoroughbred, but he wins his cousins' respect in doing so. The ending of *Gray's Hollow* is a complete rejection of Sydney values. In a later book, *'Possum* (1917), Mary Grant Bruce made a similar clash of city

and country ways a more nearly equal contest: here the country girl
has something to learn as well as much to teach the newcomers. In
general, however, the Bruce novels give the idealized image of bush
life in which Australians have always wanted to believe.

The first Billabong book, *A Little Bush Maid*, appeared as a *Leader*
serial in 1905-7 and was published by Ward Lock in 1910. Mary Grant
Bruce brought to William Steele's list of Australian children's authors
a new style and a range of characters quite different from those of the
Turner circle. Her heroine, Norah Linton, is first seen as an independent, fearless twelve-year-old, perfectly adapted to her bush life, and
devoted to her widower father and her older brother, Jim. Her father's
cattle-station, Billabong, is the ideal school of character: within it work
and pleasure are indivisible. There had been nothing quite like the
Billabong setting in Australian children's fiction. The sons and daughters in the settlers' novel share responsibility with their parents, but
the demands of pioneering life make them in effect young adults. The
children in Mrs Chaffey's *The Youngsters of Murray Home* enjoy the freedom and pleasures of country life: so do those in Ellen Campbell's *Twin
Pickles*. The difference between these novels and the Bruce series is that
the Linton children do not see the adult world as a separate one. When
Norah goes out mustering cattle with her father she has all the delights
of an exciting game of skill as well as the satisfaction of being useful.
The title of the second novel in the series, *Mates at Billabong* (1911),
indicates the children's place in their father's world; they are his 'mates'
and almost his equals. Mr Linton describes himself with characteristic
understatement as 'not exactly a poor man': the Linton children live
in equally understated luxury, with all domestic comforts, and a
motherly cook-housekeeper, Brownie, to supply the meals which are
described in loving detail. There are no conflicts in the Linton family
and no sense of loneliness in their isolated world:

It was never dull at Billabong. Always there were pets of all kinds
to be seen to. Mr Linton laid no restrictions on pets if they were
properly tended, and Norah had a collection as wide as it was
beloved. Household duties there were, too; but these could be left
if necessary – two adoring housemaids were always ready to step into
the breach if 'business on the run' claimed Norah's attention. And
beyond the range of the homestead altogether there lay an enchanted
region that only she and Daddy shared – the wide and stretching
plains of Billabong dotted with cattle, seamed with creeks and the
river, and merging at the boundary into a long low line of hills.

Norah used to gaze at them from her windows—sometimes purple, sometimes blue, and sometimes misty grey, but always beautiful to the child who loved them.

Mary Grant Bruce's Billabong became a place of wish-fulfilment for Australian children, most of whom, by 1910, lived in cities. Like Banjo Paterson's 'vision splendid' it represented the essential Australia, no less real for being idealized. And, just as Norah is the colonial girl a little further removed from her British background, so her brother Jim is the Man from Snowy River with a Melbourne public school education. The Linton trio becomes a quartet with the addition of Wally Meadows, a Queensland orphan brought home by Jim for the school holidays and thereafter unofficially adopted. Wally supplies the high spirits and sense of mischief which the sober, reliable Lintons need to enliven them. In the background is a chorus of devoted servants, stock-men and boundary riders. In their authentic Australian qualities, the Billabong men, 'all long and lean and hard, with deep-set keen eyes and brown thin faces', reinforce the Lintons' status by an evident admir-ation for 'the boss' and his children.

The city-country contrast of values is presented again and again in the Billabong series, but nowhere so heavily underlined as in *Mates at Billabong* with the visit of Cecil Linton, the cousin from town. Cecil is an almost terminal case: unlike Horace Densham in *Gray's Hollow*, he does not take the country cure. Bored, patronizing and self-satisfied, Cecil plays the new-chum role in a way calculated to show up the Lin-ton virtues of simplicity and plain living:

Dinner was very different to the usual cheery meal ... [Norah] remained unusually silent, being, indeed, fully occupied with taking stock of this novel variety of boy. She wondered were all city boys different to those she knew. Jim was not like this; neither were the friends he was accustomed to bring home with him. They were not a bit grown-up, and they talked of ordinary, wholesome things like cricket and football, and horses, and dormitory 'larks', and were altogether sensible and companionable. But Cecil's talk was of theatres and bridge parties, and—actually—clothes! Horses he only mentioned in connection with racing, and when Mr Linton inquired mildly if he were fond of dances, he was met by raised eyebrows and a bored disclaimer of caring to do anything so energetic ...

   Dinner over, Norah fled to Brownie, and to that sympathetic soul unburdened her woes ... [Mr Linton] smiled a little at the elaborate cigarette case Cecil drew out, but lit his pipe without comment, reflecting inwardly that although cigarettes were scarcely the treatment, though they might be the cause, of a pasty face and a 'nervous breakdown', it was none of his business to interfere with a young gentleman who evidently considered himself a man of the world.

At first Cecil Linton's visit to his country cousins is a matter for comedy. Cecil's letter home, with its complaints about the limitations of Billabong life, scores a few points: 'So quaint, to see the sort of mutual admiration that goes on here'. The general harmony of Billabong, and the unqualified devotion of each Linton to the others, means that the centre of interest is not in character but in event, or in the intrusion of an outsider like Cecil. Uncharacteristically, Mary Grant Bruce allows *Mates at Billabong* an element of pain for which there is no consolation: Cecil's ill-temper and poor horsemanship bring about the death of Norah's pony, Bobs. It is a measure of the security of the Billabong world that this is the only episode in the whole series without a happy resolution. In later novels the lost are found, and those believed to be dead return safely. As Brownie sums it up: 'Nothin's ever different [at Billabong] only better'.

When the first two Billabong novels brought Mary Grant Bruce wide popularity and a demand for more, she had the problem, inevitable for the writer of a series, of how to let her characters grow up. Her contemporary in Canada, L. M. Montgomery, introduced an eleven-year-old heroine in *Anne of Green Gables*, published in 1908, but placed the action in a recognizably earlier period. That allowed her to go rapidly through Anne's education, marriage and years of motherhood and take in World War I in which Anne's three sons are old enough to serve. References to telephones and motor-cars, and Norah's being allowed to ride astride, place the first Billabong books as no earlier than the turn of the century, but the outbreak of war in 1914 brought Billabong into a time-bound world. Mary Grant Bruce's own experience gave her new material and situations for the Lintons which she could use if she allowed them to grow up. In 1913 she had left Australia for Britain, to try her luck in journalism; there she met her future husband, her second cousin, Major George Bruce. They returned to Australia and were married in 1914, a few weeks before war was declared. Major Bruce was recalled to his regiment; Mary Grant Bruce travelled with him on a troop ship to Britain and spent most of the war years in Ireland, where her two sons were born. Some of the experiences of these war years are given to the Lintons in the trilogy *From Billabong to London* (1915), *Jim and Wally* (1916) and *Captain Jim*

The Billabong trio: Jim, Wally and Norah
Illustration by J. Macfarlane for the first edition of *Captain Jim* (above) and
by J. F. Campbell for the 1952 edition (opposite)

(1919). But by keeping Jim and Wally more or less to the minimum age for military service, their creator ensured that they were still boyish enough to go back virtually unchanged to a changeless Billabong in 1919. Thereafter, Mary Grant Bruce kept the clock moving at her own pace. In spite of readers' impatient demands, she delayed the marriage of Norah and Wally until *Billabong Adventurers*, published in 1927; and she made their attachment a natural extension of the mateship of their childhood: 'I was more or less forced into marrying off Norah and Wally eventually', she said, 'but beyond that I drew the line'.

With the wartime novels and later with *Billabong Adventurers* Mary Grant Bruce came into direct competition with Ethel Turner. Ward Lock published *Captain Jim* in a format identical with the Turner novel of 1917, *Captain Cub*, and presumably was happy to encourage the authors' rivalry with these parallel titles. Although Ward Lock's records were destroyed by bombing during World War II, enough survive in Ethel Turner's carefully maintained letter-books to show that William Steele and his successor constantly kept before her the challenge of the Billabong books. The younger writer was the more reliable of the two: she always produced manuscripts of uniform length with neatly planned chapters. The Turner novels were less predictable: William Steele began to find them skimpy. 'Others besides myself are noticing the lack of quantity,' he wrote in 1917 '. . . and, frankly, let me tell you Mrs Bruce's newer books are selling better than your own'. In 1928 Steele's successor, C. S. Bligh, argued for another book about the Woolcots of Misrule, whom Ethel Turner had abandoned with relief in 1902, after the lack-lustre *Little Mother Meg*. Bligh wrote:

> During the present season Mrs Bruce brought out a book 'Billabong Adventurers' containing the marriage of Norah, and this has had an exceptional sale. Next year there will not be a Billabong book, and we feel that if we had one from you dealing with the characters in 'Seven Little Australians' we have no doubt we could give it plenty of boost, and good sales could be expected.

This challenge produced *Judy and Punch* in time for Christmas 1928. With this last novel (a return to the period of *Seven Little Australians* to supply the story of Judy Woolcot's schooldays), Ethel Turner retired from writing novels. Mary Grant Bruce's status at the head of Ward Lock's list as the most successful Australian children's writer was thereafter beyond dispute. Until 1942 she kept up the regular supply to Ward Lock of a book each year for the Christmas market, and even managed three extra titles for Angus and Robertson under the Cornstalk imprint. *Hugh Stanford's Luck* (1925), *Robin* (1926) and *Anderson's Jo* (1927), for Cornstalk, as well as two stories for young children published in 1920 and 1922 by Whitcombe and Tombs, were added to the annual Ward Lock volume to make a total of thirty-eight books published between 1910 and 1942. Only once did Mary Grant Bruce falter. In 1929 her twelve-year-old son Patrick died in Ireland after a shooting accident which was an uncanny echo of a much earlier tragedy, the death of her brother, Paddy, at Sale in 1885. Financial need in the Depression period forced her back to work in 1931, and back to Billabong with a novel in which, significantly in view of her own loss, the main event concerns a little boy, lost and presumed dead, but found because of the intensity of Norah's faith and Jim's will to keep searching. Private fantasy in *Bill of Billabong* (1931) goes with the fulfilment of a dream which must have had a special appeal in the Depression years: the discovery of a gold mine on Billabong.

Although the Lintons do not need the gold, they have less fortunate friends, including an English immigrant brother and sister, whose fortunes are established by the discovery. The series needed it too. The earliest Billabong novels exhausted the obvious possibilities of cattle-station life. A fire at the homestead, a riding accident for Mr Linton, a near-fatal snake-bite for Wally—these give the necessary note of drama to the Lintons' routine. Part of the appeal of the series is its capacity to initiate the reader in bush ways and skills. There is a 'how-to-do-it' element in the novels which shows Mary Grant Bruce's journalistic training, as well as her knowledge of country life. But without some element of excitement in each volume, readers would have found too much repetition in the day-to-day life of the Lintons. Since the characters did not change, their experience must widen: hence the gold, and the private aeroplanes of the 1930s novels of Billabong, as well as a few more weedy city visitors in need of moral and physical reform.

Even with a good deal of ingenuity in bringing new elements to Billabong, Mary Grant Bruce still found it enough to devise a Linton story every other year. In between, she varied her Australian country settings and extended her range of characters a little. An early novel, *Glen Eyre* (1912) makes a useful point of comparison with the Billabong series. The family pattern is like that of the Lintons: a motherless brother and sister living with their father on a country property in Victoria. But these children, Nancy and Rob Ogilvie, have none of the emotional and physical security of Billabong. Their father still mourns his wife's death; he leaves domestic matters to a series of slovenly housekeepers, and, although the children help him outdoors, he gives them no affection or interest. The contrast with Billabong's cheerful family life and good cooking may be seen in the description of the Glen Eyre dining room: '... bare and stiff, the chairs planted round at regular intervals. There was dust on the mantelshelf, and marks of candle grease on the heavy red serge table-cloth ... unswept corners, and crumbs from the last meal still on the carpet by the table'.

Until Mr Ogilvie learns to love his neglected children, life at Glen Eyre is one of hardship and monotony. Even so, the value of a country childhood is affirmed in the Ogilvies' self-reliance. The mutual devotion of brother and sister, a characteristic pattern in the Bruce novels which may have its origin in its author's early companionship with her own brother, saves them from loneliness. One of Mary Grant Bruce's arguments against city life was its separation of boys from girls by prescribing different games: country children played and worked together. This implied plea for equality is a sign of the feminist beliefs for which the author's life gives more evidence than her work. In an article written for the London *Daily Mail* in 1913, she described the distinctive qualities of the Australian child:

> They do not play as English children play. Toys are not readily found in the country that lies at the 'back of beyond'; and the standard plaything of Australia is a string of empty cotton-reels ... The [small girl's] claim to stockwhip and bridle is no less definite [than the boy's] ... the land always dominates both. Their games are the games of the soil, and it is not easy to see just where they merge into actual work.[3]

The children of *Glen Eyre* are replicas of the Billabong set except in external circumstances. The novel reverses their fortunes to make them as happy, though not as rich, as the Lintons. Published after only two Billabong novels had appeared, *Glen Eyre* could have had a sequel. Instead, the demand was for 'more Norah'. Was this because the Ogilvie farm, at best, was cosy, without the understated splendours of Billabong Station? The complete sales figures are not available, but a statement of royalties to 1927 shows a very strong preference for Billabong:

> *Mates at Billabong* (1911) 22 127 copies sold.
> *Glen Eyre* (1912)   14 251 copies sold.
> *Norah of Billabong* (1913) 21 539 copies sold.[4]

The Linton and the Ogilvie children are alike in their unspoken delight in the natural world. With Norah's response to the Billabong land-

Riding home
Illustration by J. Macfarlane from *Glen Eyre*

scape, quoted above, may be compared Rob Ogilvie's scarcely-conscious pleasure in an early morning at Glen Eyre:

> He was no more inclined than any other small boy to notice the beauty of the sunrise. Probably he would have said, if pressed for an opinion, that the sky looked pretty decent, only it was going to be jolly hot. But something in the changing beauty of the dawn caught his small-boy eye, and he stood still to watch it, fitting one bare toe into the cracks between the boards of the verandah.

To say 'pretty decent' is about as far as a Bruce hero or heroine will go in open praise. They follow the Australian bushmen of literary tradition in being laconic and suspicious of enthusiasm, but with an instinctive feeling for the landscape to which they belong. The generations of children who recited Dorothea Mackellar's 'My Country' from their school readers met the same appeal to nationalist sentiment in Mary Grant Bruce's books. The inarticulate responsiveness of Rob Ogilvie at eight years old becomes the more reflective but equally laconic devotion of an older Bruce hero to the 'real Australia'. This extract, with its combination of the sentimental and the matter-of-fact, exemplifies the Bruce style:

> Darkness had nearly fallen when Wally Meadows came cantering down the homestead paddock at Billabong and pulled up at the gate. For a moment he sat motionless, listening: but no sound came out of the gathering gloom, save that, in a tree across the flats, a mopoke was beginning its monotonous call. Wally smiled a little, remembering certain homesick evenings in England when nightingales had poured out their song around him, and when he would have given them all to hear the dreary double note of the mopoke. Nightingales were all very well in their way, and you wouldn't really feel satisfied unless you heard one, when you got to England. But mopokes were simply part of an Australian night: just to remember the queer song made you think of the gum-trees, gaunt shadows against a star-lit sky, and brought to your nostrils the aromatic scent of their leaves. Nightingales were certainly wonderful; so were Melba and Tettrazini, only you didn't want to hear them every day. But no Australian ever got tired of a mopoke.

The nostalgia of this passage is a reminder that nine of the fifteen Billabong books were written in England or Ireland where Mary Grant Bruce spent much of her married life. She came back to Australia with her husband and children after World War I and stayed for six years.

The Bruces lived in Ireland from 1926 to 1929, when, after the death of their younger son, they moved to England. Ten years later, just before the outbreak of World War II, they decided to make their permanent home in Australia. Again, as in 1914, war changed their plans. Their son Jon, who was to have taken up farming, joined the army; and his parents spent most of the war years in a guest-house in semi-suburban Croydon, Victoria. The last Bruce novels, *Peter & Co.* (1940), *Karalta* (1941) and *Billabong Riders* (1942), belong to this period. There are Japanese spies in *Peter & Co.*, and a German spy in *Karalta*, but World War II does not disturb Billabong. It remains an idealized version of the author's own childhood: her 'land of lost content'. Norah, Jim and Wally go droving in *Billabong Riders* in the same spirit of idyllic companionship as that of *A Little Bush Maid*, written more than three decades earlier.

The timelessness of Billabong is part of its charm. No one dies; no one grows much older. Mr Linton's beard is only a little more 'grizzled' in the later volumes than in the first: Brownie is fatter, but supplies endless cups of tea and hot buttered scones with the same effortless good will. The mode in which Mary Grant Bruce wrote did not demand subtlety in characterization: she created a landscape with figures, not a series of portraits. Unlike the novelist who places his characters in time her skill was that of the choreographer, plotting movements in space.

Among Australian juvenile novels the Billabong books were an extraordinarily enduring success. It is worth considering some reasons. One is Mrs Bruce's unusual ability to find new situations for the same set of characters. This seldom works in girls' fiction: new situations in the domestic mode almost always mean growing up, with love and marriage and motherhood distancing the character from the reader. By keeping Norah active and adventurous, working and riding with Jim and Wally, Mary Grant Bruce avoided that change. Marriage and motherhood do not alter Norah. Joining the adult world, usually a defeat for individuality in a child character, is irrelevant to Billabong, since there has never been any separation. The lack of a Mrs Linton is no accident: there is no place for her in the Billabong series; and in the other Bruce novels mothers are usually absent, frail or dead. There is plenty of evidence that the Billabong series was read by boys as well as girls; it owes that double audience to its concentration on the masculine world in which Norah's special gifts win her a privileged place.

The Billabong books appealed to children, as their many reprintings and their author's enormous fan mail give evidence. They pleased adults too; they were favourite prizes in Sunday schools, held in school libraries and given by the thousand as Christmas and birthday presents. They seemed, in their author's lifetime at least, to offend no one: when she died in 1958 her novels had only just begun to look dated. It is easy to see why they were popular with parents and teachers: Jim, Norah and Wally could scarcely be more responsible, dutiful and kind. Reviewers called the books 'wholesome'. No religious sect could object to the Lintons' practical Christianity; and by apparently never going to church they avoided being claimed by any one group. They combined strong Australian feeling with loyalty to Britain, and made a special appeal to the large body of Irish-Australians. Norah's comments on her family background are relevant here: 'My grandfather was an Englishman and my mother was Irish; and though I'm proud of being an Australian, I'm prouder of them, because there wouldn't have been any Australia but for the people who had the pluck to come out here'. In 1914 Jim and Wally unhesitatingly go to war. In this, too, they flatter Australian self-esteem, because they go to the rescue of 'little Mother England'. Their bush training makes them more adaptable and stronger than any British-born soldier:

> Even when more than a year of war had made uniform a commonplace in London streets, you might have turned to look at Jim and Wally. Jim was immensely tall; his chum little less so; and both were lean and clean-shaven, tanned to a deep bronze, and stamped with a look of resolute keenness. In their eyes was the deep glint that comes to those who have habitually looked across great spaces.

With the social and political changes in Australian society in the 1950s, the Billabong era came to an end. Mary Grant Bruce's career spanned the long period between Federation and World War II. Her last book, *Billabong Riders*, was written just before the Japanese attack on Pearl Harbor brought a new element into Australian life, and a new political period began. No American visitor ever comes to Billabong, nor is the United States mentioned in any Bruce novel. It would have been hard for anyone of Mary Grant Bruce's generation to foresee the disappearance of that large political fact of their time, the British Empire. Billabong came from an imagination formed in the 1880s; it could survive only so long as Australian attitudes remained relatively unchanged.

After Mary Grant Bruce died, aged eighty, in 1958 her novels fell sharply from favour. Their assumptions about race and class were unacceptable in the 1960s, and almost overnight they vanished from the shelves of school and municipal libraries. That they are now back in print suggests the persistence of parents' memories of childhood reading; they are not approved by teachers or librarians. The reaction against them was inevitable, but in part at least misguided. There is no denying the racial stereotypes in the Bruce novels, and it should surprise no one that their author shared the prejudices of her time. Yet she has been misjudged by anxious censors who have not seen her work in historical perspective, nor read it carefully enough to see how her racial attitudes were modified over the years.[5] She has not had the indulgence given to others of her generation, like Miles Franklin whose patrician contempt for the McSwats in *My Brilliant Career* (1901) goes unrebuked, or Henry Lawson whose views on race are seldom noted. The harmless Lintons have been taken to task with a severity which can only be explained by the special vigilance given to children's reading. There is a case for protectiveness, but the perils of learning racism from reading about Black Billy have been exaggerated. There is surely at least an equal danger in falsifying the past by obliterating evidence that values other than today's ever existed. It is interesting, if uncomfortable, to consider that some at least of the moral certainties of the 1980s will be quite alien to a future generation—and to admit that we are in no position now even to guess which ones these might be.

9

The Australian Boy

'Who is capable of writing a good story about the Australian boy? . . .
We want a description from a colonial author . . .' [1] In 1880, reviewing
the latest shipment of children's books from Britain and the United
States, Catherine Helen Spence complained that there was as yet no
attempt at realistic writing in Australia to match Mark Twain's portrait
of the ordinary American boy in *Tom Sawyer* (1876). Twain wrote in
conscious reaction against the romances of Sir Walter Scott, whose
chivalric code, he believed, was a destructive influence on the American
South. He was scornful, too, of the frontier tales of Fenimore Cooper.
In *Tom Sawyer* and *Huckleberry Finn* Twain set out to demolish the heroic mode. The characterization and the language of these novels under-
mine the conventions of popular fiction: much of their comedy comes
from Tom Sawyer's devotion to the rules of literary romance and from
Huckleberry Finn's instinctive pragmatism. The originality of Twain's
work may be seen in the vernacular speech (authentic enough, in its
evocation of Huck's language, to be banned in 1885 from the Concord
public library), in the drab, small-town setting, and in the creation of
two characters whose thoughts and actions are within the range of
childhood.

It was optimistic to expect an Australian Mark Twain in the late
nineteenth century; the United States had waited a long time for the
literary independence Twain's work demonstrates. For the most part,
the Australian boys' story remained within the romance tradition, with

characters more manly than boyish, and settings chosen for their exotic qualities. In language it was standard *Boy's Own Paper* with a sprinkling of Australianisms but no sense of idiomatic speech. It may seem surprising that Australia with its tradition of laconic humour, and its affection (at least from a comfortable distance) for the larrikin type, did not produce more outsiders and iconoclasts among its juvenile heroes. The vernacular style encouraged by the *Bulletin* had comparatively little influence on children's books. One reason must be publishing policy: slang, as Ethel Turner was told, limited sales. The Sunday-school prize market could not be ignored. It was unlikely, however, that propriety was the only reason for the scarcity of 'good bad boy' heroes like Tom Sawyer in Australian children's stories. Such characters fitted best into city or small-town settings; the bush, with its harsh realities, demanded brave, hardy young settlers or explorers. The call of the bush, and the call of British publishers for something wild and strange, must have been important in directing writers away from the everyday social settings in which a comic rebel-hero could indulge his anarchic impulses.

There is one notable exception: a neglected novel by Edward Dyson, *The Gold-Stealers* (1901). A short-story writer associated with Melbourne *Punch* and the *Bulletin*, Edward Dyson, brother of the artist Will Dyson, was a miner's son, born in 1865 near the Ballarat goldfields which provided the background for much of his fiction. His stories, as Norman Lindsay said, 'are unique, for they are the only good literature that has come to us from the richly coloured era of the great mines'. [2] Like Twain's novels, with which it has an obvious affinity, *The Gold-Stealers* is on the borderline between the boys' story and the adult novel. It is worth reprinting; even if its length tests the stamina of today's children it should win some adult readers with its comic spirit, and its skilful evocation of time and place. Subtitled 'A Story of Waddy', Dyson's novel presents the minor characters of a small Victorian gold-town with the insight of Norman Lindsay's *Redheap* (1930) or *Saturdee* (1936), and with more good humour. Dyson's visual sense and his commitment to realism may be seen in such portraits as that of Waddy's schoolmaster:

> The master faced [the boys] and stood musing over them like a pensive but kindly cormorant. Mr Joel Ham, B.A., was a small thin man with a deceitful appearance of weakness. There was a peculiar indecision about all his joints that made the certainty of his spring and the vigour of his grip matters of wonder to all those new boys who

ventured to presume upon his seeming infirmities. He had a scraggy
red neck, a long beak-like nose, and queer slate-coloured eyes with
pale lashes; his hair was thin and very fine in colour and texture,
strangely like that of a yellow cat; and face, neck, and nose were
mottled with patches of small purple veins. To-day he was dressed
in a long seedy black coat, a short seedy black vest, and a pair of
new moleskins, glaringly white, and much too long and too large.

The central character of *The Gold-Stealers* is Dick Haddon, the leader
of a schoolboy gang whose hide-out is a deserted mine-shaft. Like Tom
Sawyer, Dick freely translates life into literature. Adult authority and
the threat of discipline arouse his sense of theatre. His widowed mother
sensibly ignores his habit of running away from home; pursuit, she says,
only encourages him. After a clash of wills with the schoolmaster, Dick
is delighted to hear that an official search party is on its way. One of
the gang warns him:

'They had a meetin' about youse last night—Jo, an' Rogers, an'
my dad, an' ole Tinribs, an' the rest. They're all after you. You're
fairly in fer it.'
Dick's face became radiant with magnificent ideas.
'What! You don't mean they're goin' t' form a band t' capture
us?'
'Well, they sorter agreed about somethin' like that.'
'My word, that's into our hands, ain't it? Lemme see, we must
be a band of bushrangers what's robbed the gold escort an' the
mounted p'lice 're huntin' us in the ranges. I'll be—yes, I'll be Morgan. An' Ted—! What'll we make Ted? I know—I know. He'll be
my faithful black boy, what'll rather die than leave me. You fellers
bring a cork to-morrow an' we'll pretty quick make a faithful black
boy of Twitter.'
All eyes turned upon Ted, who did not seem in the least impressed
by the magnificent prospect ... his face was pale, and funk was
legible in the diffident eye he turned upon the company. Dick noted
this and put in an artful touch or two.
'Jacky-jacky, the faithful black boy', he said; 'brave as a lion, an'
the best shot in the world—better 'n me!'
The ruse was not successful. Ted failed to respond.
'Twitter don't seem to want to be no black boy,' said Phil.

It is easy to demonstrate the debt to Twain in *The Gold-Stealers*. Even
Dick's choice of a name for himself as bushranger, Red Hand, with

The country school
The frontispiece by G. Grenville Manton of *The Gold-Stealers*

Fork Lightning for his lieutenant, echoes *Tom Sawyer*, in which Huck is 'the Red-Handed' and Tom himself 'the Black Avenger'. As in the Twain novels, the boys' fantasies turn into real danger. Dick witnesses theft and attempted murder in the old mine-shaft; he becomes as heroic as his own literary models, but does not enjoy the experience. The *Gold-Stealers* ends with a retreat into childhood games. Dick recovers from a sentimental devotion to the heroine of the adult sub-plot; he refuses an invitation to her wedding in favour of riding in a billy-goat race. His refusal, in a letter signed 'your mate Dick', ends the novel in the same spirit as the last sentence of *Huckleberry Finn*, in which 'yours truly Huck Finn' signs off before departing from 'sivilisation'. In spite of these and other resemblances of plot and tone, *The Gold-Stealers* offers more than a pastiche of Twain with an Australian accent. There is nothing second-hand about the scenes of country-town life in Waddy. Moreover, Dyson's knowledge of the mines makes Dick's ordeal underground more convincing than that of Tom and Becky lost in the riverside cave and threatened by the murderer Injun Joe. It would be too much to claim Edward Dyson as an Australian Mark Twain, but his novel stands the comparison reasonably well.

The sub-plot in *The Gold-Stealers*, a romance between the daughter of one of the thieves and the brother of his chief victim, takes up too much space. Yet the ironic presentation of local gossip about the lovers is worth having; so too, is the final scene in which the gossips find new interest in the transformation of Waddy's disreputable schoolmaster, Joel Ham, into Sir Joel Hamlyn. Leaving for England to claim his title and estates, Hamlyn says, 'I have got drunk on beer here. I shall get drunk on champagne there. That's all the difference'. Dyson could not have used the name Hamlyn here without intending a sardonic reference to Kingsley's celebrated novel of Australian life. The happy ending of *Geoffry Hamlyn* is a return to England, home and titles. It is in keeping with the tone of *The Gold-Stealers* that in recording ordinary Australian life it should ridicule Kingsley's romance. Here, too, the method recalls Twain; in *Huckleberry Finn* Twain wrecked a steamboat and called it the *Sir Walter Scott*. The best of *The Gold-Stealers* is in the episode in which Dick and his gang set out one night to steal all the goats in the neighbouring township of Cow Flat and let them loose in Waddy. Such comic narratives are rare in juvenile stories of Australian life; adventure, in particular, is a solemn business.

In the early twentieth century one other Australian writer of some talent attempted the comic adventure story with Twain as model and a 'good bad boy' as hero. This was E. J. Brady, best known as a poet, whose

Tom Pagdin, Pirate was published in 1911. Like Dyson, Brady tried to capture the everyday speech of the Australian boy, with 'cove' and 'stoush' to authenticate its local flavour in the manner of C. J. Dennis.

Twain was an obvious model for an Australian of this period who wanted to work against the grain of British writing. Brady's novel, however, is too imitative in mood, situations, characters and even idiom to mark any real progress. He openly invited the comparison: even his title matches Twain's *Tom Sawyer, Detective* of 1896. Brady's hero is a composite figure: half Tom Sawyer, half Huckleberry Finn. He has Tom Sawyer's sense of literary 'style', with Huck's habit of telling elaborate, melancholy lies and of 'borrowing' whatever food comes to hand. His mate, Dave, is the pragmatist. When the boys overhear plans for a robbery, Tom Pagdin decides to play detective:

> 'Wouldn't it be better', [Dave] asked, 'to tell somebody beforehand?'
>
> 'What!' exclaimed Tom, in unutterable scorn, 'go an' tell somebody now and spile the whole thing. You ain't got no sense, Dave Gibson—no sense whatever. You're a nice sort o' detective an' pirate, you are.'

Brady, like Tom Pagdin, does too much borrowing. The Queensland setting needs to be more firmly established to give Brady's novel a life of its own. The passage in which Tom is caught 'borrowing' a fowl, follows *Huckleberry Finn* far too closely:

> 'I got no relatives; I'm an orphan', [Tom said].
>
> 'Poor child', said the farmer's wife softly . . .
>
> 'Yes, I'm an orphan', said Tom tearfully. 'I got no father an' no mother, an' nobody in the world. I wuz put to work for a cove up there [on the Richmond] milkin' cows an' pullin' maize an' ploughin' . . . an' he treated me bad too—uster knock me about an' larrup me with a cartwhip. I never hardly got enough to eat— never—so I couldn't stand it no longer an' I run away.'

The effect of this appeal is lost when Tom, like Huck in a similar episode, forgets the name he has invented for himself.

Tom Pagdin, Pirate ends cheerfully, with the boys rewarded for their part in clearing up a robbery. They refuse the claim of Tom's drunkard father, who wants the reward, and they resist being civilized by more benevolent adults. The last sentence of the novel is in the spirit of its originals: 'So they continued to have a good time, and Tom Pagdin shot all the cats in Wharfdale with his Winchester'.

Among later novels, a story of two Bendigo schoolboys is worth noting for its comic realism: *Duck Williams and His Cobbers* (1939) by Fred Davison. Its antecedent is more likely to be Richmal Crompton's *William* series than anything by Twain, but it offers some points of comparison with *The Gold-Stealers* and *Tom Pagdin, Pirate*. The mood is anti-heroic, with the central character's imaginative impulses constantly thwarted by circumstance. The hero, Duck Williams, so named because of his flat feet, plays Ned Kelly in armour made from a kerosene tin 'borrowed' from his mother. His lieutenant in the Kelly Gang is Baldy Johnson, whose nickname, as unromantic as Duck's, refers to his shaven head and a case of ringworm. The Bendigo gold mines supply an element of real danger, but the boys meet it as inept adventurers; they lose themselves mainly because they forget to take torch or matches down the mine-shaft. With its episodes of rabbit-shooting, camping, school and Sunday school, *Duck Williams* keeps within the ordinary range of country-town life, finding comedy in the boys' attempts to enliven an obstinately prosaic adult world.

Perhaps the Australian comic spirit was too grim for children's books. Norman Lindsay's *Saturdee* is about boys but not for them; his study of country-town childhood has too much rancour in it to be pleasurable. Henry Handel Richardson described *The Getting of Wisdom* (1910) as 'a merry and saucy bit of irony',[3] but its irony would be beyond most schoolgirls even though its heroine's experience might match their own. In a different way Steele Rudd's *On Our Selection* (1899) is adult reading because of the underlying cruelty of its farce. The reasons are a matter of conjecture but the fact is plain: Australian comic realism gave almost nothing to the boys' story, and, apart from the gentle domestic comedy of *Seven Little Australians* and the absurdist fantasy of *The Magic Pudding* (1918), laughter is hard to find in any of our early writings for children. Nor is there anything to match the good humour and high spirits of Arthur Ransome's holiday adventure series. British children in the 1930s seemed to have a better time than Australians whose holidays in the outback were usually strenuous and seldom fun.

What did they do, then, the young adventurers in Australia in the early twentieth century? With pioneering virtually over, and gold-seeking a matter for companies rather than single fossickers, their fictional experiences might have turned to the irresponsible pleasures of a more settled society. Some do: Russell Allanson's *Terraweena* (1905) uses an outback station setting for a holiday adventure story. Two schoolboys, who have never seen a kangaroo 'except the tame ones in the Sydney Botanical Gardens', pack a great deal into a few weeks: they ride and shoot, lose themselves in the bush and are kidnapped by Aborigines. The novel is the Australian equivalent of countless English stories of school holidays enlivened by thieves or smugglers: as kidnappers Aborigines do just as well. For those who stay in Sydney, adventure may be found in Sydney Harbour itself, as it is in T. E. Grattan-Smith's *Three Real Bricks* (1920). The 'bricks', Ned Grattan, his sister Mel, and his chum Jim, are rather like the Billabong trio: athletic, fearless and resourceful, they capture a German wireless station in the first days of World War I. The boys try to keep Mel out of danger, but she plays her part, diving into 'water where man-eating sharks were not uncommon' and swimming ashore to report a bomb in the engine-room of an Australian troop ship. Meanwhile the boys face gunfire to board the ship and give the warning. 'While we breed such boys', the Captain says, 'the Empire has nothing to fear'. Grattan-Smith makes sure that the reader misses none of the essentially Australian qualities of the trio: Mel's mastery of the 'famed Australian crawl', Ned's 'grit' and Jim's cheerful competence. The German spies are first detected because of their un-Australian cruelty to a swaggie's dog: Mel, Ned and Jim can hardly miss that sign of the alien. *Three Real Bricks* is in the same mode as Mary Grant Bruce's *'Sea-Hawk'* (1934) and *Told by Peter* (1938): holiday stories with a dash of crime, and a spirit of cheerful assurance.

The appearance of breezy schoolboys and schoolgirls in Australian holiday adventures did not mean the displacement of earlier stereotypes. There is a surprisingly large number of juvenile stories of the early twentieth century which differ very little in plot, characterization and language from the novels of the colonial period. At first reading—and most do not encourage a second reading—they seem like Victorian leftovers, anachronistic in style and feeling. Anyone dogged enough to look more closely will find some interesting variations. I have chosen the work of Joseph Bowes and William Hatfield to show the development of the settlers' novel, with that of Alexander Macdonald and Donald Macdonald to represent the epic adventure.

Joseph Bowes wrote for Oxford University Press in the days when Oxford saw children's books mainly as commercial props for its real and less profitable business of scholarly publishing. The titles of his novels, which include *Pals* (1910), *Comrades* (1911), *The Young Anzacs* (1917), *The Jackaroos* (1923) and *The Young Settler* (1925), suggest the characteristic pattern of his work and its concentration on Australian stereotypes. *Comrades* reversed the direction of the nineteenth century settlers' novel with some 'Go North, Young Man' propaganda for pros-

The cover of *Comrades*

perous Australian boys instead of the usual 'Southward Ho!' for impoverished Britons. Joseph Bowes wrote of tropical Australia with the
enthusiasm of a travel agent. For the restless youth of the over-civilized
southern states or the jaded returned soldier after World War I the
northern Australia of his novels offers fortune and physical challenge.

The audience for these novels must have been seen as more British
than Australian: a local audience, however urbanized, would not want
such footnotes as the one explaining a jackaroo as 'a cadet or young
gentleman living on a cattle station for experience'. *The Young Settler*
reads like an immigration pamphlet, with page after page of undiluted
information about prickly pear and the rabbit-proof fence. The
question-and-answer method reminiscent of *A Mother's Offering* produces such laboured and unlikely exchanges as this conversation
between Australian nephew and British uncle:

> 'Didn't you tell me, Fred, that you went in for sugar-cane
> growing?'
> 'Yes, be jabers, we do that. Sugar, you know, is one of our staple
> industries. Queensland is the sugar State. We supply the whole Com-
> monwealth with that commodity. It grows well throughout the
> coastal belt from the south to the far north of the State. I say, uncle,
> it would be great if you and aunt were to come out for a trip and
> see for yourselves.'

The Bowes heroes differ from their nineteenth century equivalents in
several ways. The young men in Kingston's novels, for example, usually
come to Australia through necessity; the hero of *Comrades*, Sam Potts,
leaves home in New South Wales in search of adventure, dissatisfied
with the lawyer's vocation his parents choose for him:

> To become a scholar, a brilliant barrister, a judicial luminary had
> no charm for him; while, on the other hand, the adventures of the
> bush, the sport with rifle and hound, brushes with the blacks, and
> so on, made every other form of living seem stale and unprofitable
> to his imagination.

A Kingston hero would not have behaved so irresponsibly. Sam Potts
defies his parents, who are presented as affectionate and well-meaning,
by going to the Northern Territory as a stowaway on a coastal ship.
Nothing happens to make him repent: in fact the author seems to
endorse his disobedience. There is in Bowes's novels a perceptible shift
away from the Victorian moral view and the evangelical Christianity
which guided the young settlers of nineteenth century fiction. The ref-

erence, in the passage quoted above, to 'brushes with the blacks', apparently one of the diversions of life in the Far North, is revealing. There is none of the missionary impulse which kept the mid-Victorian hero from the extremes of racism: the young men of Bowes's novels do not carry Bibles or concern themselves with building churches and teaching the Aborigines. Some, at least, of the Victorian writers worry about the white man's right to tribal hunting grounds, as I have demonstrated in Part One. The sense of a common humanity in *Comrades* is minimal, as this passage shows clearly enough:

> Uncle Rod, while wishful to teach the [Aboriginal] thieves a lasting lesson, had no thought of brutally misusing them. Had he overtaken them when in red-hot pursuit, and engaged them in battle, he would have fired at them without much compunction. But to ambuscade them thus and have them at his mercy: to see them grovelling at his feet as they were now doing—well, it simply took the fire out of his anger ... After a short deliberation, he selected two of their number and bound them to trees. This done he harangued the lot, threatening summary vengeance of the utmost kind should he ever catch them interfering with the cattle. The bound men then received several strokes with a rod. He palavered again, ending with a distribution of tobacco. After receiving wholesale assurances of penitence and undying friendship, which were affably received but liberally discounted by the squatter, the party rode away.

The Aborigines in *Comrades* are divided between the savage tribes—cannibals who refrain from instantly braining a white child only because they are too lazy to carry dead weight to their camp-fire for cooking—and the tame station hands. The domesticated Aborigines are 'children of nature ... made happy by generous prizes of pipes and tobacco'. Any modern reader who is tempted to categorize all early writings of black–white encounters as equally racist needs to think about the differences between the mid-Victorian settler of juvenile fiction and his twentieth century successor. Frank Layton and the Kingston and Marryat heroes seem paternalistic to twentieth century readers, and so they are. But it should be understood that they offered the Aborigine the gifts they themselves valued most. Christian teaching, the chance to read and write, and the security of a benevolent employer are precisely what is given to the luckiest of the deserving poor in a Dickens novel: such gifts were scarce enough in Victorian England. That the early writers did not try to understand Aboriginal civilization is true enough. Nevertheless the Victorians' offerings of Christianity and literacy acknowledged a measure of human equality. The pipes and tobacco Bowes and many others thought sufficient for black happiness reflect their own cultural impoverishment.

Another novel by Joseph Bowes, *The Young Anzacs*, gives interesting evidence of the displacement of religious faith. This book, incidentally, complicates the picture of Bowes's racial views by giving its hero a part-Aboriginal grandmother from whom he inherits 'lustrous, liquid eyes' and a gift for tracking and marksmanship which is useful at Gallipoli. Bowes presents the relationship half-apologetically, stressing that a legal marriage took place, and that the bride was 'for all the mixture, comely'. She is long since dead at the time of the novel's opening; and Jack, the product of an urban upbringing in Brisbane, shows no interest in her. It is hard to see why Bowes mentions her unless to account for Jack's exceptional eyesight. The novel is almost entirely concerned with Australian boys at war. Their response is presented in the language of spiritual experience:

> Jack was so filled with the spirit of patriotic service that every other feeling was either cast out or so subordinated as to be a wholly negligible quantity ... He was born anew in the glad surrender of his free spirit to the holy cause of his country.

Given such dedication, it would be hard for the chaplain in Jack's regiment to compete. Jack describes 'the padre' as 'quite a decent sort of chap ... He doesn't preach at you; simply talks away to you, giving you good horse sense. Can handle the gloves, too, they say, just like a pro'. One example of the padre's work among the wounded bears this out. His function is to be cheerful and his manner is relentlessly facetious. When one of the men wants to know how badly he is injured, the padre replies:

> 'You curious young beggar! ... Well, let me see. Oh, that Turk sniper drilled a hole through your chest, and within a short cooee of your heart. But you'll get on famously now. No, not another word. Shut your peepers and go off to bye-bye now. I must do a skip. Here comes nursie.'

Bowes probably made the chaplain a clown more or less accidentally. It is not that the novel is anti-religious; rather that when the hero is 'born anew' for his country there is no room for another spiritual force. However, the presentation of the padre in *The Young Anzacs* helps to measure the distance from the Victorian religious values which survive in the school stories described in Chapter 10, but not in the tales of war as adventure. The 'family at war' stories of Mary Grant Bruce offer a compromise in religious styles between the fervently devotional and the clownish-secular; the chaplain in *Captain Jim* is a man of prayer and a patriot in the restrained way which suits the Lintons.

Joseph Bowes's half-dozen novels, including *The Young Anzacs*, represent one response to the taming of Australia: the writer of adventure stories could move his frontier to the north or to war. The choice of the northern journey was made later by William Hatfield, whose *Buffalo Jim*, published by Oxford University Press, appeared in 1938. Hatfield's writing is less bad than Bowes's. It must have seemed good to someone: *Buffalo Jim* was chosen as the 'scholarship novel' by the Queensland Education Department and was reprinted in an Australian edition in 1946. It follows the pattern of the first settlers' novels except that the penniless English hero finds fortune growing rice in the Far North instead of sheep or cattle in the south. The opening chapter, set in Liverpool in the Depression year of 1931, presents emigration as the only solution for British boys of spirit. The seventeen-year-old hero, Jim Westcott, sails for Australia as a stowaway because 'his sturdy independence revolted at the idea of going down to register as unemployed and getting on the dole'. The novel stresses hard work rather than luck or adventure. Jim combines a strong practical sense with the 'perfect physical development' which makes him unbeatable in a fight. He has the romantic spirit to enjoy a dangerous expedition in Central Australia, but he goes as camp cook, with no false pride about doing menial work. Gold-mining in the West does not attract him; like Frank Layton in George Sargent's novel of 1865, he sees more merit in growing vegetables.

Worthy and industrious though he is, Jim is not a Horatio Alger figure: the American success story had no exact Australian equivalent, and this may be due to our traditional mistrust of the city. No Australian hero would leave the bush for Sydney to make a million by sheer hard work in commercial enterprise. Only the risks of outback life can justify the profits, according to our popular mythology. The young factory hand of Australian fiction is not a future president: he is Lawson's little 'Arvie Aspinall, who dies clutching his alarm clock, a pathetic victim of city oppression.

Buffalo Jim is an artful mixture of adventure story and tract for the times. Because Jim constantly proves his manhood in fist-fights, shooting and rough-riding, it was presumably acceptable for him to settle for a prosaic market-garden and rice-plantation in the end. The last chapter sees the arrival from England of his parents, his sister and younger brother. The eager response to Australia of these frail, white-faced Britons echoes the last pages of a nineteenth century novel except that there is no talk of building a church, and the recipe for making an Australian girl out of Jim's sister lacks Victorian delicacy of expression:

> 'Get a bit of beef on to her limbs, and some brown into her cheeks!' said Jim. 'Ride out in the cool of morning . . . swim in the reservoir, sun-bake on the bank—anything calculated to give her an appetite.'

Except that they lack the religious note, Hatfield's comments on the Aboriginal question echo almost exactly the ideas of Kingston and Sargent. He points out the damage done by white men to Aboriginal hunting grounds, and sees it as culpable ignorance:

> No prospector would consider he was in any way interfering with a native by shooting game for food for himself, but that act alone was the most flagrant interference with the life of the nomad hunter, whose very existence depended on the natural game of the country, and whose every tribal ritual and totem belief was in some way connected with the preservation of the game.

Buffalo Jim resembles *The Young Settler* in its combination of useful facts with suspense and adventure. There is thinner bread-and-butter and more richly spread jam in Alexander Macdonald's stories of the Far North: *The Lost Explorers* (1907), *The Invisible Island* (1911), *The Mystery of Diamond Creek* (1927) and others. Published during the same period as Joseph Bowes's work, they, too, send a series of sturdy young men in search of fortune to tropical Australia. Macdonald's imaginative range is greater than Bowes's, and his prose less stodgy. From a semi-factual base, his novels move into fantasy. He specializes in finding lost treasures, lost explorers, lost civilizations. His Australia has the promise of Rider Haggard's Africa; and the recurring figure, in several novels, of a middle-aged Scot who guides the young heroes to the heart of some mystery, is wholeheartedly romantic. In action the Scot is brisk and practical, but his camp-fire reveries reveal the melancholy mystic:

> I'll no' say another word against [the boys] goin' into the Never-Never wi' me. I have wished it from the first, an' though I tried no' to influence ye, there were times when I couldna' help mysel', when the spirit o' the lonely desert sent her uncanny cry ringin' through my brain—that cry which I ken so well by this time, 'Mackay come back to your comrades; they wait for you by the mountain . . .'

Ay, they wait for me, their bleaching bones wait for me to hide them from the carrion crows. But Mackay comes—he comes . . . Get me the flute, Jack, an' let me play something cheery.

As well as searching for his comrades' bones Mackay dreams of an El Dorado beyond the Australian desert, with gold, rubies and diamonds to make the fortunes of his young companions. In *The Lost Explorers* he finds his friends (not bleached at all, but alive, well and living with a tribe of highly civilized Aborigines) and the treasure at the same time.

Because of the exotic nature of the journey, Macdonald's picture of Aboriginal life is not just the contrast between the savage and the domesticated presented by Joseph Bowes. The journey needs its dangers, so there are plenty of menacing black figures, described as 'nigs', 'murderous pests' and 'skunks' by the adventurers. But for contrast, there is the fierce but noble tribe of the 'mystic mountain': 'infinitely superior in knowledge and intellect to any other aboriginal race', from whom Mackay's party rescues the lost explorers.

Alexander Macdonald's competent boy-heroes are as uninteresting as most of their kind. His novels are crowded with indistinguishable minor figures with names like 'Never-Never Dave' and 'Emu Bill'. For villains he uses racial stereotypes: 'suave Celestials' in *The Invisible Island* and 'treacherous Dagoes' in *The Mystery of Diamond Creek*, as well as the omnipresent Aborigines. There is unintentional irony in the moral with which *The Lost Explorers* ends: 'greater by far than gold or gems is the love of our fellow-men'.

Donald Macdonald's *The Warrigals' Well* (1901) combines narrative skill with an evocative sense of place, and that rare element in an adventure story, good characterization. Macdonald, the war correspondent for the Melbourne *Argus* in the South African war, chose for his story of gold-seekers in *The Warrigals' Well* a first-person narrator rather like Buchan's Richard Hannay. His Jasper Meredith, who sees himself as a typical matter-of-fact British officer, is disarmingly hesitant about his ability to describe the Australian scene. Meredith is responsive to its weird beauty; his descriptions avoid the effect of set pieces by being carefully integrated into the narrative and given the sound and sense of the narrator's voice:

In the heat of the broad noon I was thirsty—a breakfast of cold bacon was doing its share—and I determined to have a drink at the lagoon which glittered tantalizingly between the trees, even if all the Myalls of the north were there to oppose it, the more especially as I was

Illustration by Arthur H. Buckland from *The Lost Explorers*

conscious of being anxious without sufficient reason for it. With many of us, I think, the severest discipline of all is self-discipline. I rode down through waist-high scrub to as pretty an aquatic picture as could be found in all the land. The shallows were thick with the pink and purple water-lilies, large almost as dessert plates. Amongst them stately white egrets, with airy, flowing plumes, moved like royal birds in a kingdom all their own, while, far out, flocks of black and white pelicans floated motionless. Amongst the wild-fowl a tiny goose particularly interested me, for it was as much a jewel amongst water birds as the Mandarin duck of the east, or the Summer duck of Canada.

I picked a clear spot to drink, for I had no pannikin, and conscious that I was trying to look seven ways at once, knelt down with the bridle in my hand. I had barely tasted a mouthful when Biscay gave a snort and a sudden plunge to one side, and for the fraction of a second I had a horrible sense of being left dismounted and unarmed in the midst of hostile blacks. It gave extra grip to my hold of the bridle-rein, extra vigour to the bound that brought me to my feet, and athletic skill I thought I had long forgotten, in the spring which placed me in the saddle. I had the rifle from the bucket in an instant, and was ready to shoot—what? Shadows? pelicans? water-lilies? for there was nothing else in sight. Beyond the staid water birds there was such a total absence of life of any kind that I could have laughed at myself, were it not that Billy's horse was now as nervous as his rider. I wondered, indeed, whether I had frightened him as well as myself; for fear and courage are both infectious, and a nervous rider can unnerve his horse, just as a game horse stiffens up the rider once he feels his saddle-flaps under his knees.

The Warrigals' Well is unusual among adventure stories in having an engaging and unpredictable villain. The dramatic interest of a race for gold between rival expeditions is enlivened too by some sardonic comedy. There is a welcome change from the stereotype of the heroic Australian bushman. Tom White, who accompanies Meredith's party, 'seemed to have been made to sleep in the shade of a bush'. He is lazy, but a superb horseman, stupid and cowardly, but so unconscious of his deficiencies as to arouse baffled exasperation rather than contempt. In him, as in the other members of the party, the author finds the idiosyncrasies of character which make for a good novel rather than just another 'ripping yarn' with an Australian setting.

The Warrigals' Well is the best of the romances of Northern Australia. It would be hard to award a prize for the silliest, but my own nomination would go to Bernard Cronin's *The Treasure of the Tropics* (1928) with E. V. Timms's *The Valley of Adventure* (1926) a close contender. Both give the search for hidden treasure new dimensions of absurdity; in both the prose is penny-dreadful. *The Treasure of the Tropics* was published by Ward Lock, and *The Valley of Adventure* by Angus and Robertson. That both were reprinted more than once by these reputable publishers confirms the impression that in the late 1920s Australian writing for children reached new levels of mindlessness.

The next two decades did not do much better. Allan Aldous created an Antipodean Biggles: a retired R.A.A.F. man whose wartime skills are turned to new problems. *Danger on the Map* (1947) has a Northern Territory setting, and a search for treasure in which Bluey Dowd, a twenty-three-year-old former Squadron-Leader, acts as guide and protector for an elderly professor with a scholarly interest in a seventeenth-century Dutch shipwreck. The characters in this novel are of standard cardboard thickness. Bluey is all muscle and quiet determination. The professor, too vague even to remember to pack a toothbrush, is courageous in his amateurish way. They are joined in the search by an aristocratic remittance man whose latent fighting spirit is aroused by the thought of foreign adversaries: ' "... I'm all for fighting the scum", said the Dook vehemently. "We're British stock, aren't we?" ' There is a representative 'faithful Aborigine', Johnny Jingo, who departs from stereotype only in having 'green teeth' instead of the usual flashing white. There is nothing much new in the Aldous mixture except that the treasure of the Australian North turns out to be uranium, and the adversaries of Bluey and the Professor 'a gang of munitions racketeers who had enlisted the aid of power-lusting scientists in an effort to achieve world gangster-domination'. Boy-heroes, in novels like *Danger on the Map*, are out of place. Bluey needs all his wartime experience for the final encounter with the enemy, which is not hand-to-hand fighting, but aerial pursuit and bombardment.

In another post-war adventure, *The Opium-Smugglers* (1948), Ion Idriess acknowledges the shifting borderlines of audience for such stories by saying in his preface, 'This boys' book is for your dad as well as for you'. It is evident in these two novels that the Aborigine is no longer an adequate adversary. Modern technology makes the 'wild blacks' and their spears obsolete. World War II also revived in the Australian adventure story the figure of the sinister Oriental; although *The Opium-Smugglers* is not a war story it does make use of anti-Japanese feeling in its choice of villains. When his little 'Man Friday', an Aboriginal boy, is captured, the hero of *The Opium-Smugglers* says gloomily: 'I knew the Japs thought an aboriginal life was nothing–probably [they] had strangled the boy and thrown him into the sea'.

The novels of Idriess, Aldous and others take adventure as far north as possible: to the coast of the Northern Territory or North Queensland. Chinese, Malays and Japanese, and accounts of pearling luggers and drug-smuggling gave Australia a new frontier for crime. The hero of such stories has nothing of the vulnerability of childhood about him. If he is not an adult in years, he is at least independent of family. It is worth noting that Jack and Dick, the central figures in *The Opium-Smugglers*, are old enough for cigarettes; they are constantly 'rolling another smoke' for themselves. They do not drink. That prohibition, which restricted even the middle-aged Biggles to lemonade, and the absence of any love story, keeps Aldous and Idriess on the boys' side of the fictional border. The hero is never cruel (or at least he never sees himself as cruel) but he does not worry unduly about whatever killing or violence comes his way. His code of behaviour is always clear.

The only Australian juvenile adventure story of any distinction to be written between the wars was Alan Villiers's *Whalers of the Midnight Sun*. First published in 1934, this novel reappeared under the Angus and Robertson imprint in 1949, when it won the Australian Children's Book of the Year Award. Like Aldous and Idriess, Villiers celebrates heroic action, physical courage and endurance in a place remote from everyday life. A Norwegian ship, hunting whales for oil in Antarctic waters, is the setting for most of the novel; its Australian connection, the boy-hero, is an eleven-year-old stowaway from Hobart. Alfie, presented as an outsider in the Huckleberry Finn tradition, differs from Huck in his willingness to join the adult world; he becomes part of the ship's community. He appears first on the Hobart waterfront, characterized as 'disturber of the peace of half a dozen maiden school-teachers' lives, reprobate of the waterfront, raider of all orchards within a radius of forty miles, irrepressible, uncontrollable, happy little raga-muffin of the streets'. When the Norwegians accept him as a member of the crew, he is shown to be brave and loyal, but he retains the offhand individualism and the irreverent attitude towards authority which are seen as characteristically Australian.

Whalers of the Midnight Sun shows considerable narrative skill; and its characterization, though not subtle, gives a sense of individual qualities, sufficient for a reader's interest in individual fates. It tackles the question of the morality of whaling, but resolves it in a way which today would be unlikely to find favour.

'Pouf! Whouffff!' the blue whales blew, with that strangely memorable note peculiar to those mammals, long, and slobbery, and wet, and blubbery, and yet with something in it of well-fed contentment and the joy of living, too. It seemed a pity to fire death into the midst of these harmless beasts—all for the sake of a can of margarine and a bar of soap. God had planned these beasts beyond soap, surely.

In passages like this and in others which describe in detail the slow painful dying of the whales, Villiers seems to argue the case against commerce and the Norwegians. Yet the resolution of the novel stresses the heroism of the ship's captain ('a man of steadfast purpose, unflagging courage and nobility of spirit') and finds whale-oil 'a human necessity'. The final chapters present the captain's death in terms which sanctify his achievement. In all this, Alfie and the other Australian boys on the ship are more or less forgotten. *Whalers of the Midnight Sun* is a boys' book, but it is about men rather than boys, with Captain Petersen, not Alfie, its real hero.

It will be evident from the novels I have described that the ordinary Australian boy had little to do with Australian juvenile adventure stories, except to read them. Edward Dyson's story of country-town boys in *The Gold-Stealers* had no successors, and is forgotten today. There is no hero of children's fiction in this country as well remembered as Ginger Meggs, created by J. C. Bancks for a remarkably durable 1920s comic strip which even survived its author's death in 1952.

10

Playing the Game Down Under

The English school story genre, of which *Tom Brown's Schooldays* (1857) is the prototype, came late to Australia, and understandably so. In fiction, colonial Australia was predominantly the place of outback adventure and pioneering. The sturdy young hero despatched to the colonies by Kingston or the Marryats shared many of the moral and physical qualities of the English public school boy, but his education proceeded along different lines. Not for him the delights of midnight feasts and football matches, the ordeal by roasting over a study fire or being tossed in a blanket by the school bullies. His courage was tested by bushfires, floods and Aboriginal spears, and while he might be tempted, like his stay-at-home schoolboy contemporaries, to drink or gamble, he was not endangered by the more specialized hazards of the public school code. The author whose imagination was captured by such moral crises as stolen examination papers was unlikely to go outside Britain for his setting. Australia had nothing to offer in the way of cloisters and ivy-covered towers. A gentleman might find a fortune in the colonies but not a public school education. Australia's place in nineteenth century English school fiction is neatly summed up in Talbot Baines Reed's *The Fifth Form at St Dominic's* (1887). The aptly named Loman, expelled for lying, cheating, bullying, stealing, drinking and gambling, has to leave England for moral and physical rehabilitation. After 'four or five years farming and knocking about in Australia have pulled him together', he is considered fit to take his place at a St Dominic's Old Boys' Reunion. Oliver Greenfield, Loman's chief victim, urges forgiveness: 'We must all make up a jolly party and come down together and help [Loman] through with it'. Loman is one of the lucky ones. Many disgraced public schoolboys of fiction have to spend a lifetime of expiation in Australia. Reed's point, however, is clear, and it fits a widely-held view of the value of colonial life: guaranteed to kill or cure a cad.

During the second half of the nineteenth century Australia began to build up its own system of public schools, closely modelled on the English pattern. Between 1852 and 1878 Victoria, for example, established six schools with 'public school' status. Though within this federation some were more equal than others, a kind of equality was conceded by the closed circle of competitive sports in which only these six took part. The 'Head of the River' rowing final, on the Yarra or the Barwon, aroused in Victoria something like the public interest of the Eton vs Harrow match at Lords. For many years public school sport was reported for the Melbourne *Argus* by a journalist with the pseudonym 'Old Boy'. At first these schools had to struggle against the conviction of the Anglo-Australian gentry that only English schools really counted: those who could afford to do so would send their sons 'home' for a gentleman's education. Martin Boyd's Langton novels, partly set in nineteenth century Melbourne, commemorate and mildly satirize expatriate attitudes towards an education in the colonies:

> Austin was indignant when told he was to go to Cambridge. His father said that he must have a gentleman's education. Austin said: 'I've been to the Melbourne Grammar School.' This astonished Sir William, as he had only sent Austin there from necessity, and hardly considered it a real school. 'You must have what in England will be thought a gentleman's education', he said.
> Austin said that he did not live in England, that he was an Australian.
> 'What is that?' exclaimed his father contemptuously. 'A convict—a gold-digger. You were born in England. It is your home and we shall go there when I retire.'[1]

Nothing could be done about the prejudices of Sir William, but Melbourne Grammar and others became real schools to later generations. They flourished, however, largely by being as English as possible in customs and ideals. Geelong Grammar School delighted in the informal title of 'the Eton of Australia'. Scotch College sang Harrow's 'Forty Years On'. Of the first six Victorian public schools all except Xavier College habitually imported British headmasters and housemasters. 'The typical headmaster of the church schools in the second half of the nineteenth century', Geoffrey Blainey writes, 'was the son of a well-to-do professional man, a distinguished graduate of a British university, familiar at first hand with English public schools, and unmistakably upper-class in accent and manner'.[2]

Just as Rugby, Eton, Harrow and others were celebrated in their own school stories—*Tom Brown's Schooldays*, *The Oppidan* (1922), *The Hill* (1905)—so some of the newly-founded public schools in Australia built up their own mythology in some more or less recognizable fictional versions of themselves. As in England, such novels came from schoolmasters, former pupils, and from professional writers who saw an opportunity in giving an Australian setting to a popular English fictional form. By the time the Australian public schools were sufficiently well-established to sustain their own legends, the school story convention was worn almost beyond repair. In the Edwardian period it lapsed into a feeble repetitiveness from which the only escape was self-parody or caricature. P. G. Wodehouse's elegantly subversive Psmith and Mike stories consciously deflated the conventions: 'Are you the Bully, the Pride of the School, or the Boy who is Led Astray and takes to Drink in Chapter Sixteen?' Psmith asks Mike. Wodehouse assumed in his reader some verbal sophistication and a willingness to be amused by clichés of fictional school life. For simpler readers there was another way of escape from the stodgy semi-realism of mainstream school stories. This was the comic-strip absurdity of Billy Bunter and the chaps at St Jim's: pop-art, as Isabel Quigly has described it.

World War I was to give a brief renewal to the school story genre; and such novels as *Tell England* (1922), ending with the sacrificial death in battle of the schoolboy heroes, had their counterparts in Australia. These have particular interest because of their authors' instinctive identification with England's cause: if the Australian public school boy still needed to prove himself, he could scarcely do so more effectively than by going 'over the top' on a French battlefield as gallantly as any product of Eton or Harrow.

Among the very few pre-war Australian school stories, only one is in the public school tradition. This is Mary Grant Bruce's story of a country boy at Melbourne Grammar. 'Dick's Schooldays', published as a serial in the *Leader* in 1909-10, was reprinted, slightly revised, as the second half of the novel *Dick* (1918). Although the author had a number of family associations with the school, the novel is weak in specific detail: once the 'big grey door' closes behind the young hero, the setting might just as well be that of any English boarding school. Outside, a few Melbourne scenes give some sense of place. Inside, there is nothing except the buzzing of flies against a classroom window on a hot February afternoon to give an Antipodean note. The characters and situations are all stereotyped. The headmaster is, as always, tall, calm, majestic. The French master, 'little, black-moustached' Monsieur Lenoir is predictably harmless and hasty-tempered, the victim of unruly schoolboys. The sports master, described as a 'white man' and an 'absolute brick' by the boys, has a twinkle in his eye which proves them right. They are right, too, to dislike their 'clever' form-master, Mr Wynne, who turns out to have a 'yellow streak': cleverness, the author says, is less important in a teacher than other attributes 'not easy to define'.

Dick Lester has a comparatively easy time at school. His early upbringing on an isolated country property in northern Victoria has been carefully guided by his father, a former public school man:

> Mr Lester knew that school would show what Dick was made of; and he did not believe in a boy being brought up in cotton-wool. Therefore, he had made Dick as fit as possible, physically, so that when it came to a question of bodily endurance he would be able to hold his own with other boys; and morally he had tried to make him just as strong and hardy. It was for Dick to show the result of his training.

Dick makes friends quickly, shows 'keenness' in everything but lessons, and in spite of his lack of experience in cricket, is immediately chosen for the junior team. School life proceeds normally, with only two rescues from sudden death and one bullying episode. The author adopts the public school story convention in associating bullying with smoking: Ahearne and Bayliss, the school's exceptions to the code of honour, habitually torture little boys in their study to the accompaniment of an illicit cigarette. The fagging system seems to follow English procedures, but the 'beastliness' of the bullies stops at their pleasure in inflicting physical pain. 'Beastliness' is the euphemism for unmentionable vice in many English school stories, but Mary Grant Bruce seems to use the word without this sexual implication. The punishment of the bullies by a group of determined juniors is a much milder version of a similar episode in *Stalky & Co.* (1899).

After passing all the tests of physical courage Dick has one final ordeal. He is suspected of playing a trick on the unpopular form-master; he denies it with a hesitation which suggests his guilt. The other boys think he is lying and send him to Coventry. In fact, Dick believes that his best friend is guilty. Each boy broods unhappily on the other's supposed perfidy. The whole form is punished; a cricket match is

The school bullies confronted
Illustration by J. Macfarlane from *Dick*

endangered because its best players are confined to the school grounds ... And so on. Any reader in the school story genre knows how this one ends: a sudden revelation from a third party, apologies and forgiveness all round, and the mutual suspects better friends than ever because each has suffered for the other's sake. *Dick* is consistently predictable. It does not show Mary Grant Bruce's talents to advantage. Only good characterization could have enlivened the too-familiar situations; and characterization was not one of her strengths. There is a far more engaging portrait of school life in Mrs Bruce's *Gray's Hollow*; here, with a country-town day-school, the author has the grasp of everyday detail and the sense of place to carry conviction.

Dick is Mary Grant Bruce's only attempt at the public school story. As her Billabong novels show, she believed in country life as the source of moral education: for the Bruce hero, therefore, school has little to offer. Boys like Dick Lester and Jim Linton see school as at best an interruption, a pleasant enough interval before they resume the real business of outback life. For them the schoolboy code of honour is instinctive, and they do not need to be taught the value of physical fitness. Apart from the companionship of other boys, a certain social assurance and the excitement of competitive sport, they gain nothing from school. The Bruce hero has no intellectual ambition and no need to seek a career: he returns to his father's cattle station virtually unchanged.

In Lillian Pyke's novels, school means far more than this. Like Mary Grant Bruce, Lillian Pyke was a professional writer who published regularly with Ward Lock in the first quarter of the twentieth century. Much of her work is in the school story genre. School in the Pyke novels is the moral equivalent of the cattle station in the Bruce novels: the main shaping experience of a lifetime. Her Melbourne establishments, St Virgil's and Whitefield College, and their sister schools, Riverside (also known as Riverview) and Merfield, are celebrated fervently and uncritically in a series of loosely connected narratives published between 1916 and 1925.

St Virgil's is a thinly disguised version of Wesley College, Melbourne. Its colours are royal blue and gold instead of purple and gold, but in other details, including its 'Leaving Song', it invites identification. It is one of the six Victorian public schools which compete with one another in Boat Race premierships, in football, cricket and athletics. Its rivals are easily recognized: St Andrew's (Scotch), St Joseph's (Xavier), Victorian Grammar (Melbourne Grammar), Western District Grammar (Geelong Grammar) and Mervale College (Geelong College).

In *Max the Sport* (1916), the first in the St Virgil's series, Lillian Pyke depicts a Melbourne mother with an unshakeable resolve to educate her son in the best British spirit. On the day of Max's birth, Mrs Charlton tells her easygoing husband, the improvident son of an English baronet, how the child must be brought up:

> 'I want him to play the game for the sake of the game, not for the rapture of the winning, but for the joy of playing—to be able to take his wins with restraint and to lose if it is necessary in the same way.'

The only place to learn how to play the game, as Mrs Charlton knows, is a public school. She wants her son to have as teachers 'men imbued with the education of the Old World, with its traditions, and the manner and language of gentlemen'. Her husband's death leaves her almost penniless, but she cheerfully takes in boarders so that Max may have his chance to be 'a Sport'. This comes about when, after a few years at a State School where he mixes happily with his social inferiors, Max wins a scholarship to St Virgil's.

St Virgil's headmaster, Mr Thompson, corresponds in background and outlook with Wesley's headmaster of the period, L. A. Adamson. Thompson, 'an Oxford man', combines 'the ideals of the Old World with the broadmindedness of the New'. Adamson, who came to Australia from Rugby and Oxford, set out to shape a Rugby of the Antipodes with the strenuous moral and physical spirit of the original.

From his first day at St Virgil's, Max shows his susceptibility to tradition:

> ... Max had taken an all-embracing look at the beautiful green cricket oval, the neat tennis courts, and the greystone building, which held so much unknown romance and so many hidden wonders for him.
>
> The name 'Tuck-shop' on an outbuilding gave him quite a thrill ... it called up visions of the heroes of the innumerable school books he had absorbed.

There is not much dramatic interest in Max's life at St Virgil's . Lillian Pyke sends a perfect specimen of boyhood to an ideal school: nothing can go wrong, nor does it. Max accumulates praise and prizes: he is stroke of the eight, captain of cricket, a member of the football team, and the school's champion all-round athlete. He wins a university place with first-class honours, and misses an Exhibition only because of illness on the day of the examination. Finally, his financial problems are solved when the death in England of his father's older brother makes Max heir to a baronetcy, with a comfortable income immediately available. He can choose, then, between his first ambition, to practise medicine in Australia, and the opportunity to go to England and live there as a gentleman of means. His decision to stay in Australia endorses St Virgil's teaching. Work is good in itself and a gentleman, in Australia at least, must justify himself by serving the community. Max tells his mother he does not want to go to an English university:

> 'I cannot feel just because I am heir to an English baronetcy I should look down on the education this country can provide. After all, Australia has treated me well in providing me with free learning all my life. I would like to get my degree here.'

Lillian Pyke adds an even more radical touch to her novel in foreshadowing Max's marriage to Eileen Jones, a fellow medical student whose father is in trade. This gesture towards feminism and egalitarianism is, however, balanced by Max's thoroughly traditional response to Britain's cause in World War I.

Max the Sport, like many English school stories of its period, presents the European battlefield as a heroic extension of the school playing fields. St Virgil's ageing headmaster, 'who had seen one after another of his boys go off to win their colours on a wider oval', says goodbye to Max, his pride mingled with envy of the opportunity given only to the young.

> 'Goodbye, Charlton ... I can only say to you, "Play the game" as you have always played it, and England and the school will not forget.'

'England and the school': the headmaster speaks for both. St Virgil's is England's representative, giving Australians the same dedication to the mother country (Max calls it 'home') as Rugby or Harrow give to English boys. The final endorsement of St Virgil's training comes when Max is recommended for the V.C. The last chapter, headed 'The True Sport', describes his gallantry on the battlefield. Surprisingly, he survives the war.

Max the Sport makes an interesting comparison with several other wartime novels by Australian women writers. Mary Grant Bruce sent her Billabong family to war in the trilogy *From Billabong to London* (1915), *Jim and Wally* (1916) and *Captain Jim* (1919). Ethel Turner published her 'Cub' series within the same period. The common factor in all these novels is Australia's instinctive commitment to England's cause, but there are differences. John Calthrop, the 'Cub', has no school spirit and dislikes games. Jim Linton, in the Bruce novels, has a sense of comradeship in the trenches with other public school boys, but his feeling in going to England's rescue is that of a strong dutiful member of the Empire's family. Individual conscience in *The Cub*, family loyalty in the Billabong novels, and team spirit in *Max the Sport* are the authors' characteristic responses to war. Lillian Pyke's novel differs from the others in identifying dedication to country and Empire with the sporting tradition of the Australian public schools.

It is hard to imagine anyone reading Lillian Pyke's novels today except as a source of social history. The plots are uninventive, the dialogue stiff beyond belief, and the characterization wooden. There is no trace of humour, and little suspense. The only memorable episode in *Max the Sport* is one in which boys from a rival school send opium-drugged chocolates to St Virgil's best footballer just before a big match. *A Prince at School* (1919) sets the boys of Whitefield an easy test in racial tolerance. In spite of his 'dusky complexion' and 'fuzzy hair', Prince Andi of Vilatonga is soon assimilated. His royal rank helps but, better still, he is a sportsman; he saves the day in an important cricket match and becomes a popular hero. The moral lesson, that 'colour is only skin deep' is reinforced when Andi's loyalty to Britain is contrasted with the machinations of a German schoolboy-spy, Jacob Schmidt. Apart from this wartime melodrama, Lillian Pyke keeps clear of villainy.

The last of the St Virgil's stories, *The Best School of All* (1921), makes a rare attempt at complexity of characterization in the predicament of a talented footballer, Smith, who does not want to play for St Virgil's against his old school Mervale. This situation, in which a boy resentfully changes schools and retains former loyalties, makes a neatly constructed comedy in P. G. Wodehouse's *Mike and Psmith* (1909). Perhaps Lillian Pyke's sulky Smith, exiled from Geelong to Melbourne, is an echo of the Wodehouse novel. But whether she read the irreverent Wodehouse, his unrestrainedly sentimental predecessors, or both, she did not learn that the school story succeeds through excess. It is sustained by melodrama ('that beastly Ericking' as Kipling's Stalky called the moral absolutes of Dean Farrar's world), or by caricature and self-parody. The middle ground of the solemn and more or less improbable is unrewarding. There is not enough strong feeling in Lillian Pyke's novels to sustain their basic absurdity.

The most interesting of the wartime stories of Australian public school life is Eustace Boylan's *The Heart of the School* (1920). It, too,

The cricket match
Illustration by J. Macfarlane from *A Prince at School*

concerns a Melbourne school. (For whatever reason, Melbourne produced the purest examples of the public school story; a few Sydney
schools may be found in fictional versions, but they are settings for
adventure rather than explorations of the schoolboy code.) Written by
an Irish Jesuit priest who was Prefect of Studies at Xavier College during the period in which his novel is set, *The Heart of the School* is an
entertainment with a purpose. It tries to define the place of Xavier in
the Australian public school system at a time when, for many tradition-
alists, a Catholic public school was a contradiction in terms. It was not
to be expected that the Irish or Irish-Australian Catholics from whom
Xavier drew its teaching staff and most of its pupils could respond to
the British cause in 1914 as wholeheartedly as did the Anglo-Australians
at Melbourne Grammar or Geelong. The tragedy of the Easter Rising
in Dublin in 1916 must have been as deeply felt by some at Xavier
as that of the Anzac landing at Gallipoli. The anti-conscription campaign of the Irish Archbishop of Melbourne, Dr Mannix, aroused
strong sectarian feelings; and in dividing Catholic from non-Catholic
in wartime Australia it also troubled many Catholics for whom the
Empire's claim was beyond dispute.

Eustace Boylan's novel is an attempt to reconcile these complex
loyalties and to assert Xavier's claim to be at once Catholic, Australian
and public school in feeling. Although it does not mention the schoolboy hostilities which led Victorian headmasters to cancel public school
premiership sport in 1917, the Boylan novel is an implicit reply to those
who saw Xavierians as disloyal, Irish rather than English in allegiance,
and therefore incapable of genuine public school spirit. It seeks to
resolve what the school's historian, Greg Dening, has seen as Xavier's
early dilemma: 'being a public school isolated Xavier from the other
schools of the Catholic education system. Being Catholic isolated
Xavier from the other public schools'.[3] The experience of the schoolboy
hero of *The Heart of the School* is an education in piety and in public
school spirit.

The novel's most immediate appeal must have been to boys who
recognized their own school in it, but the accounts of religious observ-
ances would have made any Catholic reader feel an initiate: for once
an insider in a public school story. Moreover, the author seems to have
tried to balance the idea of Xavier as a public and therefore privileged
school with a sense of its boys coming from ordinary families. There
are no millionaires' sons, no one with titled connections, no talk of
money, and little of the emphasis on class which is common to most
public school stories.

Home for the holidays
Illustration by Colin Colahan from *The Heart of the School*

Eustace Boylan announced his commitment to realism in the opening section. His ten-year-old hero, Peter Jackson, comes from his father's station property to board at Xavier with expectations drawn from fiction and the misleading advice of an uncle who is a former English public school boy. Expecting a world of mysterious conventions and terrifying brutality, he finds the school friendly, undemanding and almost homelike. The initiation of the gentle, bookish, literal-minded Peter has nothing in it more painful than the amused interrogation of some older boys to whom he applies for details of the fagging duties he expects.

'Your name, please, in full?' said Rigby.
'Peter Joseph Jackson.'
'Age?'
Ten.'
'What's the size of your boots?'
'I'm not sure of the size.'
'Leave a blank there, Brown, and please take him to the Physics lab. to-morrow to get his feet measured by a vernier screw, to the thousandth part of a kilometre.'
'Kilometre or millimetre?' inquired Brown.
'Kilometre will do.'
'Shall I ask Father Baker to verify the measurements?'
'As usual, of course. Have you a complete outfit, Peter? . . . Have you an umbrella?'
'No.'
'What! Not an umbrella. That's serious. Of course you've brought goloshes?'

The Heart of the School gives a deliberate invitation to identify not only the school, which is named and described in detail, but many of the characters. To read the novel against the school's centenary history is to see how closely people and events correspond with their real life originals. The Rector, Father Keating, becomes Father Keeley; Father Boylan is Father Brownless; Father Baker remains Father Baker. The author's preface announces the novel as 'non-sensational . . . very disjointed and entirely fragmentary [and] like the story of your own lives, and of all the boys you ever knew, and indeed of all normal human life, it is almost devoid of plot'. The semi-documentary style, in which minor comic incidents from classroom and recreation-time are interspersed with detailed accounts of public school football or cricket matches, is designed for nostalgic recognition rather than excitement.

It seems likely that the descriptions of public school sport are documentaries. A football match, in which Wesley's schoolboy champion, Purt, scores a record fourteen goals, matches the official account of the 1907 Xavier–Wesley match, with Harry Prout as Purt's scarcely disguised original.

The author's main difficulty is in creating an interesting central character. Peter Jackson, idealized from the beginning, progresses through the school winning all hearts, and suffering nothing more serious than a short estrangement from a friend. There is no chance of conflict for such a boy in an environment as benign and protective as the Xavier of the novel. Apart from some illicit smoking in a room behind a Hawthorn milk-bar, and a minor outbreak of cheating, none of the boys is involved in any serious breach of the codek The novel relies on its blend of comedy and sentiment rather than on any subtlety in characterization.

The epilogue, in which Peter's death is described, is an interesting variation on the final chapters of other wartime school novels like Ernest Raymond's *Tell England*. Peter does not die in battle: he survives to come back to Australia and fade gently away in his own bed at home. Father Brownless, the former Prefect of Studies who is the author's *alter ego*, is there to hear Peter's last Confession. He also hears of the comradeship of Xavierians with one another and with other public schoolboys on the battlefields of France. Peter describes a friend's rescue from 'no man's land':

> When poor Tim fell heroically in front of our position and lay there for some time, I got leave–not without some difficulty–to go out to take him some relief. Well, though the firing was terrible, an old Scotch Collegian, one of our opponents in more than one hot contest at school, at once volunteered to go with me, and together we carried him in. Wasn't he a generous fellow?'
>
> 'Yes, Pete–God bless him! It does one good to hear of a thing like that.'
>
> 'Tim died in my arms. And he died like a hero and a Christian. He was well prepared, Father. I know you will be glad to hear that. He was ready.'
>
> 'I can well believe that, Pete–with your influence about him.'
>
> 'When I was struck down myself ... I was brought in by two Public School boys–another Scotch Collegian and a Wesley boy. And they brought me in at great risk. Oh! they've great hearts, these boys.'

Here, in the final chapter, Father Boylan's theme is clearly stated.

Peter's death is exemplary, both as a public school boy who has proved his courage in battle, and as a Catholic accepting God's will. Near his bed hung a picture of the Sacred Heart, photographs of his family, and the Xavier school colours—'perhaps the very ones he had worn at the last matches he had witnessed'. There is only one thing missing: the idea of dying for England which is central to nearly all the fictional deaths of schoolboy-soldiers of 1914-18. Since Father Boylan takes such pains to name Scotch and Wesley in the comradeship of battle it is inconceivable that he forgot the ritual rejoicing at the chance to die in England's cause. No British flag, nor even an Australian one, hangs near Peter's bed. So, finally, *The Heart of the School* celebrates the public school spirit and the Catholic Church, but its author was too much an Irishman to let his hero die for England.

The Heart of the School needed a good editor; it is too long and the author talks too much. Nevertheless it is still readable. If Eustace Boylan had been a professional writer he would have shaped a neater plot, but only a teacher could be so persuasive in giving a sense of a school's day-to-day life. R. G. Jennings, the author of *The Human Pedagogue* (1924) gives another insider's view. A housemaster at Geelong Grammar during World War I, he shares Boylan's concern to show school as an extension of family life, informal, even affectionate, with all its pedagogues 'human'.

The novel, a retrospective first person narrative, recalls the arrival at Geelong of a lonely English boy who does not know what to expect of an Australian public school. Like Peter Jackson at Xavier, the unnamed hero of the Geelong novel has read his school stories and expects fagging duties. Using this perspective, the author underlines the differences between Old and New World manners: '. . . I discovered that fagging, as it is understood in English schools, is practically non-existent in Australia, which has never had a feudal system of its own, and is strangely sensitive about being a democracy.' He finds Australian boys free of class distinctions. 'Such questions as "What's your father?" "Who's your guv'nor?" are not asked in Australian schools. The descendants of pioneers do not deal in that kind of unblushing snobbery.'

As these quotations may suggest, R. G. Jennings's style is meditative, analytical. He does not attempt to create a schoolboy idiom for the narrator, who is presumed to be looking back after a number of years. There is almost no plot, and few characters. The housemaster who gives the book its dreary title, two senior boys, and two or three juniors make up the pattern of relationships which gives the book its rather awkward

shape. The 'human pedagogue' is Bolt, a vague and apparently ineffectual housemaster who is intent on reforming a lively barbarian, Barney
Vane. Barney is drawn to two older boys, loyal responsible Farr and
moody Byronic Linacre. Once close friends, Farr and Linacre are
estranged because of Linacre's cynical attitude towards school traditions. Somehow the outbreak of war in 1914 seems to settle these
emotional differences. Linacre finds a purpose in life and volunteers
after reading some verses written by a Melbourne boy for his school
magazine:

> 'The bugles of England were blowing o'er the sea,
> As they had called a thousand years—calling now to me;
> They woke me from dreaming in the dawning of the day,
> The bugles of England—and how could I stay?'[4]

The same poem inspires Farr, who leaves school on his eighteenth birthday to join the army. As Farr goes, the narrator sees the school flag
half-mast for the death of an unknown boy and wonders whether 'one
day, the flag would hang like that for Farr who loved it; for had he
not fought for it, carried it to the head of the river? It had become
part of himself, to be his through life'. With both Farr and Linacre
gone, Barney Vane makes his decision. He burns all the 'penny dreadful'
magazines which have been a symbol of his rebellion against the
housemaster's good influence. The housemaster wins Barney through
being silently sympathetic about the loss of Farr. 'He knows what it
means to Barney. He is so vastly human.'

The Human Pedagogue closes in a warm steamy bath of sentiment
for everyone. Barney loves Farr. Farr loves Linacre. The housemaster
loves Barney. The narrator loves everyone; an outsider to the end, he
watches from a distance the reconciliation of Barney and the housemaster:

> He moved forward. He was smiling. Barney looked up. Their eyes
> met.
> 'Please, sir . . .!'
> And I knew, as Barney rose to his feet, and they stood watching
> the flames while they slowly sank and flickered out, that a common
> sorrow had brought them together, and the long days of warfare
> were ended.

The Human Pedagogue is close in style and feeling to *Tell England* in
which the mutual devotion of two English schoolboys ends in their
sacrificial deaths at Gallipoli. In the heroic convention of schoolboy

fiction there is no life after school. Peter Jackson, in *The Heart of the School*, is felt to be fortunate to die in a state of absolute purity and grace. So, too, without the formal religious assurances of Father Boylan's novel, *The Human Pedagogue* affirms death in battle as the supreme good: a boy like Farr (whose death is foreshadowed, not stated) cannot live on without anti-climax. Lillian Pyke did not understand that. By letting Max the Sport win the V.C. and survive to marry Eileen Jones, she spoiled the pattern, proving thereby that women should leave the schoolboy story alone.

Writing Australian public school stories was a difficult balancing act. To keep too close to the British model was to be merely imitative, yet the genre demanded, and its readers expected, stylized characters, situations and even language. It was unlikely that British boys would want to read about the tuck-shop at St Virgil's; and Australians, too, might well prefer Greyfriars to Geelong as a place of football-field heroics, or dormitory escapades. The school story needed the genuine 'made in Britain' label. For all but the few dedicated writers whose work I have described, an Australian public school setting might give the impulse for a satisfying story, but could not sustain the central action. The best compromise was to infuse British public school spirit into a 'typical' Australian adventure story which could be read in either hemisphere.

Thus, during the 1920s, the school story merged into the boys' adventure story. A few, like Andrew Walpole's *The Black Star* (1925), brought the adventure within the school walls. In this novel a villain masquerades as a history master in order to steal a jewel, sacred to an Aboriginal tribe, from the schoolboy son of an explorer to whom the stone was entrusted for reasons which remain obscure. The plot is worked into the school story pattern with no more, or less, incongruity than the smugglers' caves and secret passages with which many British writers varied the schoolboy formula.

The public school story in its purest form could not flourish in Australia. Public school spirit was another matter. A passage from Jean Curlewis's adventure story of 1924, *The Dawn Man*, shows the internationalism of the schoolboy code. Here is an Englishman assessing his Australian allies before undertaking a dangerous enterprise:

Sir Eugene had sent him to the right men. Lithe, hard trained, sunburnt, one a little more, and one, he judged, a little less, than twenty-five, he felt for them instinctively liking and confidence. He had wondered on the voyage what sort of combination he, the Englishman, and they the Australians, would make—between men born and reared twelve thousand miles apart there might, he realized, be differences of outlook. But one glance removed his doubts. He was from a great Public School, so, obviously, were they.

The 'one glance' which brings such certainty to the Englishman reveals 'on a well-kept grass tennis court a fierce rally, . . . between two white-clad players'. There is no need, apparently, to speak to them: they are properly dressed, keen public school men playing the game at home as they can be trusted to play it anywhere in the world. As Lillian Pyke might have put it, they are trained to serve on a wider tennis court.

11

The Australian Schoolgirl

The Australian schoolgirl made an early appearance in two novels of
the 1890s: Margaret Parker's *For the Sake of a Friend* (1896) and Louise
Mack's *Teens* (1897). These novels, contrasts in style as well as in quality, show the difference, evident in girls' fiction as in any other writing
of this transition period, between genuine originals and reproductions
with an Australian veneer. Their subtitles have a revealing variation
in emphasis. *Teens* is 'A Story of Australian Schoolgirls'. *For the Sake
of a Friend* is 'A Story of School Life'. Louise Mack's interest was in
individual character; her heroines are presented as distinctively Australian, and shown in their family relationships as well as their everyday
life in a Sydney girls' high school. The realism of *Teens*, with its sharp
evocation of time and place, is in marked contrast with the artificiality
of *For the Sake of a Friend*. Concentrating on boarding school life, Margaret Parker produces only clichés of character and situation, and with
a scattering of Melbourne place-names gives the sense of an English
product with the wrong label on it.

I am not suggesting that a boarding-school story is necessarily artificial. Henry Handel Richardson's *The Getting of Wisdom* (1910) used
the enclosed world of a Melbourne school in an adult novel of strength
and subtlety; Antonia White created a finely balanced work of art with
an English convent setting in *Frost in May* (1933). However, the late
nineteenth and early twentieth century offered a boarding-school formula which could be used like a supermarket cake-mix with the same
flat and flavourless result. Margaret Parker's book shows how stylized

the schoolgirl novel had become as early as 1896, ten years before Angela Brazil began to fill the British Isles with the clash of hockey sticks.

For the Sake of a Friend takes a shy sixteen-year-old, Susannah Snow, to Melbourne's 'very grandest and most fashionable school'. Stormont House is an ordeal for a girl brought up in strict seclusion by her Quaker aunt. 'An occasional morning of shopping, a still more occasional concert, and a weekly visit to the St Kilda baths during the summer had been her only excitements.' Unfashionable clothes and a strict sense of decorum make Susannah a misfit, appreciated at first only by Miss Lorraine, the headmistress, who sees in her the school's first possible candidate for the University of Melbourne. 'Her mind is developing with quite astonishing rapidity', Miss Lorraine says with satisfaction. The queenly headmistress, who 'could be a girl with her girls when she pleased', soon wins Susannah's devotion, but the plans for Matriculation misfire. Suspected of stealing a rival's entry for the school essay prize, Susannah keeps silence because she believes her best friend to be guilty. Persecuted and ostracized, she gets brain fever, that popular literary disease, and nearly dies. The real essay-thief is caught, the girls all repent of their unkindness, and convalescent Susannah is suddenly the most popular girl in the school. This trite, conventional plot is matched by its lifeless dialogue and characterization. Its only interest is as an early specimen of the school story in Australia. It follows its literary models so closely that the changing of a few place-names— Melbourne, Toorak, St Kilda—would make it a dull English story instead of a dull Australian one.

There is more entertainment to be had from some English writers of the period who found the Australian girl a useful change from other stereotypes like the spoilt American heiress or the wild Irish rebel in an English boarding-school. The exploits of Pixie O'Shaughnessy, Mrs de Horne Vaizey's 'Irish tornado' of 1900, are easily outdone by the Australian heroines of *Dauntless Patty* (1908) by E. L. Haverfield or *That Wild Australian School-Girl* (1925) by Ethel Talbot. Colonial frankness and a regrettable accent which make these girls at first unacceptable in their English boarding-schools are counterbalanced by exceptional talent for tennis, singing and stopping runaway horses. The Australian girls' democratic ways are a rebuke to English snobbery; they are justified, too, in practical terms when, in both these novels, the shabby old lady befriended by the newcomer is found to be rich, aristocratic, eccentric and influential.

Teens has nothing to do with such clichés. The first novel published by Angus and Robertson, it is as local in flavour as *Seven Little Australians*, and some critics have thought it a finer achievement. Inevitably the two are compared, because of their authors' early rivalry and friendship, and because of the similarity of their material in late nineteenth century Sydney family life. After publishing *Teens* and its sequel *Girls Together* (1898) Louise Mack left Australia; she did newspaper work in London, wrote romantic fiction, had some adventurous months in Belgium as a war correspondent, and edited a paper in Italy. Her niece, the Sydney writer Nancy Phelan, has written engagingly of the family stories told to her as a child about *Teens* and its author:

> 'Lou was writing upstairs in her bedroom on the corner of the washstand and Ethel was writing too ... Ah! Those days, at the Sydney Girls' High School! You remember in *Teens* how Lennie Leighton— that was Lou—was running a school magazine and another girl started a rival paper called *The Bluebell*? That was Ethel ...'
>
> 'Louie wrote *Teens*, Ethel wrote *Seven Little Australians* ... Louie was NO GOOD AT BUSINESS. She took her book to George Robertson and sold it for TEN POUNDS! ...'
>
> 'Why did she only get ten pounds?'
>
> 'Because she wanted to go to ENGland. You could go steerage for ten pounds in those days. Angus & Robertson made hundreds out of *Teens*. But she didn't get a PENNY. She SOLD THE COPYRIGHT! They told her the book wouldn't sell. It sold for YEARS!'
>
> We saw it all ... the schoolgirl writing late at night on the washstand, selling her book for a pittance and going steerage to London without a penny while the villainous publisher lived it up on the fortune made from her royalties. It was with disappointment that we heard the true story from our Aunt Amy, who not only liked Mr Robertson but disapproved of her sister Louise.[1]

As the records of Angus and Robertson show, the 'ten pounds' story reflected Louise Mack's habit of self-dramatization. The sales figures are not available, but a reference to an advance on royalties of £25 shows that she did not do so badly. The *Seven Little Australians* contract gave Ethel Turner £15 and a 2½ per cent royalty: her profits came from exceptional sales. *Teens* must have brought a reasonable return for a moderate success. Neither *Teens* nor *Girls Together* had anything like the popularity of the early Turner novels. They were reprinted in the 1920s when Angus and Robertson (then publishing as Cornstalk) built up its juvenile list, but since 1927 there has been no new edition. Louise

Mack is said to have regretted not going to Ward Lock with these two novels.[2] It is tempting to believe that she paid for her independence in going to an Australian publisher at a time when even Henry Lawson, apparently, still thought of real success as a British imprint. Lawson told Miles Franklin in 1902 that if she were to change from Blackwoods (who published *My Brilliant Career*) to Angus and Robertson 'it would be a big come-down from a leading British publisher to an Australian one—no matter how big the latter'.[3] Could Ward Lock's William Steele have done better for *Teens* than George Robertson? There might have been some advantage for Louise Mack in placing her work within the Australian gift book series which William Steele established. Yet, since *Seven Little Australians* in effect created that series, it seems that *Teens*, published only three years later, lacked something, in quality or luck, which would have brought a similar popular success. In format the first edition of *Teens* is almost a replica of *Seven Little Australians*: a handsome three-and-sixpence-worth in red cloth and gilt. Frank Mahony's lumpish schoolgirls, however, were a mistake; he was the wrong illustrator, and so was George Lambert who makes the characters of *Girls Together* look too mature.

Re-read today, *Teens* has considerable charm. A family story as much as a school story, it begins with its heroine Lennie Leighton, just thir-

The school reunion
Illustration by G. W. Lambert from *Girls Together*

teen, anticipating her entry into the outside world of school. The opening scene in which Lennie enjoys the envious attention of her three
younger sisters is typical of Louise Mack's skill in using the commonplaces of family relationships to give a sense of character and mood.

> Lennie plaited on to the end of her long, brown hair, then turned
> the ends up, and tied them tightly with a piece of black tape. Then
> she threw the plait over her shoulder, and looked sideways at it in
> the glass.
> 'I shall always wear a plait now,' she said.
> 'It would be horrid to have one's hair all hanging round one in the
> train.'
> The others were all silent.
> 'I wonder what it will be like', said Lennie, sitting on the edge
> of the bed, and looking at them. They hazarded no suggestions.
> 'There will be crowds and crowds of girls, of course. Heaps of
> nice ones; some nasty ones. I think I'll know at a glance which I
> shall like, and which I shall hate. And we'll all be sitting in a big
> room together, and we'll write our [examination] papers without
> being allowed to say one word. It will be awfully exciting.'
> 'You won't know one of them', said Floss.
> The element of the wet-blanket would keep creeping into the tones
> of the other three – the three who were not going up for an examin-
> ation tomorrow.
> 'I dare say I will be introduced', said Lennie.
> 'The headmistress told Mother she would look after me.' A tremen-
> dous sigh burst forth suddenly from nine-year-old Brenda.
> 'I *wisht* I were going', she wailed. 'Oh, I *wisht* I were going.'
> 'Oh, it's lovely', said Lennie, heartlessly. She had curled her round,
> black-stockinged legs up under her, and was crouched in a ball-like
> attitude on the bed.
> 'No more Miss Middleton! No more *Philosophe*! No more of those
> silly drawing-copies! No more writing essays, and getting no marks
> for them! It will be so heavenly to get marks, and to have girls to
> work against. And to beat them.'

Lennie's fortunes are recounted without any of the heroics of the usual
schoolgirl story. None of the labels of formula fiction are appropriate
for Lennie or her friend Mabel; they are not exceptionally popular or
gifted; no one misunderstands them, and they do nothing particularly
wrong or dangerous. *Teens* depends on the truthfulness of its feeling

and the humour and shrewdness of its observation. Perhaps it is too quiet a book to win a mass readership.

A comparison of the events in *Teens* with Nancy Phelan's account of the Macks' childhood suggests that the book was deliberately toned down. Lennie, the author's version of her younger self, is much less striking in personality than the flamboyant Louise. Some of Louise's exploits are transferred in the novel to minor characters. Others are brought within the range of the timid and usually law-abiding Lennie. The episode in which Lennie and the other girls, on holidays at Black-heath, get up at half past three to see the sunrise at Govett's Leap takes place in *Teens* with their mother's approval. As Louise and her sisters recalled it in later years, they went at 2 a.m., without permission, and added to their guilt by throwing stones at the window of a nearby house to wake a friend.

> 'Then Maggie's mother opened the door. She had her hair in curlers. What a fright she looked! It was *two o'clock*! She said, "What do you want?" And Lou said calmly, "*Is Maggie in?*" '[4]

The Mack household with its thirteen children, comparatively poor, with a distinctly idiosyncratic family style, is reduced in *Teens* to the more prosperous and sedate Leighton family of five children and an ideal father and mother. Lennie's friend Mabel, with four lawless brothers and an eccentric father, is given some of the Mack experiences. It is surprising that Louise Mack, adapting her own childhood for a schoolgirl audience, changed from the 'tuppence coloured' which happened to be the truth, to the 'penny plain' of probability.

Girls Together takes up the story of Lennie and Mabel two years after the last episode of *Teens*. It is Lennie's last year at high school, and Mabel has just returned from studying art in Paris. As in the earlier novel, the emphasis in on character rather than event. Lennie, still a schoolgirl in outlook as well as fact, is left behind by Mabel and the other friends who are joining the adult world, with careers, love, marriage and babies as their new preoccupations. The novel is low-spirited, with Lennie's feeling of exclusion the predominant emotion. There are some comic episodes, mainly centred on Brenda, the youngest and most inventively naughty of the Leightons. This portrait, drawn from Louise Mack's sister Amy, has all the life and unpredictability which the central characters lack. As first Mabel and then Lennie move into the adult world, Louise Mack's tone becomes uncertain. The balance between irony and sympathy is lost, and the author's natural warmth towards her characters becomes sentimentality. The novel ends with Mabel's engagement, and Lennie's acceptance of the eldest sister's role with the care of her invalid mother. The last page echoes the plaintive note which is characteristic of *Girls Together*.

> A new interest had crept into Mabel's life – the widest, warmest, deepest she had ever known – but Lennie could have no part in it. Mabel's feet had gone into a foreign country, whither Lennie's could not follow yet.
>
> The Mother looking on from her low couch by the window, saw it all.
>
> She could only sigh for the cloud that hung about her eldest daughter's heart. Yet she hoped for the time when the cloud would scatter, in a burst of light as warm and radiant as the light now shining on Mabel.

It seems ungenerous to give only qualified praise to Louise Mack's novels. A comparison with the schoolgirl stories that followed them should make any reader value their real merits of accurate observation, good dialogue and the ability to evoke through small details suburban Sydney of the 1890s. Few writers for children have given a firmer sense of place; even the changing weather is as much a part of these novels as the moods of the characters.

In Louise Mack's work the schoolgirl is more important than the school. In that, her work resembles such novels as the American Susan Coolidge's *What Katy Did at School* (1873) or the more sedate stories of English girls at boarding-school published by Mrs Molesworth during the 1890s. In these stories the real values are those of home and family relationships. More numerous in the twentieth century, and on the whole much less interesting, are the stories in which the school is the moral centre. L. T. Meade's Lavender House in *A World of Girls* (1886) is an early example of the English girls' school as a self-sufficient world. Who needs a home when there is a headmistress to give a 'mother-kiss and a murmured blessing' to her girls on Sunday nights? From this kind of school story and the more robust classroom and playing-field dramas of Angela Brazil came the undistinguished and apparently popular Australian novels by Lillian Pyke and Constance Mackness.

It is almost enough to say of Lillian Pyke that her girls' schools were created for the sisters of her St Virgil's boys. Her Riverside, Merfield and Riverview, all Melbourne schools, vary only in name. Their pupils learn to play the game in the same spirit as the St Virgil's boys. The civilizing influence of Riverside extends even to the Pacific island of Vilatonga whose Princess is as loyal to her old school in Australia as her husband is to his. Prince Andi of Vilatonga whose flashing white teeth are celebrated in Lillian Pyke's *A Prince at School* (1919) makes his 'dusky servants' wear the blue and gold of his Melbourne public school. Princess Lala, 'the sweetest thing . . . was educated at Riverside, and she dresses her servants in the school colours too'.

The Lone Guide of Merfield (1925) is as good an example as any of Lillian Pyke's version of Australian school life. There is nothing in it of incident or character which could not be matched in the work of Angela Brazil or Ethel Talbot. Schoolgirl friendships and misunder-standings, the Girl Guide movement, and a good deal of melodramatic adventure come in a package to which Lillian Pyke added a few local touches. Among these are some sporadic and unconvincing attempts to reproduce the Australian idiom.

> 'Fancy', [says one of Merfield's sporting champions] 'just because I was so silly as not to wear my mask, I shan't be able to play base-ball again t his season.'
> 'It is bad luck for you and Merfield, too', agreed Mary. 'You're such a bonza-catcher, too.'
> 'Well, Miss Graham says she's going to try you in that possie, Mary.'

Among all the verbal clichés of the English school story, 'bonza' and 'possie' stand out. The Australian habit of abbreviation is caught again when some Merfield girls enjoy 'bonza cakes and sandies and things'. The use of 'good-oh' seems to go with the unpretentiousness of the truly well-bred girl. Enid, the school snob, never says it. But Brenda, the daughter of 'people of considerable importance in Sydney', is a Guide, informal and enthusiastic:

> 'Tell me about the people on board, [Enid] said. 'Anybody worth knowing?'
> 'Oh, lots!' said Brenda. 'I think we're in for a jolly trip. It is good-oh for me to have discovered another Guide on board. She's such a bonza girl too.'

The dropping of 'good-oh' into a formally constructed sentence recalls the early efforts of Shaw's Eliza Doolittle. It is just as well that Lillian Pyke often forgets the local colour and lets the girls say 'jolly good' as well as 'good-oh'. It would be interesting to know whether the 'bon-

The school picnic
Illustration by J. Dewar Mills from *Sheila the Prefect*

zas' were Mrs Pyke's own idea, or whether her English publishers, Ward Lock, thought that school stories so similar to their English contemporaries needed some Australian touches.

Unlike the schoolboy novel, the schoolgirl story need not stop with the last day at Merfield or Riverview. For heroes of schoolboy fiction, anything except a war is an anti-climax after the last big match. The emotional attachments between boys have to end: ordinary life cannot accommodate them. It is different for girls. Many of the school novels of the 1920s and 1930s follow the heroine's fortunes through a career to marriage. The English writer, Dorita Fairlie Bruce, for example, began her heroine's career with *Dimsie Goes to School* (1921) and followed her progress year by year, volume by volume, until Dimsie serves her term as Head Girl and leaves. That is not the end of it. She takes up a career, becomes engaged ('I'm marrying my mate') but returns to her old school to see her beloved headmistress through a crisis of discipline involving an illicit traffic in lipstick, powder and slimming creams.

Lillian Pyke's 'Sheila' series is the Australian equivalent of the Dimsie books, and their exact contemporary. *Dimsie Among the Prefects* and *Sheila the Prefect* were published in 1923. Sheila reappears in *Three Bachelor Girls* (1926) in which she rejects a career in favour of marriage to the brother of her school chum Beryl. This novel shows the continuing attachment of the Riverview College girls to their old school and its headmistress: they meet constantly at their Collegians' Club in Melbourne, do charitable work together, and organize an Old Pupils' Dramatic Club, with St Virgil's boys to play the male roles. There is a good deal of nostalgia for schooldays:

> As the opening bars of 'The Rustle of Spring' rippled out under Patricia Merriman's skilful fingers there was immediate silence and Beryl Lindsay left her post at the entrance and slipped into a chair, the familiar sight of Pat seated at the piano bringing back a crowd of memories, of ping-pong in the prefects' study, the old tuck-shop and her rivalry for the music scholarship with Sheila Chester.

Such memories indicate the traditional nature of Lillian Pyke's school stories. Like most of their English counterparts they are only mildly feminist. Although their heroines are often unusually gifted and therefore tempted to try a career, there is no question of their choosing it instead of marriage, nor of being able to combine the two. Sheila, in Lillian Pyke's series, has great promise as a singer but, without even telling her fiancé, she refuses a concert tour which would have made her reputation. This choice is recommended during schooldays by the teacher who overhears Sheila singing a baby to sleep: ' "That's the kind of audience for a voice like yours, Sheila", [Miss Champion] said softly'. Just as the school takes the mother's role in directing its girls' moral education, so the teacher underlines in her own brave acceptance of the single life the ideal of marriage and children. 'Sometimes an ambition can be purchased too dearly', Miss Champion tells Sheila. In their emphasis on the role of the school as moral guide Lillian Pyke's novels are outdone only by Constance Mackness, herself a teacher, whose *Miss Pickle* (1924) is dedicated to the ex-students of Presbyterian Ladies College, Croydon, New South Wales.

Miss Pickle's central theme is seen in a confession of failure from one of the prefects. None of her achievements, she says, is worth anything because she did not work for the sake of the school. The heroine of the title, the reformed 'pickle', consoles her:

> 'Poor old Phyll! I know how you feel. I could howl like a hungry dingo when I think of my past record.'

The 'hungry dingo' is a touch of local colour, but *Miss Pickle*, like Constance Mackness's other school stories, follows a long-established pattern. The 'dear old grey College . . . with its garden of flowers and its garden of girls' is just like L. T. Meade's Lavender House of 1886. 'As I see the school', one of the Mackness girls remarks, 'she's a mother with her hand resting in benediction on our heads. Every school makes its girls a little wiser, I suppose; but ours is a Church one, and aims at character-making too. The resting hand is the old school's influence . . .'

In 1948, when the wartime paper shortages still restricted publishing enterprise, Oxford University Press reissued *Miss Pickle* with the Dimsie books and some Biggles titles in a special Australian five-shilling edition published in Melbourne. Formula fiction must have seemed the safest choice in a period of restraint. There was no incongruity in placing the Australian and the English volumes side by side. Dorita Fairlie Bruce's prose is less gauche and gushing than that of Constance Mackness, but both bring only naïve enthusiasm to a fictional form which had resisted change throughout its history. Transportation to Australia did nothing for the schoolgirl heroine. Only in Louise Mack's work, which owes nothing to literary stereotype, is there any sense of reality.

12

The Spirit of Place

Australian boys are at a disadvantage, in that there is little of romantic interest in the short history of our country and the associations
of our streams and mountains ... [They live] in a new country,
which as yet has had but little romance in its history, and on whose
soil no fighting has been done—fighting which would inspire our
people with love of country, and pride in its achievement. Yet while
this is so, every Australian boy knows, or ought to know, that he
can claim kinship with a great nation whose history goes back
through many centuries, and many of whose citizens have been very
great and famous men ... [this] gives pleasure to Australian boys
and does, to a wonderful degree, inspire them with the noble feelings of patriotism.   *Australian Boys' Paper*, 1903[1]

History

For the early writers of Australian juvenile fiction, colonial history was
arid ground. Writing for adults, Marcus Clarke found the romantic
possibilities of convict days, in *His Natural Life* (1874), an immensely
readable melodrama in the tradition of Dumas' *The Count of Monte
Cristo*. It is likely that many children enjoyed Clarke's novel, but it
is too brutal to have been approved juvenile reading. Moreover, to
dwell on the convict past was not the best way to strengthen love
of country.

Henry Lawson's poem of 1895, 'The Star of Australasia', prophesied

181

true nationhood for Australia only when 'the Star of the South shall rise in the lurid clouds of war':

> There are boys out there by the western creeks, who hurry
> away from school
> To climb the sides of the breezy peaks or dive in the
> shaded pool,
> Who'll stick to their guns when the mountains quake to the
> tread of a mighty war,
> And fight for Right or a Grand Mistake as man never fought
> before.

One does not need to endorse the confused ideas about nationhood in this poem to see that Australia's lack of a 'Grand Mistake' was an impediment to the writing of successful historical fiction, at least for children. The potential villains—convicts, Aborigines, bushrangers— have an awkward habit of arousing sympathy. If society's enemies are its underdogs there is no place for a hero: there is nothing romantic about being on the side of law and order. That leaves the possibility of a romantic, wronged outlaw: a mythic Ned Kelly or Captain Starlight. Such figures are, however, risky models for children, safer to use as peripheral figures than as central characters.

Among the few attempts to write a novel of the convict period for a juvenile audience, Joseph Bowes's *The Honour of John Tremayne* (1920) may be noted: a stodgy romance about a man unjustly convicted of murder, who clears his name and makes good in the colony. John Macarthur has a minor role in this undistinguished story.

In general, the public conflicts of nineteenth century Australia were awkwardly shaped for fictional treatment and too close in time for romance. The troubles of Governor Bligh, for example, have considerable historical and psychological interest: Ray Lawler's play *The Man Who Shot the Albatross* (1971) has demonstrated the dramatic possibilities of Bligh's situation. Yet even now with a longer historical perspective it would be hard to make any of the early governors, no matter how besieged and betrayed, take on the picturesque qualities of a martyred Charles the First, or Mary, Queen of Scots. To think of Parramatta Gaol and the Tower of London is to be conscious of the power of time, tradition and pageantry. The handful of early Australian historical novels for children demonstrates some degree of struggle against the colonial handicap, but not much achievement. Only in the last ten or fifteen years has any work of distinction been done in this genre to establish Australia as a place with a history of its own.

There were real possibilities for historical fiction in stories of exploration within Australia. The most interesting—the expeditions of Burke and Wills, and of Leichhardt—have everything for a juvenile audience in heroism, suspense and mystery, except a solution and a happy ending. Ernest Favenc, himself an explorer, tried to overcome this problem by placing the Leichhardt story within a fictional framework and having his heroes solve the mystery of the lost explorers. In the preface to his *Secret of the Australian Desert* (1896) Favenc discusses the material and treatment of his novel:

> Although the interior of the continent of Australia is singularly deficient in the more picturesque elements of romance, it was, for nearly two-thirds of a century, a most attractive lure to men of adventurous character. Oxley, Sturt, Mitchell, Kennedy and Stuart have left deathless names on the roll of Australian explorers, but the unknown fate of Ludwig Leichhardt has always centred most of the romance of story about his memory ... This, the great mystery of Australian exploration, I have taken for the groundwork of my story.

Favenc's narrative is competently handled, and there is genuine suspense in the sequence of discoveries about the Leichhardt party. The limitation of the novel is in its characterization: the men who find the explorer's trail are scarcely individualized and their motive for the expedition (many years after Leichhardt's disappearance) is inadequate, given their heroic efforts. The reader's interest is focused on the personalities and experiences of the lost men; these are partially revealed in the diaries which occupy several central chapters. It is natural that Favenc's imagination should be more deeply engaged with Leichhardt and his group than with the men who follow in their path. But, since Favenc plays fair with historical fact in not allowing a survivor to be found, the novel trails off in anti-climax when the fictional characters are given the consolation prize of a reef of gold in the desert. It is one way of turning a story of heroic defeat into something more cheerful. But having made his readers care more about the 1848 expedition than its fictional sequel in the 1870s, Favenc misjudges the tone of his ending.

The Secret of the Australian Desert shows the imaginative possibilities of the harsh Australian landscape. The arbitrary, impersonal cruelty of the desert makes it unnecessary to supply human adversaries; the hostile Aborigines in the novel are dramatically superfluous. In Jack Lindsay's *Rebels of the Goldfields* (1936) the emphasis is on the clash between individuals and authority on the Ballarat diggings. Like Favenc, Lindsay dramatizes a historical event by presenting it as part of the experience of some fictional characters; this novel is a boy's view of the Eureka rebellion. The hero, Dick Preston, is the idealistic son of an unsuccessful prospector. From a distance, the boy watches Lalor and Carboni prepare to defend the miners' rights. He listens to the monotonous eloquence of their Welsh ally, Humffray: 'Borne have we as much as a freeman can bear—and something more'. Jack Lindsay presents his story mainly as a class struggle. While Carboni urges the miners to support 'the cause of holy Liberty', he is watched 'with bored contempt' by 'a young Englishman with clear-cut aristocratic features'. The point of view resembles that of the English writer, Geoffrey Trease, in *Bows Against the Barons* (1934), but Lindsay's novel, lacking energy and written in the flattest of prose, suffers in the comparison. Part of the novel's weakness is the failure to give Dick any individuality; Lindsay mentions him as often as possible but cannot make much of the boy's response to the mood of Eureka:

> As dusk came on, camp-fires were lighted and songs were sung under the summer stars. Irish insurrection songs, English Chartist songs, German songs of the barricades. Near Dick sang a group of men who had been jailed in England, condemned as criminals for their part in the Chartist Movement for vote by ballot, and sent as convicts to Australia. Their song stirred Dick deeply.

Remove Dick from *Rebels of the Goldfields*, and what remained would be a civics lesson. Leave him at his observation post, and it is still a civics lesson. Even though the boy runs into dangers of his own when he escapes from the goldfields, it is hard to take any more interest in his ordeal than does his indifferent creator.

Will Lawson's *When Cobb & Co. Was King* (1936) is an entertainment which comes just within the juvenile range. It follows the fortunes of Buster White, a penniless bush orphan with an extraordinary gift for managing horses, who becomes a famous driver in the coaching days of Victoria and New South Wales. The episodic structure is neatly worked out: each chapter marks a stage in Buster's progress and also gives a glimpse of a new place or event in pioneer history. Moving from a small country town to Ballarat, and then to Melbourne, where Buster drives an eight-in-hand to Flemington races on Cup Day, 1861, the novel uses the boy's viewpoint to show the colony's expansion. Buster's sense of wonder is the author's means of commemorating the pioneer past. There are echoes of Paterson and Gordon in the boy's feeling for the bush and for horses. He resists an offer to train racehorses in Melbourne and explains to the city-bred owner's daughter why he cannot give up his coach and team:

'After a long night trip under the stars, with the hoofs and harness and wheels making a song, and all the people drowsy and comfortable, when it is dawn, you get a new team, and swing out again on to the road, and it stretches away ahead, all bends and dips and hills and gullies ... So when you ask me to come [to Melbourne], I want to, but I just can't because the roads and the teams pull too strongly ...'

Bushrangers and stolen gold, several violent deaths and a love story give *When Cobb & Co. Was King* its variety. It has some factual basis: Buster White's career is drawn partly from the reminiscences of a famous driver for Cobb & Co., as well as from Lawson's own memories of the coaching days. Its literary merit is slight, but it is worth noting as one of a very small group of juvenile novels to look back nostalgically to the 'golden days' of the colonial past.

Eric Bedford's *Scum o' the Seas* (1944) suffers from a garrulous narrator and a cluttered plot. The hero, a guileless fifteen-year-old, finds bad company at the Bathurst goldfields in 1853 and is forced to join the crew of a pirate ship. In spite of constant temptations to drink, steal and murder, George comes safely home from his Pacific adventures to his father's blacksmith's shop in Windsor, New South Wales, with no fortune, but a clear conscience. There are only the most perfunctory attempts at establishing a sense of time and place; these include the hero's complaint that Englishmen still think of Australia as a place for convicts, not free men. *Scum o' the Seas* is a conventional blood-and-thunder tale with some appeals to national pride. It was published in Sydney by the Currawong Press, presumably with an Australian audience in mind. Surprisingly, in a period of wartime paper rationing, it reached a second printing.

The Adventures of Margery Pym by Rosalind Miller reworks the material of nineteenth century settlers' novels. It describes the fortunes of an English family at the time of the gold rushes with more attention to character and domestic arrangements than to action and adventure. Although the events of *Margery Pym* are those of any number of colonial narratives—the discovery of gold, an attack by bushrangers, a search for a lost child—the treatment shows its twentieth century origins very plainly. Its concentration on the children's perspective is characteristically modern: so is the dialogue. The author sensibly avoids archaisms of phrase but does not succeed in the more difficult task of making the Pyms' speech convey a sense of difference in their thinking. There is a competent reconstruction of Melbourne life in the 1850s

Illustration by Jean Elder from *The Adventures of Margery Pym*

which stresses the strangeness of the landscape to the newcomers' eyes. Less skilfully, the author reminds the reader at regular intervals that the heroine is a child of her time; this is done mainly by such obvious hints as 'she came rushing round the veranda with crinoline skirts held high'. Except for the crinoline, Margery Pym is indistinguishable from any tomboy heroine of the 1940s. Active, brave, forthright and disobedient, she gallops around the countryside, solving the problems of brother, father and uncle, and subduing a gentlemanly bushranger by an exercise of will. Whatever the author's intention, the characterization of the novel seems to assert that only the picturesque details of costume separate the past from the present.

Margaret Kiddle's *West of Sunset* (1949) is the work of a historian rather than a novelist. Like *Margery Pym*, it describes the arrival in Australia of an English child and explores colonial life from that child's perspective. Margaret Kiddle, the author of *Caroline Chisholm* (1950) and *Men of Yesterday* (1961), can be trusted not to shrink from the harsher aspects of life in Sydney in the 1840s: her young heroines are

repelled by the city, 'ramshackle and dirty in the strong sunlight'.
When they move to the country, their achievements in new surroundings are recorded; so are their fears:

> She sat beside the oven with a lighted lamp on the table beside her.
> The small light threw giant shadows which crowded the walls and
> pressed about Harriet. She huddled closer to the fire, and held her
> breath to listen for the frightening sounds of the night—the cry of
> a curlew or the howl of a dingo. But was it a dingo? In the flickering
> darkness the memory of yahoos and bunyips came to terrify her, and
> the thud of her heart sounded loudly in the stillness. The howl
> sounded closer as the wild dog wailed his hunger and loneliness to
> the moon. Then there was silence; the enormous silence of the plains.
> Harriet pressed her fingernails into the palms of her hands, and bit
> her lip until she could taste the blood . . .

West of Sunset succeeds better in creating a landscape than in peopling
it with lifelike characters. Caroline Chisholm makes a brief appearance
in an early chapter as guide and friend to the young English girls, but
in this and most other scenes in the novel, the dialogue is stiff and
there is little sense of any distinctive human qualities. Yet, if *West of
Sunset* is disappointing as an entertainment, it has its special interest
as an attempt by a distinguished historian to discover for children the
experience of early colonial days.

It is clear today that pioneering experience in Australia offers much
to the writer of historical fiction; it seems surprising that in the first
half of the twentieth century so few writers for children attempted to
work in this genre. Pioneering sagas of Australian life were common
enough in adult writing of this time; such novels as Martin Boyd's
The Montforts (1928), Brian Penton's *Landtakers* (1934) and Eleanor
Dark's *The Timeless Land* (1949) are a few among many backward
glances at early settlement in Australia. In the United States many talented children's writers found material in their nation's past: Carol
Ryrie Brink's *Caddie Woodlawn: a Frontier Story* was published in 1935
and Laura Ingalls Wilder's first prairie chronicle, *Little House in the Big
Woods* in 1937. *Johnny Tremain* (1943), by Esther Forbes, is an exciting,
well-shaped narrative of the War of Independence. The critical and
popular success of this novel, as well as that of the frontier stories of
Ingalls Wilder, Brink and others, emphasizes the strong interest in the
past among children's writers and readers of the 1930s and 1940s. Books
of the quality of *Caddie Woodlawn* and *Johnny Tremain* are rare in any
period, but it is still worth asking why so few Australian writers even

attempted to follow international fashion at this time. For one *Margery Pym*, a mediocre Australian historical novel, there are dozens of feeble and imitative Australian schoolgirl stories, like Constance Mackness's *Miss Pickle* and Dora Potter's *With Wendy at Winterton School* (1945). Why did England's Angela Brazil supply a popular literary model while the American Laura Ingalls Wilder, apparently, did not? The fact that international publishing agreements favoured the importation of British books is only part of the answer.

As an insight into Australian attitudes to the past, the novelist Shirley Hazzard's memories of a Sydney childhood in the 1930s are worth considering:

> History was the folding coloured view of the Coronation that had been tacked on the classroom wall–the scene in the Abbey, with the names printed beneath. The Duke of Connaught, the Earl of Athlone, the slender King in ermine ... That was History, all of a piece with the Black Prince and the Wars of the Roses ... Australian History, given once a week only, was easily contained in a small book, dun-coloured as the scenes described. Presided over at its briefly pristine birth by Captain Cook (gold-laced, white-wigged, and back to back in the illustrations with Sir Joseph Banks), Australia's history soon terminated in unsuccess. Was engulfed in a dark stench of nameless prisoners whose only apparent activity was to have built, for their own incarceration, the stone gaols, now empty monuments that little girls might tour for Sunday outings ... Australian History dwindled into the expeditions of doomed explorers, journeys without revelation or encounter endured by fleshless men whose portraits already gloomed, beforehand, with a wasted, unlucky look–the eyes fiercely shining from sockets that were already bone.
>
> That was the shrivelled chronicle–meagre, shameful, uninspired; swiftly passed over by teachers impatient to return to the service at the Abbey. The burden of a slatternly continent was too heavy for any child to shift. History itself proceeded, gorgeous, spiritualized, without a downward glance at Australia.[2]

Too heavy for children: that, until the late 1950s, was the implicit verdict on Australian history. Lacking a War of Independence, Australia could have no *Johnny Tremain*. So long as pageantry was a British monopoly and the past for children a matter of kings and battles and lost causes the historical novel was unlikely to flourish in Australia. The discovery that the pioneering family was a subject for romance would come only when the Australian literary tradition recovered from its pre-occupation since the 1890s with survival stories in the Henry Lawson mode. Instead of the circle of warmth and safety guaranteed by a strong, resourceful father in the American 'Little House on the Prairie' novels, the dominant image of Australian family life has been the gaunt figure of the drover's wife, left alone with her children in a comfortless hut in an arid, indifferent landscape. Although 'The Drover's Wife' (1894) was not intended for children, its wide popularity and inclusion in many collections of short stories helped to form a vision of pioneering days: a matter for stoic endurance, not celebration.

Fantasy

Just as Australia's colonial past for many years resisted translation into historical fiction for children, so too the elements of mystery and magic in the land proved elusive. Many writers felt the strangeness of the landscape; Marcus Clarke's response, in a celebrated essay, to the 'weird melancholy' of the bush, in which he saw 'the strange scribblings of Nature learning how to write' is one of many nineteenth century literary evocations of the spirit of place in Australia.[3] D. H. Lawrence's *Kangaroo* (1923) echoes Clarke's idea of the Australian bush as a place of terror, with 'weird, white, dead trees'; Lawrence felt its 'terrible ageless watchfulness, waiting for a far-off end, watching the myriad intruding white men'.[4] As such responses show, there was no lack of mystery in the landscape, but those who felt its sombre power most strongly did not write for children. In a period of children's literature dominated by *Alice in Wonderland* (1865) and *The Wind in the Willows* (1908) Australian writers seemed most at home in the realistic mode. Fantasy had a slow, awkward, self-conscious development, with many false starts.

That Australian children should have their own kind of magic was acknowledged in the 1890s and afterwards in a number of ways. Some writers tried to introduce into the Australian landscape the traditional figures of European folklore, and to re-work familiar stories in new settings. Charles Marson's *Faery Stories* (1891), published in Adelaide, had the merit of not being too specific in the creation of a setting for his stories of children beguiled by wicked trolls or malicious dwarfs. There is enough detail to give a sense of physical reality, but no gratuitous local colour. The trolls go about their business without incongruity. Marson's stories do not fail for lack of skill in bringing Old World magic into a new setting; his South Australian coastal region is suitably mysterious and timeless. Yet they do fail. They are too macabre for children, and the ending of each story in a mood of pain or loss is arbitrarily punitive. Marson's book is a curiosity which, because of its odd qualities, plain format and local publisher, is unlikely to have been widely read. There would have been more interest, a few years later, in Ward Lock's first venture into Australian fantasy. Having failed to persuade Ethel Turner to write a collection of fairy stories with a local flavour, Ward Lock published Atha Westbury's *Australian Fairy Tales* in 1897. This volume opens unpromisingly, in an arch, self-conscious style which shows the author's uneasiness with her material and her audience:

> Australia! Hast thou no enchanted castles within thy vast domain? Is there not one gallant youth, ready armed to do battle for the fair ones sleeping 'neath the spell of wicked genii?
> Come, youngsters, draw up your chairs ... I am going to draw aside the magic curtain which hides the great continent, marked on our map UNKNOWN.

The enchanted castles thus revealed are placed somewhere in Central Australia. For all the difference it makes, they might as well be in Abyssinia. One example from the Westbury stories should be enough to suggest the effect of the author's use of imported literary machinery with local labels. 'Twilight' opens in Gertrude Street, Fitzroy, a Melbourne place-name which is left to be its own guarantee of a homemade product. Tom Brock, the barber, has an unexpected customer, Baron Thimble of Faydell, a vast kingdom in Central Australia. The Baron wants the barber to go with him to Faydell, and there to shave a Gorilla who has claimed the Princess Lollypop as his bride. The formula is that of Beauty and the Beast, with the Gorilla a bewitched prince whom shaving restores to human shape. In payment for the journey and the mammoth task, the barber is given a mansion 'in the aristocratic suburb of Toorak'. The story would be feeble whatever its setting or origin. As an Australian story it offers only the assertion that magic is within reach of Melbourne, and that a Toorak mansion is a suitable reward for bravery.

Jessie Whitfeld's *Spirit of the Bushfire and other Australian Fairy Tales*, published by Angus and Robertson in 1898, resembles Atha Westbury's book in its consignment of mermaids, witches, dragons and enchanted princesses for duty in Australia. Apart from the title story, in which the destructive Bush Fire Spirit is presented in a simple but effective narrative, Jessie Whitfeld's Australian connections are forced.

The book was handsomely produced, with illustrations by G. W. Lambert, but Angus and Robertson's files show no enthusiasm for the stories. The publishers' reader, A. W. Jose, complained of too much moralizing and thought many of the stories were feeble.[5] He did, however, see some use in the local labels: he thought that 'The Mermaids' Ballroom' should be renamed 'Why the Mermaids Left Manly'. Like Angus and Robertson's decision to advertise Louise Mack's *Teens* as 'A Story of Sydney Girls' High School',[6] Jose's comment suggests not only the importance of the local readership, but the publisher's judgement that Australian children wanted to see their own world reflected in their reading.

A similar assumption may be found in Ernest Favenc's *Tales for Young Australia* (1900). This collection includes 'The Two Fairies', a fantasy in which narrative is almost entirely displaced by a debate about national attitudes and manners. The Australian fairy, 'pretty ... although quite black', is energetic and high-spirited: she enjoys stirring possums, riding on locusts and throwing sticks at koalas. Her prim English counterpart is shocked: such behaviour, she says, is fit only for elves and sprites and other 'rough sorts of creatures'. Favenc's creation of a new kind of fairy, like yet unlike her English model, is an indication of the sense of incongruity felt by many Australian writers of fantasy in bringing figures from the European tradition into the Australian landscape. Some devised literal-minded and often absurd strategies of adaptation. Olga Ernst's depiction of the Fairy Sunridia resting on a couch of eucalyptus blossom beside the Goulburn River is as synthetic as the title of her book: *Fairy Tales from the Land of the Wattle* (1904). These stories have no sense of place. Fairy Sunridia is a movable stage property, and the whole work a consciously dutiful effort. A later volume of the same kind, Hume Cook's *Australian Fairy Tales* (1925), constructs a mythology for Central Australia with half a dozen 'fairy tribes' ruled by King Eucalyptus. Among these the most powerful agents for good are the Shower Fairies; they wage war constantly against the vicious Desert Fairies. It is hard to take much interest in this, or in the central event of the book which is the marriage of Prince Waratah to Princess Wattle Blossom. Expensively produced, with full-page colour illustrations by Christian Yandell, *Australian Fairy Tales* has nothing in it more surprising than a foreword by the former Prime Minister, W. M. Hughes, in praise of the author's discovery of 'the enchanted Bush, with real Australian Fairy Princes and Princesses'.

Among those who believed that imported magic was a mistake was Donald Macdonald. His fantasy, *At the End of the Moonpath* (1922), is set in a place of dreams where children and native animals meet in a cheerfully nonsensical world of Lewis Carroll word-games. There are no fairies in Moonland:

> We tried some fairies of different kinds long ago ... but they were not a success ... The Banshees were always calling themselves exiles from Erin, and talking about green fields far away; the Pixies were ever singing one song about the Bonnie Hills of Scotland, and the Fairies complained that there was no old castles or haunted oaks or nut copses or ivy ruins, where they could dance in the moonlight. The place didn't seem to suit them at all—they were so particular.

On the whole, Macdonald was right: the mixture of gauzy wings and wands with gum leaves and wattle blossom did not work. The insistence on being Australian tended to destroy the illusion of otherworldliness essential to the fairy story. Only those writers in whom the European literary tradition was stronger than any nationalist impulse managed to strike a balance. In the work of Annie Rentoul, Ida Rentoul Outhwaite and Tarella Quin (Tarella Quin Daskein), a mood rather than a precise setting is evoked. Ida Rentoul Outhwaite's drawings recall Kate Greenaway, and the best of Tarella Quin's dialogue suggests Lewis Carroll. A careful reader of the rather insipid texts of *The Enchanted Forest* (1921) and *The Little Fairy Sister* (1923) will discover a kookaburra and some koalas—the latter called 'teddy bears'—but they are minor details in a fully-populated fairyland which English children would have found thoroughly traditional. Ida Rentoul Outhwaite's place in Australian children's literature is as an illustrator: none of the stories she or her husband Grenbry Outhwaite wrote could match the charm of her drawings. Working with a text by her sister, Annie Rentoul, she had livelier narrative material: *The Little Green Road to Fairyland* (1922) shows their partnership at its best. She also found the right mood and tone for Tarella Quin's *The Other Side of Nowhere* (1934) a collection of fantasies, mainly comic, which are all the better for having almost no local colour; they create miniature worlds with their own logic and motion. 'The Binnajig and the Tattyoon' in this volume is an outer-space race meeting, at which each competitor rides his own miniature planet, perilously spinning and bumping against other worlds. The title story, a child's nightmare of a visit to the moon, takes its gum trees for granted, as part of the increasingly lonely, threatening landscape through which she travels:

> After a while the trees grew thinner and the saplings were neither so leafy nor so tall. They left behind them the sound of the stringy-

bark blowing, tapping, knocking on the straight white trunks of the gums ... Here Lou-Lou's frock blew out in front of her, and her wild brown hair got tangled across her eyes. The imp's thin brown wings were rumpled, and blew in any and every direction, while the tail of his cap flew ahead and fluttered in the gale. They scampered with flying steps across the great moonlit spaces; and dead bracken, withered leaves, and bark accompanied them in their flight.

There was an obvious source of fantasy in the distinctive Australian animals; and one by one the kangaroo, the wallaby, the koala, the bandicoot and others appeared in fiction, speaking in human voices. Among the first sustained narratives of this kind are 'His Cousin the Wallaby', the title story in a collection of short stories (1896) by Arthur Ferres, and *Dot and the Kangaroo* (1899) by Ethel Pedley. Both are moral tales. Their message is kindness to animals and in form they draw on a long tradition of stories of role-reversals in which humans learn self-improvement by seeing themselves through innocent, non-human eyes. *Dot and the Kangaroo* is the better of the two, partly because it attempts less. Its earnest simplicity has worn better than the forced whimsicality of 'His Cousin the Wallaby'. It is framed within a realistic story: the familiar Australian narrative of a child lost in the bush.

The perspective is that of Dot herself who at first feels threatened by 'the cruel wild bush', but comes to see her surroundings differently when she has learned the language of its creatures. The Kangaroo, characterized as wise, gentle and maternal, adopts Dot as a temporary substitute for her own lost joey; with her protection and tutelage, Dot learns a new philosophy. The moral of the story emerges through a series of incidents in which man's destructive habits are dramatized, and through the Kangaroo's direct instruction:

'See', she said, 'how easily one can live in the bush without hurting anyone; and yet Humans live by murdering creatures and devouring them. If they are lost in the scrub they die, because they know no other way to live than that cruel one of destroying us all. Humans have become so cruel that they kill, and kill, not even for food, but for the love of murdering. I often wonder', she said, 'why they and the dingoes are allowed to live on this beautiful kind earth. The Black Humans kills and devour us; but they, even, are not so terrible as the Whites, who delight in taking our lives, and torturing us just as an amusement. Every creature in the bush weeps that they should have come to take the beautiful bush away from us.'

There are echoes of *Alice in Wonderland* in Dot's rediscovery of the world from a new perspective, but there is none of Carroll's irresponsible comic inventiveness. A basic difference in mood may be seen in comparing the effect of Alice's tactless reference to her cat Dinah, which upsets the Mouse, with that of Dot's promise to be 'an Improved Human' and 'never, never eat kangaroo-tail soup'. There is no sense in Carroll's Wonderland that the human world may threaten it; it exists for delight, with no lessons to impose. Ethel Pedley's Kangaroo has a human voice and viewpoint; she is there, like Anna Sewell's saintly horse Black Beauty, to show what a human might feel in being treated as property or object. The final scene, in which the Kangaroo risks being shot by Dot's father in order to take the child home, derives its pathos from the reader's seeing the animal as an embodiment of motherly love. Although the story ends with an implicit recognition of the separateness of animal and human worlds, the force of its moral argument depends on their being much the same.

Mary Grant Bruce's *Timothy in Bushland* (1912) follows *Dot and the Kangaroo* in its anthropomorphic approach. Timothy is rewarded by a bushland court of justice for his gentleness to animals and birds and his love of trees. Like *Dot and the Kangaroo* this novel shows some ingenuity and humour in characterizing Australian native animals. Both books are competent, readable narratives. As moralities they are quite persuasive. If neither shows the liberating imaginative power of true fantasy, it must be conceded that in the literature of any country such a quality is comparatively rare.

Dot and the Kangaroo shares with some other Australian children's books of the 1890s the sense of its author's being at home in the landscape and using it without artificiality. It began the slow assimilation into the human world of the strange creatures which, in colonial fiction, were simply observed as curiosities, material for a natural history lesson. Like Eden, Australia needed its 'naming the animals' day before the white settlers could take imaginative possession of the land. It took centuries of English country life as well as the individual genius of Kenneth Grahame to produce *The Wind in the Willows*. Such a close relationship between man and the natural world is harder to achieve in Australia; its distances, its climate and the characteristic separation between city and bush work against it. The English village, with its nearby fields and woods, is indispensable to the style and mood of *The Wind in the Willows*; its pattern of living is reproduced with unforced charm in such scenes as that of the carol-singing field-mice outside Mole's house:

. . . sounds were heard from the fore-court without—sounds like the scuffling of small feet in the gravel and a confused murmur of tiny voices, while broken sentences reached them—'Now, all in a line—hold the lantern up a bit, Tommy—clear your throats first—no coughing after I say one, two, three.—Where's young Bill?—Here, come on, do, we're all a-waiting—' . . .

In the fore-court, lit by the dim rays of a horn lantern, some eight or ten little field-mice stood in a semi circle, red worsted comforters round their throats, their fore-paws thrust deep into their pockets, their feet jigging for warmth. With bright beady eyes they glanced shyly at each other, sniggering a little, sniffing and applying coat-sleeves a good deal.

The convention of the English story can accommodate field-mice choristers, like village children, within this traditional scene. It is hard to imagine any analogy within an Australian country town.

The strength of the English tradition, shared by Kenneth Grahame, Beatrix Potter, Alison Uttley and many others, comes from close knowledge of the natural behaviour of animals and the imaginative tact required to place them in a human domestic setting without cuteness or sentimentality. Australian writers have too often entered this dangerous literary territory equipped with nothing but the conviction of the inherent quaintness of a koala or a kangaroo. One of the best-known, Dorothy Wall, the author and illustrator of the immensely successful Blinky Bill stories, had the artist's gift for creating some engagingly stylized 'dressed animals' but she wrote clumsily. *Blinky Bill*, which appeared in 1933, to be followed by *Blinky Bill Grows Up* (1934) and *Blinky Bill and Nutsy* (1937), begins an interminable saga of a young koala and his friends and relations in an over-populated bushland-suburbia. The drawings cannot compensate for the lacklustre prose and the pervasive coyness of tone, which may be seen, for example, in this account of the koala christening:

> The Reverend Fluffy Ears looked very important with a white collar made from the bark of the paper-tree. He also held in his paws a book of gum-leaves from which he read.
>
> Mr and Mrs Koala smiled at everyone, and everyone smiled at Blinky Bill . . . Angelina [Wallaby] looked sweet in her nut-brown coat, and her large eyes watched Blinky Bill all the time. She had made a ball of fur for him to play with, and he cuddled and hugged it closely all the time.

It is hard to know for what age group *Blinky Bill* was written. The chapters are too long and the narrative too crowded for the young children who would enjoy the pictures and some, at least, of the situation comedy of koala-as-naughty-child. Here and there among the stories of the disobedïent, quarrelsome, destructive behaviour which makes Blinky Bill a genuine indestructible all-Australian animal (or boy), there is a conservation message which emphasizes his vulnerability. Mrs Koala's friend Mrs Grunty has suffered in human captivity; she survives to report to her friends some newspaper statistics she overheard during her ordeal, and had the presence of mind to commit to memory:

> 'During the year 1920 to 1921, two hundred and five thousand six hundred and seventy-nine koalas were killed and their skins sold to the fur market, under the name of wombat.'
> Hearing this Mrs Koala gave a jump with fright and nearly fell off her perch.
> 'Oh! how dreadful! It is only a short time ago that my husband was shot. And we are supposed to be protected and allowed to live. What will I do if Blinky is killed?'

Much of the pleasure of the 'dressed animal' story depends on the perception of incongruity. A mother koala who cooks and knits and occasionally spanks her son for riotous behaviour is perfectly acceptable within her tree-house setting so long as the author maintains the inner consistency of this humanized animal world. Dorothy Wall's protectionist message, too explicitly presented, is at odds with the narrative. The reader who is told that the koala cannot survive without gum leaves, and can eat nothing else, is not necessarily troubled by the fact that Blinky Bill steals peppermints from a shop and raids a pantry for jam, eggs and milk. Yet it seems a failure in tact, at least, to make so strong a point of the koala's special dependence on gum tips and then to negate it. *Blinky Bill*'s narrative is at best predictable and mildly comic; at worst, coy. No one remembers the text or quotes from it. What remains in the memory is the single visual image of an irrepressible small-boy bear: a Ginger Meggs of the bush.

There were many Australian bushland fantasies in the first half of the twentieth century and most of them show that to create talking animals is not easy. Pixie O'Harris's *Marmaduke the Possum* (1942) is like *Blinky Bill*: better to look at than to read. Michael Noonan's garishly illustrated *The Golden Forest: the Story of Oonah the Platypus* (1947) works out the central situation—the identity crisis of the unclassifiable platypus—with too large a cast of bush characters to make any one of them memorable. There are many labels—Dick Rosella, Ben Bandicoot, Constable Emu, Postman Koala—but no sense of individuality. The labels could be exchanged without making any difference, because no distinctive qualities, animal or human, have been communicated. To get a group of native animals together and hope that something will come of it seems to be the only impulse behind most books of this kind.

Some Australian writers bypassed the domestic, humanized animal story for a genre which looks like documentary but has an element of fantasy. *King of the Ranges* (1945) by C. K. Thompson, a story of a kangaroo, concentrates on the animal's natural life, and almost avoids anthropomorphism. Yet not quite: there is a concession to human sentiment at the end when the much-battered and hunted kangaroo is soothed in the loneliness of old age by finding a new mate. A companion volume, *Monarch of the Western Skies* (1946), celebrates the fierce strength and endurance of a wedge-tailed eagle; it too endows its hero with some human feelings: anger, pride, ambition. The documentary element in these stories, as well as in Frank Dalby Davison's better-known *Man-Shy* (1931) and *Dusty* (1946), is dominant. The animals have no powers of speech and the author seems content to observe and record their way of life. The books are not, however, empty of human emotion, as this passage from *Dusty* will show:

> In the night, when [Dusty] failed to return, his mate stirred uneasily. She missed him from his place in the least comfortable part of the lair. The tides of life were turning. It would soon be time to teach the pups to hunt a little for themselves. She was inclined to disregard Dusty in presence, but became acutely aware of him in absence. The moon was shining in the opening of the lair. She stirred uneasily, and at last got up and crept out into the open. She stood for a while, lifting her nose, listening, waiting, wondering. The night was clear and quiet. The moonlight, falling between the branches, lit every hair of her back. She was an image of worn motherhood—lean frame and drained dugs.

There, with only a few words to be changed, stands The Drover's Wife.

The literary tradition of such books as *Monarch of the Western Skies* and *Dusty* is that of Henry Williamson's *Tarka the Otter* (1927) in Britain and the late nineteenth century Canadian stories of Ernest Thompson Seton. During the 1950s Mary Elwyn Patchett and Elyne Mitchell were among the Australian authors who continued these semi-documentary accounts of animal life. Given the nature of the Australian landscape and man's comparative remoteness from its wild creatures, it may seem surprising that so few earlier writers chose this form of fiction. It may be that the apparent hostility or indifference of the land strengthened the urge to reduce and domesticate it. More likely, writers brought up in the English tradition of Beatrix Potter, not that of Ernest Thompson Seton, thought of animal fantasies in terms of smallness and social comedy, and tried, with varying success, to subdue the Australian bush and its animals to that scale and mood.

Australian animals were strange enough in shape and habits, and sufficiently new to stories for white children, to make it unnecessary to invent mythical creatures; until recently the bunyip has been the only unverifiable figure of any importance in animal fantasy. It appears in a children's story of 1871, J. S. Lockeyear's *Mr Bunyip*, as a large finned shape, something between an elephant and a whale; and it speaks with considerable moral authority and eloquence. Mary Grant Bruce chose a Bunyip to preside over the animal court of justice in *Timothy in Bushland*, but avoided giving it more than a vague physical description. For Timothy, it is a majestic presence and a voice: it is the essential spirit of the bush. The difficulty of visualizing it may have kept the Bunyip out of children's fantasies; it presents the illustrator with as much difficulty as the Loch Ness Monster, and it is probably best left as a voice and a threat. Except in the Aboriginal stories to which it properly belongs, the Bunyip has not come to imaginative life.

The first notable creatures to be invented for the Australian bush, and from it, are May Gibbs's Gum-Nut Babies, in *Snugglepot and Cuddlepie* (1918) and its successors. The babies, small and naked except for a gum-nut hat, were first used as part of a decorative motif in a design of gum leaves for the cover of *The Lone Hand* in 1914.[7] They took on independent life in a bush melodrama in which they are constantly threatened by the wicked Banksia Men. Snugglepot and Cuddlepie are brothers, identical in appearance, but not in temperament: Snugglepot is venturesome, and his brother timid, clinging and demonstratively affectionate. Another gum-tree creature, Little Ragged Blossom, becomes their adopted sister. May Gibbs's texts are long and complex enough to make the Snugglepot and Cuddlepie stories more than picture books, but the narrative, with its repetitions, and its direct address to the child ('You remember how ...') is best suited to being read aloud. The Banksia men conspire with a good deal of sinister chuckling and incantation:

'... if we destroy these stupid Nuts, their friend Mr Lizard will die of anguish, and he is our greatest enemy.'

'Our hated foe,' said one.

'Smoke and burn him,' growled another.

'Drop and drown him,' snarled another.

'Ha,' said the biggest Banksia man, 'that's a good idea.'

'We'll drown them. Ha! Ha! Listen.'

Then all the bad Banksia men put their heads together and made a wicked plot.

May Gibbs's stories are still in print, but in luridly coloured revised editions which retain none of the charm of the originals. The primary

Illustration by May Gibbs from *Snugglepot and Cuddlepie*

appeal of the books is visual. Their author has something of a child's vision, perceiving menace in the grotesque shapes of the Banksia tree and babyish innocence in the small round gum nuts. Verbally the stories are less inventive, although such words as 'deadibones' and 'quicksticks' tend to linger in a child's memory, along with the enigmatic tongue-twister password: 'She stood in the door of the fish-sauce shop welcoming him in'. The plots are one chase after another, with Little Ragged Blossom enacting a bushland version of *The Perils of Pauline*, constantly endangered and rescued.

In most of the animal fantasies so far discussed adult human beings are no more than a threat or a distant presence. Children may enter the bush, as they do in *Dot and the Kangaroo* or *Timothy in Bushland*, to learn its wisdom and then return to their own world. There are problems of scale and tone involved in admitting adults. If *Dot and the Kangaroo* were to end with Dot's grateful parents inviting the Kangaroo in for a cup of tea, the story would lapse into absurdity, its mood of serious magic destroyed. There is no place for adult humans in the comic episodes of *Blinky Bill*, because the comedy depends on Mrs Koala's behaving exactly like any suburban housewife, gossiping with neighbours and complaining about her tiresome son. The protectionist theme of the Blinky Bill stories demands that some threatening human figures be introduced, but they remain outside the domestic scenes. Probably most children like the division between animal and adult human lives to be maintained, or, at least, they like adults to be excluded from the privileges of magic. Some writers of fantasy have successfully broken the convention of separateness. Kenneth Grahame took the risk of undermining the illusion of a self-contained miniature animal world in *The Wind in the Willows* when he sent Toad out on the open road in a stolen motor-car. How big is Toad? Could he drive a car, or be disguised as a washerwoman? That these questions seem irrelevant is proof of the assurance of Grahame's art; so, too, with the best Australian fantasy, Norman Lindsay's *The Magic Pudding* (1918), in which dressed animals and human figures take their places in the narrative without forced whimsicality.

The Magic Pudding is the only Australian work which bears comparison with Lewis Carroll or Kenneth Grahame. Simpler in outline than *Alice* or *The Wind in the Willows* and with less variety of mood, it shares something of their wit, their use of parody, and their inconsequential humour. It has no moral lesson. The struggle for possession of the magic pudding—the central situation—has nothing to do with rights. The adversaries are all tricksters and victory goes to the more ingenious strategists. In a letter to his publishers, Angus and Robertson, Lindsay disclaimed all moral purpose except the determination not to exploit his readers' emotions:

> I may warn you before hand that the sole appeal I have made to childhood in this book is for the humour of adventure. Sentimental tenderness and prettyness are strictly repudiated. I am sorry to intrude a moral consideration, but even in the sacred name of business I cannot lend a hand to the sentimental perversion of youth.[8]

As his central character, Lindsay chose an insouciant koala, Bunyip Bluegum, who sets out to see the world carrying a walking-stick and 'assuming an air of pleasure'. Along the way he makes friends with Bill Barnacle, a sailor, and Sam Sawnoff, a penguin. These two are the possessors (though with doubtful rights of ownership) of the delicious, everlasting, self-renewing Puddin', which they must constantly defend against 'a Possum, with one of those sharp, snooting, snouting sort of faces, and . . . a bulbous, boozy-looking Wombat in an old longtailed coat, and a hat that marked him down as a man you couldn't trust in the fowl-yard'. The narrative is shaped by the Puddin's fate: stolen, retrieved, stolen again and finally restored to safekeeping, to be shared among friends and happily eaten ever after. The lasting popularity of this story confirms Lindsay's belief that 'if a kid were to be given his choice between food and fairies as delectable reading matter . . . he would plump for food'.[9]

The characterization of *The Magic Pudding* depends partly on Lindsay's own drawings. A timid, quavering Bandicoot and a garrulous overweight Rooster come to quasi-human life through their poses and facial expressions as well as their voices. The perception of likeness between animal and human figures works both ways: the Rooster looks like a man who looks like a rooster. Lindsay is as likely to have seen his original in a bar, boring his fellow-drinkers, as in a fowl-yard. The language of the story is versatile enough to establish the variations in character among the principal and minor figures. There is a difference of class and idiom between the well-bred, bookish Bunyip Bluegum and his humble sailor friend Bill Barnacle. The speech habits of these two have a strong flavour of Dickens, with Bill playing unpretentious Joe Gargery to Bunyip Bluegum's grandiloquent Wilkins Micawber:

> 'If them Puddin'-thieves ain't sufferin' the agonies of despair at this very moment, I'll eat my hat along with the Puddin',' said Bill exultantly.

'Indeed,' said Bunyip Bluegum, 'the consciousness that our enemies are deservedly the victims of acute mental and physical anguish, imparts, it must be admitted, an additional flavour to the admirable Puddin'.'

'Well spoken,' said Bill admiringly. 'Which I will say, that for turning off a few well-chosen words no parson in the land is the equal of yourself.'

There is a stolen pie in *Great Expectations*, stolen pudding in *David Copperfield*, and a great deal about food in both. It is possible that Joe Gargery's heroic attempt to describe his disappointment on first seeing London ('which I meantersay as it is . . . drawd too architectooralooral') is echoed in Lindsay's country town of Tooraloo. Scholarly source-hunting is too solemn a game for *The Magic Pudding* but it suggests something of the verbal richness of Lindsay's book that it can stir memories of Dickens, of Lewis Carroll and of W. S. Gilbert without sounding derivative and without losing its Australian accent. Few of the bush creatures have Bunyip Bluegum's superior style of address, and many are rude in an unequivocally Australian way:

> To start off with, they had an unpleasant scene with a Kookaburra, a low larrikin who resented the way that Bill examined him.
>
> 'Who are you starin' at, Poodle's Whiskers?' he asked. 'Never mind,' said Bill. 'I'm starin' at you for a good an' sufficient reason.'
>
> 'Are yer?' said the Kookaburra. 'Well, all I can say is that if yer don't take yer dial outer the road I'll bloomin' well take an' bounce a gibber off yer crust,' and he followed them for quite a long way, singing out insulting things such as, 'You with the wire whiskers', and 'Get onter the bloke with the face fringe.'

Lindsay's Tooraloo, the country town in which the pudding-thieves are brought to trial, is sufficiently generalized to be a place for fantasy yet in its afternoon heat and drowsiness it has a typical local quality which invites recognition:

> The town of Tooraloo is one of those dozing, snoozing, sausage-shaped places where all the people who aren't asleep are only half awake, and where dogs pass their lives on footpaths, and you fall over cows when taking your evening stroll.

However, the town is only one of the many stopping-places in the long chase which makes up the narrative. *The Magic Pudding* has no particular setting; it gives the impression of unlimited spaces and roads without destination. It ends only because, as Barnacle Bill points out, 'we are pretty close up to the end of the book, and something will have to be done in a Tremendous Hurry, or else we'll be cut off short by the cover'. Bunyip Bluegum has the solution: 'We have merely to stop wandering along the road, and the story will stop wandering through the book'.

The 'on the road' story was one way of meeting the difficulty of place in Australian fantasy. Norman Lindsay tried a similar narrative direction in another children's book, *The Flyaway Highway* (1936), but found none of the unforced comedy of his earlier work. That road led nowhere else. *The Magic Pudding* remains in print, after more than sixty years and numerous editions, to make its own comment on national taste and temperament. It must mean something, surely, that there have been no witches worth mentioning, nor wizards, in Oz, and that our one undeniable classic of fantasy is about food. Colin MacInnes' comments on *The Magic Pudding* suggest some of the reasons for its enduring appeal:

> What a happy world this is of bush and endless summer, a perpetual diet of meat, suet, jam and billy tea, [and] a sockdolager on the snout to solve every problem ... In his final tableau of sloth and bliss we have Lindsay's vision of the Australian Dream. There they all are, in their home in the tree with its corrugated iron water tank and the Southern Cross fluttering at the masthead, in an idyllic rural setting with a charming township on the skyline ... doing *absolutely nothing*.[10]

Aboriginal Life and Legend

In the nineteenth century children's books set in Australia, the Aboriginal past is scarcely contemplated. Aboriginal life and customs are shown mainly in the here-and-now of white settlers' stories; there is little interest in their history. Towards the end of the century, at the time when Andrew Lang's collections of traditional European fairy stories were being published in Britain, a few Australian writers began to gather Aboriginal legends and re-tell them for children. Mary-Anne Fitzgerald published *King Bungaree's Pyalla* in 1891, with a dedication 'To the Boys and Girls of My Native Country ... hoping it may interest them in the Folk-lore of that simple people, now fast expiring, but who were once lords of this glorious land'. In her preface she admits the difficulty of transmission: '... in my efforts to render intelligible

Illustration by Norman Lindsay from *The Magic Pudding*

the legends told in imperfect English, by the Black King, I may have
weakened their original force and beauty'.

Since the stories attributed to King Bungaree are said to have been
told to the author in her own childhood, memory as well as language
is likely to have been imperfect. They are, however, a serious attempt
to present for young children the way in which Aborigines saw the
natural world. The Fitzgerald volume belongs only in part to King

Bungaree's tales of the Bunyip and the Kukuburra; they are supplemented by anecdotes of the recent past with the unifying theme of friendship between black and white. Although these stories are not fantasies, each has an element of mystery within it to represent some aspect of Aboriginal custom or belief. 'The Faithful Koogaree', for example, is presented as a reminiscence of the early days of white settlement. Its narrator, a white grandmother, begins with 'many years ago' to tell the story of how her son saved an Aboriginal youth's life, and many years later had his own life spared by members of a savage tribe. The second encounter explained the strange reaction of the Aboriginal youth in the first episode, in cutting a deep wound on the face of the white boy before disappearing, with a few muttered but apparently grateful words. The scar from this wound is recognized in the second encounter: the wild Aborigines drop their spears before a sign they must revere.

The Fitzgerald collection as a whole is more fanciful than factual but its attitude towards the Aboriginal past distinguishes it from most of its contemporaries. Mr Everdale, the kindly squatter of *The White Kangaroo* (1890), announces confidently that the Aborigines have no past, no religion, no hope and no future. Without making so blunt a summary, other writers of juvenile fiction of this period implicitly agreed on one point at least: the close study of the Aboriginal way of life had no interest. The most important exception to the general indifference was a very skilled and sympathetic collector of Aboriginal legends, Kate Langloh Parker. Her *Australian Legendary Tales* was published in London and Melbourne in 1896, and *More Australian Legendary Tales* in 1898. Both volumes were introduced by Andrew Lang who stressed their importance in the context of world folklore:

> ... till Mrs Langloh Parker wrote this book, we had but few of the stories which Australian natives tell by the camp-fire or in the gum-tree shade.
>
> These, for the most part, are *Kinder Märchen* [children's fairy stories], though they include many aetiological myths, explanatory of the markings and habits of animals, the origins of constellations, and so forth ... Man, bird, and beast are all blended in the Australian fancy as in that of Bushmen or Red Indians. All are of one kindred, all shade into each other; all obey the Bush Law as they obey the Jungle Law in Mr Kipling's fascinating stories. This confusion, of course, is not peculiar to Australian *Märchen*; it is the prevalent feature of our own popular tales. But the Australians 'do it more natural': the stories are not the heritage of a traditional and dead, but the flowers of an actual and living condition of the mind.

Kate Langloh Parker wrote these stories down partly for their intrinsic interest and partly from a sense of urgency: she did not believe the tradition would last much longer. A squatter's wife, living on a remote station in north-western New South Wales, she made the most of her daily opportunities to study the language and custom of the Noogaburrah tribe. 'I was much in touch with the natives the whole time I was on the station', she wrote, 'and during the eleven years I practically devoted to the study of their folklore, I had as many about me as I could, in various capacities, the result of which was often scraps of folklore revealed incidentally'.[11]

The importance of Kate Langloh Parker's work was acknowledged in the re-publication in 1978 of *Australian Legendary Tales*, followed in 1982 by *My Bush Book* in which her own chronicle, edited by Marcie Muir, was placed in context by a substantial biographical account. Its relevance here is her contribution to Australian children's literature. It is probably fair to say that *Australian Legendary Tales* needed to concede more to its audience to achieve popular success, and that Kate Langloh Parker was too serious a folklorist to make the changes. The language is demanding, not because of the author's prose, which is admirably clear and direct, but because of her decision to use a large number of Aboriginal words which are not always readily explained by their context. Passages like the following make the glossary a necessity except for the attentive reader who notes each unfamiliar word on its first appearance:

> Goomblegubbon the bustard, his two wives, Beeargah the hawk, and Ouyan the curlew . . . had their camps right away in the bush; their only water supply was a small dungle, or gilguy hole . . . One day the wives asked their husband to lend them the dayoorl stone, that they might grind some doonburr to make durrie.

Although 'dayoorl', 'doonburr' and 'durrie' have been explained in earlier stories, their appearance here within the same sentence has the effect of a translation exercise. Read carefully and in sequence, and preferably read aloud, the stories offer a great deal to the child's sense of wonder and delight in the unfamiliar. Many are comic, and told as comic stories should be, without the verbal nudging and winking which, in too many children's books, makes the joke fall flat. A few, like 'Ouyan the Curlew', are too macabre for pleasure; a folklorist would not want to omit them but a writer for children might well have done so.

The author's claim on a double audience, of adults and children, is made in her preface:

Though I have written my little book in the interests of folk-lore, I hope it will gain the attention of, and have some interest for, children – of Australian children, because they will find stories of old friends among the Bush birds; and of English children, because I hope that they will be glad to make new friends, and so establish a free trade between the Australian and English nurseries – wingless, and laughing birds, in exchange for fairy god-mothers and princes in disguise.

Although most local reviewers gave *Australian Legendary Tales* a measure of dutiful praise on its publication in 1896, there was none of the excitement with which *Seven Little Australians* had been greeted just two years earlier. The Turner novel was 'authentically Australian' in a way which suited its time; the Langloh Parker collection was not. The *Bulletin*'s attitude is as always illuminating. Its policy, during the 1890s and afterwards, of fostering a national tradition in literature, could not take in the Aboriginal, past or present. The journal's mast-head, 'Australia for the White Man', was the crudest expression of its narrow, pragmatic attitude towards Australian life and culture. A. G. Stephens, reviewing *Australian Legendary Tales* for the *Bulletin*, dismissed the book as 'a literary curiosity – the prattlings of our Australia's children, which even in their worthlessness must have charm for a parent'.[12] The irony of that curious phrase, 'our Australia's children', cannot have been intended; it does, however, underline the contradictions of 1890s nationalism.

It may be worth noting here that when the favourite literary children of the 1890s first appeared in *Seven Little Australians*, their experiences included being told an Aboriginal legend as they made their way to a bush picnic. This four-page episode was left out of the 1900 edition and has never been restored. It is impossible to be sure why the cut was made. Perhaps the episode was thought tedious. Perhaps Ward Lock simply wanted the space for the four pages of advertisements which were added to this volume. Whatever the reason, it is interesting that the Aboriginal legend was so readily expendable.[13]

In 1905 Jeannie (Mrs Aeneas) Gunn, best known for *We of the Never-Never* (1908), published a story for children, *The Little Black Princess*, which makes a useful comparison with *Australian Legendary Tales*. There are similarities in the lives and experiences of the two authors. Each of them, as the wife of a station owner or manager on an isolated property, came into daily contact with Aborigines. Each combined a position of some authority with a good deal of leisure. Childless and

lacking the companionship of other white women, Kate Langloh
Parker and Jeannie Gunn found an occupation, and an outlet for
human affection and curiosity, in the Aborigines of the homestead. The
results, in their writings, are very different. Jeannie Gunn had only a
short time in the Northern Territory. She went there as a bride in 1902
and returned a year later as a widow. Her two books owe much of their
appeal to the idealizing power of her memory of that brief period of
happy married life. She had not the time, and perhaps not the intellectual curiosity, which Kate Langloh Parker devoted to her work. *The Little
Black Princess* shows that she was willing to observe and to take pleasure
in learning Aboriginal customs, but the main focus of the book is the
relationship between one little girl, Bett-Bett, and her 'Missus', the
author. Tribal beliefs and legends are presented to the reader through
the doubly simplifying perspective of Bett-Bett and her friends and the
author's indulgent, amused perception of their naïvety. The white children for whom the book was written are invited to share gentle comedy
with Mrs Gunn who is always there as first-person narrator to control
and direct their sympathies:

> The first time I met Goggle-Eye, he was weeding my garden, and
> I didn't know he was a King; I thought he was just an ordinary
> blackfellow. You see, he didn't have a crown, and as he was only
> wearing a tassel and a belt made from his mother-in-law's hair, it
> was no wonder I made the mistake. It takes a good deal of practice
> to tell a King at a glance—when he's naked and pulling up weeds
> . . . I was always ready to listen to any old blackfellow telling about
> the strange laws and customs of the tribe. Very soon Goggle-Eye
> found this out, and as sitting in the shade, yarning, suited the old
> rascal much better than gardening, we had many a long gossip.
>
> I never laughed at their strange beliefs. I found them wonderfully
> interesting, for I soon saw that under every silly little bit of nonsense
> was a great deal of good sense. At first it appears great nonsense to
> tell the young men that fat turkeys and kangaroo tails will make
> them old and weak; but it does not seem so silly when we know
> that it is only a blackfellow's way of providing for old age.

The portrayal of Bett-Bett, the eight-year-old girl who is informally
adopted by the 'Missus', is almost free of the condescension with which
Goggle-Eye is shown. As a portrait of childhood, Bett-Bett's is close
to the little larrikin stereotype of the period: fearless, mischievous,
unpredictable, and loved for these qualities by the mother-figure of the
story. The book's freshness comes from the novelty of its incidents and

setting, and from the reversal of relationships when Bett-Bett's superior bushcraft reduces the narrator to helpless admiration. The white child reader can identify in turn with white adult and black child. Bett-Bett's difficulty with 'Mumma A *and* piccaninny belonga Mumma A' in the reading lesson is balanced by the Missus's inability to recognize the tracks of the 'Maluka', her husband, as anything but marks on the ground. It is essential that *The Little Black Princess* should end with Bett-Bett still a small child, and that the final glimpse of her is of a solitary figure disappearing into the bush. There could be no sequel: a 'Bett-Bett Grows Up' would have involved the author in material too complex to manage. The portrait of Bett-Bett, like *We of the Never-Never*, still has considerable charm but it is the charm of unreality. *The Little Black Princess* is an idyll of childhood in which the relationship of black and white, mother and child, retains its warmth and simplicity in a timeless world. It is, indeed, the 'Never-Never'.

Bett-Bett is one of the very few Aboriginal child characters to be portrayed in the context of her tribe and her beliefs. Even if the treatment is superficial and the viewpoint limited, Mrs Gunn's book created something quite different from the 'faithful black boy' stereotype of countless adventure stories. Mary Grant Bruce has been much derided in recent years for her Black Billy in the Billabong novels, a figure almost completely summed up by blackness, horsemanship, fidelity, a wide grin and the all-purpose word 'Plenty'. She developed Billy a little in the later Billabong novels, but within that fixed framework of family chronicles she could not alter much. She did, however, show an interest in the Aboriginal past which could not have been inferred from the Billabong books. *The Stone Axe of Burkamukk* (1922) is a collection of legends which the author introduces with a plea to white children 'to collect and preserve what they can of the ancient life and legends of Australia'. There is a more or less explicit assumption that the Aborigines are soon to disappear:

> The folk-tales of a people are the story of its soul, and it would be a pity if the native races of our country were to vanish altogether before we had collected enough of their legends to let their successors know what manner of people lived in Australia for thousands of years before the white man came.

The dozen stories in *The Stone Axe of Burkamukk* are presented for the most part in a carefully formal language which makes its gesture to the past by using 'Nay' for 'No', and inverting the natural word order here and there. A comparison of the Bruce version of the origin of the

Emu with that of Kate Langloh Parker shows the advantages of the more matter-of-fact Parker treatment. There is too much in the Bruce version about the Emu's feelings. In general *The Stone Axe of Burkamukk* explains too fully; the stories lack the authority which assumes belief. Nevertheless, they are competent, coherent narratives which do not trivialize their material except by default. A sense of the mysterious or magical was outside the author's range.

The Stone Axe of Burkamukk sold poorly; booksellers reported that the title was unattractive to buyers.[14] The disappointing fortunes of this work by a popular author may have affected Angus and Robertson's initial response to James Devaney's manuscript for *The Vanished Tribes*, which was published after a great deal of hesitation in 1929.[15] Devaney saw his book as 'pioneering literary work', giving the Aborigine 'a definite place in Australian literature, apart from the comic half-civilized station black'. Angus and Robertson weighed favourable readers' reports against the views of a committee of booksellers, and refused it. When the author offered to forego his royalties, George Robertson reconsidered the matter and offered £10 for the copyright. He told Devaney: 'Notwithstanding what the literary advisers think, the book-selling side of A. & R. think it has hardly any chance'. Only the persistence of the author and Robertson's good will overcame the book trade verdict that the public had no interest in the Aborigines.

The Vanished Tribes was an attempt to describe Aboriginal life before the coming of the white man. It concentrated on life rather than legend. The crusading spirit in which the book was written may be seen in Devaney's own comments on it:

> The chief criticism I anticipated ... was that I made too much of and claimed too much for the Australian blackfellow. No one seemed to see any romance in him, and in our young literature he has been quite neglected. In print he has been the butt of the comic artist and the par-writer who have exploited him as a kind of blundering native Handy Andy; but these have given us only the "civilized" aboriginal, the hanger-on of the white man's settlements and the picker-up of his vices. I have tried to go back to the tribes as they were before the coming of the whites ...
>
> ... what was really necessary for them they could do surpassingly well. They had to be hunters and they were matchless trackers and hunters. They invented the boomerang and the spear-thrower and even a simple spindle for making string. Their legends and folk-lore were ingenious and often beautiful. They were born humorists and

inveterate song makers. Their marriage laws were intricate and admirable, and their moral code very strict. Their corroborees were really aboriginal dramas or primitive operas and their message sticks the rudimental beginnings of a written language ... Their tale has been perhaps the blackest blot on the early pages of our history; it is a tale of terrorism and reprisals, wholesale shootings, poisonings, opium, the Black Police. These things cannot now be undone, but at least we can be just to the memory of the exterminated tribes.

To the surprise of George Robertson and, presumably, the booksellers who thought no one would read *The Vanished Tribes*, its first cautious printing of 1016 copies sold quickly. With the encouragement of the Director of Education, Frank Tate, selected stories from the book which Devaney intended for adults were abridged for children, in four separate volumes. These 'Vanished Tribes Readers' sold nearly 3000 copies by June 1930 and a second edition of the unabridged book was produced. The interest was only within Australia; Robertson told Devaney in 1929 that British bookshops 'don't care a damn about Australia', and that the lack of British reviews of *The Vanished Tribes* was to be expected. It took less than three decades to turn *The Vanished Tribes* from pioneering work into cliché. An Angus and Robertson reader's report of 1957 recommended against reprinting it because of its 'faded' style and its 'veil of whiteman's sentiment'.[16] Much the same would have to be said of all the other attempts, in the first half of the twentieth century, to introduce white Australian children to Aboriginal life. None of the authors sounds at home with his material or his audience. W. M. Fleming had a promising idea for *The Hunted Piccaninnies* (1927): two white children, lost in the bush, join forces with three Aboriginal children who are running away from their tribe's wicked Medicine Man. The story is told by one of the white boys in a ponderous style which flattens a potentially exciting narrative. The pooling of the skills and resources of two groups of children in a shared ordeal of escape and survival is interesting in itself, but the voice of the narrator gives the story a lethal dose of boredom.

The Prince of the Totem by Tarlton Rayment (1933) is subtitled 'A Simple Black Tale for Clever White Children'. That first note of arch condescension to the white readers as well as to the Aboriginal protagonists of the novel is fair warning. There is, of course, no easy solution to the problem of language in such narratives, but there seems no reason for the conversations of the tribal Aborigines of the story to be presented in this sort of pidgin English:

'When will rain no more come down?' Gor-ree asked his new mother, Ba-lum-bir.

'No want rain go back!' she answered. 'Plenty more rain, make plenty more Nardoo; plenty more Mun-yer-roo; plenty more cakes for Gor-ree.' She laughed at the little fella, because she had a bright, happy nature, like the butterfly after which she was named. 'You like Nardoo cakes, Gor-ree?'

'Yes, mummie, but I like Mun-yer-roo better!'

The Aboriginal hero and heroine of Frank Dalby Davison's *Children of the Dark People* (1936) are allowed to speak normally and naturally. Like the children in *The Hunted Piccaninnies*, Jackadgery and Nimmitybelle in Davison's story are running away from a Witch-Doctor who has taken a dislike to them. The book is an odd mixture of realism and fantasy, with the author at his best in the realistic scenes, showing how the two children use their skills in finding food for themselves when they are alone and lost in the bush. But because they have to struggle not only against natural hazards but against the Witch-Doctor's magical powers, their own resources are not enough. They find new protectors: the Spirit of the Billabong, the Spirit of the Caves, Grandfather Gumtree, and Old Mr Bunyip who is the most powerful of all. The author makes these representatives of the bush the children's allies during their long flight from the Witch-Doctor. There is no reason why Davison should not mix his magical figures, and yet these bush spirits seem ill at ease. Part of the trouble is that they are presented in trite conventional phrases. Here, for example, is the Spirit of the Billabong: '. . . a being clad in a filmy garment decorated with water-lily buds, while a fully open bloom was bound to her forehead. She was very lovely'. Grandfather Gumtree, a stout hospitable personage with a hollow trunk for hiding in, is the only one of the spirits who is adequately visualized and he seems to belong to a different kind of story. Altogether, *Children of the Dark People* does not succeed in what its author described as 'an attempt to possess four worlds within one pair of covers, Reality and Fantasy, and the Past linked with the Present'. There is less sense of mystery than there should be, and more muddle.

The literary achievement of sixty years of white interpretations of Aboriginal life and legend for children is not impressive. This chapter would be lengthened but the record unimproved if it were to take in books about white children in which there are some Aboriginal characters. I have chosen to concentrate here on the few authors who were interested and ambitious enough to try to explore an alien culture.

Ion Idriess's *Nemarluk* (1941), a story of conflict between black and white in the Northern Territory, is told from the point of view of the losing side. Idriess had already written about Nemarluk, the 'King of the wilds', in his adventure story of 1935, *Man-Tracks*. In the later novel, which, he claims, is 'a true page from our frontier history', he takes the Aborigine as his hero and shifts the balance of sympathy away from the Mounted Police who capture him. The novel ends thus: 'And then it was a long, long march to Darwin—and Fanny Bay Jail. He saw it again, the big fence that shut out the sweet, free bush, that shut out liberty. Nemarluk died, only recently. Died of a broken heart'. There are no psychological subtleties in Idriess's novel; it is routine adventure except for the imaginative enterprise of re-working the events of *Man-Tracks* and finding heroism on the other side.

Mary and Elizabeth Durack's *The Way of the Whirlwind* (1941) establishes the right tone of voice for fantasy. Neither coy nor condescending, it has the resources of language to ensure the reader's assent. There is a simple narrative structure: a search by two Aboriginal children for the little brother whom they believe to have been stolen by Here-and-There the Whirlwind. As they travel, Nungaree and Jungaree ask questions of the animals and birds of the bush. One of the strengths of the book is the sharp visual detail with which these creatures are described:

> They came upon the flying-foxes farther down the river, clustering all together among the drooping palms. There were great furry grandfather foxes with scalloped, vampire wings like folded parachutes, father foxes and mother foxes, little black timid baby foxes clinging to them with their little clinging claws. They hung down from the branches, looking out of bright ferrety eyes. When Nungaree and Jungaree drew near they pricked up their little black pointed ears and twitched their black pointed noses. 'Squeak, squeak, squeak!' they said irritably, for they hated being disturbed in the daytime.

Setting and narrative work neatly together in *The Way of the Whirlwind*. The children's quest, and the series of questions they ask as they make their way to the 'Nowhere' of the Whirlwind's home, create a coherent world of fantasy which is also the natural world of the bush. The illustrations have a touch of the eerie and the grotesque which counterbalances a tendency to blandness in the text itself.

In the books discussed above, the most common authorial attitude is that of memorialist. Aboriginal tales are re-told or invented so that white children may know something of Australia's past. The idea of a continuing culture scarcely exists. Nor is there any suggestion that Aboriginal children might read these stories; it is white on black for white. Readers today will notice the changing forms of reference: Mrs Gunn uses 'nigger'; James Devaney has 'blackfellow'; Davison and the Duracks say 'dark people'. That self-conscious attempt at tact, which remains in the 1979 revised edition of *The Way of the Whirlwind*, shows the beginnings of awareness that Aborigines might be present as well as past.

There is a more confident tone and a well-shaped narrative in Rex Ingamells's *Aranda Boy* (1952). Although its publication date makes this a post-war work, it should be mentioned here as a late expression of the Jindyworobak literary movement which was at its strongest during the 1930s and 1940s. The writers of the Jindyworobak group tried to bring Australian art into close contact with the natural environment. Their cultural campaign, Ingamells said, 'rested on the uniqueness of the Australian continent among the lands of the world'.[17] *Aranda Boy* attempts to express for children a sense of the special qualities of Aboriginal life. Although there is something of the literary exercise about it, the novel for the most part achieves a welcome simplicity and directness of style. The ideas which prompted *Aranda Boy* are more interesting than the novel, but it is important as an early recognition that the Aboriginal tradition must be understood, not for the sake of the Aborigines, but because the white settlers need it.

Illustration by Rex Backhaus-Smith from *Australian Legendary Tales*

PART THREE
1950–1980

13

Post-war Pastoral

Although the first post-war decade brought new talent and energy to Australian children's fiction it did not at first seem to take a new direction. The happy homestead story established by Mary Grant Bruce in 1910 was continued in the early work of Joan Phipson and, with some change in emphasis, by Nan Chauncy. The success of these two writers, both of whom won their first Australian Children's Book of the Year awards during the 1950s, suggests that the celebration of rural life suited the mood of the period. Their novels presented traditional images of the Australian family in an idealized landscape. With enough hardship cheerfully overcome to flatter national self-esteem, the fictional families of Chauncy's Tasmania and Phipson's New South Wales symbolized continuity in a time of recovery from war and the beginnings of social change. A little later the South Australian writer Colin Thiele drew from memory a nostalgic portrait of childhood on a Barossa Valley farm. There are important differences in mood and characterization in the work of these writers, but they share a strong feeling for the natural world and an unequivocal rejection of urban Australia. Nan Chauncy is the most singleminded of the three. Her ideal state is to be as remote from the modern world and as self-sufficient as Robinson Crusoe.

Nan Chauncy's own history is illuminating in any consideration of her work. Born Nan Chauncy Masterman in 1900, she came to Australia from Britain as a child of twelve with her parents, sister and four brothers.[1] Her father, an engineer, took up ninety acres of scrubland near Baghdad, Tasmania, not far in miles from Hobart but in a secluded valley which made it seem remote. The incongruity of those place-names—Baghdad and Tasmania—is in keeping with the timeless quality of Nan Chauncy's fiction. Her early experiences in a close-knit idiosyncratic family had as much in common with those of nineteenth century pioneers as with most of her contemporaries. As an immigrant child Nan Chauncy saw with sharpened perception; in her new world she took nothing for granted. So atypical were her memories of growing up during World War I that she could transfer them in her fiction to a period thirty years later without altering mood or circumstance. She wrote of isolated families like her own, living contentedly in primitive simplicity: whether the date in the outside world of London or Hobart was 1914 or 1944 made no difference.

In an autobiographical note Nan Chauncy recalled her first years of Tasmanian life:

> Picture the delight of conventionally brought up children of those days, let loose in this wonderland ... the long twisting valley with its steep tree-covered walls, its wild mountain creek, and endless sandstone caves. Everything was a huge adventure, the world full of glorious discoveries. Naturally the valley, the animals, and the adventures have found their way into my books.
>
> Animals were our special friends. While the axes rang and the trees fell, the children had to look after the poultry, feed and milk the cows, harness the horses, drive a harrow sometimes and take the buggy ten miles to fetch the mail. We had no other children to play with, and we didn't need them.[2]

The pleasures of outback freedom, hard work on equal terms with adults and a sense of exclusiveness in family life are recurring motifs in all Nan Chauncy's fiction. The perspective of her first three novels is that of the newcomer to Tasmania and the bush. *They Found a Cave* (1948), *World's End Was Home* (1952) and *A Fortune for the Brave* (1954) share the theme of making a home in a new land. In these books some rather contrived plot manoeuvres remove the central characters from everyday life and teach them the skills and delights of self-reliance. There are four English children in *They Found a Cave*, wartime evacuees to Tasmania for whom the adult world turns temporarily hostile. They escape to a hidden mountain valley, taking with them a herd of goats to milk, and are comfortable and secure in the cave they make their own. Happiness, in a Chauncy novel, is to create a private world in the wilderness, to domesticate it and to hold it like a fortress. The cave in the first novel represents that ideal:

> She eased her shoulders and had a drink of tarn water before carrying her load into Capra Cave. It looked just as they had left it. She felt it queer to be standing alone in this small, cool world, wedged above an immense space of tree tops and blue sky. It was queer to walk that stone floor and plan a sleeping place where only a bushranger had slept before; most queer of all to look out and see far below the Homestead, as unimportant and unreal now as if made of empty matchboxes.
>
> Cherry would have liked to linger on, enjoying the first thrill of the escape, but a head coming into view far down the track reminded her of home-making activities yet to be done . . . She tied gum-leaves to a stick and swept [the cave-shelves] free from dirt and loose sand. She had just begun to sweep the whole floor in the same way when she heard a shout and ran to look out.

The third Chauncy novel, *A Fortune for the Brave*, sees fortune as a barren private island off the Tasmanian coast on which the English boy who inherits it can make a sparse living from bee-keeping. The 'home' of *World's End Was Home* is a hundred acres of pasture in 'a most strange and secret valley', walled in by rock and inaccessible except to the most determined. The last two Chauncy novels, *Lizzie Lights* (1968) and *The Lighthouse-Keeper's Son* (1969), present, with the author's obvious approval, children who want nothing more than the island seclusion of a remote lighthouse. Few children's authors so consistently reject the outside world as Nan Chauncy does: for nearly all her heroes and heroines the ordinary life of towns and cities is either trivial or frightening. A comparison with Mary Grant Bruce is relevant here. The Billabong novels endorse the absolute value of country life, but they do so without any of the panicky self-protectiveness of the Chauncy novels. The Lintons find Melbourne boring, but not threatening. The Billabong children are hard-working and resourceful, but they have no need to be pioneers. Billabong Station is an achievement, not a struggle; it gives a guarantee of everlasting, unostentatious prosperity. It is also a kind of mission station; it takes in waifs and strays from Melbourne and reclaims all but the weediest for wholesome country living. By contrast, Nan Chauncy takes little interest in reform; she is much more inclined to reject those who do not immediately adapt themselves to the strenuous life of the wilds. If anything marks the Chauncy novels as products of the 1950s it is their inward-looking, defensive quality: they build family fortresses against a dangerous world.

Nan Chauncy's fullest portrait of a family is that of the Lorennys who appear in *Tiger in the Bush* (1957), *Devils' Hill* (1958) and *The Roaring 40* (1963). Her hero, Badge Lorenny, is a shy eleven-year-old, whose home is a hidden valley in south-western Tasmania, unknown to surveyors and cut off from Outside (as the Lorennys call the rest of the world) by a semicircle of mountains and a river with no bridge. Except in a dry summer when the river—the Gordon—is low, the Lorennys can reach Outside only by means of two stout wires slung between trees on either side of the river. Their valley was discovered by Badge's father, Dave Lorenny, who claimed it for himself, built a slab-and-bark house, and brought up his three children there. Dave is presented as a simple bushman, an individualist and a visionary for whom the valley is much more than a place to make a living:

> ... Dad found himself not a step away from a drop of about eight hundred feet, with a wide unknown valley at the bottom of his precipice. The mists cleared, the sun shone briefly, but Dad was still there—still staring down. For Dad was learning every feature of the valley, he was telling himself this was 'it', the place he had always hoped to find ... Who knows how long Dad stood there with a gleam in his eye? What held him? Was it the peace of this wild place, its ancient air, its freedom from the taint of man? Was it because he was busy selecting the slope where he would build his home, and marking with his eye the line of a zigzag track he would cut to the valley floor? He may even have been worrying then about how to cross the Gordon with supplies.
>
> It was Uncle Link who suggested the Wire and helped to build it. He also told Dad there was no point in paying for land he had discovered himself. The valley was his—by right of pioneering conquest and hard work. 'You don't want to let those lawyer chaps chip in', said Uncle Link. 'It's your place as long as no one else knows about it.'

A revealing phrase in the passage just quoted, 'freedom from the taint of man', might suggest that the Chauncy novels are misanthropic, and so in a sense they are, but only by implication. Outsiders are seldom characterized as evil; they are scarcely seen at all. Only two or three representatives of Outside come to the valley; they are tolerated rather than welcomed and they go away, leaving Badge and his parents in peace. The older Lorenny children, Lance and Iggy, eventually leave home for a Hobart high school; their talk of 'careers' is presented with a slightly amused tolerance. Dad and 'Liddle-ma', as his wife is called,

Illustration by Geraldine Spence from *Devils' Hill*

neither approve nor disapprove of their children's moving Outside. There is no anger or rebellion in the Lorenny family, and although Badge's complete endorsement of his parents' way of thinking is obviously the ideal, the other two are allowed to decide for themselves. Lance is said to be 'clever'—a word which Nan Chauncy uses without enthusiasm—and Iggy is sociable. Badge, by temperament a solitary, more at home with birds and animals than with people, is the natural heir to his father's territory.

The characterization of the Lorenny family is a matter of simple outlines. The parents are defined largely by the atmosphere of peace and self-confidence they create. Dad is the archetypal outback Australian; resourceful, wryly humorous, laconic. His wife, whom he calls 'mate', is as much at home chopping wood as making scones. The warmth of fires and food, shared work, and relaxation after it in companionable silence are Nan Chauncy's indications of family harmony. Much of the pleasure of these novels, for city children especially, must come from the Lorenny family's reversal of categories of 'ordinary' and 'extraordinary' experience. Badge has never seen a house with glass in its windows nor a bed with legs; such things as electric light and radio he associates with the distant, legendary Hobart he has no wish to explore. What would be an adventurous holiday camp for most Australian children is Badge's everyday routine. This family tableau from *Tiger in the Bush* suggests not only the quality of the Lorennys' family life but its separateness from ordinary human interchanges:

> Liddle-ma filled the mugs with strong black tea and stirred each one before she passed it over. There was a steamy fragrance in the warm room, a rich scent of frying, and gum wood burning, and tea. There was also a sound coming from outside, a small sound heard clearly through the walls above the usual sounds of eating and drinking and tea-stirring.
>
> 'What's that?' asked Dad, listening intently. 'What's outside?'
>
> 'On'y an ole possum?' suggested Badge through a delicious mouthful '–or a 'roo?' They sat transfixed, for they knew–even Badge knew that the sound was not that of a possum on the roof, nor a kangaroo in the garden, nor any wild creature.
>
> Liddle-ma stood by the table as Dad moved to the door: Badge, his scone sticking in his throat, glanced from one face to the other and shivered in the warm room at their silence. *What was it? . . . What was it? . . . What was it?*
>
> It was the sound of footsteps crunching in the frost–human footsteps, not harmless animals at all.

All animals (and even snakes) are harmless in the Lorennys' world. The bush has no dangers for the initiated few. Human beings are another matter; as representatives of Outside they are likely to upset the Edenic order of the Lorennys' valley. The plot of *Tiger in the Bush* concerns Badge's first direct experience of Outside values. When an American cousin comes uninvited to camp in the valley, bringing with him a scientist friend, Badge does not at first share his father's wariness of the newcomers. With naïve pleasure in seeing such novelties as cameras, zip-fasteners and tinned fruit, Badge responds to the genuine good will of the two Americans and becomes their guide to the wilderness. Without meaning to do so he betrays a secret, by telling the visitors that he knows where to find a Tasmanian tiger. Having let the information slip, he is appalled by their eagerness to track and photograph the tiger, and to publish their discovery of an animal thought to be extinct. His efforts to repair the damage done by his indiscretion and to keep the tiger from prying Outside eyes give the book its suspense.

Nan Chauncy's Americans are caricatures. Their portrayal rather clumsily reinforces the book's theme of self-reliance and its rejection of modern society. Even in the first physical description of Cousin Russ and his scientist friend Doc, the author's prejudices show clearly. Russ has a face 'like an egg . . . smooth and clean'. Doc's hands are 'plump, clean, pink and white'. All the Lorennys are brown and wiry with hard and often grimy hands. The Lorennys are quiet and reticent; the Americans talk too much, fulsomely praising 'this grand land of yours and the little-known inhabitants of the forests and plains, the bush and the rivers'. The American interest in wild animals is a matter of textbook curiosity; they are incapable of understanding what Badge knows by instinct. There is no attempt to reconcile Inside and Outside points of view; the Americans go home still innocent barbarians, not worth the trouble of conversion. Badge has some regrets about having to deceive them in order to save the tiger, but, as he explains it to his sister, he has no choice:

'. . . they'd get [the tiger] and hundreds of people would go to stare at it, and it'd die; then they'd stuff it and put it in a glass cage and people would stare at it dead. Hundreds–thousands of people. And just because there was hundreds of them they'd reckon it was right. They wouldn't think of the tiger . . . only of something new to look at.' His voice dropped still lower, and his face twisted suddenly. 'Even Russ thinks that way!'

'Yeah, it's the way they look at things. "Scientific", they call it.'

Badge Lorenny is the least assertive of heroes. The strategy he uses to defend the tiger is characteristic: an ingenious hoax, quietly carried out, sends the Americans away without any suspicion that they have been outwitted. His parents and sister take Badge's victory as an enjoyable though private family joke; he remains a little uncomfortable about winning. Shy, awkward and often fearful, Badge is the novels' best guarantee against complacency: like the other wild creatures in the Lorennys' valley he threatens no one but is himself endangered. Nan Chauncy's conservation theme includes Badge, for whom the threat of school, in *Devils' Hill*, is the equivalent of a cage for a wild creature:

'Aw, well . . . well, I best get going,' Badge muttered reluctantly, still turning his back on the thin track leading through dense Tasmanian rain forests to the world Outside. He was Badge Lorenny going to school for the first time. In all his eleven years he had never seen so much as the outside of a school building.

'I best get going', he repeated, still facing the west—the wrong direction—with eyes fastened on his mother's like the lost stare of a possum disturbed in daylight. His fingers clutched nervously at the rope round his pack . . .

Badge's experience of school is delayed in *Devils' Hill* by a series of lucky accidents. Nan Chauncy described his ordeal briefly in the third novel of the trilogy, *The Roaring 40*, before rescuing the boy once more and returning him to the wilds. She will have nothing to do with the well-worn theme of the bush boy proving his worth in the outside world. Since Outside, in Chauncy terms, offers Badge nothing, he is right to go home without a fight.

The Chauncy novels were ahead of their time in a concern with environmental questions which was later to turn to cliché. Although they could be reprinted today with a 'Save the Wilderness' sticker on the dust jacket, they are not formula novels. Nan Chauncy wrote with authority of a region she knew, and the Lorenny novels have the authenticity of emotion recollected. There is more feeling in them than in the obviously autobiographical *Half a World Away* (1962), which describes the emigration to Tasmania in 1911 of a middle-class English family. The Lettengars of Overlooking, Kent, correspond very closely with the Mastermans of Highover in their English and Australian experiences. The breezy confident mood of this novel matches its late Edwardian setting. It is no more than a pleasantly written period piece about a self-sufficient pioneering family. Perhaps it hampered Nan Chauncy to write so directly from life. Whatever the reason, her imagination seems to have been more engaged by the Lorennys' wary defence of their small, known world than with the Lettengars' cheerful venture into the unknown.

The New South Wales families in Joan Phipson's novels of the 1950s and early 1960s are more conventional than Nan Chauncy's Tasmanians, but they too affirm that bush ways are best. *Good Luck to the Rider* (1953) an Australian Children's Book award-winner, is in the Mary Grant Bruce tradition. It combines an idyllic outback setting with an agreeable, affectionate family group. Mr Trevor has all the qualities of the ideal Australian father: 'a powerful figure', tall, quiet and weather-beaten, with eyes that occasionally twinkle reassuringly. He sounds just like David Linton. His wife is the embodiment of maternal strength: quiet like her husband, with a 'wise tranquil smile'. The mood of the novel is established in the opening paragraph:

> It all began when Barbara was twelve, during the Christmas holidays before she first went to boarding school. They were lying under the elm-tree on the lawn one hot afternoon in January. Behind them the long veranda of the Tickera homestead lay dark and cool, shaded by its curtain of grape and wistaria. In front the garden sloped downwards and fell away to an expanse of dazzling yellow paddocks that stretched, gathering mauve shadows with the distance, to a line of sharp blue hills some thirty miles away. The fresh summer smell of hay came strongly off the dry grass in the slight northerly breeze. Beyond the garden fence to the right, the stock-yards stood deserted and silent under the sun, for the men had not yet come in from the day's work. Even the fowls in the yard behind the house lay quiet in their dust-baths beneath the marshmallow leaves. It was too hot for cackling.

It is hardly necessary to note the boarding-school and the men out working to see that this will not be a story of pioneering. Everything is in its proper place. There has been time to establish a garden, and even a lawn, as well as to build stockyards; the homestead and paddocks are serene, cultivated and prosperous, like their owners. Against this background Joan Phipson sets some not-quite-perfect children. Of the four Trevors, only one, George, fits easily and naturally into his surroundings. His twin brother, Clive, is clever and conceited, and one sister, Sheila, is preoccupied with social success. The plot of *Good Luck to the Rider* concerns the youngest of the Trevors, Barbara, who lacks the physical courage and competence of a true country child. In choosing to rear and train an unpromising brumby foal, Barbara asserts independence; she learns confidence as her awkward pupil accepts her authority. There is something of the wish-fulfilment of *National Velvet* (1935) and other girl-and-pony stories in the ending of *Good Luck to the Rider* when Barbara rides her 'ewe-necked, slab-sided pantaloon' to win a hurdle event in the local Show.

From the Trevors in this early novel Joan Phipson turned to a less prosperous family. The Barkers, who appeared in minor roles in *Good Luck to the Rider*, are at the centre of *The Family Conspiracy* (1962), (another Australian Children's Book of the Year award-winner) and its sequel *Threat to the Barkers* (1963). Mrs Barker is idealized: Mr Barker is not. She is the archetypal bush mother, worn, patient, overworked, uncomplaining. Her husband is well-intentioned but he lacks the quiet authority and competence of Mr Trevor; he is inclined to shout and bluster, and to be obtuse about his family's needs. The description of his property reflects bad luck and some degree of bad management. In the Barker outhouses 'doors sagged at their hinges, roofing iron flapped loose at the corners and many of the timber supports were quite obviously feeling the pressure of sheer old age'. However, in spite of a good deal of hard work in a dispiriting season of drought, the six Barker children show no signs of discontent. The property 'was more than their home; it was their world . . . they knew no other. Nor did they wish to, for they led full and busy lives'. The 'family conspiracy' of the first Barker novel makes them busier than ever in an effort to raise money so that their mother can go to Sydney for an operation. If the reader is willing to accept the plot contrivance of Mrs Barker's mysterious illness, there is a pleasant mixture of comedy and suspense in the working out of profitable schemes within the children's capacity. There are disappointments and quarrels among the children, and some misunderstandings with their parents who must, of course, be kept from knowing why they are all looking for extra work. The success of the conspiracy is almost entirely due to the self-reliance and the special skills of a bush upbringing. The boys earn their money by rabbit-trapping, and droving for a neighbour. Lorna, almost as competent as her mother in household matters, takes a holiday job in Sydney looking after the two small children of an affluent young couple. In this episode Joan Phipson emphasizes the contrast between the spoiled city mother and the country schoolgirl who instinctively 'began to create order . . . where there had never been any order before'.

'Tell me, Lorna' [asks her bewildered employer], 'do you *never* stop working? Do you do this sort of thing at home?'

Lorna put the trousers down, and swung round . . . 'Well, I help Mum with the mending', she said in some surprise. 'But I do a lot of outside things too.' She drew in her breath quickly, thinking with a sudden surge of regret of the old weatherboard homestead, the rambling garden that always needed attention, and the brown, hay-smelling paddocks in which she spent so many active hours. 'There's always work to do on a farm,' she ended lamely.

The pleasure of the two Barker novels depends less on the events, which are generally unremarkable, than in the building up of a pattern of family relationships against a closely observed rural background. They make an even firmer claim than *Good Luck to the Rider* on behalf of bush values. Life is comparatively easy for the Trevors; the Barkers'

Illustration by Margaret Horder from *The Family Conspiracy*

combined response to difficulties strengthens them as a family unit. In this, and in their rejection of city life, these early Phipson novels re-state a less extreme version of Nan Chauncy's family fortress theme. In her later fiction Joan Phipson moved away from rural settings and began to portray troubled children with absent or inadequate parents. One example may be given here to suggest the persistent association made in Phipson's work between family happiness and rural living. In *The Crew of the Merlin* (1966) Joan Phipson brings a spoiled city boy and his country cousin together in a holiday sailing adventure. Even though Charlie, the country boy, is the younger of the two, physically frail, clumsy and inarticulate, he becomes the expedition's real, though unassertive, leader because he has the inner certainties which do not, apparently, come with an urban upbringing. When the two boys talk about their families, Jim shows impatience and resentment; he feels misunderstood by his busy, ambitious father. Charlie thinks of life on the farm with simple nostalgia:

'Tell us what it's like up there in the scrub, Charlie,' [Jim] said. And Charlie, who had never felt farther from his home in his life, began to talk about the small brick house with its deep veranda in the middle of wide yellow paddocks over which his father's sheep and their few milking cows grazed ... 'I like it best at home in the summer,' he said. 'When you can sort of smell the grass. Mum likes it all green when we've had some rain, but then she always goes on about bringing mud into the kitchen. Elsie always remembers to wipe her feet. I hate girls.' His eyes roved towards the blue line of the horizon, but they saw a parched expanse of rolling country, aromatic and dusty under the summer sun.

The Crew of the Merlin and some of Joan Phipson's later novels reaffirm the pastoral ideal from a distance, or indirectly by attacking city life. The arrival during the 1960s of 'realism' and 'relevance' in children's literature made the happy homestead story seem outmoded. The Billabong books disappeared from library shelves to the accompaniment of disapproving murmurs about their élitism and wish-fulfilment. Harsher pictures of country life began to appear, like Mavis Thorpe Clark's *The Min-Min* (1966) and Margaret Paice's *The Bensens* (1968), both of which will be discussed in Chapter 15. The rural idyll survived in the work of Colin Thiele but with a significant change in perspective. His immensely popular first novel, *The Sun on the Stubble*, which appeared in 1961, is the story of a country childhood during the 1920s. Based on the author's memories of growing up in rural South Australia, it is a celebration and a farewell. The central part of this very engaging book is made up of a series of episodes, mainly comic, in the life of a German-Australian farming family. An opening and a closing scene provide the frame and the nostalgic mood; in both, the author marks the end of a childhood and implies the end of an era. Here is the prelude:

Bruno sat in the car beside his father and stared stolidly through the windscreen. They were climbing out of the valley. Behind them the farm lay like an oil-painting in yellows and ochres as the sun swung up above the ridge and touched the stubble paddocks with long-handled brushes of golden light. A tear drained slowly along the lower lid of his eye into the corner near his nose, and he tilted his face upwards as if his nose were bleeding, to prevent it from suddenly sliding down the round curve of his cheek. 'The train for Adelaide leaves at half past six,' said Dad woodenly. 'You'll be in plenty of time.' Bruno said nothing.

This scene recalls one already quoted, in which Nan Chauncy describes Badge Lorenny leaving home for school and the world of Outside. The difference is that, for Colin Thiele's hero, the rescue will not take place.

The incidents in the novel are those of Bruno's last year in the valley. He is one of the six children of Marcus and Emma Gunther, who belong to a well-established German Lutheran farming community in the Barossa Valley. *The Sun on the Stubble* is comparatively rare in Australian children's fiction, in giving the sense of a particular region and its people. Thiele's Barossa Valley families, in this and in later novels, retain the differences of speech, customs and religion which make them a distinctive group. They are not one of the embattled minorities of life or fiction. There are no cultural identity crises, and, writing from inside the tradition, Thiele is free to enjoy its eccentricities. The stories of Bruno's childhood are told with a good deal of comic embellishment; they give the impression of coming from a family's collective store of memory, and having been re-told and touched up for new audiences until the line between fact and invention ceases to exist. The opening chapter, 'The Possum in the Kitchen', is an anecdote of domestic chaos which gains its effect from going just a little beyond belief. Because everything is seen from the selective, backward-looking point of view which Thiele establishes in the prologue, exaggeration is not only permissible but appropriate.

In characterization as well as in narrative, the child's perspective allows for caricature. Bruno's view of his aunt Emily is rather like David Copperfield's of Miss Murdstone; though less frightening, it is equally metallic:

Aunt Emily and Uncle Emil came up from Adelaide for the weekend in their new car, and Mum installed them ceremoniously in the front room. Aunt Emily was a great talker. Bruno thought he had never known such a noisy person in his life. Everything about her was noisy—noisy chains of beads and shiny ornaments about her neck (ironmongery, Dad called it caustically), noisy ear-rings that bobbed and clinked, great noisy hats with clips and brooches all over them; and whenever she spoke, which was all the time, her ear-rings bounced vivaciously and her chins waggled like turkey-wattles. Just like a gobbler, Bruno thought to himself.

'But Emma, no 'lectricity!' said Aunt Emily. 'After ten years in Adelaide I don't think I could ever live in the country again. It's the convenience. Not only the 'lectricity, but the water laid on, and a proper bath-heater and deep drains in the lav.'

Illustration by Margaret Horder from *Threat to the Barkers*

It seemed to Bruno that deep drains would be pretty awkward and dangerous in such a place, but he said nothing, just kept gazing at Aunt Emily in fascinated astonishment.

So much for Adelaide: a noisy aunt with an obsessive interest in plumbing. The author makes his point against city life through the boy's simplifying point of view. In a later Thiele novel, *Uncle Gustav's Ghosts* (1974), the stereotyped figure of the cousin from town is reduced to a non-human absurdity. Cousin Arthur is not a character but the embodiment of all the qualities that threaten and repel a country twelve-year-old: he is 'scarves and warm socks and health tonic', pretentious cleverness and patronizing laughter. 'Arthur adjusted his glasses on the tube of his face and opened up a horizontal split underneath them, full of cackling noises and teeth.' This image of a machine laughing has nothing to do with the reality of Arthur; indeed he has been given none. What Colin Thiele wants the reader to feel is the angry defensiveness of the perceiver. So too with *The Sun on the Stubble*: the narrative strategy gives the world as Bruno perceives it. He is an observer as well as a participant in the action. The central figure and the source of comedy in many episodes is his exuberant, accident-prone father, the hero and victim in these tall tales of Australian family life.

The rural novels of Nan Chauncy, Joan Phipson and Colin Thiele are as different in tone as they are in place. They have in common the celebration of country life, the rejection of urban progress, and the identification of family strength and happiness with the outdoor work shared between parents and children. That pastoral vision of Australia, long cherished by a nation of city-dwellers, was increasingly hard to maintain in the second half of the twentieth century. Nan Chauncy's way was to stop the world and get off. Joan Phipson admitted imperfection and for a time held on. Colin Thiele conceded change and defeat but created his ideal childhood world in the past, where it might have been so.

14
Survival Stories

In the Australian adventure story of the 1960s and 1970s the characteristic theme is survival and the main adversary is the land itself. The certainties of the pastoral mode yield early in the 1960s to doubt, panic and despair as vulnerable children struggle against overwhelming natural forces. Left to themselves in a hostile landscape, they are tested to their limits. Throughout these two decades it is as though the most talented Australian authors competed with one another in devising appalling situations, turning the screws of anxiety and physical pain a little tighter with each new volume. There are none of the quick solutions of earlier fiction in which 'with one bound our hero was free', nor can the adult world be relied on for shelter or rescue. Human evil is irrelevant. The hero does not set out to search for fortune or conquer villainy; he just happens to be underneath when the sky falls. Survival has to be its own reward, and in the deepening gloom of the period its value is questionable.

The dominant figures in the creation of catastrophe are Ivan Southall and Joan Phipson. Both established themselves in the 1950s as writers of the most comfortable kind. Southall's Simon Black series was as predictable as the Biggles books; his former Australian Air Force ace was always on call to save civilization whenever statesmen were baffled by the master-minds of international crime. In Joan Phipson's early novels cheerful, resilient family groups proved the worth of good sense and hard work. One of these, *The Boundary Riders* (1962), shows signs of something more. Although it has the thoroughly conventional form of the family adventure story with the security of home and parents reaffirmed at the end, its concern with character under pressure in the ordeal of three lost children, and its presentation of a vast featureless landscape make this novel more interesting and emotionally fuller than the other Phipson novels of this early period. A nicely controlled comic sense and good dialogue establish the relationships between the children. In a quiet revolution the eleven-year-old country boy, Bobby, displaces his confident city cousin, Vincent, as leader of the group. Vincent knows the proper procedures and with diminishing assurance tries to follow them. Bobby is the pragmatist:

> It was even too overcast for them to guess at the direction of the sun. They had, by now, hopelessly lost their bearings and might just as well go one way as another. But Vincent said, 'Of course, we ought to stay just where we are and not move at all till they find us.'
> 'Who?' said Bobby. 'Nobody's looking for us yet.'
> And then they realized that they would not be missed for another two days . . .
> 'Another thing we ought to do,' said Vincent with a spark of his old energy, 'is to light a fire. People will see the smoke.'
> This was one of the very few occasions on which Bobby was ever known to smile. His tired eyes twinkled, his thin mouth stretched into an unaccustomed grin. 'How?' was all he said.

The Boundary Riders is demonstrably the same kind of novel as *The Family Conspiracy* and *Threat to the Barkers*; even though the children need luck as well as endurance to find their way out of the 'desolate wilderness', no one can doubt their ultimate safety. The natural world is indifferent but not hostile, and the human world of parents and other adults is emotionally and physically a sanctuary.

There is less certainty to be found in Ivan Southall's *Hills End* (1962), published in the same year as *The Boundary Riders*. Having had enough of the invincible Simon Black, Southall took a new direction, beginning to write about children as well as for them, and choosing gritty realism instead of comic-strip simplicity. In the ordeal of the seven children of *Hills End*, nature is fiercely destructive, parents are useless and the sanctuary of home proves an illusion. The novel opens by establishing the isolation and apparent self-sufficiency of the township of Hills End, a small mountain community of timber-workers and their families:

Eighty-five miles it was, across the mountains, from Hills End to
the town of Stanley, over a dangerous road ... The drivers knew
the road and were ever careful, but even they would not venture
over it once the rains began. Sometimes for two months, sometimes
for three months of every year, Hills End was cut off from the world,
except for the occasional hardy or eccentric bush-walker, and the
mailman, arriving once a week in his jeep, nerve-racked and mud-
splashed, always vowing that he would never make the trip again
...
   Life might have been hard in some ways at Hills End but the
people were not poor, or unhappy, or without the better things of
life. Their homes were comfortable, and their community shop was
well stocked. They attended a social get-together on Friday nights,
a film show on Saturday nights, and chapel on Sunday mornings
(all in the one building) when Ben Fiddler [the mill-owner] took
the pulpit and usually preached on the sins of city life.

One summer day Hills End is empty. Nearly everyone has gone to the
picnic races at Stanley, across the mountains. By chance seven children
are left behind with their schoolmistress, Miss Godwin; they go with
her to explore some mountain caves for the Aboriginal rock-paintings
one of the boys claims he has seen. There is danger enough in that
expedition, but Ivan Southall supplies a natural disaster for Hills End:
a cyclonic storm which destroys most of the town and kills the one
man left in it:

   The heavens split apart and rain and hail fell from the clouds. A
   mighty wind roared up the valley, and sheets of iron were blasted
   from rooftops. Chimneys collapsed. Outbuildings vanished. Trees
   split like stick, and Frank Tobias couldn't reach shelter. He couldn't
   stand up. He was beaten into the ground. Again and again he tried
   to run. Again and again he was stunned and driven back to the earth.
   He couldn't see in any direction for more than twenty yards. He
   couldn't draw a breath without pain. Crashing ice and water were
   as near to solid as they could be. 'It's the end of the world,' he kept
   telling himself. 'The end of the world. The end of the world ...'

The novel describes the ways in which the children respond to the
storm and flood, the disappearance and probable death of their teacher,
and the shock of returning to Hills End with no adults to shield them
from chaos, new dangers, and the apparently hopeless task of surviving
alone in the ruins, cut off from the outside world. The second half

of *Hills End* is in effect a desert island story. More optimistic than William Golding's *Lord of the Flies* (1954) which in some ways it resembles, it shows the children capable of working together to re-establish order. There are quarrels and rivalries within the group; there is cowardice and self-interest as well as courage and forbearance. The children establish themselves in the general store and live on tinned stew and lemonade while they solve the problems of having no electricity and a polluted water supply. They search for the injured schoolmistress and carry her to safety. But after two days of heroic effort they lapse into despair. One of them sums up:

> 'We *can't* take it. We can't survive. Every single one of us, one after the other . . . Surviving is so much more than just finding something to eat. We haven't even got a leader . . . We're all arguing and squabbling and being nasty.'

The turning point in the children's fortunes is the emergence of a leader, the only one who takes time to withdraw for a few hours into silence, to think and plan. When he presents the group with a programme, giving each member clearly defined responsibilities, morale improves and survival is assured. By the time their fathers reach the township order has been restored and the children are able to rebuke the adults for saying that Hills End is dead.

Hills End established Ivan Southall as a novelist of considerable subtlety and narrative skill. The children are made convincing as individuals and as a group. The success of their leader, Adrian, does not depend on his being extraordinarily strong or skilful; his plan works because it takes account of the particular capacities of each child. With the balance of mishaps and achievements which make the township's revival more or less plausible, there is the satisfaction of disproving the adults' belief that, left to themselves, the children would die. In the last scene, an arrogant father has to apologize for underestimating his son. Although there is relief and warmth in the family reunions, the ending is a satisfying variation on the more predictable rescue by superior forces.

Ivan Southall followed *Hills End* with *Ash Road* (1965) which won the Australian Children's Book of the Year award in 1966. Instead of the arbitrary natural disaster of the cyclone of *Hills End*, *Ash Road* centres on a bushfire accidentally caused by three city boys camping out in the hills in summer heat. The action takes place within the space of one day and brings together the members of four households threatened by the fire. Confusion, arguments, panic and obstinate denial are presented as the characteristic responses to the emergency. The novel moves jerkily from group to group revealing everywhere human inadequacy and muddle. Southall describes the bushfire as an apocalyptic vision:

> It came upon [Peter] as something living and evil, shapeless and formless, constantly changing, huge beyond comprehension, an insane creature of immense greed consuming everything around it whether the taste pleased it or revolted it, rejecting what it did not care for only after it had mauled and savaged it, then pitching it aside or spitting it into the heavens. The heavens shrieked with the indigestible things that the fire hurled from its mouth, spraying after them a froth of fury, flaying them with its ten thousand tongues, whipping before it the terror-stricken survivors of the deep green forest: screaming rabbits and wallabies, bush rats and mice, milch goats and cows, dogs and cats, children's ponies and wombats as fat as pigs, lizards and snakes, and creeping and crawling and flying things.

The children in *Ash Road* are not seen as a single group, as they are in *Hills End*. The fire scatters members of each family and creates a number of temporary alliances which include the three city boys whose camp-fire caused the whole disaster. Their guilt and their fear of being discovered by the police at first makes them turn away from the country children who take them for fire-fighters and appeal to them for help. But they find isolation unendurable; it is easier, in the end, to give help and accept responsibility as well as forgiveness by admitting what they have done. *Ash Road* takes a relatively benign view of human nature. There are displays of selfishness and stupidity from some adults, 'kind people with hard masks', in the crisis; there is a great deal of fumbling, useless activity, and many courageous efforts to save life and property. Children and grandparents seem to behave better under stress than the able-bodied parents who should take charge. Ivan Southall, in this novel and in others, shows a particular affection for eccentric old age. The real hero of *Ash Road* is a solitary eighty-seven-year-old, Grandpa Tanner, who is not at all concerned with his own survival. Having carefully lowered two small children to shelter down a forty-foot well, he prays for their safety, expects his own death, and does not welcome being reprieved by rain:

> Grandpa had not meant the prayer for himself. Surely he had made it clear that it was for Julie and the Robertson baby and for little children everywhere.

But God had sent the rain. Of course He often did, though not always. He had built that provision into the plan of nature. Great fires drew to themselves ... great rains. But not always. Just sometimes. Perhaps when men forgot themselves and prayed for little children; not when they shook their fists in fury and defiance.

Since these are almost the last words of the novel, Grandpa Tanner's belief in a benevolent ordering providence comes to the reader with authority. *Ash Road* is as optimistic as *Hills End*. Most of the children seem to be the better for their ordeal. As the author moves from one to the other, summing up, he finds in one the elation of reaching manhood; another feels 'complete'; a third is 'ready for whatever life was going to do to her. No longer lost. No longer frightened'.

There is an interesting comparison with *Ash Road* in Colin Thiele's bushfire novel of the same year, *February Dragon*. Southall concentrates on the actions of a single day, and the testing of human strength. Thiele brings a placidly episodic domestic novel to an appalling, sudden close. There is no reconciliation, nothing to comfort three children who find their house destroyed, and their pony, trapped in the stable, burned to death like all but one of their other household pets, and all their father's sheep. The novel ends with the children's realization that 'there was no such thing as "home" any more'. *February Dragon* was written as a cautionary tale, with the encouragement of the South Australian Bushfire Research Council. Its horrors, therefore, have a purpose outside the novel: to teach children the dangers of kindling even a spark in summer. With such a direct lesson in mind, Thiele cannot afford to celebrate heroism; his children do not take part in fighting the fire and they see only desolation. The impact of *February Dragon* is the harsher because of the predominantly comic mood of all but the last two chapters, and for the lack of anyone to take the blame. The reader is told that the fire was caused by the children's complacent Aunt Hester, but she never knows it, nor do any of the other characters in the novel. The ending shows Aunt Hester 'fussing in with cool drinks' for the survivors and moralizing about careless people who start fires and are never caught and punished as they deserve to be. Thiele is hard on aunts; this one is a facsimile of Aunt Emily in *The Sun on the Stubble*, equally loud-voiced, 'gabbling and clacking', all jangling ear-rings and suburban self-importance. The main point of resemblance between *Ash Road* and *February Dragon* is their harsh vision of the Australian bush: unpredictable, savage, beyond the control of man. Thiele's novel ends as Southall's does with rain; in oth, man may survive natural disaster but he cannot subdue it.

Survival is the theme of another 1965 novel, Reginald Ottley's *By the Sandhills of Yamboorah*, which was placed second in the Australian Children's Book of the Year awards of that year. Set on a cattle-station near the 'desert edges' of South Australia, the story belongs to the 1930s but in its primitive simplicity of background it would be hard to date if the author did not offer the information. The landscape is the principal character; in the foreground is 'the boy', a station hand who is never named, and whose anonymity and stoic endurance signify his adaptation to a harsh monotonous routine. There is not much plot. The boy's wish for a dog of his own, a commonplace of juvenile fiction, has added meaning in the isolated setting. He rears a cattle pup, knowing its owner will claim it eventually, but when the time comes he is desperate enough to leave the station on foot, with the dog, and try to cross the sandhills. He has been told that such a journey is almost impossible:

> Always, during the day, he could see them from any angle: the woodheap, the shed, or the stables—even from the kitchen, just outside the door. Wave after wave of sand, washing away to the skyline. Desolate and wind-ridged, the hills shimmered daily under a blazing sun. He hugged his knees when he asked, low-voiced, 'Are they bad? As bad as the fellers say?'
>
> 'Bad?' Ross grunted. 'I'll say they're bad. There's a hundred miles of 'em, stretchin' away out there. An' they're raw. Raw as hell an' twice as hot. If you don't know the lay, there ain't a chance. Wind changes 'em from day to day.'

Ottley's desert is no more amenable to man than Southall's storm and bushfire. The boy plods on, hopelessly lost, until he collapses from heat exhaustion. He is rescued just in time by the dog's owner, who then decides not to claim his property. Ottley's 'boy' differs from a Southall character in being by nature and upbringing a laconic battler in the literary tradition of Lawson. He is heard singing his version of an 1890s bush ballad:

> Wrap me up in my blankets an' stockwhip
> An' bury me deep down below
> Where the dingoes an' crows won't molest me
> Down where good stockmen go.

Like the stockman of the ballad, the boy has low expectations. He reappears in two further volumes, *The Roan Colt of Yamboorah* (1966) and *Rain Comes to Yamboorah* (1967). In all he is a symbol of endurance in a harsh environment.

Illustration by Robert Hales from *Rain Comes to Yamboorah*

Southall's heroes—or anti-heroes—are less self-reliant and have led easier lives. They are not bush boys, and they are certainly not laconic; they usually talk too much, panic easily and turn confusion into chaos. Good sense and calm consideration are more likely to come from one of the girls in a Southall grouping; the shrewdness of Maisie in *Hills End* and the patient strength of Lorna in *Ash Road* help to maintain the precarious balance of the boys.

To the Wild Sky (1967), Southall's next novel, makes its predecessors seem as cosy as Enid Blyton. After storm, flood and bushfire, Southall uses an air crash on a desert island to give a group of six country-town children a painful, prolonged ordeal. *Hills End* and *Ash Road* assert some value in the experiences they describe; *To the Wild Sky* seems as indifferent in mood as the barren island on which the children are left, presumably, for a life sentence. The misanthropic attitude of this novel is established in the opening scenes, in which three mothers say good-bye to their sons and daughters who are to go by private plane for a weekend birthday party on a New South Wales sheep-station. The first mother is characterized by her 'nagging' voice, 'a sound [Mark] scarcely bothered to listen to'. The second is also a voice, this time 'yelling from the back of the house'. ' "Mum's havin' hysterics. The lunch is spoiling, she says." ' The third is silly and socially ambitious, embarrassingly gratified by her daughter's being invited to the Hennessy homestead:

'Hullo, Mrs Bancroft' [Gerald Hennessy said], '. . . so nice of you to allow Carol to come.' Mrs Bancroft didn't mind. Not where anything with people like the Hennessys was concerned. 'She'll be in good hands,' she simpered, 'and it'll be a marvellous experience for her. You've never been on a sheep station before, have you Carol?' 'No, Mother.'

There are only three more adults in the novel. Gerald Hennessy's aunt says goodbye perfunctorily: '. . . she pecked him on the cheek and shut the door before he reached the front gate'. The boy knows she does not want to miss even a moment of her 'drippy old film' on mid-day television. A bad-tempered taxi-driver with a 'coarse face', and an irritable pilot ('yet another grown-up of uncertain humour') make up a thoroughly disagreeable set of adults. The men snarl; the women yell or nag. From the children there is a great deal of howling, sobbing, sniffing and squealing even before the plane takes off. The pilot at least has some excuse for his irascible temper: he dies of a heart attack in mid-flight. That is the end of the adult world and of civilization as the children know it in *To the Wild Sky*. Gerald, who has some flying experience, manages to take over and bring the plane, hours later, to a crash landing on a desolate island beach. Without food or shelter, without fresh water or the means of making a fire, the chances of survival are very small. Gradually the children understand that the outside world offers no hope; they are too far off the map. None of them has any of the special skills usually given in more conventional desert island stories to the castaways. The only signs of earlier human habitation speak of failure and death:

> It wasn't a settlement at all. It was as though men had come here just for the sake of a stupid fight against the bush, just to show how clever they were, just to show how brave they were, but had never looked like winning; had been whipped and beaten and broken and stamped on ... These were strangled ruins, where people had been lonely and desperate and cut off. Mad people surely. If not mad before they came, mad before they got away; or dead before they got away.

Although Southall does not commit himself to predicting a similar fate of madness and death for the children, it is at least a likely one. For their first few days on the island they have some hope and energy; they think about building a raft, sending a message in a bottle, waiting for an air search. They co-operate with one another as well as they can; they are unselfish and mutually protective as often as they are sulky and aggressive. There are a few signs of achievement. One of the girls, who is part-Aboriginal, wonders whether her inheritance may not give her an advantage over the others; after many hours of digging with a stick she brings back 'a heap of little fruits, nuts and the roots of plants swollen with juices, and a dead lizard'. Another, a Girl Guide, manages after many failures to light a fire. The narrative ends with the children's elation at the warmth and the sense of familiarity given by the fire to their alien world. It is just possible to read this as a happy ending; the group may, after all, survive. But against this Ivan Southall weighs all the practical circumstances and, even more heavily, a vivid dream in which one of the girls foresees their dying, one by one, until she is left alone. 'And then there would be no one.'

The resolution of *To the Wild Sky* is a matter of speculation because Ivan Southall did not supply it. The dream may be a delusion. The fire may be no more than a moment of hope. Perhaps it is enough for Southall to affirm that the children are still capable of hope after several days of near-starvation, but it is unlikely that the reader will be satisfied. This desert island story invites comparison with R. M. Ballantyne's *The*

Illustration by Jennifer Tuckwell from *To the Wild Sky*

Coral Island (1858) and Golding's *Lord of the Flies*. Golding reconstructed Ballantyne's novel, turning its Victorian optimism about man's capacity for order into a bleak modern fable of his reversion to savagery. In some ways, *To the Wild Sky* gives a more depressing view than *Lord of the Flies*: the children want order but their efforts to achieve it are futile and pathetic. The most likely outcome is a repetition of the fate of the earlier settlers on the island ('whipped and beaten and broken and stamped on') in their 'stupid fight against the bush'. Whatever the fate of the children, the reader is entitled to know it. It does not help to suggest that the real interest is psychological and that the inner meaning of the experience makes physical survival irrelevant. Try telling that to the twelve-year-old for whom, presumably, Southall is writing. It will not deflect his justifiable irritation that a writer of cliffhangers should decide to leave the heroes hanging over the precipice. In any case, the story is as unsatisfying on the level of individual experience as on that of narrative. *To the Wild Sky* begins in misanthropy and ends—or stops—in doubt. Only the author can say why it does so, but given the nature of his vision of the adult world he may not have thought it worth while to foreshadow a future for the castaway children. A William Golding Prize for Cultural Pessimism would have been more appropriate for Southall at this stage of his career than the Australian Children's Book of the Year award which he won in 1968 for *To the Wild Sky*.

It is a relief to know that Southall's next catastrophe novel, *Finn's Folly* (1969) did not win any prizes. Although many 1960s critics of children's literature still tended to believe, like Victorian nannies, that a dose of nasty medicine was good for children, the new Southall mixture made them pause. In a double accident on a lonely mountain road, a car crashes into an overturned truck. The driver of the car and his wife are killed. The truck-driver, trapped in his cabin with his fourteen-year-old daughter Alison, dies slowly of his injuries. Before he dies, he tells the girl that 'there are problems':

> 'It's our load, love. There was enough poison on the back to wipe out half the State. Cyanides of different kinds, other chemicals too; awful, deadly stuff. Takes only a few grains to kill a man. You can't roll a transport like this and leave the load intact. Where's it ended up? I heard it go, thudding off downhill. Thirty-eight drums of poison, love. There's a dam down there; and people must drink. What am I going to do; how am I going to get out of the cab before people start falling dead?'

If the poison were the only problem, *Finn's Folly* would be relatively simple. The truck-driver also tells Alison that her mother, whom she believes to be dead, had deserted them both, and that she was 'as cold as a fish', hard and ambitious, with no maternal feelings. If the girl ever escapes from the wrecked truck and its load of poison, she will be alone in the world. Some miles away in a lakeside cabin, the fifteen-year-old son of the man and woman who died in the car has heard the crash. He and his sister set out with a torch in heavy fog to see what has happened, leaving their two younger brothers behind. One of these, David, is severely retarded, incapable of speech and uncontrollable in action. He runs away into the fog, where he is lost for hours, and nearly dies from exposure. The girl, Brenda, stumbles in the darkness into a pool of cyanide; we never know whether it does her any harm or not, because there is too much else going on. The eldest boy, Max, finds the car with his dead parents in it and the truck nearby. He cannot free Alison from the cabin, so for several hours he talks to her, strokes her hair and falls in love. Meanwhile, in another part of the wood, a television 'personality' (whom the reader knows to be Alison's mother) taunts her vacillating husband because he seems unable to decide whether to look for the lost child or go to the scene of the accident. It remains dark, cold and foggy. Everyone stumbles about looking for everyone else, except Max and Alison who keep talking.

There is no way of predicting how, in such a situation, Max and Alison would behave. The discovery of mutual love, with the bodies of three parents nearby, and cyanide leaking everywhere, seems improbable but it is scarcely more grotesquely incongruous than the other events of the single night which makes up *Finn's Folly*. John Rowe Townsend gamely tries to make the best of what he admits to be a 'difficult' and 'disturbing' book. 'It seems', he says, 'that girl and boy are taking the place of lost mother and lost father for each other, and it could be that there is a deeper significance still, for here at the moment of death is the rebirth of love'.[1] Could be. Anything could be, in *Finn's Folly*. Walter McVitty understandably finds the dialogue 'inane and appalling', and the prose pretentiously glib.[2] There are any number of passages to illustrate the crassness and banality of *Finn's Folly*; here is a sample:

> 'Max,' she said, not asking a question, not expecting a reply.
> 'Alison.' He knew what she meant because he said nothing other than her name and that was enough for a while.
> 'Max, I love your hand there, but you'd better take it away. I'm dirty. I've been sick.'
> 'I don't care. I don't mind.'
> It didn't seem strange in the least to be huddled against the wreck with one aching arm extended inside . . . It was as beautiful as being alone, as not having to strike a pose but it was more than that; there was nothing troublesome about it, nothing that bothered him, only a wonderful calm strangely related to sadness, yet different in an unfathomable way.

Anyone who wants to fathom this novel will have to figure out what Frank Fenwick (husband of Alison's mother Phyll) feels for Alison, and why Alison's father set out for Finn's Folly, which is really Phyll's Folly, which is his ex-wife's lakeside cabin. Would an ex-husband call in on a foggy night, after ten years separation, with a truck-load of cyanide? Well, as John Rowe Townsend says in his essay on Southall, 'human nature is infinitely strange'.[3] Could be.

Lilith Norman's first novel, *Climb a Lonely Hill* (1970), resembles Southall's work in several ways. There are some parallels in plot with *To the Wild Sky* and *Finn's Folly*, and in mood with *Hills End* and *Ash Road*. *Climb a Lonely Hill* has the 'left to themselves' motif; it is concerned with the child's capacity to endure physical and emotional pain; and it presents the natural world as indifferent or arbitrarily cruel. For Norman, as for Southall in *Hills End* and *Ash Road*, to survive a catastrophe is to gain strength for re-entering the unreliable human world. Her novel begins with a car crash in a remote part of outback New South Wales. Two children on a summer camping holiday with their uncle are left alone when he dies in the crash, impaled on the broken steering column. The children, fourteen-year-old Jack and his younger sister Sue, have no bush experience. Grief for their uncle, whose cheerful strength has been the only compensation for the inadequacies of their alcoholic father, turns to panic. They quarrel over whether or not to leave the wrecked car and their uncle's body. Jack, whose method of dealing with everyday matters is always to evade responsibility, is overwhelmed by Sue's demand that he take charge; he 'hates' her for pressing him to decide:

> Behind the hatred lay fear. Fear of not knowing what to do. Hatred, suddenly, of the vast, bleached bush around them. It lay silent in the noonday heat, yet seemed to hum and pulsate as though a hidden dynamo were vibrating just out of earshot. Dirty, stinking, hot, horrid *bloody* country. Fear of what was in the front seat. Fear and a choking nausea when he thought of what the days could bring ... and the summer heat.

Although the children are not much injured in the crash, and they have supplies for some days, inexperience and bad luck soon bring them close to despair. They lose most of their water supply when Sue carelessly up-ends the heavy container; it falls on her foot and cripples her. With almost nothing to drink, it becomes clear that they must start walking towards the hills where water might be found. Sue can scarcely move, even with the crutch Jack manages to make for her. They set out, slowly, 'a frightened boy, and a frightened crippled girl, trudging towards nowhere—two forlorn specks of nothing on the face of this alien, hostile land'.

Lilith Norman spares none of the painful details of eleven days in the bush, in which the two children come close to starvation. When at last they find water, their food supplies are exhausted and they must rely on Jack's capacity to hunt. They survive, growing physically weaker day by day, on snakes, lizards and emu eggs. Emotionally, however, the experience strengthens them; for the first time they talk openly about their mother's death and their father's degeneration into 'the town drunk'. Jack has a new perception of himself as something more than 'the town drunk's son', neglected and pitiable.

> Suddenly he understood that he and Sue were the strong ones: they would go on surviving, no matter how long it took. He thought back over their trek to the hills, the awful struggle to carry Sue up to the pool, and the endless hunt for food. *They* had fought the odds and survived—it was Dad who was weak and sick and defeated . . . His own battles weren't over, yet, Jack knew. He would have to go on fighting—and winning—because he'd still hate to see Dad drunk, and he'd still be hurt by other people's gibes and laughter.

At this point, the realization of inner survival, the author brings external relief; the children's camp-fire is seen from the air and rescue is assured. As Lilith Norman's later novels show, her main interest is in character. Although the landscape in *Climb a Lonely Hill* is the children's immediate adversary, it is also an image of their harsh and arid private world. The novel's resolution comes without any easy consolations; there are no promises of return to a reformed father or a more sympathetic neighbourhood. It does, however, have a satisfaction denied to readers of *To the Wild Sky* or *Finn's Folly*; the author has made up her mind about what happens at the level of narrative and what it means to the individuals whose ordeal she describes.

Joan Phipson, too, has her certainties. Her theme, in three novels of the 1970s in which children survive catastrophe, is that of man's estrangement from the natural world and the possibilities of reconciliation. The first, and to my mind the least successful, is *The Way Home* (1973). It is the most obviously didactic, with a narrative awkwardly manipulated in the interests of a message. It begins, like *Climb a Lonely Hill*, with a car accident. There is a storm and a flood. The driver is missing presumed drowned; and her son, niece and nephew find themselves in a vast unfamiliar landscape, uncannily empty of other human life. They walk for days, expecting to find a road, a house, other people, but even though their accident must have happened on a main road some hours' drive from Sydney all signs of habitation have vanished. The mood is one of dream or nightmare as the three survivors react to the loss of the familiar world. With the idea of home before them

like a mirage, they must make their way without signposts. Each responds differently. The oldest, Richard, a seventeen-year-old Sydney boy, suffers the most from the shock of displacement and from physical privation. His two cousins, Prue and Peter, accept the unknown more easily; Peter, who is only seven, is the most resourceful and the only one who seems never to be afraid of the bush. Prue has some moments of fear when she thinks of herself and the boys as 'three small and helpless people in a vast and empty plain, covered by a remote and even vaster sky ... [with] nothing and no one to know or care that they existed'. But as she accepts her dependence on the natural world, her fear diminishes. Sheltering from a bushfire, she feels safe:

> As she lay there she lost the sensation of being a body on the ground; it seemed to her that she was close to some protection, some calm, healing presence with which she had always been deeply familiar but which she had never before known how to approach.

Joan Phipson categorizes Richard, Prue and Peter according to their backgrounds. Richard lives in a 'tall building' in the middle of Sydney; he is at home and confident there in 'the surge and press of city life'. His cousins belong to 'the very outside edge of the city, where they could see the open country not far away'. Peter is at home with earth and water, fishing in the muddy creek at the end of the garden. Of Richard it is said 'earth was something he never touched'. He is clear-minded, rational, unable to leave a question unsolved or to tolerate the idea of mystery. In Richard, the author sets out to show man's estrangement from nature; although – or because – he is the oldest and most self-confident of the three, he is physically and emotionally the most fragile. Peter survives easily, Prue learns, Richard fails the test and dies unhappily, still wanting his questions answered. The author sets up her moral antitheses of reason and intuition, city and country, in a semi-allegorical story which does not quite work either in literal or symbolic terms. At the literal level the novel seems arbitrarily cruel and punitive. Richard's death is predetermined by his city upbringing and a rational habit of mind. Just as arbitrarily, his cousins are saved and led home by the protective Presence whom Richard cannot see.

> 'Didn't you see *him* at all', Prue asked once, as they walked along.
> 'I saw those horrible little insect things just before we got back – got –' His voice trailed off doubtfully. 'That's all I saw,' he added finally. 'That's all there was to see.' She slid her arm through his. 'Never mind. One day you will.'

'Why shall I? Why must I see something that isn't there?' Peter answered him. 'Because he–she–*is* there.'

'You keep saying it. But how can I believe it? We've got to a place where nothing makes sense. Nothing rational or logical. Nothing adds up. I think you and Prue have gone mad. And I can't stand it any more. I wish I were dead.'

It was a cry of despair, and it silenced them, and after this, little by little, Richard seemed to retreat further and further into himself. He withdrew from them and lived only in some grey remoteness of his own.

The journey of *The Way Home*, which takes the three wayfarers into the future as well as the past, does not have the narrative interest needed to sustain its symbolic meaning. There is little suspense. The landscape changes; there are dangers from fire and prehistoric monsters, from volcano and glacier, but there is not much variety of mood. Because most of the experience comes to the reader through Prue's consciousness, her trance-like state tends to muffle its effect. The three trudge on and on; there seems no reason for the journey ever to end. The supernatural Presence appears from time to time, rather too explicitly delivering the message in heavily portentous tones. Richard turns on her with the unlikely epithet of 'Hater': an anagram of Earth, in case anyone is still in doubt about Richard's distorting vision or the Presence's identity. 'He had my name but the wrong way round', Prue and Peter are told.

The moral pattern of *The Way Home* resembles that of Patricia Wrightson's Wirrun trilogy in which white Australians are divided between the deluded, ironically named 'Happy People' of the city and the sounder, stronger 'Inlanders' of the country. Within the impersonal mythic structure of the Wrightson novels such categorization may be more easily accepted than in *The Way Home*. Richard has to be both a bewildered victim, realistically portrayed, and a representative of mankind's moral blindness. In her later novels of survival, Joan Phipson moved away from abstractions and supernatural machinery; the didacticism remains, but is not so obviously in charge.

The Cats (1976) returns to the theme of man's relationship with the natural world, but does so within a self-sustaining and exciting narrative. Two country-town boys, Jim and Willy, whose parents have just won a lottery, are kidnapped on their way home from school and driven to a derelict house in a wild bush region. The two kidnappers, Socker and Kevin, are amateurs in crime, and only a few years older than their victims. Neither is at home in the bush; Socker is all ignorant bluster

and Kevin is afraid of the unknown, the silence and the faint sounds
of wild creatures. As the four move further away from the town there
are signs that the younger of the two prisoners, Willy, is gaining in
confidence as Kevin becomes more uneasy. Willy is a silent fourteen-
year-old, accustomed to solitary camping-out in the bush; he is the only
one who knows the region well. Watching him, his brother Jim is
comforted by the younger boy's air of confident expectation. When
a tree falls, blocking the road back to the town, Willy knows without
looking exactly where it fell. Joan Phipson stops short of making the
boy unambiguously a clairvoyant; his powers of 'reading' the bush are
just on the edge of the supernatural. His importance in plot and theme
come from his being unselfconsciously in harmony with his surroundings. He is the only one of the four who is unperturbed by the stormy
landscape through which they travel:

> About midday Socker stopped the car. When it came to a standstill
> he switched off the engine and flopped forward across the wheel with
> his forehead on his hands. Still no one spoke or moved. Now that
> the car was silent the sounds outside poured in through the open
> window. The bush was roaring still, and above the deep, hollow
> notes of the wind in the gullies the shrill screaming of the treetops
> added a note of hysteria to the general hubbub. The sun blazed
> down, implacable and searing, and the west wind carried with it all
> the parched heat of the central Australian desert.

The Cats draws its narrative interest, not only from the series of disasters
which turn the kidnappers' plan upside down, but from the interplay
of character. Isolation brings new alliances. Kevin, left with the gun
to guard Jim and Willy, cannot bear the silence; he becomes more and
more dependent on his prisoners. Socker holds obstinately to his idea
of himself as a tough, independent leader, but he too needs human allies
in the hostile bush. The particular ordeal to which the author subjects
Socker and Kevin is a series of attacks by huge feral cats. Socker is to
blame; by killing a kitten he invites his own death. Willy saves him—
more, it seems, for the sake of the cats than for Socker. He explains
it to Jim:

> 'Jim, it wasn't only the kitten. These cats have never seen people—
> only me. I never hurt them and they never hurt me. Now Socker's
> shown them people are dangerous. What's going to happen now?
> . . . There are so many cats.'
> 'Then they can look after themselves, can't they?' . . . 'And what

happens to animals that think they can defend themselves against people?'

Jim knew the answer to that, and thought better of giving it.

The survival of all four boys is due to Willy's ability to make a truce with the cats and to find a way home. The kidnapping is never reported; Socker and Kevin go back to work, having suffered rather more than their victims from the experience. They seem at least to have been cured of playing master criminals, and in the final chapter Socker earns Jim's respect by showing a strength of character which has nothing to do with aggression. *The Cats* makes a satisfying adventure story with the bonus of good characterization and an edge of mystery. Through Willy it asserts the possibility of establishing the right relationship with the natural world, and in its refusal to adopt the simple moral scheme of *The Way Home* it comes to an appropriate ending in human terms.

Joan Phipson's *Keep Calm* (1978) takes up the city–country debate again, but places the physical dangers, for once, in city living. The ordeal of this novel is caused by a power strike in Sydney. A brother and sister, Nick and Binkie, are left alone in a tenth-floor apartment, not knowing why their mother has not come home. The central idea of *Keep Calm* seems to be the fragility of urban life. The lights go out, the trams and buses stop, and as all the assumptions of normal living are undermined, a large, bewildered population begins to panic. The children take the advice of the most reliable adult they know; predictably, in Joan Phipson's scheme of values, he is an exile from the country. He tells them to leave Sydney:

'I reckon the city's enough to frighten a cove at any time. When everything starts collapsing, like now, you got to go. In this street they can't see it yet. They'll put up with it for a while. They'll scavenge about when they can't buy no more food, but in the end they'll go, even though they are city born and bred . . .

'When a city like this stops, you begin to notice things that were blocked out before. Take last night's storm. I reckon that panicked more people than anything that's happened. They seen it coming an' they heard it, an' for once they saw what a real storm was like . . . They think their city's proof against anything. Well, it ain't and now they're learning. I could 'a told 'em.'

As in *The Way Home*, survival in *Keep Calm* means a long walk. The children in this novel, however, are less isolated; they find friends, and except for the fear that their mother may be dead, they endure nothing more than hunger and exhaustion. The main dangers are bypassed when they leave the inner city; as they move away from scenes of looting and violence the open spaces promise safety. 'You sleep easier on earth than on asphalt', they are told, and their first night in the open gives 'a wonderful sense of relief in being out and away from walls and kerbs ...' A friendly truck-driver takes them home with him, and his wife, the embodiment of country hospitality, looks after them until the lights go on in Sydney and their mother is found.

Keep Calm has less to offer in characterization and suspense than *The Cats*, and it is a little too heavily loaded with message. The crack in what Nick calls the 'eggshell' of city life provides the novel's unifying idea, and it is distracting to make the disruptive power strike part of an anti-nuclear protest. Although the anti-nuclear theme could have been used to underline the idea of urban vulnerability, the novel would probably have foundered under its weight. Joan Phipson, perhaps unintentionally, makes it a side-issue, and finds her dramatic interest in a series of well-staged scenes of city nightmare. The power of the natural world and the frailty of man and man-made structures link *Keep Calm* with the other survival novels discussed in this chapter. This is made explicit in Nick's vision of Sydney Harbour:

> It would look now as it had when the first ships came from over the ocean—dark, secret and brooding. It had been there when the brown men came. It was there now they had gone, or almost gone, and it would still be there when the last white man had gone too.

The perception of man's insignificance in the landscape is a recurring note in Australian literature. It is there, for example, in the recollections of Graham McInnes, as an essential part of an Australian childhood: 'The bush was cryptic, ageless and self-contained; it was we who were totally irrelevant'.[4] That uncomfortable sense of human irrelevance is for the most part subdued in Joan Phipson's work. She asserts that man and nature can be reconciled, and that 'the earth abideth forever'. Ottley and Norman, and Ivan Southall in *Hills End* and *Ash Road*, make survival in a hostile world the test of inner strength. Southall's late work, doubtful, dismal, chaotic, leaves children dangling in a meaningless universe, surviving to no purpose.

15

Family Life Wasn't Meant to be Easy

The domestic tradition in Australian children's literature established by Ethel Turner in the 1890s began to revive in the late 1950s with a renewed interest in family relationships. Even in the first few decades of the twentieth century the family study in the Turner style was displaced by fiction of an increasingly girlish kind; it turned into 'flapperature', with love and marriage the chief concern of its heroines, or into a tangle of hockey sticks and prefects' badges. The family adventure story lasted a little longer. Norah of Billabong rode on serenely until 1942, but the idyll of outdoor family life, only briefly renewed by Joan Phipson after World War II, did not outlast the 1950s. As I have shown, the self-sufficient rural family was already an endangered species in Nan Chauncy's 1950s novels of the Tasmanian wilds. The next phase for Australian domestic fiction was a return to the indoor world of the early Turner novels, to creative, introspective children with difficult, unlucky or absent fathers and impoverished suburban settings. Family emotions rather than family adventures or schoolgirl romances were the preoccupation of a new group of writers, and from the late 1960s juvenile domestic fiction became more and more concerned with problems and crises. There is not much comedy; the analogy with Ethel Turner breaks down if one looks for the irresponsible liveliness of Misrule. There is, however, a close correspondence with some late Turner novels. *Mother's Little Girl* (1904), which concerns an adopted child and the relationship with her natural mother, is similar in theme to Lilith Norman's *The Shape of Three* (1971). In *Nicola Silver* (1924) the heroine's escape from domestic drudgery and a brutal father has a modern equivalent in Mavis Thorpe Clark's *The Min-Min* (1966). The victimized slum child in *St. Tom and the Dragon* (1918) endures as much and as stoically as the hero of Reginald Ottley's *The War on William Street* (1971); both have alcoholic fathers. I am not arguing that any of these modern writers has a specific debt to Ethel Turner; it is rather that the fictional Australian family of the 1960s and thereafter is often presented in the emotional situations she was accustomed to use. Inheriting from the domestic literary tradition of Victorian England and from Louisa Alcott's *Little Women* (1868), she showed the family circle as a place of conflict as well as comfort. In her time she took the juvenile novel as close to adult territory as her publishers would allow, and on certain matters, such as divorce, she was censored. Modern writers, free of the pressures of the Sunday-school prize market, and working in a literary climate which favoured harsh realism, began again to move the boundary lines that separated adult and juvenile fiction. After a long period in the early twentieth century in which it was thought right to shelter children from reading about unsheltered children, the late 1960s and 1970s bring a return to something like the sombre moralities of the Victorian era, but with moral certainties diminished. There is no sudden change of direction; there are cheerful domestic novels of this period as well as bleak ones. The first move is, as it was in the 1890s, to bring the children indoors and see them as individual characters within a family setting. Putting comfort before conflict, I shall look first at the happy families from the 1950s to the mid-1970s.

Some early signs of the revival of the indoor family story may be seen in the first novels of Eleanor Spence. Her 1959 novel, *The Summer In Between*, matches the cheerful mood of the first post-war decade, and with its interest in character and family relationships it prepares the way for the more complex domestic patterns of her later fiction. The setting, just outside a New South Wales coastal town, is the ideal combination of suburban and rural life, with the sea not far away. The heroine, Faith Melville, the clever ambitious twelve-year-old daughter of the local high school's headmaster, has everyday outdoor pleasures as well as the world of books and music. The healthy state of the Melvilles' family life may be deduced from this description of their surroundings:

The house itself, of grey weatherboard with a red iron roof, was neglected somewhat in favour of fowl-yards and the small orchard, but with its broad veranda and wide french windows, it had an undeniably friendly and homely appearance . . . the main meal of the day was eaten in the living-room, a large apartment furnished with shabby comfortable old arm-chairs, an enormous early Victorian bureau that Mrs Melville had inherited from her grandparents, a straight-backed settee that was regarded as Faith's particular property, and a piano that every member of the family used . . .

This is comfort and culture without ostentation, almost a guarantee of good fortune for the heroine. Faith is an Australian version of Anne of Green Gables, less volatile than L. M. Montgomery's heroine, but similarly inclined to self-dramatization, and with the same literary tastes and ambitions. Her wish to find a 'kindred spirit' in a newcomer to the neighbourhood brings a verbal echo from the Montgomery novel; and the Avonlea Story Club, founded by Anne, has a counterpart in the Kenilworth Valley Literary and Dramatic Club for which Faith writes a play. Eleanor Spence centres the novel on Faith's discovery of her talents and her limitations; pride and satisfaction in finding that she can write is temporarily dampened by her failure as an actress. When she loses a leading role to a girl she dislikes, Faith resigns from the club and sulks. Her quietly observant parents prescribe a visit to Sydney where a performance of *A Midsummer Night's Dream* persuades her that while actresses come and go, a playwright's work may last for centuries. The novel ends with Faith as buoyant as before, but singleminded in ambition, and less self-centered.

The events of *The Summer In Between* scarcely ruffle the surface of the Melvilles' placid life, and the summer holiday mood is as idyllic as that of *Good Luck to the Rider*. The difference between early Spence and early Phipson may be seen in the choice of heroine and of setting. In *Good Luck to the Rider* Barbara is a contented outdoor child with horizons bounded by her father's fences and needing only a little more self-confidence to become another Norah of Billabong. For Faith Melville, who reads poetry, likes *Little Women*, and is just starting *Wuthering Heights*, the imagination is at least as important as the natural world and aspiration is unlimited. She does not see the city, as Phipson heroines do, as a place of grey oppressiveness; she responds to the pleasures of the Sydney theatre, and enjoys a shopping expedition, 'riding on the escalator, and staring back at the bustling crowds and the glittering counters and the bright street beyond'.

Eleanor Spence won her first Australian Children's Book of the Year

Illustration by Geraldine Spence from *The Green Laurel*

award with *The Green Laurel* in 1964. This is a more substantial novel than *The Summer In Between* and its other predecessors, with more difficulties for the heroine than a shock to self-esteem. Lesley Somerville, another introspective twelve-year-old, belongs to no particular place. Her father makes an itinerant living by driving a miniature train at country showgrounds; his two daughters go with him and 'home' is re-created at each stopping place by his serenely competent wife:

Small, plump and apparently tireless, she cooked, washed, packed and unpacked, helped dismantle and set up the train, sold the tickets, drove the car and trailer between stops, made her own and the girls' clothes, and still found time to transform two rather battered tents into a cosy and welcoming home.

With that faultless mother, and an equally idealized father who is Lesley's 'shield against the world', the most likely problem for the Somervilles could be predicted as one of health or money. It is both. Mr Somerville has to spend a year or more in a sanatorium while his wife finds work in Sydney and gives the two girls their first permanent home, in a drab housing settlement. Lesley, who has read the Yeats poem from which *The Green Laurel* takes its title, has an imaginative ideal of home as the 'one dear perpetual place' which reality does nothing to satisfy. The ideal is re-created in another way when she submerges her disappointment by drawing houses and planning a career as an architect. Gradually her early dislike of the settlement is modified; she makes friends with a group of migrant children and with them learns to be patient with imperfection, doing what she can to improve some aspect of her surroundings. Eleanor Spence underlines the moral by contrasting the emotional unity of the Somervilles, which survives the father's physical absence and their cramped ugly house, with the vague discontent of their affluent friends the Brents. Mr Brent, absorbed in business all the week and in golf at weekends, pays too little attention to his children; their beautiful house is no compensation. Lesley admits the unimportance of surroundings: 'With all of us together, a home can be any sort of place', she says.

There is no contrast of values between city and country in *The Green Laurel*. Lesley sees Sydney as a place of excitement and promise, no less beautiful than the New South Wales countryside. It is characteristic of Eleanor Spence to present the city and its Harbour as a scene of human work and pleasure; it would not occur to her to shudder at man's disturbing the peaceful waters:

The shape of the city grew, white and grey and fawn above silky blue water, and across the foreground spread the silver arch that seemed to touch the sky. A business-like tug guided a snowy tanker towards one of the oil depots up past Pyrmont; a green ferry was coming out of the Quay and approaching the squat brown island of Fort Denison. Out off Bradley's Head there were white sails dipping, the crowded launches following the race; southward, at Rose Bay, a flying boat had just come in from Lord Howe, and its wake fanned across the water . . . Ships berthing, a place called The Rocks, big boats and little boats, coming from as far away as Northern Europe and as near as Kirribilli, old sandstone buildings jostled by shining glassy office-blocks—it was confusing and exciting and enchanting all at once.

Gentle, decorous, observant, Eleanor Spence's early fiction depicts family life without conflict or crisis except of a minor and external kind. The limitation of these engaging, literate novels is their restricted emotional range; they need more variety of mood and character. By changing the setting from one novel to the next Spence does something to diminish the reader's sense of having met most of the characters before. But what happens to them is always much the same: becoming accustomed to a new place or discovering a new talent are recurring themes which link *The Green Laurel* and its successor *The Year of the Currawong* (1965) with the historical novels Eleanor Spence published in the late 1960s. These will be discussed in Chapter 17. They are, however, a natural extension of the interest in the Australian past with which Spence endows her contemporary characters. The child as amateur historian may be found in *Patterson's Track* (1958), *The Summer In Between* and *The Year of the Currawong*, and the sense of tradition in *The Green Laurel* is expressed in the heroine's enthusiasm for old houses. The children in the early Spence novels, with their perfect parents and understanding teachers, have very little to be angry about; they do, however, find a focus for indignation in *The Year of the Cerrawong*. Here their impersonal enemy is a motel company with plans for developing an historic site. An instinctive feeling for 'old things' marks a Spence heroine or hero as surely as love of animals goes with moral worth in the work of Phipson or Chauncy.

Conservation in Eleanor Spence's fiction is a habit of mind rather than a crusade. It is more central to the plot in some of H. F. Brinsmead's 1960s novels of adolescence; the real estate developer is the target of protectionist energies in *A Sapphire for September* (1967), and tourism is seen as threatening and destructive in *Isle of the Sea Horse* (1969). In a number of Australian family novels a conservationist cause is the means of bringing together a group of brothers and sisters, and answering the essential question: what will they do? The happy family story may become insipid if the children are too much confined to small matters; many depend for their energy on a cause, an adversary, an absorbing task. In the Victorian family novel there were good works in plenty to be done among the deserving poor. The heroine of Charlotte Yonge's *The Daisy Chain* (1856), Ethel May, helps to build a church in a neglected district. The March girls in *Little Women* (with less enthusiasm than Ethel shows for her project) give their Christmas dinner to a poor family and help to take care of its sick baby. With the virtual disappearance of religion as a motive for altruism and the displacement of private charities by social services, the writer of children's stories in the mid-twentieth century found an acceptable cause in the conservation movement. Children with nothing much to do could go out and save something.

One of the best family stories with a conservationist theme is Celia Syred's *Cocky's Castle* (1966). With a New South Wales country-town setting, it centres on the attempt of four cousins to save their great-aunt's deserted old house from demolition by restoring it to its mid-nineteenth century state and entering it in a Historic Homes competition. If this sounds a large task for the school holidays, it is made more plausible by giving one of the boys some professional skill; he is already working as an apprentice for his father, a builder who takes a benevolent interest in the plan:

> 'Though I must say', [Mr Smeaton] said, 'you've taken on a big job ... I think you should be able to manage most of what needs doing. But no tackling the roof, mind. Too dangerous a job for amateurs!'
>
> 'It sounds a very good idea to me ,' said their mother, secretly thankful that they would have some definite activity for the holidays. 'I hope you win a prize with Cocky's Castle. It's a dear old house!'
>
> 'It won't be a dear old house for long if the Pitt Street farmer buys it ... Plenty of money to throw around and ambitious to be a country property owner. Bet your life he'll buy himself a broad-brimmed hat!'
>
> Barry grinned. 'The bigger the brim the smaller the property,' he said ...

At times *Cocky's Castle* reads too much like a newspaper column with hints for amateur decorators, but in showing the children at work, the author adds suspense to information, leaving their capacity to finish the task always in some doubt. The fate of the old house is in the end less important than the discovery of the central character, Fran Smeaton, that she has artistic talent. Her sketch of Cocky's Castle ensures a kind of permanence for the house even though the attempt to save it is finally frustrated. The ending of Celia Syred's novel is thus rather like that of *The Green Laurel*, with the physical reality of a house shown to matter less than the heroine's imaginative possession of it. The clash between country and city values expressed in the Smeatons' antagonism to the 'Pitt Street farmer' does not remain a simple matter of moral opposites; the Sydney businessman proposes a satisfactory compromise between clearing the land for his farm and keeping the bush unspoiled.

Joan Phipson's *Helping Horse* (1974) is not quite a conservation story, unless saving a migrant qualifies as part of the cause. In this country-town novel four children appoint themselves guardians of a helpless adult, a newly-arrived German antique dealer who is trying to establish a business in a derelict cottage. Besieged by a bikie gang and handicapped by his primitive English, Horst (whom the children call Horse) is a figure of innocence who depends on the children for friendship and encouragement. They enjoy having an unusual protégé, and make themselves as useful in restoring his cottage to order as Celia Syred's children do in *Cocky's Castle*. *Helping Horse* is pure comedy with none of the earnest pleas for tolerance that too often turn a migrant story into a tract. The domestic scenes, in which the children manipulate the four sets of parents in Horse's interests, are neatly balanced to show differences and likenesses in family idioms and attitudes. In all these households, the children are as much in charge as they are in Horse's cottage. This inventive, unpretentious situation comedy must be one of the most enjoyable domestic stories of recent Australian writing.

There is more subtle comedy and fuller characterization in Margaret Balderson's *A Dog Called George* (1975). Perhaps its title, which suggests something for very young children, has prevented this novel from winning the recognition it deserves. The author is known mainly for an earlier work *When Jays Fly to Barbmo* (1969), a story of growing up, with a Scandinavian wartime setting. That book was welcomed as a turning-point in Australian children's writing because it refused ready-made Australianism and moved confidently outside the local scene. *A Dog Called George*, set in Canberra, is a family story with the dog of the title no more than a source of comedy and the means of illuminating the relationships between parents and children and between a boy and his friends. Temporary ownership of an enormous, ingratiating Old English sheep dog opens up a new view of the world for Tony Brent, the unremarkable youngest in a talented sharp-tongued group of children. Before George's coming Tony feels insignificant; with him he feels important, popular, respected by the outside world and necessary to the dog's well-being. Although the novel is clearly one for the 'happy families' category, the Brent family life is not quite as it should be. Mr Brent spends all his spare time studying for a university degree, his wife is overworked; the older brothers patronize Tony, and a strong-willed sister pushes him into the background. Without spelling it out, the author makes it clear that Tony's wish to keep George to himself is a sign of his having too small a share of attention. This is not a *Lassie-Come-Home* formula novel of simple wish-fulfilment; George is not the 'one-man dog' Tony wants him to be. When he is eventually claimed by his owner, Tony is deflated by the dog's easy

Illustration by Nikki Jones from *A Dog Called George*

acceptance of the change. He is told that no one really 'owns' George:

'He gives his loyalty to anyone who stops to scratch him behind the ear or shake a paw for him.'

'Well, then—what's the point of having a dog?' Tony couldn't understand the man at all . . .

'Oh—he's a good fellow, that George. And I wouldn't swap him for a gold-mine. But I've never asked his single-minded devotion in return. Do you think I'd be happy knowing that if I died tomorrow he'd give up the ghost and do a Greyfriars Bobby act on my grave? Do you think I'd rest happier under the daisies knowing that George was right there on top of me—a languishing bundle of abandoned misery? No. That dog's got his head screwed on right. He'd cotton on to somebody else and make the best of whatever they offered him. That's not disloyalty. That's just his compulsion to survive coming up stronger than anything else. I wouldn't have him any other way.'

The merits of Margaret Balderson's book are its shrewd portrayal of family life, its dialogue which economically and often wittily explores the relationships between parents and children and some good comic scenes of home and school life.

None of the books I have described so far is a problem novel; all concern fortunate children with loving parents, living in modestly comfortable surroundings, and beginning to explore a benign world from that solid base of family life. Alongside these families may be seen other groups of children, troubled or insecure, with a high proportion of missing or inadequate parents, and a future that seems to promise little but struggle.

City settings, including slums, and unhappy, impoverished families were not new to Australian children's fiction; they returned, however, in greater numbers in the 1960s and with some interesting differences from their predecessors in treatment and style. The Carruthers boys, in Ethel Turner's 1890s novel *The Little Larrikin*, are only fringe-dwellers in their disreputable street; in background and education they are middle-class, and it is always clear to the reader that they will one day regain their proper place in society. So, too, with the heroine of *St Tom and the Dragon*, Ethel Turner's temperance novel. Anne Godwin is the daughter of a scholar and a gentleman who is also an alcoholic. When he kills himself in a mood of sober despair in order to save the child from his violent drunken rages, there is no question of her remaining in the Sydney slum of her early years. She is adopted by a millionaire brewery-owner who sees in her suffering and her father's the human cost of his trade; he then gives up the manufacture of everything except light ale and devotes his time and fortune to philanthropy. It is not difficult to see why such a resolution was adopted in this and in other Turner 'problem' novels; the idea of a happy childhood in the slums would have been unacceptable both to the author and to most of her readers. Only by sentimentalizing poverty could a consoling ending have been found without removing Anne from her surroundings. Moreover, most parents and teachers, choosing books for children in the early twentieth century, expected a good example in speech and manners from fictional heroes and heroines which a realistic portrait of slum life would not provide. Even the mild colloquialisms of *The Little Larrikin* brought protests, as did the language of the neglected children in Turner's *The Camp at Wandinong* (1898). The children in Mary Grant Bruce's novels are occasionally allowed a lapse in syntax, which the author carefully brings to the reader's attention; in general they are as correct in speech as they are polite. The runaway from a Melbourne orphanage in Bruce's *The Happy Traveller* is a middle-class casualty; in spite of years of neglect his accent and manners indicate his 'good family' background.

There are signs of a change in attitudes towards 'correct' language in the novels of the 1960s which goes with an increasing readiness to write not only about children in poverty but about the children of poverty. In books of this decade the ideal of correctness, in life as in speech, came to be seen as less important than that of realism: authors were exhorted to 'tell it like it is', and to enlarge the child's experience of life rather than to give him models to follow. Thus the pattern of development which may be seen in Australian children's fiction during the 1890s, with its move away from idealization towards realism, was repeated in the 1960s. L. H. Evers's *The Racketty Street Gang* (1961) reflects that transition in language, setting and domestic situation. The large numbers of European migrants who came to Australia after World War II provide the main theme for this family story. The central figures in Evers's novel are Anton Smertzer, a German-born twelve-year-old who is just beginning to make friends with Australian boys, and his parents who are still isolated in their new society. The German family is idealized; except for a shadow on Mr Smertzer's reputation which is dispelled in the course of the novel, there is nothing to prevent them from being perfectly happy and prosperous. Their little house in shabby 'Racketty Street', in a disreputable Sydney district, marks an early stage in their Australian fortunes; they are not likely to stay there. Evers contrasts the secure family life of Anton with that of his three new friends in the 'Racketty Street gang'. One boy is motherless, with a drunken father and a dirty, dispiriting house. 'He was always putting his father to bed and looking after him generally, but the truth was he was ashamed of him and ashamed of being ashamed . . .' Another member of the gang has a violent-tempered father who is present in the novel only as a distant angry voice shouting for his son:

. . . from the direction of Racquetier Street came a sound of hammering on the Smertzers' back gate, and an angry voice shouting words which were with some difficulty translated into, 'You come out of there you lazy little beggar—c'mon, come out of there—I'll half kill you when I lay hands on ya—you hear?'

The Australian boys, all in some way neglected by their parents, are impressed by Anton's mother, her neat, hospitable kitchen, and her cooking. 'Any old time your mother gets sick of seeing too many cakes cluttering up her cupboards, just give me a call,' one of them says. The studied casualness of his words, presented as characteristically Australian in their understatement, are contrasted with the formal courtesies of the German family. It is part of the design of the novel and characteristic of many fictional treatments of the migrant theme, that Anton should learn to value the rough-and-ready manners and mateship of the Australians while they find gentleness, refinement and maternal warmth in the migrant household. The story ends with the solution of the Smertzers' problems. It does not, however, provide happy homes for the other boys; one violent father and one who is habitually drunk remain unreformed. The ending is made cheerful by a reward to be shared among the boys for their part in capturing a bank robber; this makes their ambitions seem feasible. One plans to 'work hard at school and go on to the university'; another speaks of saving up and buying 'a bit of a farm' some day. In the meantime, the solidarity of the Racketty Street gang is a compensation for comfortless homes and inadequate parents.

Reginald Ottley's *The War on William Street* (1971) resembles *The Racketty Street Gang* in its picture of urban poverty and deprivation. It is a period piece, with a 1930s Depression setting, but its three Sydney boys are used very much as Evers used his gang, with the main emphasis on family life or the lack of it. As in the earlier novel, there is one fortunate boy from a secure home, complete with mother, and two waifs who envy their friend:

'Snow knows,' [Corro] thought, 'the way me an' Spud live. But it goes beyond knowing. He'd have to live like we do to understand, an' he don't. That house of his is a flamin' mansion. An' his Mum an' Dad are pretty well the best there is.'

Like Evers, Ottley stops short of showing in close-up the brutality of parents towards their children. The domestic scenes presented in *The War on William Street* are those of the ideal family, that of Snow. His friend Corro says, 'My place is rough, an' me Mum an' Dad lay into us, sometimes', but the narrative does not take the reader uncomfortably close. The convention of the gentle, loving mother is seldom broken in juvenile fiction of this period; fathers may be violent, but mothers usually fail their children only by absence or death. In *The War on William Street*, the third member of the gang, Spud, is starved, beaten and exploited by an old woman whom he calls 'Gran', but who is not his grandmother. His father, who is absent somewhere in the country, drinks and forgets to send money for Spud's maintenance. His mother is dead. Like the children in Reginald Ottley's stories of Australian country life, Spud is a battler and a stoic; the pathos of his situation is emphasized by his refusal of self-pity. He maintains a dogged loyalty for the appalling Gran, and records her doings with some admiration:

> 'Yer know,' Spud's eyes shone for a moment with the exciting memory, 'before you could say Ned Kelly, a dozen blokes were pounding up the stairs. One of the other blokes had grabbed me round the neck, an' I was punchin' away at 'im, but it didn't last for long. The blokes comin' up the stairs saw to that. They had them two bottled in a trap, an' they beat the daylights out of 'em. An' ol' Gran sat at the table drinkin' a bottle of beer while she urged 'em on. Boy oh boy, they were two sick jokers when the neighbours threw them down the stairs.'

The Racketty Street Gang and *The War on William Street* enlarged the territory of the family novel in several ways. Their attempt to capture the life of inner-city, working-class boys, and their refusal to move them either into the country or into the middle class was unusual; so was the acceptance of weak or harsh parents as a fact to be endured rather than an aberration to be corrected. The emphasis on the relationship between fathers and sons, and on boys' friendships, with scarcely a female figure in sight, makes these two novels distinctive among family novels, which are usually dominated by daughters and written for girls. In spite of the violence and crime which make up part of the narrative, the emotional centre in both novels is the family; they are not simply adventure stories.

With Mavis Thorpe Clark's *The Min-Min*, one of the best family novels of the post-war period, we are back in the feminine domain, but the situation and its treatment are original and moving. There can be few heroines of fiction as isolated as Sylvie, whose home is one of a row of ten fettlers' cottages on a railway siding on the Nullarbor

Illustration by Genevieve Melrose from *The Min-Min*

Plain. This little settlement in the desert and others like it, many miles apart, exist to maintain the railway track which links the east coast of Australia with the west. For Sylvie the main event of the week is the arrival of the goods train ,which brings provisions every Saturday to a settlement too barren to grow its own food:

> The engine siren gave a long impatient blast as the train lessened speed. It wanted all the siding people down at the track with their baskets and money quickly ... Sylvie edged to the front of the crowd, leaving her barrow in an accessible spot. She wanted to be first in when they opened the door of the provision van. Light spilled like liquid then on to the stones and turned the weathered bits of broken bottle into diamonds. But it was the inside of the van she

liked. It was fitted like a shop. There was colour and light and order-
liness . . . and much to look at.

The weekly shopping excursion is the only one of Sylvie's household
tasks to give her pleasure; for the rest she looks after younger brothers
and sisters and waits on her low-spirited, pregnant mother and her ill-
tempered father who escapes from disappointment and boredom into
drunkenness. The symbol which gives the novel its title is the phantom
light on the horizon, the beckoning 'min-min' which represents for Sylvie some possibility beyond her dreary experience of life. When she
decides to run away from home she is at once rebelling against her
father and affirming the idea of the 'min-min'. She is also prompted
to escape in order to take her brother out of reach of the police who
are about to charge him with vandalism and have him sent to a reformatory.

Mavis Thorpe Clark does not make Sylvie exceptional in anything
but her circumstances; she does not need to, because the relationship
between character and setting carries the novel's emotional weight. The
girl is unusual only in her capacity for wonder, her responsiveness to
experiences which most of the novel's readers would take for granted.
A few families, an ordinary domestic routine, a vast desert which is
crossed daily by one fast modern train, are elements incongruous
enough to sustain *The Min-Min*'s dramatic interest. To say that the children 'run away' is a euphemism; there is nowhere to go, and running
is impossible. They stow away on a freight train for fifty miles or so,
then walk thirty miles to an out-station in the hope of getting advice
from a woman whom Sylvie remembers, from one chance meeting, as
sympathetic and knowledgeable about the outside world. Everything
in the novel emphasizes the contrast between the railway siding and
the world beyond it, between the insignificant human figures and the
wide indifferent spaces they must cross. Distance, in Nan Chauncy's
novels, is security; in *The Min-Min* it is tyranny. The answer, in the
human terms of the novel, is to admit defeat and to move, as Sylvie's
father does when he understands the cost to his family of staying at
the siding. In the domestic contest, the real conflict is between father
and daughter, with the ailing mother off-stage and the delinquent
brother a weak-willed nonentity. Sylvie is able to make her own terms
for coming home to look after the younger children; her father takes
a labouring job in an industrial town, stops drinking and makes the
boys help with the housework. She learns dressmaking at the technical
school and looks forward to having a shop of her own with her name

in gold letters on a plate-glass window. It is a low-key but satisfying ending to a novel which gains its effects without flourishes. Mavis Thorpe Clark's matter-of-fact prose works well in making the essential contrasts of the story. For the reader, the Nullarbor Plain will be strange and surprising, while the commonplaces of most Australian experience—trees, flowers, and running water as well as streets and shops—come to Sylvie as the wonders of civilization.

Margaret Paice's novel of outback Queensland, *The Bensens* (1968), shows a happier family than that of *The Min-Min*, but it too draws its emotional interest from the struggle to maintain family life in an isolated place. There is little of the pastoral idyll about *The Bensens*. The father is an itinerant bush worker and the Bensen home is a caravan. A cheerful, indomitable mother keeps the family together, accepting her husband's restlessness without resentment. 'Sometimes I think the kids and I should stay in a house in some town whilst Alec goes off on a job, but I don't know—we've done it so long now, and it's not a bad life. Besides, we like to be all together.' The author balances the pleasures the Bensen children find in the freedom and variety of their nomadic outdoor life against its limitations. The heroine, Kylie, resembles Sylvie of *The Min-Min* in her wish for wider opportunities; and she has artistic talent which cannot be developed through the haphazard correspondence lessons which make up the Bensen education. She shares her mother's desire for permanence, but regretfully accepts the fact that the family 'must move on, as they always did, with only memories to take with them'. The portrait of Mr Bensen has a sharp edge of irony; the author lets the incidents of the novel reveal the selfishness that his wife and children do not appear to notice. 'Mr Bensen was sorry he had forgotten Kylie's birthday, but hang it, one day was just like another in the bush. You forgot to look at the calendar.' In setting and characterization *The Bensens* is a skilful and observant novel. Its open ending, with Kylie's future still a matter of hope rather than assurance, is characteristic of the 1960s reluctance to hand out prizes and promises to all deserving characters in the final chapter. Characteristic, too, is the author's interest in the children of a wage-earning bush worker instead of the graziers' or farmers' children more familiar in earlier Australian juvenile fiction.

With the 1970s came an increasing tendency to examine family life in acute emotional crisis. Instead of the measurable difficulties of a parent's illness or loss of money, writers of Australian children's fiction followed their American and English contemporaries in producing insoluble psychological or social problems. Some of these novels have a case-book quality about them; they are issues in search of characters. Some examine material too painful or too complex for juvenile fiction to accommodate without exceptional skill and subtlety; the result is usually superficial and banal. Others succeed in using an extraordinary domestic crisis to explore ordinary family relationships. A good example of the latter is Lilith Norman's *The Shape of Three* (1971). The 'whose baby?' plot, with or without the complication of identical twins, has been used for centuries as the literary material of comedy, tragedy or melodrama. It very often ends with the discovery of the rightful place for the mixed-up children; prince and cottager change places, a mother is reunited with her own son, a young man finds out how and why he was left as a baby in a handbag on a British railway station. Lilith Norman takes up the more interesting question of what happens after the discovery is made. Two Sydney schoolboys meet face to face in a crowd at the Easter Show, and each sees his mirror-image twin. One believes himself to be the only child of a prosperous real-estate agent. The other has grown up with a non-identical 'twin' brother in a large working-class family. Rearrangement soon follows the discovery. The twins are reunited and the third boy—odd-man-out in the trio—becomes an only child. No one is happy. The mother who insisted most strongly on reclaiming her own son feels uncomfortable with an alien, hostile newcomer. There are differences between the two households which make difficulties for both boys. To some extent these are stereotyped; the mother of the large working-class Catholic family, overworked but serene, is too neatly contrasted with the discontented, status-seeking mother in her harbourside house with its Regency-striped chairs and carefully subdued pale-gold carpets. One of the boys considers the differences between the two women:

> Mrs Herbert was partly dressed [for breakfast] in a cotton print, but she was wearing slippers and her hair was still in rollers. Ugly blue veins knotted out on her legs. Fancy someone like her being called Grace! Bruce was ashamed of this thought even as it flashed across his mind. In lots of ways she was nicer than Mum—easier to get along with, happier. No, that was being disloyal. No, it wasn't; Grace was his mother now. But Mum was so neat and clean and tidy; Grace was sloppy but sort of comfortable, while Mum was all tensed up. Oh hell, what a muddle.

The unhappiest of the three boys is the one who has gained the most in material possessions but lost the companionship of a 'twin' brother and the warmth and energy of a large household. He resolves matters by running away. Both sets of parents are then forced to admit that nurture means more than nature and to take back the boys they had accidentally adopted as new-born babies in a maternity hospital muddle. The exceptional circumstances of *The Shape of Three* give suspense and some degree of thoughtfulness to an engaging and persuasive study of everyday family relationships. There is no great subtlety in any individual characterization, but the group portraits and backgrounds are convincingly detailed.

Noreen Shelley's *Faces in a Looking Glass* (1974) handles complex material with sensitivity and a resourcefulness in narrative structure which avoids over-simplification. A story of teenage parents in a highrise flat with a six-week-old baby in danger of being battered sounds like a social worker's case-history. By treating this theme only indirectly, as part of the vicarious experience of a sheltered Sydney schoolgirl, the author makes her social protest on behalf of the unhappy high-rise trio without coming uncomfortably close. The novel is mainly concerned with the discovery of the heroine that her moral categories of good, gentle mothers and evil, angry mothers are too simple. As a reluctant witness in a kidnapping case she at first resists the idea of helping a 'cruel' mother get her baby back. When she sees both young parents on television appealing for help in tracing the kidnapper, she cannot reconcile their obvious distress with her own image of their callousness:

> Dad got up and switched off the television set . . .
> 'She was nothing *like* herself!' said Kylie, sounding dazed.
> 'She looked like a different person . . .' Her father was studying her unhappily. 'You're judging that poor woman unfairly, Kylie', he said. 'You met her *once* – when she happened to be in a bad mood. You can't judge a person on one chance meeting.'
> Kylie looked at him despairingly. 'You don't understand . . .'

Faces in a Looking Glass encloses the battered baby theme within the main story of Kylie's growing up and makes it an essential part of her experience. The central idea of withholding absolute moral categorization applies not only to the immature, resentful mother but to the kidnapper, a lonely unbalanced woman, whose decision to 'rescue' the baby translated into action Kylie's own certainty about what ought to be done. Noreen Shelley's first novel, *Family at the Lookout* (1972), was an Australian Children's Book of the Year award-winner. *Faces in a Looking Glass*, with better characterization and a stronger narrative interest, deserved but did not win a second award for its author.

Eleanor Spence's novels of the 1970s follow the fashion for unhappy families. In *The Nothing-Place* (1972) Spence moved rather uncertainly among problems and conflicts to show a boy coming to terms with deafness and a girl accepting the fact of her parents' divorce. She found a stronger though more difficult theme in *The October Child* (1976), and managed it with assurance. She asks what it might be like to have an autistic child in the family, and shows the mixed emotions of two brothers and a sister. The Marriners of this novel are not very different from the Somervilles of *The Green Laurel*; pleasant parents with agreeable, affectionate children living in modestly comfortable circumstances. Their sedate existence is disrupted by the birth of Carl, 'the October child', who grows into a physically sturdy, uncontrollably violent, unteachable boy. He cannot speak, and responds to the world in unpredictable rages and short periods of apparent contentment. The main focus of the novel is his older brother, Douglas. Of the first three Marriner children, Douglas does most to help Carl, and rebels most strongly against the emotional burden. Eleanor Spence leaves the problem unsolved, but gives Douglas a compensating gift and a means of escape in the world of music. The novel is carefully balanced, with scenes of chaos relieved by periods of comparative serenity. As a central figure the awkward, anxious, conscientious Douglas is sufficiently well realized to hold the narrative together, and his sudden explosive anger is released at the right moment as necessary emotional relief for the reader:

> He held out his arms. Carl's hair flashed golden in the lamplight as his head swung round, and he fastened his teeth in his brother's wrist, ripping like tissue paper the worn flannelette of Douglas's shirt.
>
> Douglas stumbled backwards. He stared at the small upraised face of his brother, and could see in the round blue eyes nothing but rage and hate. There was no fear, no remorse—worst of all, there was no recognition. It was the face of a hostile stranger.
>
> 'You're *not* my brother!' Douglas whispered. 'You never *were* my brother!'
>
> He turned and ran.

That moment of fury is needed before the final resolution in which Douglas accepts Carl as part of his life but no longer the dominant part. The guilt, at least, has gone; and, by leaving the parents in the background, Eleanor Spence contrives an ending which is neither painful nor tritely reassuring.

In her next novel, *A Candle for Saint Antony* (1977), Eleanor Spence moved into another difficult emotional area with the story of a brief homosexual attachment between two fifteen-year-old Sydney school-boys. One is a conventional, unimaginative outdoor Australian, the other a sensitive, withdrawn Viennese migrant. Against a rather too schematically drawn background of cultural contrast the boys become mutually and exclusively devoted to one another. The author scores some points against Australian hedonism and ockerism. Europeans are presented as less rigid and self-conscious than Australians in their emotional and cultural lives. The Viennese boy has a gentle, loving widowed mother whose shabby Sydney flat, with its classical music and good cooking, re-creates a tradition in exile. A genial, generous Greek café-owner is there to reinforce the ideal of Europe against the Philis-tinism of Australian middle-class ways. The Australian household is dominated by money and possessions; a discussion between father and son is presented in the terms of a business deal. 'All right,' said Mr Vincent. 'I'll talk terms.' Religion has meaning for the Europeans; for the Australians it is a Sunday occasion for being seen in expensive clothes. Granted its simplification of national types, the clash of cul-tures is well dramatized. The main weight of the novel, however, rests on the relationship between the two boys. In spite of Eleanor Spence's skill, it does not quite succeed. *A Candle for Saint Antony* is a love story of adolescence, and because it is homosexual it is written with particular care and restraint. It is not a protest novel. Its comment on the limi-tations of a society which misunderstands innocent love is made part of the Australian-European theme. In style and structure the novel is skilfully managed, but the final effect is less than might have been expected. The central emotions are not implied; they are simply not there. A comparison with the absurd but unselfconscious passions of early twentieth century schoolboy novels like *Tell England* may help to suggest a reason. Ernest Raymond, writing at a time when homo-sexuality was unmentionable, wrote about its emotions with a freedom not available to a contemporary writer of juvenile fiction. Eleanor Spence can tentatively use the terms which tell the reader the nature of the schoolboys' scarcely-expressed feelings, as when a reference to 'gay' Vienna suddenly makes one of them self-conscious. She cannot allow anything like the strength of emotion which would be demanded by a teenage heterosexual romance. I am not arguing for more uninhibi-ted treatment, but if a subject must be approached with such caution, it is probably best left off the juvenile list.

A Candle for Saint Antony shows a gifted writer in difficulties. A less gifted one, Elisabeth MacIntyre, is in more difficulties with her story of a teenage unmarried mother, *It Looks Different When You Get There* (1978), but does not seem to know it. The bright superficial narrative voice in which the heroine tells her own story gives the beginning and the end, but leaves out the central event of the baby's birth. The progress from apprehensive pregnant girl to brave competent mother has an emotional as well as a chronological gap. It looks easy, and it doesn't get anywhere.

Two novels which lie just outside the period of this survey may be mentioned to close this brief account of Australian post-war family fiction. Mavis Thorpe Clark's *Solomon's Child* (1981) is a competent narrative with a touch of the social worker's case-book about it; it has little of the subtlety of *The Min-Min*. Illegitimacy, teenage crime, and a dispute over the custody of the heroine are the main issues, and, for once, there is an interesting mother-and-daughter relationship. Joan Phipson's *A Tide Flowing* (1981) does not take up social questions, but is concerned with an even more troubled child than Mavis Thorpe Clark's heroine. The initial tragedy in the Phipson novel, a mother's suicide, is known only to her son who witnesses what is thought to be an accident. The boy expects his father to try to compensate for the mother's act, and perhaps explain it. He suffers a second betrayal when the father clearly shows that he does not want to know the truth about the supposed accident, and that he proposes to marry again and to leave the boy with grandparents. In a long period of extreme loneliness and depression the boy regains some hold on human affections in a friendship with a crippled girl. The girl's death, after a painful illness, helps him move back towards normal life. *A Tide Flowing* is more sombre than most juvenile novels. It breaks the convention of the reliable loving mother in the suicide scene, and in the crippled girl it gives a modern counterpart of the Victorian set piece of a child's redemptive death. Instead of the Christian consolation of the nineteenth century novels, it affirms a pantheistic vision of harmony:

> . . . sea and sky and air and water held them together still, and always held them, part of the great tide, part of the harmonies of a living universe. Just as he was held together with his lost mother and with Connie.

As always, Joan Phipson's writing is intelligent, and *A Tide Flowing* does not lack narrative interest. It raises again the recurring, unanswerable question of appropriate emotional range, and leaves a bleak image of family life: a solitary boy, looking from a window at an empty beach, sustained by belief in the ultimate order of nature. Little Paul Dombey had an easier time of it; Dickens let him go out with the tide.

16

The Outsiders

The campus cult book of the 1950s, J. D. Salinger's *The Catcher in the Rye* (1951), established a literary image of alienated youth in the United States. In that decade and the next, the colloquial style of Holden Caulfield's first person narrative, as well as his attitude towards what he sees as the pervasive 'phoniness' of adult society, was widely accepted as representative of the new generation. Salinger wrote for a general audience but his sixteen-year-old hero was quickly claimed by college and high school students for whom the book seemed both to reflect and to reinforce the mood of their time. The hero as drop-out had arrived. Anxiety, depression, and a passive withdrawal from society characterized the new hero. American children's fiction of the 1960s followed adult fiction in a preoccupation with outsiders, victims and minorities and with questions of identity. Australian children, however, did not find extreme states of alienation in their own literature until the early 1970s. It is relevant to recall here that *The Catcher in the Rye* was banned by Australian Government authorities in 1956, as an indecent publication; we were not ready then for Holden Caulfield whose idiom is inseparable from his point of view. Without television (which came to Australia in 1956) and before jet planes, Australians were given ample time during the 1950s to absorb American culture shock. Holden Caulfield, released by the Australian Censorship Board late in 1957, has slowly made his way to sixth-form prescribed-text status, and fifth-form recommended reading in Australian schools.[1] Meanwhile his counterparts in Australian juvenile fiction have appeared; Ivan Southall's central characters in *Bread and Honey* (1970) and *Josh* (1971) are well advanced in alienation, and J. M. Couper's narrator in *The Thundering Good Today* (1971) echoes the Caulfield tone of controlled panic.

The first important Australian children's writer to deal with alienation in a mild form and with the 1960s counter-culture was H. F. Brinsmead. In her first novel, *Pastures of the Blue Crane* (1964), which won the 1965 Australian Children's Book of the Year award, she presented a very traditional story with a few contemporary touches. The heroine, sixteen-year-old Ryl Merewether, is an outsider who comes inside as soon as she is given her first home and meets her grandfather for the first time. The home is a dilapidated house and a small banana farm in north-eastern New South Wales in which she and her grandfather inherit equal shares according to her father's will. They travel together to their property as two self-willed, unloving individuals, unused to sharing anything. For the old man, Dusty Merewether, the journey is a rediscovery of his own past. For the girl, brought up in a city boarding-school, it is the first glimpse of the countryside which the author calls 'the heart of Australia'. Characterized in the early chapters as cold and arrogant, a 'lone wolf' at school, Ryl has felt no ties of affection to any place or person. She responds to the natural beauty of the land and to her grandfather's laconic, undemanding companionship. Together, but disputing every decision with one another, they reclaim the derelict property; they make friends in the district and learn to accept and to give help. In theme and mood *Pastures of the Blue Crane* recalls Frances Hodgson Burnett's *The Secret Garden* (1911) in which two spoiled, solitary children come to emotional life in 'making things grow'. The traditional theme is given individuality in the Brinsmead novel by the author's sense of place. Its contemporary flavour comes mainly from an element in the plot which also provides suspense. There is a mystery about Ryl's parentage, to which the author supplies a sequence of clues. The heroine remains unaware of these emphatic signals until she is ready for the knowledge that her great-grandfather was a Kanaka labourer on a sugar plantation. She has dissociated herself from local racial prejudice before she realizes that she is by definition one of White Australia's rejects. There is nothing painful in this discovery: Ryl, beautiful, confident, clever and rich, has nothing to fear from society, and her sense of self has been assured by the experiences of her new life.

Pastures of the Blue Crane is a buoyant and charming tale. It has worn much better than its successor, *Beat of the City* (1966), in which Brinsmead attempts a group portrait of some young urban outsiders, rebel-victims of the 1960s counter-culture. The trouble with this story is that the author has too little sympathy with three of her four central characters and too much for her fourth. The narrative voice of the novel is uncertain; it swings for no justifiable reason from using the teenage jargon of the protagonists to some very sententious, formal prose. It is as though the author tells the story sometimes as the comfortable policewoman with whom she clearly identifies, and sometimes as the absurd Raylene, 'the scruffy little sort in purple', for whom she has limited patience:

> Raylene sniffed and smeared her face with a dirty hand. The policewoman, who hated inefficiency, wiped the face herself vigorously with the paper handkerchief, and pushed back the hair. It was strange, but in this vulnerable hour something was happening . . . to Raylene. The toughie, the fisher girl who despised all authority, wanted nothing so much as to weep out loud and long on that blue serge shoulder. All night she had been hating authority, with the vicious and hysterical hatred of the fanatic. Now suddenly with the daylight, this was gone. All that was left was an empty weariness, and a longing for a shoulder to cry on. And oh, what a broad shoulder this blue one was! How firm and warm it looked to a cold, tired scrawny prisoner with empty brown velvet eyes!
>
> 'Come on, love,' said the policewoman. 'Drink up your tea and I'll pour you another.'

The passage just quoted sounds like the author as a blue serge shoulder. Elsewhere, the narrative voice comes closer to Raylene's idiom:

> But Aunty Denny—well I dunno, thought Raylene. She wasn't square. Even though she bossed you around if your shoes needed cleaning or you hadn't picked up the bathmat after you. I dunno.

The antithesis of Raylene, the blank-faced rocker, is Mary, the angelic singer of folk songs, to whom the author attributes extraordinary powers. Mary can subdue evil with one fearless glance, and, if that does not work, 'it was not for nothing that her adopted brother had taught jujitsu at the Police Boys' Club . . .' It may be argued that the characterization of *Beat of the City* is deliberate caricature of a kind to encourage the comic illustrations drawn for the novel by William Papas. If so, it is self-defeating; it works against the moral earnestness with which the author attacks the 'Instant, Ready-mixed, King-sized Plastic Substitute' for happiness which the young pursue. The most surprising aspect of *Beat of the City* as a 1960s novel is its wholehearted approval of the

Illustration by William Papas from *Beat of the City*

adult world; there are no caricatures among the parents, police and others who represent authority. With so much kindness and common sense among the elders, there is no case for the rebels, and no real conflict in the story.

There is cause for rebellion in Colin Thiele's *Blue Fin* (1969), with its harsh, demanding father's contempt for an awkward, accident-prone son. Snook Pascoe is everyone's victim, and his father's most of all:

> The truth was that his father had no faith in him. Snook was a thin gangling fellow of fourteen who looked for all the world like the fish he'd been named after. He had the same straight tube-like body, the same long tapering nose with closely set eyes and elongated jaw. The kids had been cruel to him about it; all through his primary school days they'd jeered at him over his nose and his nickname, and now it had followed him to high school. The teachers didn't help either; some of them didn't seem to know that his real name was Steven any more than the children did, and Mr Smart, his class teacher, was as ruthless as a barracuda. He usually referred to Snook as 'that poor fish' and suggested that even if he was such a dolt in the classroom, perhaps with a shape like his he could make up for it at the swimming carnival. But Snook couldn't swim very well either, and he was hopeless at football, so everybody wrote him off as a dead loss, his own father most of all.

Although the author's sympathies are firmly on the side of his misfit hero, there is no question of the boy's refusing to compete for adult approval. In a deftly-handled, exciting narrative of sailing and shipwreck Thiele shows Snook proving his courage to his father. The boy keeps calm when a waterspout almost destroys the *Blue Fin*, when the three crew members are drowned, and his father is critically injured. After five days of heroic endurance, Snook brings the boat safely home from 'the voyage that had ended his boyhood as suddenly as if he had dropped it over the edge of a cliff'. Proud of his son at last, Mr Pascoe exclaims, 'Oh, he don't look it, but he's a tiger, that boy. By God, he's a tiger'. The sadness with which the author tempers the satisfaction of the boy's victory marks *Blue Fin* as a modern story. The father still does not understand, and the boy knows it. He also knows that he will follow his father and 'live by the sea—while he lived'. The resolution is rather like that of a Hemingway story in its recognition of the cost as well as the necessity of courage. An earlier writer of boys' books would have made it wholly affirmative; a later one might well have ended the story with the father being rejected by the son. In Thiele's fiction there are outsiders, but no drop-outs. Even the solitary child of his *Storm Boy* (1963) agrees, in the end, to go to school.

Thiele's conservationist concerns may be seen in *Blue Fin*, and these, of course, are very much of their time. In this story they are hard

Illustration by Margaret Horder from 'I Own the Racecourse!'

to assimilate; the reader must somehow balance the author's idea of
tuna-fishing as an affront to nature against his endorsement of the
needs and good conscience of the fishermen. I am not suggesting that
the moral themes should have been simplified, but that some way
might have been found to hold them together.

    To call Patricia Wrightson's 'I Own the Racecourse!' (1968) a novel
about an outsider is to risk simplifying a subtle and delightful story.
The hero, a mentally-retarded Sydney boy, is outside society in more
than one way, but the most obvious way, which is his intellectual

deficiency, is not the most important. This is not a protest novel, and it has only a little more to do with the mentally-retarded than *The Great Gatsby* has to do with gangsters. Its central idea is like that of Fitzgerald's novel; it is the difference between imaginative and material ownership. The schoolboys' game from which '*I Own the Racecourse!*' takes it title is a variation on Monopoly; the players outbid one another by declaring themselves the owners of more and more impressive assets. '*I own the timber-yard! I own the Town Hall! I own the ferries!*' Andy, the novel's hero, has never understood how to play this game, but has always tried to join in with his friends. When, through a misunderstanding with a drunken tramp, he believes that he has bought a racecourse for three dollars, he is triumphant and the others are dismayed. They try to protect him from the results of his illusion. 'The problem, it seemed to [them] was to make Andy see what was real and what was not.' As Andy, with growing confidence and delight, begins to assert the rights of ownership, the other boys are astonished to see how strongly the dream is sustained. The workers at the racecourse and Andy's neighbours are kindly and amused; they nourish the dream with their assent until, finally, the boy claims too much privilege. The author has to find a way to make him relinquish possession without his dream being shattered, and to show his friends that what he owned went beyond the physical realities of the track itself. The solution is as ingenious as the comic episodes at the racetrack during the boy's illusory rule.

'*I Own the Racecourse!*' does not come with a detachable message for its readers about being kind to the mentally handicapped. The arguments among the boys who try in different ways to protect Andy bring the story to its understated conclusion about the nature of reality and dream, and material and spiritual possession. It is the central idea of *The Great Gatsby* but without Fitzgerald's tragic vision. Patricia Wrightson keeps the fable within the comic world she has created: here the outsider wins.

There could scarcely be a greater contrast in styles than between '*I Own the Racecourse!*' and Ivan Southall's *Bread and Honey* (1970). Wrightson's gentle, ordered narrative and limpid prose have little in common with the murky stream-of-consciousness of Southall's novel. There are thematic connections which reinforce the contrasts. Southall, like Wrightson, is concerned with the value of the imaginative world; unlike her, he shows its suppression by materialistic adults who are determined to destroy any sustaining illusion. His confused thirteen-year-old hero, Michael, is told by his father to 'face facts':

'Don't put your faith, my boy, in silly imaginations. There are no fairies, no ghosts, no magicians, no angels with harps. There are no mysteries in heaven or earth that can't be expressed mathematically as formulae or dismissed as poisonous nonsense. The rock that hangs on the cliff is hard; you can analyse it, you can break it down into invisible particles; but when that rock falls and hits you on the head it kills you dead. That's life, my boy. That's nature. Blood and claw.'

Southall clearly dissociates himself from this attitude, and he presents its antithesis in Michael's grandmother, an indomitable eighty-three-year-old who believes in God, Santa Claus, and Anzac Day. '*Believe* in things, Michael', she says. 'It doesn't matter if you're wrong.' The final page of the novel finds Michael echoing his father's words when he tells the grandmother to face facts. Although he regrets his harshness, and immediately tries to console her, the implication of the novel is that if Michael can survive it will be by becoming strong in his father's way.

Bread and Honey is one day in Michael's life. Although nothing much happens in external terms, he suffers a great deal. A narrative technique which imprisons the reader for very long periods in a disturbed consciousness needs more careful control than Southall gives. We have no means of placing such outbursts as the following, which is a fair example of Michael's habitual desperate state:

It was like the end of the world, like failing in everything he had ever tried to do; like dying, only worse, because maybe with dying that'd be the end. Being like this meant there was more. It was terrible being alive. Why couldn't he be dead like Mum, like those ten million fellows who marched off to war? Thinking exhausted him; half-thinking, half-feeling; it made him want to cry, made him want to die.

Michael is beside himself, his usual position. If the reader takes him seriously, the novel will be painful from beginning to end. The only alternative reaction is boredom. In so far as one can deduce its author's place in this chaotic novel, it seems that Southall would like to share the grandmother's illusions, but feels impelled to tell his readers what he believes to be the truth about their dangerous world. And that, in effect, is what the coldly rational scientist father does to Michael, in the name of 'facing facts'.

Josh is easier reading than *Bread and Honey* and it repays the trouble of finding one's way through the hyperactive prose. The difficulties include a new Southall mannerism which with repetition becomes tiring: the use of the present participle instead of the present indicative:

> Crumbs flecking Josh's lips, panting for breath, crumbs spraying right and left, Aunt Clara shrilling with shock, 'Take a drink. Good heavens, boy, you'll choke.' Josh reeling to the edge of the veranda, somehow balancing his cup, and spitting the shortbread as far as he could spit. Drooping there as if he had been whipped, then trying to wash down the bits with tea that was scalding hot.
> 'Are you all right?'
> Josh nodding in despair.

Josh's reactions to the hazards of a few days in the country staying with a formidable great-aunt make a caricature of sensitivity. Yet the author knows it and so does Josh who is capable of some humour and self-appraisal. The reader does not have to take the ordeal of tea and shortbread with the serious compassion apparently demanded by Michael's struggle to find a handkerchief in *Bread and Honey*. Josh fails most of the tests of his country visit and evades the rest: he is wary, embarrassed and, with reason, afraid of the local boys and he chooses to walk home alone to Melbourne rather than to see them again. Southall creates in Josh a likeable anti-hero whose world is limited but not entirely self-enclosed. A later Southall novel, *What About Tomorrow?* (1977) has another hero-victim, but the emphasis is rather different from that of *Bread and Honey* or *Josh*. The pressures on the runaway newsboy, Sam Clemens, are external; he falls in love without difficulty and shows little of the psychological fragility of Michael or Josh. Perhaps in borrowing his hero's name from Mark Twain Southall gave him something of the resilience of Huckleberry Finn. Even though from its 1930s setting Sam's death in war is foreshadowed, *What About Tomorrow?* is not a novel of defeat. It combines the narrative skill of Southall's early work with the psychological interest of *Josh*; and its prose is demanding without being chaotic. Perhaps it marks a new direction for a very talented author; it is a welcome contrast with the unmediated anguish of *Bread and Honey*.

In choosing an Aboriginal boy as the hero of *Hughie* (1971), David Martin took the most obvious outsider figure in Australian literature and the one who presents the most difficulties for a satisfying literary treatment. In the nineteenth and early twentieth century children's stories already discussed, the Aborigine appears in various guises: noble primitive, sub-human savage, faithful slow-witted servant or quaint child of nature. Such stereotypes, hostile or benevolent, have one thing in common: their authors did not know their own ignorance. As racial attitudes, inside and outside Australia, began to change after World War II, and the civil rights movement in the United States suggested some parallels in this country, such confident simplifications broke down. White Australian writers who were disturbed by reading James Baldwin or Ralph Ellison during the 1950s, or soothed by Sidney Poitier in *Guess Who's Coming to Dinner?* (1967), could no longer unselfconsciously use Aborigines as minor stock characters in their fiction. They did not often need them; with the increasing preoccupation of children's writers of the 1960s with urban or suburban settings, there were few roles for an Aboriginal character to play. There are exceptions: an important one is Patricia Wrightson's *The Rocks of Honey* (1960) in which an Aboriginal boy is central to the action and presented with warmth and individuality. In this novel of country-town schoolboys, the expected roles are reversed: the white boy is the outsider in a plot which concerns Aboriginal cultural inheritance. David Martin takes a more predictable situation in *Hughie*, focusing on white society's exclusion of an Aboriginal boy who wants to come inside, quite literally, to swim in the country-town's handsome new Olympic pool.

Hughie is a protest novel, and stronger in argument than in characterization. The situation is neatly contrived to make the moral issues clear. The opening scene describes the drowning of an Aboriginal girl in the dangerous water-hole which is the local children's alternative to the Olympic pool. In trying to save her Hughie is himself almost drowned; he is saved by his friend Clancy, a white boy who uses the water-hole instead of the pool so as to have Hughie's companionship. The accident gives Clancy's parents a pretext for breaking his friendship with Hughie; they tell their son not to swim with the Aboriginal children again. As a promising competition swimmer, Clancy has every reason to train in the Olympic pool, and reluctantly he submits. Hughie, who has never questioned the colour bar, does so when it deprives him of his friend. Naïvely, he appeals to an influential local businessman, and is told to be patient:

> 'One day, I've always said, we'll outgrow all this—this black and white rigmarole. We Aussies don't really like it, it's not made for us. But it'll take a bit of time, and meanwhile the good Lord, who knows best . . . has arranged it so that white is still white and black is still black. Who are we to rush Him, if He wants to take His time?'

Hughie is depicted as an innocent who develops a sense of his rights

only under extreme provocation. Without intending it, he starts a political campaign which is taken over by a group of university students
and directed by his confident radical cousin from Sydney. Although
their demonstration ends in violence and the battle for the pool is lost,
there has been something of a change of heart in the town, with a fair
proportion of its citizens willing to consider integration. For Hughie,
it is more important to regain the friendship of Clancy; the novel ends
in their reconciliation. This final scene, with mateship reaffirmed
between black and white, is in keeping with the author's view of human
nature; he depicts a good deal of stupidity, but little malice. Apart from
two brutal Sydney policemen and one obnoxious businessman, the
adults of this novel are at least capable of being reformed. In the characterization of Hughie, an exceptionally gifted artist as well as a brave,
gentle, loyal and sensitive boy, Martin yields to the temptation to
idealize which is one of the risks of novels of this kind; it leaves the
Aborigine in stereotype.

The students who sing 'We shall overcome' in *Hughie* are the contemporaries of J. M. Couper's heroes in *The Thundering Good Today*
(1970) and *Looking for a Wave* (1973). Like Martin, Couper is concerned with political and social questions, and states of alienation. In
The Thundering Good Today the narrator and main character, Guth, is
expelled from school for painting an anti-conscription slogan on a
statue just before it is to be unveiled, 'with lots of blah-blah and local
hallelujahs', by the State Governor. The time is that of the Vietnam
war, and the issue the 'lottery' system by which Australian boys were
chosen for military service. Guth is not so much depressed by his expul-
sion as by the fact that his gesture changes nothing:

> Apparently the grim fact was that school was much the same as it
> had ever been, as comfortably lousy as ever. It wouldn't have made
> any difference if I'd scratched my head instead of the statue. And
> the statue had had a shower, and some pumice stone, and with a
> bit of armpit lotion it all smelt great. Wouldn't it bog you? Made
> me very nearly gnash my milk-shake and all ... You could go to
> the moon, so help me, and inside two days nobody would be talking
> about it, I bet. And couldn't maybe name you the guys that had
> gone there. It's a waste of time, political action, must be.

The voice here and elsewhere in the novel is like that of *The Catcher
in the Rye* in its idiom, its direct address to the reader and its tone of
wry despair. Unlike Salinger, however, Couper does not know when
to stop. The language which has an engaging liveliness and informality,

is often too clever and allusive, drawing attention to itself at the expense of theme and characterization. 'I was incensed', Guth says, 'incensed as a stained-glass window'. Couper's *Looking for a Wave* is much the same in tone, but with a different set of issues. Bikies, pack-rape, an unmarried mother with V.D., and a child born with a deformity caused by pre-natal drug-taking are some of the elements in this overcrowded novel. Both have statements to make about victimized youth in a society which Guth describes as 'a valley that's all dry bones ... a derelict car dump. And they expect us to fight to keep it derelict'.

The 'us' and 'them' of Couper's novels is youth against the consumer society. He does, however, find some adults who share the scepticism and anti-materialism of the new generation, and there is companionship to be found within the groups of young people. In Esta de Fossard's *The Alien* (1977), a Greek migrant boy is solitary and desperate in a world of indifferent or brutal human relationships. Home, school and city are presented as places of sexual violence. The parents of Nick, the sixteen-year-old hero, migrated to Australia in search of a higher standard of living; and the father, at least, is punished for his materialism by the near-destruction of his marriage. Although the author gives an idealized vision of Greek society in Nick's memory of the order and beauty of his early years, she sees Greek women as its victims. Nick's mother takes a job in a Melbourne factory and learns from the other women workers her right to resist male authority. Unhappily, the boy hears his parents quarrelling and his mother's refusal to submit to 'crude love-making'. The sex-and-violence motif pervades the novel. At school Nick is tormented by Australian boys for his apparent effeminacy; he responds by trying to rape a girl whose 'openly seductive behaviour' encourages the attempt. Near the school a younger girl, for whom Nick feels the sympathy of a fellow-outcast, is raped and murdered. Nick discovers her body, which is described with all the grisly relish of a Sunday newspaper. In a state of shock, he turns for refuge to his only other friend, a middle-aged European migrant, but there, instead of comfort, he finds his second body for the day. Although this one is a natural death it is, understandably, too much for Nick who collapses and is taken to hospital. When he recovers a little, he considers his problems with a new detachment which the author seems to see as maturity:

But now it no longer seemed important to Nick whether his parents stayed together or separated—perhaps for them, as for him, this new country was leading them to a realisation of their individuality for the first time. He understood that if he was seeking freedom to explore his personality in this new land, perhaps his parents had the same need.

So we leave Nick, deep in platitudes, searching for his identity. *The Alien*, a crude, mechanical novel, must have fitted someone's notion of a children's book. It appears under a reputable publisher's imprint with a dust-jacket prediction that it 'will be enjoyed by young people everywhere of twelve years and over'.

Simon French's *Hey Phantom Singlet* (1975) announces its Australian origin in its title. In the United States it would have to be *Hey Phantom Tee-Shirt* and in Britain *Hey Phantom Vest*. Singlets are all-Australian, and so is the idiom of this fresh and likeable novel. Written when the author was still at high school, its narrative and dialogue take full advantage of that perspective; the author did not have to guess how boys talk to one another. The central character, Math Roxon, is a Sydney twelve-year-old in his first term at an inner-city high school, wearing a uniform for the first time and disliking it. His orange 'phantom singlet' and a Dr Zhivago fur hat are worn as signals of non-conformism; they assert a self-confidence within the group which Math does not possess. His background makes him feel an outsider among his school-friends, he misses his father, who appears to have deserted the family, and his mother has little energy to spare from housework and a full-time job. Math's search for his father gives the book its rather slight plot. Its theme is loneliness, with Math's attempts to assert his difference from the other boys seen finally as his means of defence.

In his next novel, *Cannily, Cannily* (1981), Simon French gave a fuller and more accomplished study of an outsider. Again, the situation is that of a boy starting school. The setting is a country town and the boy's parents are newcomers, itinerant workers for whom home is a succession of caravan parks. Their nomadic life is a matter of choice; they are middle-class drop-outs from the affluent society who take to the road so as to be free of suburban pressures to conformity. In the settled society of the country town, among men 'who wore riding boots and Akubra hats and talked about crops and stock', Kath and Buckley Huon and their son Trevor are seen as irresponsible gypsies. Society's disapproval is just what pleases Kath and Buckley, but Trevor, who did not choose to be unconventional, feels ill at ease. His mother's complacent amusement at the conventions of his new school is no help. In an attempt to show the other boys that he is not an ineffectual freak, Trevor decides to train for the football team. He consults his mother:

'What would you and Dad reckon about me playing football?'

'Don't think we'd mind.'

'I mean, playing in a team . . . if I played in a proper team, what would you and Dad think?'

'We'd think you were nuts. But it's your decision.'

In Trevor's predicament, Simon French captures a relatively new fictional situation. Kath and Buckley made their bid for independence as members of the counter-culture in the 1960s. Their son, in the late 1970s, is an outsider with nowhere to go, except inside. The author does not argue for the virtues of fitting a social pattern, but he does show the illusory nature of the freedom offered by the parents. *Cannily, Cannily* is shrewd, amusing and well-constructed: an interesting look at a new kind of alienation.

Alienation could go no farther than it does in Lee Harding's *Displaced Person* (1979), an Australian Children's Book award-winner which was simultaneously published in the United States. Perhaps some minor changes in vocabulary were made with an American audience in mind; the hero, for example, talks about getting good 'grades' at school. Its tone and idiom would present nothing unfamiliar to American readers. The literary antecedents of this story of psychological nightmare are Poe, as the author indicates in his epigraph ('All that we see or seem is but a dream within a dream') and Ellison's *Invisible Man* (1952), which it resembles closely in situation. Ellison used invisibility as a metaphor for being black and alienated in the United States; Harding uses it for being young and alienated in Melbourne, or anywhere else. The hero tells his own story in a tone of suppressed panic. From the vague alarm of finding that people no longer hear or see him clearly, he comes to the realization that he is a ghostly invisible figure, without form or substance in his own world. Then that world fades, leaving him isolated in an eerie twilight, neither living nor dead:

> I somehow managed to keep moving . . . And while I walked I wondered about the vast, silent greyworld and people who disappeared without trace, missing persons whose absence left no logical explanation. I wondered how many of them had suffered my fate. Perhaps God was a clumsy bookkeeper . . . And I asked myself: Had I ceased to exist in the outside world because people had ceased to notice me?

There is nothing exceptional about the hero of *Displaced Person* except his predicament. The book gives a vision of an arbitrary universe, of lost people and lost connections, in which there is nothing to do except

Illustration by Margaret Paice from *Run to the Mountains*

to 'keep moving'. It draws its suspense from the hero's efforts to maintain reason and to learn the rules (if there are rules) of non-existence. It is an ingenious, well-constructed and assured piece of work which gains its effects through understatement.

There can be few more familiar figures in children's fiction than the orphan; and the orphanage child is an obvious choice for an outsider role. Two intelligent and well-written Australian novels of the last decade take an institutional 'home' as the starting point for exploring the emotional problems of social misfits. Margaret Paice's *Run to the Mountains* (1972) is a picaresque tale of three runaways from a Melbourne reformatory. Its strength is in the narrative rather than the characterization, with the question of when and how the boys will be caught taking precedence over their states of mind. Nevertheless, the author places them unambiguously as society's rejects, showing with varying degrees of intensity their reasons for resentment. *Dingo Boy* (1980) by Michael Dugan is a sourly memorable novel which reverses the happy-ever-after formula of such rescued orphan stories as L. M. Montgomery's *Anne of Green Gables* (1908) and Jean Webster's *Daddy Long-legs* (1912). An elderly farmer and his wife take a boy from a Melbourne orphanage to live with them. The boy, Carl, who has been happy enough in the Home, is wary of the new arrangement; he has heard stories about foster-parents who take children only for the cheap labour they can give. His suspicions are fully justified by Ray and Ena, a dreary, self-centred pair whose cruelty takes the form of bland indifference to Carl's feelings. They feed him well, work him to exhaustion and notice neither his loneliness nor his distaste for some of the tasks he is given. The point of rebellion comes when, after unwillingly helping to set traps for dingoes, he sees one of them dying slowly and painfully. Ray will not disturb himself to shoot the trapped animal, so with repugnance the boy puts an end to its struggles.

The episode strengthens his feelings of identification with the outlaws who threaten Ray's sheep:

> As he sat there Carl felt a bond with the dingoes. Useless to human society, they had been forced into an environment that was unnatural to them—these rugged hills offered little sustenance. Nor had his coming here been of his choosing. Yet the dingoes hung onto what was left of their freedom, whatever the cost . . . Carl could not help admiring such a struggle for freedom.

With no one to talk to, the boy becomes increasingly resentful. Ray and Ena remain delighted with their own good sense in finding a sturdy young farm worker who costs them almost nothing, and congratulate themselves on giving a home to a city waif. The boy then devises a means of escape and revenge. It must be something to make forgiveness impossible, so that he can be sure of being left in the Home. He cuts a hole in a fence to let the dingoes in and, as they fall hungrily on Ray's sheep, he starts walking to the railway station:

> Once on the train he ate his sandwiches and began re-reading *The Wind in the Willows* . . . It would just about last him to the city.
> At the next stop an old lady got into his compartment. She was large, cheerful, laden with shopping bags, and chatty.
> 'Off for a holiday in the city?' she asked as she settled herself and the train pulled away. Carl closed his book.
> 'No,' he said, 'I've had my holiday. I'm going home.'

With this neat, ironic ending Michael Dugan undermines the literary convention which identifies happiness and wholesome living with country life. *Dingo Boy* recalls, though with less power and less bitterness, a story by Saki which shows a child's revenge on adult cruelty. In Saki's 'Sredni Vashtar' the victimized child arranges to have his oppressor killed by proxy, using a pet animal as his agent. The dingoes of Dugan's novel, like Saki's polecat-ferret enact the child's anger, but their action is limited to killing sheep. They do not, however, spare Ena's pampered pet sheep Cynthia, the object of all the attention she denies to the boy. Briefly, the boy regrets Cynthia's death, but on the whole he is satisfied as he turns towards his orphanage 'home'.

The novels considered in this chapter are as varied in tone as they are in quality. They have in common a concern with the relationship between a more or less troubled protagonist and a society in which he, or she, cannot easily find a place. It is usually he; alienation and rebellion are seen in general as masculine states of mind. It may be argued that Sylvie of *The Min-Min*, discussed in Chapter 15, is an alienated heroine. Yet there is an important difference; Sylvie's quarrel is with her father, not with society as a whole, and her reconciliation takes place within the family.

There is nothing surprising about this uneven division of nonconformist roles. Children's fiction in Australia has so far heard few echoes from the women's movement, and although the 1980s will almost certainly bring changes, the first three post-war decades confirm traditional patterns. Feminine conflicts begin and end at home; masculine conflicts are with the wider world and do not necessarily end in reconciliation. Again, it is worth remembering *The Catcher in the Rye*. Holden Caulfield could not endure home, school or society. His sister Phoebe could and did.

17

The Uses of the Past

'. . . I was born in the sub-tropics of Australia. Not that I spent all my life there, only my young years, and most of it far from cities. I lived a life that was at once new and old. The country was new and the land itself very old—the oldest in the world, geologists say, and in spite of the brash pioneering atmosphere that still existed, even a child could sense the antiquity of it . . . My body ran about in the southern sunlight but my inner world had subtler colours, the greys and snows of England where little Joe swept all the crossings and the numberless greens of Ireland which seemed to me to be inhabited solely by poets plucking harps, heroes lordily cutting off each other's heads, and veiled ladies sitting on the ground keening.'

P. L. Travers[1]

In the passage just quoted the Queensland-born creator of that very English nursery fantasy, *Mary Poppins*, describes a division between past and present, between inner and outer worlds, which for her was not resolved. Her feeling for the past, nourished by the myths of Ireland and the novels of nineteenth century England, found no sustenance in her Australian surroundings; the land, lacking an accessible mythology, offered nothing to her imaginative inner world. Thus, a very gifted writer for children could create nothing directly from her own childhood: she was never culturally at home.

The great challenge for the early white settlers in Australia was the land; they took physical possession of it with difficulty. Imaginative possession was even harder to achieve, yet to do so has been felt as a necessity by most Australian poets, novelists and painters. The dominant tradition of landscape painting, and the preoccupation with rural settings among writers of fiction to the present day give evidence of the need of the European imagination to make itself at home in a strange land. The urge to find or create a past is reflected not only in the many historical novels for adults but also in semi-autobiographical novels or memoirs such as Hal Porter's *The Watcher on the Cast-Iron Balcony* (1963), George Johnston's *My Brother Jack* (1964), and Randolph Stow's *The Merry-Go-Round in the Sea* (1965) and many others in a genre which has been seen as distinctively Australian.[2] These reminiscent narratives of Australian childhood are attempts to unite the inner and the outer worlds, to reconcile the division which Travers describes.

In children's literature of the post-war period three distinct yet related approaches to the past may be seen. There is the realistic historical novel, represented by the pioneering chronicles of Mavis Thorpe Clark and Eleanor Spence or by David Martin's period pieces. Another way back is the memoir: H. F. Brinsmead's *Longtime Passing* (1973) and its sequels are the only notable examples of this genre to be written for children, although there are many for a general audience. A third approach is that of fantasy. Nan Chauncy's *Tangara* (1960) and Ruth Park's *Playing Beatie Bow* (1980) bring past and present together by means of a time-travel story. Patricia Wrightson, from *An Older Kind of Magic* (1972) to the Wirrun trilogy (1977-81), explores 'the spirit of place', using Aboriginal myth as a means to understanding the land and its past.

Most of the realistic historical novels concentrate on capturing a sense of place and period in the individual fortunes of anonymous and relatively unimportant people. Few characters are drawn from life; if they are, their roles are usually minor ones at the edge of the action. In a country without pageantry whose history has no major internal conflicts, a few Governors with gold braid and unused swords would not go far; it is only sensible to leave them alone in favour of the man in moleskins with the broad-brimmed hat. The struggle to conquer the land or the search for gold are the recurring themes, and the emphasis is social rather than political. The first three of Mavis Thorpe Clark's historical novels differ very little in style from 1940s stories like *Margery Pym*, or in material from the nineteenth century settlers' novels. *The Brown Land Was Green* (1956), *Gully of Gold* (1958) and *They Came South* (1963) are competent narratives of pioneering life in Victoria, with the careful accumulation of details of settlement their main merit. Although, like the early settlers' novels, they have hardy, hard-working English immigrant boys in the foreground, they show their modern origin in creating important active roles for girls. The need to make good in the new country is the main impulse, with the physical dangers and reversals of colonial fortunes and some human villainy supplying the series of events. Mavis Thorpe Clark has less need to explain Australian conditions than her predecessors, and she is more economical with such special effects as bushfires, floods and Aboriginal raids. Yet she has new obligations. The nineteenth century reader needed to be told a good deal about the strange qualities of the new country. The modern reader, better informed about Australia, has to have facts of a different kind worked into the narrative: an observation about child labour in the 1830s, for example, in *They Came South*, or a reminder in *Gully of Gold* that 'schooling was neither free nor compulsory'.

The modern story offers dialogue as an easy way of presenting facts in digestible form. At times, in Thorpe Clark's books, it is awkwardly done, with characters solemnly trading unnecessary information in unlikely exchanges:

'Good rations, too; ten whole pounds of flour, twelve pounds of butcher's meat, two pounds of sugar and a quarter pound of tea. When shepherds can have that much to eat, sir, it must be a good place!'

'Yes, indeed,' Edward agreed. 'This is August 1839—little more than four years since John Batman said, "This is the place for a village". Yet I'm told that before this year is out, a superintendent is to be appointed—Charles Joseph La Trobe.'

In characterization, none of the three is more than adequate. There are melodramatic plot contrivances—a lost ex-convict father in *Gully of Gold*, rival heirs to a fortune in *They Came South*—and some mild boy-and-girl romance, yet, in spite of such attempts to add human interest to these pioneering chronicles, there is more fact than feeling in their total effect.

With her fourth historical novel, *Blue Above the Trees* (1967), Mavis Thorpe Clark achieved a much more interesting and coherent narrative with better characterization. This book gains from its comparatively narrow focus; with one family, one setting and no sub-plots, there is room to develop conflicts of personality, and create inner tension as well as external action. The single setting gives scope, too, for the author's sense of a particular place: the Great Forest of South Gippsland before the work of clearing it began. The story is as much about the forest as the family of invaders, the Whitburns, who come from England to repair their fortunes during the 1870s. William Whitburn, the father, plans to spend no more than ten years in the colony, and with the profits of the enterprise to fulfil a long-held ambition to farm in Devon. He does not succeed so easily; the land he claims and clears finally holds him so strongly that he forgets about going home to England. Meanwhile, the new environment tests his relationship with his wife, his daughter Clarissa and his son Simon, all of whom resist his will in different ways. It is in the working out of these family conflicts that *Blue Above the Trees* most clearly separates itself from the nineteenth century juvenile novels whose pattern of external events it follows. Although there are plenty of marital disputes in Victorian fiction—those of Bishop and Mrs Proudie, Tertius and Rosamund Lydgate among many others—such conflicts tend to be kept out of children's fiction of the period, and rebellion against parents is not endorsed. When seventeen-year-old Clarissa, restless and bored in the solitude of the forest, runs away to Melbourne, she is made as unhappy by the 'deceit' of a man as many Victorian heroines. Her defiance is not only forgiven by her father; it is approved by the author. Clarissa returns, disenchanted, to the bush but she is seen as the city's victim, and not as a disobedient daughter whose wilfulness invites punishment. The dialogue, which keeps to a middle course between nineteenth century formality and colloquial idiom, places the balance of sympathy on Clarissa's side:

> She glared across the flickering lamplight first at her brother, then at her father. 'It's not what I want! Can't you see father. I don't want to live out here . . . out in the bush . . . walled in by that forest. I like people—I want to be with people. Let me go back to Melbourne—where I can earn my own living.'. . .
>
> William thumped the table and the lamp sputtered. 'No daughter of mine is going to run loose in a city!' he said. 'This is your home, girl—and your work is here. To pay our debts and win fortune for ourselves, we all have to do our share. You'd better get to like it.' She answered him before she sat down. 'At least . . . I shall never give thanks for it.'

If Clarissa sounds a decade or two ahead of her time in her New Woman consciousness, and even more modern in her idiom ('I like people—I want to be with people'), her brother Simon is as contemporary as last week. His rebellion against his father goes against the whole Whitburn venture: the clearing of the forest for farming. Simon discovers a pair of lyrebirds and becomes their friend and protector, he pleads with his father to spare twenty acres of forest so that the birds will be undisturbed. His father (surprisingly well informed about lyrebirds) at first refuses:

> 'Simon, this is not the only part of the eastern coast of Australia where there is rainforest, and lyrebirds and the rest. Lyrebirds can be found—certainly only in a narrow mountain belt—as far north as southern Queensland. They're not going to be lost altogether.'
>
> 'Maybe not. But why should they be lost to this area, which seems so specially their own? And where the most beautiful of the species live?'

Mavis Thorpe Clark's conservation theme is hard to reconcile with a pioneering story. She makes an acceptable compromise, in which Simon gets his twenty-acre sanctuary but accepts the idea that the loss of the forest must be balanced against the family's survival and the needs of hungry city-dwellers: 'there are so many people in the world', Clarissa reminds him, 'to be fed from these pastures'.

Even though Simon talks like a conservation pamphlet, the clash of viewpoint he initiates adds life and energy to the story. His arguments, of course, are not as new as his rhetoric; they may be found, for example, in Louisa Meredith's *Tasmanian Friends and Foes* (1880). Yet he is not a typical figure of his time, or a representative fourteen-year-old. He is the author's spokesman in the novel, her means of interpreting the past for the present. Although his views are at times awkwardly presented, they give the conventional pioneering story a unifying idea as well as a source of suspense. Like most historical novels, *Blue Above the Trees* reveals at least as much about the time of its writing as that of its setting; it is a twentieth century perspective on nineteenth century Australia. Mavis Thorpe Clark finds the meaning of the Australian past in the individual achievements of the pioneers and in their close, uneasy relationship with the land. The best of her prose may be seen in long descriptive passages such as an account of a forest fire, in which she shows the land's destructive power.

Eleanor Spence's historical novels have less conflict, and they depict a softer landscape. *Lillipilly Hill* (1960), *The Switherby Pilgrims* (1967) and *Jamberoo Road* (1969) are all primarily stories of family life. Their pioneering background, presented unobtrusively, provides a set of challenges for the characters who are always the essential concern. There are close resemblances between *Lillipilly Hill* with its 1880s setting and Spence's *The Seventh Pebble* (1980), a story of the 1930s; both show con-

trasting family groups, divided in the later novel by religion and class
and in the early one by nationality and class. The English immigrant
family of *Lillipilly Hill* does not undergo any of the physical hardships
of colonial life; its difficulty is in accepting new ideas about ways of
living. The heroine, Harriet Wilmot, is an enterprising twelve-year-old
who enjoys the outdoor freedom of a New South Wales farming district and quickly makes friends with the local children. She has no
regrets for England and the 'tall, blank-faced sedate old house in a quiet
Kensington square'. The other Wilmot children, as quiet and sedate as
the Kensington house, at first dislike the new country; Mrs Wilmot
worries about snakes, unladylike behaviour and other colonial dangers,
and wants to go home. The narrative describes Harriet's campaign to
assimilate these reluctant colonials and, in a series of encounters
between the native-born and the newcomers, shows genteel English
manners giving way to easy informality:

> 'The butter nearly runs away while I look at it', [Polly] observed
> cheerfully. 'And I've been half the morning making it too.'
> 'Why do you put it in the well?' asked Harriet.
> Polly stared at her.
> 'Why indeed! You don't know much, do you? To keep it cool, of
> course.' Her voice was rough, but far from unkind. She was a plump,
> brisk, red-headed girl, eighteen years old—Harriet had certainly never
> encountered a servant quite like her. Polly 'lacked respect', Mrs Wil-
> mot said, and could rarely bring herself to address the children as
> 'Miss' or 'Master'. She was a Colonial born and bred, and although
> she had been in domestic service for six years, she had lost none of her
> native toughness and independence.

Harriet Wilmot has an almost exact counterpart in temperament in
the heroine of *The Switherby Pilgrims*, Cassie Brown. Cassie, too, finds in
Australia the opportunities denied her in England, and the new country
is again seen as a place of social equality and opportunity. This novel has
a more substantial story than *Lillipilly Hill*. It describes the colonial
adventure of Miss Arabella Braithwaite, an intrepid lady from an English vicarage who collects ten semi-destitute village children and takes
them to start a new life in Australia. *The Switherby Pilgrims* and its
sequel *Jamberoo Road* show the various ways in which the children learn
to work together, transforming themselves in the process into a united
family. An eleventh child is added when a young Aboriginal boy follows the English group from Sydney to their land in the Illawarra district. The circle is complete with the addition of Eben, a young convict,

assigned to Miss Braithwaite as a servant, but soon to be given older-brother status by the children.

Eleanor Spence's modern version of the settler's tale is characterized by a strong interest in individual talents and ambitions and by its attitudes towards race, class and opportunities for women. Cassie Brown, who would have been an uneducated servant in England, learns Latin and mathematics and becomes a governess; she is given the chance to marry her employer's son and return to England as a lady. She refuses, and marries the ex-convict Eben, with whom she lives happily and prosperously in Sydney, combining the roles of wife, mother and part-time author. As with Cassie, so with the other children; all are given a vocation to suit their gifts. The Aboriginal boy, who in a nineteenth century story would have been taught prayers and useful work, is left to come and go as he pleases. He is not seen as a victim; Miss Braithwaite does not rescue him for white civilization, but allows him to join her family because he shows a liking for the children's company and seems to have been cut off from his own tribe. The three Spence novels of nineteenth century Australia do not ignore the difficulties of pioneering, but they stress its pleasures. Even the most testing part of *The Switherby Pilgrims*, a journey through wild country, has compensations:

> For her own part, Cassie was positively enjoying it. She slithered and stumbled along, knowing that it did not matter in the least if she muddied and tore her frock, or displayed too much ankle, or let her hair be caught in overhanging twigs. She felt as light and free as any native bird in this wild undisciplined land, where every privilege must be fought for.

Spence's dialogue, in these novels as in her modern stories, is good, plain and natural. It presents the Anglo-Australian contrasts easily and economically, without the burden of information which weighs down so much historical fiction. The state of England in the 1840s and the likely fate of workhouse children are described in the conversations between Miss Braithwaite and her brother. The picture of the colony is built up as the newcomers discuss among themselves its surprises and its problems, and in some descriptive passages, usually functional rather than decorative, such as the glimpse of a prosperous settler's garden with wilting English flowers in *Jamberoo Road*. Eleanor Spence's Australia is a landscape with figures. Its wildness and freedom correspond with the energy and enterprise of her heroines. The theme, in *Lillipilly Hill* and in the two Switherby novels, is the making of a colonial girl to match a vigorous new society.

Illustration by Doreen Roberts from *Jamberoo Road*

David Martin's novels of the past stress the strangeness, the oddities and contradictions of Australian life. This Hungarian-born Jewish author grew up in Germany, joined the International Brigade in Spain in 1937, spent the war years in Britain and worked in India as a foreign correspondent before settling in Australia in 1949. With that diverse experience of societies in times of crisis it is not surprising that he should be an alert observer, finding variety and contrast where the Australian-born might see sameness. Commenting on the use of the past in his fiction, Martin says: 'I seem to be approaching Australia somewhat obliquely . . . Am I still building half-way houses, perhaps?'[3] His first historical novel, *The Chinese Boy* (1973), is set in the 1860s, on the goldfields of Kiandra and Lambing Flat, with the main perspective that of an unwilling exile, the fourteen-year-old Ho. Ho sees Australia as anything but a land of sunshine and fortune; its people are hostile, the weather wet and cold and even the stars seem different from those that shine at home. At Kiandra in the Australian Alps, the gold-seekers are made insignificant by the landscape, 'man-ants in their thousands [living] practically in the open, between the earth they were gouging and the sky they had no time to look up to'.

With Ho as the unifying figure, *The Chinese Boy* looks at the life of the goldfields. A motley collection of various nationalities, the prospectors are shown, on the whole, as greedy, suspicious and violent. They live by improvised rules which barely constrain chaos. The legal system, to which the Chinese appeal when they are swindled, lacks the impersonal dignity of justice:

> Ho had never been inside a court of law, but his uncle [Hong] . . . was ready to make allowances for the simpler customs of this raw country. Yet he was shocked when the public was called to order and the magistrate entered and took his seat. Was this supposed to be a Mandarin, even of the seventh and lowest grade, a dispenser of justice in the prosperous colony of a great kingdom? . . . He was a quite ordinary, rather stout gentleman, dressed like a tradesman, who could have walked in straight from the Taproom. So far from feeling reassured by this alien informality, Hong was frightened by it.

The substance of justice is as deficient as the form. The court case, in which the Chinese are inevitably the losers, becomes a goldfields entertainment, watched with contemptuous amusement by more than a hundred diggers. It is one of many diversions: a circus, a prize-fight, a Sportsmen's Ball, a travelling phrenologist's demonstration. David Martin adds to these murder, attempted murder, a bushranger's attack and the anti-Chinese riots of Lambing Flat. The novel is not only about being Chinese in a hostile society; it is a panorama of Australian life in the 1860s period, with the emphasis on contrasting moods of hope and defeat, casual kindness and sudden brutality among the people. The Chinese, with their sense of order and their loyalty to the family group, are used to comment on the individualism of the British, American and Australian miners. Ho, the central figure, is scarcely developed as a character; he is observer, representative victim and, because he speaks English better than most of his group, interpreter. He is the author's means of viewing Australian society in a time of rapid growth. The parallels with the period of post-war migration to Australia may have roused Martin's interest in the gold rushes; the racial and ethnic prejudices of the late 1940s and the 1950s were expressed in ways not so different from those of *The Chinese Boy*:

> You're mad, you don't know how to live! Toil like convicts and die before you spend a shilling. You never have a good time, 'cept you get rotten on opium. Never join in no new rush—too mean-minded, wouldn't take the risk. The likes of us tear our tripes out, and you come and fossick through our old tailings, which we might have to go back to some day. You hang on where a sparrow would hop the twig. Like to starve us out, eh? Maybe you won't though! God knows what you do in your temples, those Joss Houses of yours. You're asking for trouble, crowding decent folk. It's us what own this country!'

The idiom, contemporary rather than mid-Victorian, reinforces the sense of *The Chinese Boy* as a comment on modern Australian society, obliquely made in a historical excursion. *The Man in the Red Turban* (1978) resembles the earlier novel in choosing another period of social unrest, the Depression of the early 1930s, and setting an exotic, alien figure against a changing Australian landscape. The alien in this novel is an Indian hawker, friend and ally of an Australian boy and girl who travel in his wagon across the Victorian countryside. The picaresque mode suits David Martin's talent for describing eccentric people and odd happenings; it is part of the convention of 'on the road' stories to vary mood with place, bringing comic and terrifying incidents together without the need for causal connections. The frauds and tricksters who flourish in times of economic hardship are made more or less plausible in this period setting. There are some contrasts with *The Chinese Boy* in the treatment of the racial question. The Indian is less vulnerable than the Chinese; he is a familiar figure, welcomed by most of the isolated country women who buy his goods. But, like the Chinese, he wants to go home as soon as he has the money. He knows, too, that his day is over: with cars and buses and closer settlement, the travelling shop is outmoded. 'I like Australia', he says, 'but is not my country'.

The Cabby's Daughter (1974), set in 1903, has a single focus, and one Victorian country town accommodates all the action. It is the first-person, reminiscent narrative of Bess Tillick, the cabby's daughter of the title. Her mother's death and her father's habitual drunkenness leave Bess in charge of the almost destitute household she is determined to keep together; on the edge of society she forages for herself and her brother. The country town is quite unlike the prosaic place usually presented in Australian fiction; it is a shady, neo-Dickensian underworld.

Bess is threatened by an escaped maniac, sexually attacked by an unctuous pawnbroker and swindled in a mail-order fraud by a 'Magnetic Healer' to whom she appeals when she thinks she might be pregnant. There are a few kindly, ordinary adult figures in Martin's freakish gallery, but his imagination is more engaged in depicting oddities like Bess's half-crazy grandmother who lives by scavenging for old clothes. Although Bess's situation resembles that of some of Dickens's neglected children, she is more resilient and except in sexual matters less innocent than most of his heroines. The author does not present her as a pathetic victim; she tells her own story calmly, looking back with some pride and almost no self-pity at her younger self. Like Martin's other novels of the past, *The Cabby's Daughter* is an exploration of the fringes of Australian society, where he finds and celebrates the grotesque.

Valerie Thompson's trilogy of the gold rush period, *Rough Road South* (1975), *Gold on the Wind* (1977) and *The Mountain Between* (1981), is a leisurely re-working of some situations familiar in nineteenth century novels of Australian life. The main themes are gold-seeking and its dangers, the land, and the contrast between English and Australian manners. They are brought together in the story of Rob Howell, a fourteen-year-old English boy from a well-to-do family who, by the sudden death of his older brother, is stranded in Sydney without

Illustration by Edwina Bell from *Rough Road South*

friends or money. The first of the three novels uses Rob's journey from Sydney to Melbourne as a means of describing the colonial scene. The friendships he makes on the road show the contrasting ways in which men responded to the opportunities of the new land. Two men, in particular, befriend and influence him. The first is a good-natured American prospector with a weakness for gambling and an obsessive ambition to be the first to strike gold in a new field. The other is a prosperous, reliable squatter who sees the gold-seekers as a threat to the settlement:

> 'I just hope', said Uncle Alec fervently, 'that no one finds gold round here. I shudder at the thought. All my good work gone for nothing. The sheep disturbed—probably disappearing as fast as they could be eaten. A crowd of ex-convicts and ticket-of-leave men all over the place. The ground all turned to mullock heaps.'

Necessity as well as loyalty to his first protector, the American, takes Rob for a time to the goldfields, but prospecting does not capture his imagination as the land does. In Melbourne, he finds city life disagreeable and dangerous. In Sydney, when he is reunited with his family in the final book of the trilogy, it is boring and restrictive. Valerie Thompson shows the land as the authentic Australia, and she finds a prospective wife for Rob in a fearless colonial girl, Elizabeth, the squatter's niece. The Thompson novels resemble those of Eleanor Spence in using the new society as a means of discussing matters of class and the role of women. Rob's 'mate' from Melbourne, an illiterate, semi-reformed pickpocket, strains the Howell family's notions of suitable friendships for a gentleman's son. There is strong feminist feeling in a sub-plot concerning Rob's aunt, a deserted wife who starts her own school, and in the portrayal of his discontented sisters. The model Australian is the strong-minded, unpretentious squatter, Alec Barker, for whom the land is not a means to fortune but a source of continuing challenge and reward. Those who come to plunder, the author implies, will be punished by the natural forces they do not understand. The Thompson novels differ from their nineteenth century counterparts in attributing to the landscape an independent life. Rob's awareness of its power as well as its subtle beauty marks him as one of those whom it will not destroy. After at first seeing only 'a terrible inhospitable country', he looks more closely:

> . . . it was only now when he found himself surrounded by the desolation of the previous summer's bushfires, and the great contrast with the untouched green furrow of the valley, that he became fully

conscious of the drama in the landscape. The backdrop of white-topped mountains, asleep in a timeless brooding, gave rise to a feeling that they would be watching over him as he rode on . . . lying there he could see things to which he had been blind before. Endless variety in the trees, the patterns and colours of limitless distance, the variations in the evergreens and winter browns that surrounded him . . . there was so much to see if one knew how to look.

Like David Martin's Chinese boy, Valerie Thompson's hero is less a character than a point of view; the trilogy's central concern is the relationship between the newcomers and the land. There is more individual interest, and an actual historical event, in Paul Buddee's *The Escape of The Fenians* (1971). This novel, set in Western Australia in 1875, describes the successful Irish-American adventure in which six Irish political prisoners were rescued by a group of their supporters in an American whaling ship. This must be one of the most cheerful episodes in Australian convict history as well as one of the last. There was no loss of life, and at least from Irish-Australians there was a good deal of local sympathy for the prisoners. As narrator, Paul Buddee uses one of the few fictional characters in the story: thirteen-year-old Jamie O'Mara who acts as courier for the rescue party. The episode makes a good suspense story, and it has the added interest of showing the convict system in its final stage, an anachronism after nearly a century of settlement.

Joan Phipson's *Bass & Billy Martin* (1972) is an exploration story of early colonial days. Instead of the more familiar thirsty trek into the Australian desert with Leichhardt, she describes the series of sea voyages in which Bass discovered the strait between New South Wales and Van Diemen's Land. Billy Martin, a headstrong fourteen-year-old who sailed with Bass, is there to give humour and human interest to the narrative. He is also there to ask questions; a naïve newcomer from Britain to whom all things Australian are strange, he is a useful means of giving the reader the facts and sensations of colonial life. As Bass's willing pupil as well as his servant, Billy absorbs information of all kinds. The narrative method is a modern version of such nineteenth century documentaries as Howitt's *A Boy's Adventures in the Wilds of Australia*, but with an important difference in emphasis. Although the feelings of Howitt's boy-narrator—fear, pleasure, wonder, disgust—give a human dimension to the journey of exploration, these appear as a series of reactions, not a process of change. Joan Phipson sees Billy, Bass, Flinders and, by implication, other white men in Australia as undergoing a profoundly disturbing experience. When Billy explores a cave and finds signs of Aboriginal habitation he is troubled by 'the life that he sensed was all about him, but that he could not understand . . . [and] he was more alone, more desolate than he had ever been in his life'. Alone in a storm he is even more deeply disturbed:

> About him on the bare patches of rock the dust and twigs and dead leaves whirled and flung themselves at his face. He clung to the rock face behind him, bewildered and lost. Even the secrets of the cave faded into insignificance before this great upheaval of nature. Humans, black or white, were quite unimportant to this empty landscape. Never before had he felt that the earth he stepped upon was anything but a background for himself and the people around him. Now he understood that he—and Bass and Thistle and all of them— and all the miserable jetsam in the colony, were, like the natives, no more than one of the species of animal life crawling on its face.

Although *Bass & Billy Martin* at first glance seems an uncharacteristic Phipson venture into costume drama it is closely linked with such novels as *The Way Home* and *The Cats* by its psychological dimension and its concern with the relationship between man and the natural world. Billy's sense of human insignificance is not necessarily a twentieth century state of mind. There is, for example, a scene in Clarke's *His Natural Life* in which an escaped convict, alone in a sea-cave, has a similar vision of his own irrelevance. Nevertheless Phipson's novel clearly separates itself from most earlier historical novels in making an inner journey part of the external action.

H. F. Brinsmead's reminiscences of a pioneering family in *Longtime Passing* (1973), *Once There Was a Swagman* (1979) and *Longtime Dreaming* (1982) differ from the historical fiction so far described in tone and in their semi-autobiographical form. The approach to the past is by way of Brinsmead's own family history; and the shaping spirit is memory. The narrator's early experiences and her inheritance of family stories come together in a leisurely narrative of a 1920s childhood in the Blue Mountains of New South Wales. *Longtime Passing* is partly a story of exploration. Man's efforts to subdue this wild, hostile region are shown as dangerous; many destroy themselves in the attempt. Apart from the obvious physical hardships and the loneliness, the invaders of the Longtime district risk retribution if they disturb 'the silent secret land' of the Aboriginal tribe, the Daruk. The Truelances of the Brinsmead stories respect the spirit of the region, and so, the author says, they became 'part of the mountains'.

Longtime Passing opens with an account of the first white explorer's venture into Longtime's sacred tribal region, in the early nineteenth century. This episode frames the chronicles of the Truelances who came a century later; their story is personal, domestic and predominantly serene. The author describes a secure family life in which the pleasures of pioneering and the sense of achievement by far outweigh the difficulties. The form of the novel is anecdotal and the mood skilfully balanced between comedy and nostalgia. The characterization of the Truelance parents in particular helps to give the novels their individuality; both are eccentrics whose pioneering is as full of comic miscalculations as of stoic endurance. Just outside the immediate family circle, some equally eccentric uncles, aunts and neighbours make up a close-knit community, held together by their isolation from the ordinary world of streets, shops and schools. The Truelance kitchen, 'full of warmth, and a smell of clean sheets and bread baking', is the safe family centre from which the children go out to explore an exciting and beautiful natural world. The Longtime stories give an idyllic picture of an Australian childhood. They bring together time, place and emotion with the authority of direct experience, and they convey the sense, through family recollections going back beyond the author's own memory, of a shared, accessible past. Better than any other realistic Australian historical fiction for children, the Longtime novels solve the problem of linking past and present.

Most of the historical novels described in this chapter show some degree of awkwardness in projecting contemporary ideas into the minds of their fictional characters. To comment on such questions as the conservationist rhetoric of Mavis Thorpe Clark's *Blue Above the Hills* or the post-Darwinian consciousness of Joan Phipson's Billy Martin is not to argue for a 'pure' form of historical fiction in which only the habits of thought typical of their time might be admitted. Apart from the difficulty of knowing what was typical, it would impose a crippling limitation on a genre which largely justifies itself by new ideas and perspectives. Nevertheless, anyone writing Australian historical fiction today will find a cautionary tale in Randolph Stow's *Midnite* (1967), a comic reinterpretation for children of colonial history. Stow's bushranger-hero, Midnite, meets an anguished explorer in the 'Cosmic Symbolical Desert':

> This explorer was a rather miserable German man called Johann Ludwig Ulrich von Leichardt zu Voss, but in Australia he called himself Mr. Smith, and his two bad-tempered camels were called Sturm and Drang . . .

'May I ask where you are going?' [Midnite said.]

'I too am exploring,' said Mr Smith. 'I am exploring me.'

'How can you explore you?' asked Midnite.

'I will not explain,' said Mr Smith. 'You would have to be me
to understand.'

Midnite and Smith belong to different worlds and different novels. To
have them collide is a nice touch of absurdity which suits Stow's purpose.
In historical fiction which attempts a realistic effect, however, incongruities may be damaging; the genre needs tact as well as imagination.

There is a close correspondence between a sense of the past, a feeling
for place and the writing of fantasy. So long as white Australian writers
thought of themselves as newcomers in a traditionless land and drew
mainly on their European past for imaginative sustenance, their best
literary work was likely to be in the here-and-now of the realistic mode.
Although all literature, including realistic fiction, needs a sense of tradition, it is in the creation of fantasy that its lack is most obviously
felt. The first Australian writer to bring past and present together in
a successfully realized fantasy was Nan Chauncy, whose *Tangara* (1960)
is a time-travel story with a Tasmanian setting.

The design of *Tangara* resembles that of many English fantasies of
the twentieth century, from E. Nesbit's *The Story of the Amulet* (1906)
to Alison Uttley's *A Traveller in Time* (1939) and Philippa Pearce's
Tom's Midnight Garden (1958). Such stories re-create the past for two
sets of present-day children: the time-travelling fictional characters and
the modern readers who share their imagined journey. *Tangara* is given
a firm foundation in period, place and character. The central figure,
a solitary, imaginative eight-year-old, Lexie Pavemont, belongs to a
family long established in Tasmania. The Pavemonts, according to family legend, were among the few early Tasmanian settlers whose record
of relationships with the Aborigines was totally free of hostility on
either side. During the 1830s one of the Pavemont children, Rita, is
said to have made friends with Merrina, a little Aboriginal girl of her
own age; they played together and each learned to understand something of the other's language. A shell necklace given to Rita by Merrina
now belongs to the twentieth century child, Lexie, who closely
resembles her great-great-aunt in appearance. Wearing the necklace,
Lexie goes into Blacks' Gully, the place where, more than a century
before, Merrina's tribe had been shot by escaped convicts. Lexie's point
of entry into the past, however, is just before this massacre; she meets

Merrina as her ancestress had done, during the last peaceful days of the tribe. The shell necklace is the magic object which works, like Nesbit's amulet, to admit Lexie into the past. Once there, she plays happily with Merrina by day and goes home each evening scarcely conscious of the magical dimension of her experience. She meets the rest of the tribe and learns that something has happened to make them feel unsafe in their secluded gully; the reader will know this to be a threat from white men, but Lexie guesses nothing. Unprepared, she witnesses the convicts' attack on the tribe; she escapes with Merrina's help, but is injured in a fall in the gully, and later found unconscious by her father. So far, what happens to Lexie is a re-living of Rita's experience. It is implied that after guiding the white child to safety, Merrina returned to find herself the only survivor, and that she lived on for a time mourning the lost tribe. Shock and grief killed Rita; for Lexie the same experience becomes a troubling dream. It returns to her conscious mind a year later and a second journey in time takes place. In this episode Merrina responds to Lexie's call for help and makes the time-journey into the present day. Lexie then remembers the scene of the massacre, and she accepts Merrina's reappearance as proof that their friendship was not destroyed by the convicts' guns. In spite of this proof of forgiveness, the book ends with Lexie still haunted by her experience, returning in imagination to Blacks' Gully:

> Greetings and laughter rang through the house, coming nearer, but Lexie was far away.
>
> She was in a hidden place in the bush under the cold stars. A small red fire glowed in the half-moon of space before the ring of cliffs, and there for ever squatted Merrina, her thin arms reaching up imploringly.
>
> Merrina alone—alone, and calling to her dead.

Nan Chauncy's novel succeeds because of her firm grasp of the present-day world of Lexie, and her ability to create the friendship between the two children in convincing dialogue and narrative. The wild Tasmanian bush is as appropriate a setting for nineteenth century episodes as for modern ones; externally, little had changed between the time of Rita Pavemont and that of her great-great-niece.

After *Tangara*, which won the 1961 Australian Children's Book award, Nan Chauncy returned to the Aboriginal theme with *Mathinna's People* (1967). The second novel makes an interesting contrast with the first; more ambitious, in its attempt to view tribal life partly from the insiders' viewpoint, it is, I think, less successful. There is no magic time-travelling in *Mathinna's People*. The story of the Tasmanian Aborigines' experience of white invasion is told with sympathy and insight, as it might have been felt. As an imaginative venture it is impressive but, lacking the unifying individual viewpoint of the child in *Tangara*, it has less emotional force. However, Nan Chauncy's matter-of-fact prose allows the facts to speak for themselves; she avoids the coyness and the uneasy assumption of intimacy with which many earlier writers present the Aboriginal consciousness. Even so recent a work as Beth Roberts's *Manganinnie* (1979) which, like *Mathinna's People*, describes the last days of the Tasmanian Aborigines, founders on the question of language and viewpoint. On the one hand *Manganinnie* makes demands on the reader's concentration with its very liberal scattering of Aboriginal words. On the other, it represents the thoughts of the central character in jerky sentences which give the impression of naïvety rather than simplicity. Children old enough to use the much-needed glossary in *Manganinnie* will be too old for its narrative style and its cosy First Reader tone:

> Manganinnie loved planning and she loved teaching Common Knowledge. Now she had a very special little one to teach: a child with the markings of *Parnuberre* in her hair. She felt proud and happy. Today they would stay inside the cave and sing songs in praise of *Parnuberre* and play games and talk. There was so much to be taught. Soon Tonytah must learn to see and listen, how to sit very still and move very slowly for stalking, to run fast and climb and jump and swim. All these things could be taught as games. It would be very easy. Manganinnie loved little children and they knew this.

Manganinnie and *Mathinna's People*, both set in early nineteenth century Tasmania, describe the Aboriginal way of life just before its obliteration. Both commemorate what was lost in a region of Australia in which white settlement was totally destructive. Except by implication they are not protest novels; they are laments for a heritage irretrievably gone. Children's books which give a sense of a continuing Aboriginal tradition are rare; the only notable examples may be found in the work of Patricia Wrightson and Bill Scott in the late 1970s.

Patricia Wrightson's career, which began in 1955 with a mild, conventional story, *The Crooked Snake*, moved slowly from realism to fantasy and, in her most recent work, to the creation of an Aboriginal mythic hero. The link between these three groups of Wrightson novels is a strong feeling for place, an awareness of man's relationship with the land, and an interest in discovering the strange and uncanny

Illustration by Margaret Horder from *The Rocks of Honey*

beneath familiar surfaces. In *The Rocks of Honey* (1960) a sense of mystery, evoked in an Aboriginal legend, gives an added dimension to a story of country-town children and inter-racial friendship. Although the supernatural element in this novel is unobtrusive, the central theme is the power of the past over Eustace the Aboriginal boy. For him place and tradition have an importance which he neither desires nor understands; they are part of the racial inheritance he must learn to accept. From mystery in *The Rocks of Honey*, Patricia Wrightson moved to magic in *Down to Earth* (1965), a fantasy of a Martian visit to Sydney.

This whimsical suspense story gains its effect from the puzzled, slightly patronizing view of modern city life given by 'Martin the Martian'. Like E. Nesbit's Psammead, Martin solemnly explores a new world in search of the rational principles he believes must explain its apparent oddities. The outsider's perspective of *Down to Earth* prepares the way for the next Wrightson novel, *'I Own the Racecourse!'*, in which there is no magic except in the transforming vision of the central character, whose simple belief in the impossible creates its own reality. *'I Own the Racecourse!'*, discussed in an earlier chapter, is mentioned here as an example of Wrightson's continuing preoccupation with ways of seeing beneath the surfaces. The city of Sydney in *Down to Earth* and *'I Own the Racecourse!'* is made magical by a perceiver who does not accept the limitations of ordinary experience. With a third Sydney novel, *An Older Kind of Magic*, Wrightson found another way of seeing the city; this time, fantasy is a means of linking past with present, and the land with the people. The nature of the magical element in the novel, and the way in which it was created, are explained in the novel's epilogue. Wrightson says:

> Those of us who were bred in the old lands and live in the new ... have tried to plant here the magic that our people knew, and it will not grow. It is time we stopped trying to see elves and dragons and unicorns in Australia. They have never belonged here, and no ingenuity can make them real. We need to look for another kind of magic, a kind that must have been shaped by the land itself at the edge of Australian vision.
>
> So I have tried, in a small way. I have pictured Pot-Koorok, Nyol and Net-Net, unsuspected in their own water or rock; creeping from tunnels and drains into our streets; never seen, but perhaps to spring out at us some day. I have put beside them for contrast a shabbier, pretended magic that has shrunk to an advertising gimmick and is real for only a moment in a thousand years. Perhaps this may be a beginning.

The spirits in *An Older Kind of Magic*, drawn from Aboriginal tales, are a source of mischief as well as supernatural power. Although they act capriciously, with no sense of purpose, their intervention in human events is decisive; they save a large part of Sydney's Botanical Gardens from being turned into a car park. In the foreground of this story three children campaign for what they see as *their* garden but, using the inauthentic magic supplied by an advertising agent, they can do nothing effective. The plot is simple: it describes the battle for the

Illustration by Noela Young from *An Older Kind of Magic*

Gardens, with the millionaire businessman, Sir Mortimer Wyvern, as the villain and the children as his opponents, defenders of the inner city's breathing space. The children's ally, the modern magician of mass advertising, produces a *Save Our Gardens* demonstration in which figures from a shop-window display march on Parliament House. But the temporary animation of these 'petrified people' does far less for the cause than the actions of the rock-spirits, the Nyol, who capture Sir Mortimer and keep him prisoner in the Gardens. Later, by another piece of 'old magic', he is turned to stone and remains for ever among the trees, just as still, though more solid, than a figure in one of his own shop-windows.

The Sydney of Patricia Wrightson's novel has its own magic—in the shop-windows, 'magic caves full of light and colour' and the tall, brightly illuminated buildings. The main characters, Selina and Rupert, live on the top floor of the government offices in which their father works as caretaker; for them inner-city Sydney becomes a place of adventure and delight after the workers go home each evening. The theme of the novel might suggest a didactic conservation story, with all things urban automatically condemned, but there is an undeniable sense of romantic excitement in the bustle and stir of 'the lovely terrible city'. For the children it is more lovely than terrible, and the author clearly intends that its attractions should be felt as well as the constricting power suggested in such passages as this:

> The city hummed and grumbled, never sleeping. It whispered in the splashing of its fountains and breathed in the tides of its harbour. It spread its net of lights to shut out the stars, and held the land in a grip of concrete and steel. Yet deep under the city, forgotten under the concrete, the land was still there.
>
> Its soil was there, stripped of ferns and shut away forever from the sun. Its stone was there, deep and abiding; and out of the stone the Nyols crept, the old creatures of the land. They found their way up through tunnels . . . into the darkest places. The lights did not please them, for they liked their lights to be far and pale, and lit by distant suns. They found the city a harsh dead place; but still they came to feel the wind.

The spirits of rock and water who stir beneath the city in *An Older Kind of Magic* are almost undisturbed in the country setting of *The Nargun and the Stars* (1973). It won Patricia Wrightson the second of her three Australian Children's Book of the Year awards, and must make a strong claim, with *'I Own the Racecourse!'*, to be her best work. The Nargun of the title is a powerful rock-spirit, neither good nor evil, but capable of immense destruction. It has moved slowly, inch by inch, across the Australian continent until, after a journey measured in centuries, it came to rest in a Hunter Valley farming district. Past and present are brought together when a boy from the city, Simon Brent, discovers not only the ancient Nargun, but other more genial local spirits. Of these the most sociable is a swamp-creature, whom Simon coaxes into conversation:

'What's your name?' It was a stupid thing to say to a swamp-creature, but how else could you start?

The swamp-creature made a sound like the calling of frogs.

'Eh?' said Simon.

The creature made the sound again. 'Potkoorok.'

'Is that your own name? Or is it what you are?'

'That is my name that I am,' said the creature a little grandly. 'You are Boy. I am Potkoorok.' . . . 'Pot-koo-rok,' said Simon. The creature chuckled.

'And what are they? The ones in the trees?'

'Turongs. Tu-rongs. Their name that they are is Turongs.' It was watching Simon with sly attention.

'Turongs,' repeated Simon thoughtfully. '—Hey!' He had lost his apple. A green hand with flattened webbed fingers had plucked it lightly from his own hand while he spoke. The Potkoorok chuckled with glee and munched the remains of the apple. Simon supposed that if you wanted to be friends with it you would have to put up with that sort of thing.

Patricia Wrightson creates her local spirits deftly and economically with a few visual details to suggest colour and shape, and with voices which at first are almost indistinguishable from the sounds of wind and water. The landscape comes to life for Simon; he listens and watches with increasing wonder and delight. Except for the Potkoorok, the spirits remain elusive, scarcely visible. They show no human qualities, apart from a teasing humour at Simon's expense. By resisting the temptation to domesticate them, Wrightson avoids the sentimentality which often spoils a fantasy world. Comedy and mystery are carefully balanced, never predictable. The Nargun, who threatens the human world and is defeated, evokes from Simon a kind of pity as well as terror, but the pity is shown to be inappropriate, since it attributes to the Nargun emotions which it cannot feel.

The Nargun and the Stars combines a simple but exciting story—the challenge of the Nargun—with a strong sense of place. The three main characters, Simon and his two elderly cousins, are drawn with warmth and an engaging, gentle humour. Their spare, laconic dialogue is convincing in idiom and in feeling, and their matter-of-fact acceptance of strange happenings helps to guarantee the reader's suspension of disbelief. There are no false notes, and none of the didacticism which at times diverts *An Older Kind of Magic* from narrative into sermons on the seductive power of commercial advertising. The fantasy of *The Nargun and the Stars* is unforced, and the novel achieves the authentic magic for which Australian children's writing waited so long.

With her next work Patricia Wrightson took the more difficult step of bringing an Aboriginal hero into imaginative possession of his own land. The trilogy, *The Ice is Coming* (1977), *The Dark Bright Water* (1978) and *Behind the Wind* (1981), all celebrate the achievements of Wirrun, a young man specially chosen to serve his people and to restore the land to its natural order. The time is the present day. Following the tradition by which heroes are found in unlikely, obscure places, the author makes Wirrun a young garage hand from an unnamed country town in 'the old south land'—the term for Australia throughout the trilogy. White people are as irrelevant to the Wirrun stories as is their name for the country or for themselves; there are no 'Australians'. Instead there are the city-dwellers, contemptuously labelled 'the Happy Folk' and shown to be totally absorbed in their synthetic consumer-culture, and 'the Inlanders', country men and women who gain some small degree of recognition for attempting, however ineptly, to come to terms with the land. The Aborigines are 'the People'.

The Wirrun stories are an attempt to create a mythic hero with power to summon and control the spirits of the land. In the first novel Wirrun must find a way to repel the ice-people whose spell threatens to imprison the whole continent. With the aid of the Eldest Nargun, who holds the power of fire, Wirrun wins the battle and establishes himself as an authentic though unwilling hero. He returns temporarily to his prosaic job among the 'Happy People', but is soon summoned to solve another problem. In the second volume of the trilogy, *The Dark Bright Water*, Wirrun's immediate challenge is the erratic behaviour of inland waterways. When he finds a beautiful displaced water-spirit to be the cause of the trouble, he falls in love with this seductive siren-figure. He takes her into the human world, but his power is not strong enough to hold her there. In the final volume, *Behind the Wind*, she eludes him until, having conquered Death, Wirrun becomes a spirit and is permitted to claim a fellow spirit:

> . . . he knew he had been changed as ancestors and heroes and lesser men before him had been changed. The land was silently peopled with them; among its ancient rocks their stone bodies lay in warning or in promise while they themselves lived on; behind the wind as the old men said. Now he too lived behind the wind. He had grown out of now into forever.

Among the problems Patricia Wrightson faces in the Wirrun trilogy are those of characterization and appropriate language. How much individuality should Wirrun have, and how should he speak? The mythic hero, of course, is primarily a man of action; psychological complexity may be as out of place in Wirrun as in Beowulf. Yet Beowulf and other ancient heroes belong to a single world. Wirrun must move from the commonplaces of petrol pump and pub and rented room to the ceremonious occasions of his heroic calling. The transition is not easy to manage, and it is one of the weaknesses of this ambitious work that Wirrun seems not quite to fulfil the demands of either context. In his everyday setting, drinking beer with his friends, he is uninteresting: nothing he says or does gives an impression of any special quality. In the final pages of the trilogy, when he has become pure spirit, he is still the inarticulate boy from the petrol station. 'Don't be scared', he says to Murra, the water-spirit. 'Everything's fine. Tell me what's up.' Murra's language is formal. 'I am here, Great One', she says, before confessing her shame at not having guarded him from death. Wirrun's response is awkwardly facetious. Sounding more an Ocker than a Great Spirit he forgives her with: 'Well I'll just have to beat you, I reckon. A man's gotta beat his wife now and then'. The incongruities of tone in much of the dialogue are one indication of the author's failure to link the worlds of fact and fantasy. A comparison with a similar kind of novel, Susan Cooper's *The Dark is Rising* (1973) may be useful. In that novel an ordinary English boy is totally convincing in his everyday role at home, with friends and in his village; transported in time and given magical powers he grows into the heroic role without ceasing to be himself. Perhaps the special difficulty of the Wrightson trilogy is that Wirrun, a fringe-dweller in white society, is given almost none of the human context which might help to define him. It is easy to see why the author might be unwilling to place him in a tribal group; as an outsider she would hesitate to claim the necessary insight. There are good reasons, too, not to involve him in the dehumanized white society which is presented, with heavy-handed satire, as 'the Happy Folk'. The result, however, is a lifeless central figure and, consequently, an almost total dependence on narrative and descriptive interest. In the first volume Patricia Wrightson's inventiveness is equal to the task: *The Ice is Coming*, with its strong sense of place, its variety of scene and its well-controlled suspense is an impressive and imaginative work. With the two succeeding stories invention falters, the strong, flexible prose stiffens, and the central figure remains inadequate. Nevertheless, the best of the Wirrun trilogy confirms Patricia Wrightson's achievement as the first writer for children to discover in Aboriginal legend, and in close, loving observation of the landscape, the imaginative possibilities of the Australian past.

Bill Scott's *Boori* (1978) and *Darkness Under the Hills* (1980) resemble the Wirrun stories in their creation of an Aboriginal mythic hero. They do not, however, attempt to link past and present, but set Boori's exploits in a period 'after the Dreamtime' and before white settlement in Australia. The problems of language and characterization in the Wrightson novels do not arise in Scott's work. Boori is not individualized. He accepts his heroic role without hesitation, and when the old men of the tribe doubt his magical powers he rebukes them with dignity and assurance:

> Doubters, I will not come to live among you. I will be a solitary man, living alone and keeping the Law within the boundaries of the country I take from you. One day you will need my help and I will not be here among you. When that time comes, you will know where to find me, in the country of the Cave of Honey. Remember my words!

Within the single world they create, the Boori stories are convincing. The viewpoint assumes belief in Boori's magic and the prose has an appropriate seriousness. Because the teller respects the tales and presents them simply and directly, *Boori* and *Darkness Under the Hills* succeed in bringing Aboriginal customs and beliefs within the imaginative range of modern children, and suggesting a living tradition. Scott does not trivialize the system of beliefs he describes, nor condescend to his readers.

There is another perspective on a quite different past in Valerie Weldrick's *Time Sweep* (1976) and Ruth Park's *Playing Beatie Bow* (1980). These two time-travel fantasies link present-day Sydney children with their predecessors by giving them an inside view of the lives of early settlers from nineteenth century Britain. *Time Sweep* consists of a series of visits to the London of 1862, in which a Sydney boy and girl, Laurie and Clare, make friends with a London crossing-sweeper. The magical device for the backward journey in time is Laurie's Victorian brass bed; absent-mindedly rubbing the lapis-lazuli bed-knobs he gets as unexpected a result as Aladdin with his lamp. An ill-prepared intruder in a mid-Victorian household, Laurie finds a friend and ally in Frank, the crossing-sweeper, who believes his story and helps him steal some clothes to cover his inadequate summer pyjamas. From that point Laurie becomes more and more interested in Frank's predicament; he is astonished that there is no 'welfare' or school system to look after a semi-destitute illiterate waif. More surprising is the fact that Frank expects so little. As Laurie masters the magical travel system he makes nightly visits to London, taking warm clothing, and some ball-point pens which he sells as a miraculous invention from the colonies. With the proceeds, he and Frank explore London, dine out magnificently and go to the theatre. They go together to the 'ragged school' where Frank is trying to learn to read; here Laurie is outraged by the teacher's assumption that the poor must not presume to rise from the class in which they were born. He takes over Frank's education, and encourages him to go to Australia, not as a convict (Frank's first impulse is to get himself transported for a small offence) but as a free settler. By day, back in Sydney, Laurie and his friend Clare, who shares some of the time-travelling, pester Sydney librarians for details of life in London in 1862, and on Frank's behalf discover the opportunities for emigration to New South Wales. Between them, they give the sturdy ambitious Frank his start, but the magic fades before they know what happens to him.

Months later a school project in local history completes the story. Laurie and Clare interview the great-grandson of one of the early settlers in North Sydney. Surprising him by their interest in every detail of his family history ('My goodness, how youngsters throw themselves into their school work these days . . .') they discover that Frank had done exactly what they advised, and had lived a long and happy life in Sydney. They read a diary, written in the late nineteenth century, in which Frank indulges in a private joke about the building of the Sydney Harbour Bridge in 1932. This confirms Laurie's belief that all Frank's careful records had been made in the hope of their reaching 1977 and delivering his message to his friends.

Time Sweep is lively and entertaining. The contrasts between twentieth century Sydney and nineteenth century London arise naturally from the situations; there is nothing of the disguised social history lesson about this well-shaped novel. If it suffers by comparison with Ruth Park's *Playing Beatie Bow*, that should not diminish its achievement. *Time Sweep* is a very successful first novel by a newcomer to children's fiction. *Playing Beatie Bow* is one of the best works of an established and unusually gifted writer for adults as well as for children.

The central idea of Ruth Park's novel is like that of *Time Sweep* in showing a modern child's discovery of an alien way of life in an earlier period. This time-traveller is Abigail Kirk, an unhappy Sydney fourteen-year-old who wanders through a gap in time to become part of a struggling immigrant family in the Rocks district of Sydney in

1873. The implication of *Time Sweep* is that the Victorian age was a hard time for children; Laurie and Clare see Frank as someone in need of rescue. The nineteenth century characters in Ruth Park's novel have some problems which the twentieth century could solve, but they do not invite pity. At first the child of 1973 sees only squalor:

> The houses were like wasps' nests, or Tibetan houses as Abigail had seen them in films, piled on top of each other, roosting on narrow sandstone ledges, sometimes with a lighted candle stuck in half a turnip on the doorstep, as if to show the way. The dark was coming down, and in those mazy alleys it came quicker. The lamplight that streamed through broken grimy windows was sickly yellow ... Where the Bradfield Highway had roared across the top of The Cut there were now two rickety wooden bridges. Stone steps ran up one side, and on the other two tottering stairways curled upon themselves, overhung with vines and dishevelled trees, and running amongst and even across the roofs of indescribable shanties like broken-down farm sheds. These dwellings were propped up with tree trunks and railway sleepers; goats grazed on their roofs; and over all was the smell of rotted seaweed, ships, wood smoke, human ordure, and horses and harness.

Ruth Park re-creates the two Sydneys in bifocal vision, with an assured sense of time and place in both. She has an equally firm grasp of character. Neither Abigail nor the wary, pugnacious Beatie, her counterpart in the early period, is a mouthpiece for an interchange on progress or a comparative cultural study. The novel avoids the easy simplifications of setting nineteenth century wholesomeness and godliness against twentieth century decadence. There are divisions within the modern family which make Abigail lonely and resentful. But Beatie, too, is restless, eager to know and do more than a girl of her time can easily achieve. She is not particularly impressed by Abigail; although she envies superior knowledge and wider opportunities, she finds the modern girl ignorant in many important matters, and morally unreliable. Even the information Abigail can give Beatie about the future is received with scepticism:

> 'But where is the Empire?' Beatie asked, baffled.
> Abigail did not know. 'It just seemed to break up and drift away,' she admitted lamely.
> 'But who's looking after the black men?'
> 'They're looking after themselves,' said Abigail. But Beatie could not understand.

'Black men canna look after themselves. Don't be daft!'

For Abigail the past has subtler lessons than anything she can teach Beatie. These come from her affinity of feeling with Beatie's grand-mother, a serene old woman whose capacity to survive hardships and loss become for the modern child a guarantee of human strength, reassuring in the shaky family life to which she returns. Having felt like a prisoner in the nineteenth century she goes back through the time-gap with a sense of exile. She has also a strong desire to know what happened to her friends, long dead before the 1970s. Like the chil-dren in *Time Sweep*, she finds out by meeting a descendant of the family, who is astonished by her interest in his past. The author makes the last connecting link between past and present in a neatly-contrived happy ending.

In *Time Sweep* and *Playing Beatie Bow*, Australian children's fiction produced two good novels in a genre which Britain has made particu-larly her own. Weldrick's reference to *A Traveller in Time* (among the favourite books of Laurie and Clare) is her tribute to a well-established tradition—one in which she shows herself to be thoroughly at home. *Playing Beatie Bow* is a stronger and more satisfying novel because of the fullness and complexity of its characterization. Moreover, it has a special importance in the development of Australian children's fiction because the past which Abigail visits is not London, as in the Weldrick story, but her own Sydney. The two cities, past and present, are created in this novel with the authority of knowledge and imagination: they are seen, known and felt. The shadowy figure of Beatie Bow, revisiting the Rocks district, is as authentic a ghostly presence as the child in *Tom's Midnight Garden*, Philippa Pearce's much-admired story of time-travel in an English setting. Bush fantasy and a sense of the past have eluded Australian children's writers until this decade: now, with Wrightson's *The Nargun and the Stars* and Park's *Playing Beatie Bow*, the magical dimensions of the land have been realized; and after nearly two hundred years of European settlement, one Australian city at least is sure enough of its own reality to admit a ghost.

Australian Children's Book Awards

The Australian Children's Book Awards were first given by the Australian Book Society. From 1951 to 1956 they were given by the Children's Book Council of New South Wales. Judges from the Children's Book Council of Victoria were appointed in 1957, and from that of South Australia in 1958. The Children's Book Council of Australia, which represents all the States, was established in 1958 and has administered all awards since 1959. The list below does not include the prizewinners in the Picture Book of the Year category.

1946   Leslie Rees *Karrawingi The Emu*
1947   No award
1948   Frank Hurley *Shackleton's Argonauts* (non-fiction)
1949   Alan Villiers *Whalers of the Midnight Sun*
1950   No award
1951   Ruth Williams *Verity of Sydney Town*
1952   Eve Pownall *The Australia Book* (non-fiction)
1953   J. H. and W. D. Martin *Aircraft of Today and Tomorrow* (non-fiction)
        Joan Phipson *Good Luck to the Rider*
1954   K. Langloh Parker *Australian Legendary Tales*
1955   N. B. Tindale and H. A. Lindsay *The First Walkabout* (non-fiction)
1956   Patricia Wrightson *The Crooked Snake*
1957   Enid Moodie-Heddle (ed.) *The Boomerang Book of Legendary Tales*
1958   Nan Chauncy *Tiger in the Bush*
1959   Nan Chauncy *Devils' Hill*
        John Gunn *Sea Menace*
1960   Kylie Tennant *All the Proud Tribesmen* (not set in Australia)
1961   Nan Chauncy *Tangara*
1962   L. H. Evers *The Racketty Street Gang*
        Joan Woodberry *Rafferty Rides a Winner*

1963   Joan Phipson *The Family Conspiracy*
1964   Eleanor Spence *The Green Laurel*
1965   H. F. Brinsmead *Pastures of the Blue Crane*
1966   Ivan Southall *Ash Road*
1967   Mavis Thorpe Clark *The Min-Min*
1968   Ivan Southall *To the Wild Sky*
1969   Margaret Balderson *When Jays Fly to Barbmo*
        (not set in Australia)
1970   Annette Macarthur-Onslow *Uhu* (picture book)
1971   Ivan Southall *Bread and Honey*
1972   H. F. Brinsmead *Longtime Passing*
1973   Noreen Shelley *Family at the Lookout*
1974   Patricia Wrightson *The Nargun and the Stars*
1975   No award
1976   Ivan Southall *Fly West* (non-fiction)
1977   Eleanor Spence *The October Child*
1978   Patricia Wrightson *The Ice is Coming*
1979   Ruth Manley *The Plum Rain Scroll* (not set in Australia)
1980   Lee Harding *Displaced Person*
1981   Ruth Park *Playing Beatie Bow*
1982   Colin Thiele *The Valley Between*
1983   Victor Kelleher *Master of the Grove*

Abbreviations

ML   Mitchell Library, Sydney
MS   Manuscript
NLA   National Library of Australia, Canberra
SLV   State Library of Victoria, La Trobe Library, Australian
       Manuscripts Collection

Notes

Introduction

[1] (London, 1952). Revised as *British Children's Books in the Twentieth Century* (London, 1971).

[2] Eleanor Spence to Brenda Niall, 14 January 1982.

[3] *Books, Children and Men* (Boston, 1963), p. 128.

Chapter 1

[1] (London, 1830).

[2] *Australia and its Settlements* (London, c. 1854).

[3] Quoted by J. S. Bratton, *The Impact of Victorian Children's Fiction* (London, 1981).

[4] Frank Eyre, *Oxford in Australia, 1890-1978* (Melbourne, 1978).

Chapter 2

[1] E. S. Turner, *Boys Will Be Boys*. New revised ed. (London, 1957), p. 73.

Chapter 4

[1] Marcie Muir, *Charlotte Barton* (Sydney, 1980), *passim*.

Chapter 6

[1] A fuller account of the life and literary career of Ethel Turner and a complete listing of sources may be found in Brenda Niall, *Seven Little Billabongs* (Melbourne, 1979).

[2] Quoted by Susan Eade in her introduction to *Clara Morison* (Adelaide, 1971), p. xvii.

[3] *Bulletin*, 23 November 1895, Red Page.

[4] *Daily Telegraph* (London), 7 September 1894, p. 6.

[5] *The Diaries of Ethel Turner*. Compiled by P. Poole (Sydney, 1979), p. 262.

Chapter 7

[1] William Steele to Ethel Turner, 20 November 1893, Turner Papers (ML), MS.667/5/3.

[2] *The Diaries of Ethel Turner*, p. 115.

[3] William Steele to Ethel Turner, 19 October 1896, Turner Papers (ML), MS.667/5/206.

[4] Bernice May, 'Vera Dwyer', *Australian Woman's Mirror*, 10 June 1928, p. 12.

[5] William Steele to Ethel Turner, 19 October 1896, Turner Papers (ML), MS.667/5/206.

[6] *The Diaries of Ethel Turner*, p. 129.

[7] *Bulletin*, 11 November 1915, Red Page.

Chapter 8

[1] 'Ships I Have Known', *Blackwood's Magazine*, 246, November 1939, p. 598.

[2] A fuller account of the life and literary career of Mary Grant Bruce and a complete listing of sources may be found in Brenda Niall, *Seven Little Billabongs* (Melbourne, 1979).

[3] 'Bush Babies', 28 July 1913.

[4] Bruce Papers (SLV), MS.9975/1309/2.

[5] For a detailed discussion of this question see *Seven Little Billabongs*, ch. 8.

Chapter 9

[1] *Sydney Morning Herald*, 15 December 1880.

[2] Introduction to *The Golden Shanty: Short Stories* by Edward Dyson (Sydney, 1963), p. viii.

[3] Quoted by Nettie Palmer, *Henry Handel Richardson* (Sydney, 1950), p. 195.

Chapter 10

[1] Martin Boyd, *The Cardboard Crown* (London, 1952), p. 34.

[2] Geoffrey Blainey, *Wesley College* (Melbourne, 1967), p. 92.

[3] Greg Dening, *Xavier: A Centenary Portrait* (Melbourne, 1978), p. 136.

[4] The author, J. D. Burns, was vice-captain of Scotch College in 1914. He was killed in action in September 1915. (*Flosculi Australes: An Anthology of Poems and Songs from the Scotch Collegian*, Melbourne, n.d., pp. 6-7.)

Chapter 11

[1] Nancy Phelan, *A Kingdom by the Sea* (Sydney, 1980), pp. 42-3.

[2] Nancy Phelan to Brenda Niall, 10 November 1982.

[3] Henry Lawson to Miles Franklin, September 1902. Quoted by A. W. Barker (ed.) in *Dear Robertson* (Sydney, 1982), p. 34.

[4] *A Kingdom by the Sea*, p. 226.

Chapter 12

1 'Our Imperial Heritage', *Australian Boys' Paper*, vol. 6, no. 1, 1 August 1903, p. 7.

2 *The Transit of Venus* (London, 1980), p. 32.

3 Preface to *Sea Spray and Smoke Drift* by Adam Lindsay Gordon. Reprinted in *Marcus Clarke*. Edited by M. Wilding (Brisbane, 1976), pp. 645, 647.

4 *Kangaroo* (Harmondsworth, 1950), p. 19.

5 Angus and Robertson Papers (ML), MS.314/36.

6 Ibid., MS.314/56/45.

7 Marcie Muir, *A History of Australian Childrens Book Illustration* (Melbourne, 1982), p. 81.

8 Angus and Robertson Papers (ML), MS.314/52/128.

9 Quoted by A. W. Barker (ed.), *Dear Robertson*, p. 62.

10 'Lotus Land', *Bulletin*, 30 May 1964, p. 52.

11 Quoted in *My Bush Book*. Edited by Marcie Muir (Adelaide, 1982), p. 146.

12 *Bulletin*, 9 January 1897, Red Page.

13 Marcie Muir, *A Bibliography of Australian Children's Books* (London, 1970), vol. 1, pp. 863-4, records this change in pagination.

14 Bruce Papers (SLV), MS.9975/1310/2.

15 The subsequent comments on the publishing history of *The Vanished Tribes* are drawn from the Angus and Robertson Papers (ML), MS.314/27/433-625.

16 Angus and Robertson Papers (ML), MS.3269.

17 Introduction, *Jindyworobak Review, 1938–1948* (Melbourne, 1948), p. 25.

Chapter 13

1 K. C. Masterman, 'Nan Chauncy, 1900-1970'. *Reading Time*, July 1975, pp. 35-42.

2 'Nan Chauncy', Oxford University Press publicity material, July 1970.

Chapter 14

1 *A Sounding of Storytellers* (Harmondsworth, 1970), p. 183.

2 *Innocence and Experience* (Melbourne, 1981), p. 253.

3 *A Sounding of Storytellers*, p. 183.

4 *The Road to Gundagai* (Melbourne, 1967), p. 179.

Chapter 16

1 For details of the case of *The Catcher in the Rye* see *Australia. Senate Debates*, 1957, vol. S.11, p. 237 ff., 1958, vol. S.12, p. 211 ff. *House of Representatives, Votes and Proceedings*, 1957, vol. 16, p. 974 ff., 1958, vol. 17, p. 1582 ff. The

novel was prescribed reading for Higher School Certificate English in Victorian schools in 1971.

Chapter 17

[1] 'Only Connect' in S. Egoff, G. T. Stubbs and L. F. Ashley (eds), *Only Connect* (Toronto, 1969), pp. 184, 186.

[2] Richard Coe, 'Portrait of the Artist as a Young Australian', *Southerly*, June 1981, pp. 126-62.

[3] 'Notes by David Martin', in McVitty, *Innocence and Experience*, p. 191.

Bibliography

Year of publication is given for first publication in book form.

Australian Children's Books

The titles listed below are those discussed in the text. For further reading, see Marcie Muir's *Bibliography of Australian Children's Books*.

ALDOUS, Allan. *Danger on the Map*. Melbourne, F. W. Cheshire, 1947.

ALLANSON, Russell (pseud.). *Terraweena: A Story of a Mid-Winter Vacation in Australia*. London, Wells, Gardner, Darton, 1905.

BALDERSON, Margaret. *A Dog Called George*. London, Oxford University Press, 1975.

[BARTON, Charlotte.] *A Mother's Offering to Her Children*. Facsimile edition. Brisbane, Jacaranda Press, 1979 (first published 1841).

BEDFORD, Eric. *Scum o' the Seas*. Sydney, Currawong Publishing Company, 1944.

BOWES, Joseph. *Comrades: A Story of the Australian Bush*. London, Henry Frowde, Hodder and Stoughton, 1912 (first published 1911).

——. *The Honour of John Tremayne*. London, Epworth Press, 1926.

——. *The Jackaroos: Life on a Cattle Run*. London, Humphrey Milford, Oxford University Press, 1923.

——. *Pals: Young Australians in Sport and Adventure*. London, James Glass, n.d. (first published 1910).

——. *The Young Anzacs: A Tale of the Great War*. London, Humphrey Milford, Oxford University Press, 1917.

——. *The Young Settler: The Story of a New-Chum in Queensland*. London, Epworth Press, 1927 (first published 1925).

BOWMAN, Anne. *The Kangaroo Hunters, or Adventures in the Bush*. London, Routledge, 1859.

BOYLAN, Eustace. *The Heart of the School: An Australian School Story*. Melbourne, J. Roy Stevens, 1920.

BRADY, E. J. *Tom Pagdin, Pirate*. Sydney, N.S.W. Bookstall Company, 1911.

BRINSMEAD, H. F. *Beat of the City*. London, Oxford University Press, 1966.

——. *Isle of the Sea Horse*. London, Oxford University Press, 1969.

——. *Longtime Dreaming*. North Ryde, N.S.W., Angus & Robertson, 1982.

——. *Longtime Passing*. Sydney, Angus and Robertson, 1971.

——. *Once There Was a Swagman*. Melbourne, Oxford University Press, 1979.

——. *Pastures of the Blue Crane*. London, Oxford University Press, 1964.

——. *A Sapphire for September*. London, Oxford University Press, 1967.

BRUCE, Mary Grant. *Anderson's Jo*. Sydney, Cornstalk Publishing Company, 1927.

——. *Bill of Billabong*. London, Ward Lock, 1931.

——. *Billabong Adventurers*. London, Ward Lock, 1927.

——. *Billabong Riders*. London, Ward Lock, 1942.

——. *Captain Jim*. London, Ward Lock, 1919.

——. *Dick*. London, Ward Lock, 1918.

——. *From Billabong to London*. London, Ward Lock, 1915.

——. *Glen Eyre*. London, Ward Lock, 1912.

——. *Gray's Hollow*. London, Ward Lock, 1914.

——. *The Happy Traveller*. London, Ward Lock, 1929.

——. *Hugh Stanford's Luck*. Sydney, Cornstalk Publishing Company, 1927.

——. *Jim and Wally*. London, Ward Lock, 1916.

——. *Karalta*. Sydney, Angus and Robertson, 1941.

——. *A Little Bush Maid*. London, Ward Lock, 1910.

——. *Mates at Billabong*. London, Ward Lock, 1911.

——. *Norah of Billabong*. London, Ward Lock, 1913.

——. *Peter & Co*. London, Ward Lock, 1940.

——. *'Possum*. London, Ward Lock, 1917.

——. *Robin*. Sydney, Cornstalk Publishing Company, 1926.

——. *"Seahawk"*. London, Ward Lock, 1934.

——. *The Stone Axe of Burkamukk*. London, Ward Lock, 1922.

——. *Timothy in Bushland*. London, Ward Lock, 1912.

——. *Told by Peter*. London, Ward Lock, 1938.

BUDDEE, Paul. *The Escape of the Fenians*. Camberwell, Victoria, Longman, 1971.

CAMPBELL, Ellen. *An Australian Childhood*. London, Blackie, 1892.

——. *Twin Pickles: A Story of Two Australian Children*. London, Blackie, 1898.

CHAFFEY, M. Ella. *The Youngsters of Murray Home*. London, Ward Lock & Bowden, 1896.

CHAUNCY, Nan. *Devils' Hill*. London, Oxford University Press, 1958.

——. *A Fortune for the Brave*. London, Geoffrey Cumberlege, Oxford University Press, 1954.

——. *The Lighthouse-Keeper's Son*. London, Oxford University Press, 1969.

——. *Lizzie Lights*. London, Oxford University Press, 1968.

——. *Mathinna's People*. London, Oxford University Press, 1967.

——. *The Roaring 40*. London, Oxford University Press, 1963.

——. *Tangara*. London, Oxford University Press, 1960.

——. *They Found a Cave*. London, Geoffrey Cumberlege, Oxford University Press, 1948.

——. *Tiger in the Bush*. London, Oxford University Press, 1957.

——. *World's End Was Home*. London, Geoffrey Cumberlege, Oxford University Press, 1952.

CLARK, Mavis Thorpe. *Blue Above the Trees*. Melbourne, Lansdowne Press, 1967.

——. *The Brown Land Was Green*. Melbourne, Heinemann, 1956.

——. *Gully of Gold*. Melbourne, Heinemann, 1958.

——. *The Min-Min*. Melbourne, Lansdowne Press, 1966.

——. *Solomon's Child*. Richmond, Victoria, Hutchinson of Australia, 1981.

——. *They Came South*. Melbourne, Heinemann, 1963.

CLELAND, E. Davenport. *The White Kangaroo: A Tale of Colonial Life Founded on Fact*. London, Wells, Gardner, Darton, 1890.

COLE, E. W. *Cole's Funny Picture Book: The Funniest Picture Book in the World*. Melbourne, E. W. Cole, n.d. (first published 1876).

COOK, Hume. *Australian Fairy Tales*. Melbourne, J. Howlett-Ross, 1925.

COUPER, J. M. *Looking for a Wave*. London, Bodley Head, 1973.

——. *The Thundering Good Today*. London, Bodley Head, 1970.

CRONIN, Bernard. *The Treasure of the Tropics*. London, Ward Lock, 1928.

CURLEWIS, Jean. *Beach Beyond*. London, Ward Lock, 1923.

——. *The Dawn Man*. London, Ward Lock, 1924.

——. *Drowning Maze*. London, Ward Lock, 1922.

——. *The Ship That Never Set Sail*. London, Ward Lock, 1921.

DASKEIN, Tarella Quin. *The Other Side of Nowhere*. Melbourne, Robertson & Mullens, 1934.

DAVISON, Frank Dalby. *Children of the Dark People: An Australian Folk Tale*. Sydney, Angus & Robertson, 1936.

——. *Dusty: The Story of a Sheep Dog*. Sydney, Angus and Robertson, 1946.

——. *Man-Shy*. Sydney, Angus and Robertson, 1962 (first published 1931).

DAVISON, Fred. *Duck Williams and His Cobbers*. Sydney, Angus and Robertson, 1939.

De FOSSARD, Esta. *The Alien*. Melbourne, Nelson, 1977.

DEVANEY, James. *The Witch-Doctor and Other Tales of the Australian Blacks*.

Sydney, Angus and Robertson, 1930.

DUGAN, Michael. *Dingo Boy*. Harmondsworth, Middlesex, Puffin Books, 1980.

DURACK, Mary. *The Way of the Whirlwind* [by] Mary and Elizabeth Durack. Sydney, Consolidated Press, 1941.

DWYER, Vera. *The Kayles of Bushy Lodge: An Australian Story*. London, Humphrey Milford, Oxford University Press, 1922.

——. *A War of Girls*. London, Ward Lock, 1915.

——. *With Beating Wings: An Australian Story*. London, Ward Lock, 1913.

DYSON, Edward. *The Gold-Stealers: A Story of Waddy*. London, Longmans, Green, 1901.

EMMETT, George. *Tom Wildrake's Schooldays*. London, Hogarth House, n.d. (first published c. 1870).

ERNST, Olga. *Fairy Tales from the Land of the Wattle*. Melbourne, McCarron Bird, 1904.

EUROPA (pseud.). *The Fernythorpe Choristers: A Tale for Boys*. Melbourne, George Robertson, 1876.

EVELYN, J. *Captain Kangaroo: A Story of Australian Life*. London, Remington, 1889.

EVERS, L. H. *The Racketty Street Gang*. London, Hodder & Stoughton, 1961.

FARJEON, Benjamin. *The Golden Land, or, Links from Shore to Shore*. London, Ward Lock, 1886.

FAVENC, Ernest. *The Secret of the Australian Desert*. London, Blackie, 1896.

——. *Tales for Young Australia* by E. Favenc [and others]. Sydney, Empson, 1900.

FERRES, Arthur (pseud.). *His Cousin the Wallaby and Three Other Australian Stories*. Melbourne, George Robertson, 1896.

FITZGERALD, Mary Anne. *King Bungaree's Pyalla and Stories Illustrative of Manners and Customs That Prevailed Amongst Australian Aborigines*. Sydney, Edwards, Dunlop, 1891.

FLEMING, W. M. *The Hunted Piccaninnies*. London, Dent, 1927.

FOUINET, E. *Allan le Jeune Déporté à Botany-Bay*. Paris, Eymery, 1836.

FRASER, Alexander A. *Daddy Crips' Waifs: A Tale of Australasian Life and Adventure*. London, Religious Tract Society, [1886].

FRENCH, Simon. *Cannily, Cannily*. Sydney, Angus & Robertson, 1981.

——. *Hey Phantom Singlet*. London, Angus & Robertson, 1975.

GIBBS, May. *Snugglepot and Cuddlepie: Their Adventures Wonderful*. Sydney, Angus & Robertson, 1918.

GRATTAN-SMITH, T. E. *Three Real Bricks: The Adventures of Mel, Ned and Jim*. Sydney, Australasian Publishing Company, 1920.

GUNN, Jeannie. *The Little Black Princess: A True Tale of Life in the Never-Never Land*. Melbourne, Melville and Mullen, 1905.

HARDING, Lee. *Displaced Person*. Melbourne, Hyland House, 1979.

HATFIELD, William (pseud.). *Buffalo Jim*. London, Oxford University Press, 1938.

HAVERFIELD, E. L. *Dauntless Patty*. London, Humphrey Milford, Oxford University Press, n.d. (first published 1908).

[HEMYNG, Bracebridge]. *Jack Harkaway and His Son's Adventures in Australia*. London, Harkaway House, n.d. (first published 1876).

HENTY, G. A. *A Final Reckoning: A Tale of Bush Life in Australia*. Colonial ed. London, Blackie, 1896 (first published 1887).

HODGETTS, J. F. *Tom's Nugget: A Story of the Australian Gold Fields*. London, Sunday School Union, 1888.

HOWITT, William. *A Boy's Adventures in the Wilds of Australia, or Herbert's Note-Book*. London, Routledge, n.d. (first published 1854).

HUGHES, Mrs. F. *My Childhood in Australia: A Story for My Children*. London, Digby, Long, 1892.

IDRIESS, Ion. *Man-Tracks*. Sydney, Angus and Robertson, 1935.

——. *Nemarluk: King of the Wilds*. Sydney, Angus and Robertson, 1941.

——. *The Opium-Smugglers: A True Story of Our Northern Seas*. Sydney, Angus and Robertson, 1948.

INGAMELLS, Rex. *Aranda Boy: An Aboriginal Story*. London, Longmans Green, 1952.

JENNINGS, R. G. *The Human Pedagogue*. Melbourne, Australian Authors' Agency, 1924.

KENNEDY, E. B. *Blacks and Bushrangers: Adventures in Queensland*. London, Sampson Low, Marston, Searle & Rivington, 1889.

KIDDLE, Margaret. *West of Sunset*. Sydney, Australasian Publishing Company, 1949.

KINGSTON, W. H. G. *The Gilpins and Their Fortunes: An Australian Tale*. London, Society for Promoting Christian Knowledge, [1865].

——. *Milicent Courtenay's Diary: or The Experiences of a Young Lady at Home and Abroad*. London, Gall & Inglis, [1873].

——. *The Young Berringtons, or, The Boy Explorers*. London, Cassell, n.d. (first published 1880).

LAWSON, Will. *When Cobb and Co. Was King*. Sydney, Angus & Robertson, 1936.

LEE, Sarah. *Adventures in Australia, or, The Wanderings of Captain Spencer in the Bush and the Wilds*. London, Grant and Griffith, 1851.

LINDSAY, Jack. *Rebels of the Goldfields*. London, Lawrence & Wishart, 1936.

LINDSAY, Norman. *The Flyaway Highway*. Sydney, Angus & Robertson, 1936.

——. *The Magic Pudding*. Sydney, Angus & Robertson, 1918.

LOCKEYEAR, J. R. *Mr. Bunyip, or, Mary Somerville's Ramble: A Story for Children*. Melbourne, Dawson, 1871.

MACDONALD, Alexander. *The Invisible Island: A Story of the Far North of Queensland*. London, Blackie, 1911.

——. *The Lost Explorers: A Story of the Trackless Desert*. London, Blackie, 1907.

——. *The Mystery of Diamond Creek*. London, Blackie,1927.

MACDONALD, Donald. *At the End of the Moonpath*. Melbourne, Whitcombe & Tombs, 1922.

——. *The Warrigals' Well: A North Australian Story*. London, Ward Lock, 1901.

MacINTYRE, Elisabeth. *It Looks Different When You Get There*. Lane Cove, N.S.W., Hodder and Stoughton, 1978.

MACK, Louise. *Girls Together*. Sydney, Angus and Robertson, 1898.

——. *Teens: A Story of Australian Schoolgirls*. Sydney, Angus and Robertson, 1897.

MACKNESS, Constance. *Miss Pickle: The Story of an Australian Boarding-School*. London, Humphrey Milford, Oxford University Press, 1924.

MARRYAT, Augusta. *The Young Lamberts: A Boy's Adventures in Australia*. London, Frederick Warne, n.d. (first published 1878).

MARSON, Charles L. *Faery Stories*. Adelaide, E. A. Petherick, 1891.

MARTIN, David. *The Cabby's Daughter*. Hornsby, N.S.W., Hodder and Stoughton, in association with Brockhampton Press, 1974.

——. *The Chinese Boy*. Hornsby, N.S.W., Hodder and Stoughton, 1973.

——. *Hughie*. Melbourne, Nelson, 1971.

——. *The Man in the Red Turban*. Richmond, Victoria, Hutchinson of Australia, 1978.

MEREDITH, Louisa Anne. *Tasmanian Friends and Foes Feathered, Furred, and Finned*. Hobart, J. Walch, 1880.

MILLER, Rosalind. *The Adventures of Margery Pym*. London, Hutchinson, n.d.

NOONAN, Michael. *The Golden Forest: The Story of Oonah the Platypus*. Sydney, Angus and Robertson, 1947.

NORMAN, Lilith. *Climb a Lonely Hill*. London, Collins, 1970.

——. *The Shape of Three*. London, Collins, 1971.

NORRIS, Emilia Marryat. *The Early Start in Life*. London, Griffith & Farran, [1867].

O'HARRIS, Pixie (pseud.). *Marmaduke the Possum*. Sydney, Angus and Robertson, 1942.

OTTLEY, Reginald. *By the Sandhills of Yamboorah*. London, André Deutsch, 1965.

——. *Rain Comes to Yamboorah*. London, André Deutsch, 1967.

——. *The Roan Colt of Yamboorah*. London, André Deutsch, 1966.

——. *The War on William Street*. London, Collins, 1971.

OUTHWAITE, Ida Rentoul. *The Enchanted Forest* by Ida Rentoul Outhwaite and Grenbry Outhwaite. London, A. & C. Black, 1921.

——. *The Little Fairy Sister* by Ida Rentoul Outhwaite and Grenbry Outhwaite. London, A. & C. Black, 1923.

PAICE, Margaret. *The Bensens*. London, Collins, 1968.

——. *Run to the Mountains*. Sydney, Collins, 1972.

PARK, Ruth. *Playing Beatie Bow*. West Melbourne, Nelson, 1980.

PARKER, K. Langloh. *Australian Legendary Tales*. London, Nutt, 1896 (reprinted, Bodley Head, 1978).

——. *More Australian Legendary Tales*. London, Melville, Mullen & Slade, 1898.

PARKER, Margaret. *For the Sake of a Friend: A Story of School Life*. London, Blackie, 1896.

PEDLEY, Ethel C. *Dot and the Kangaroo*. London, Thomas Burleigh, 1899.

PHIPSON, Joan. *Bass & Billy Martin*. South Melbourne, Macmillan, 1972.

——. *The Boundary Riders*. London, Constable, 1962.

——. *The Cats*. London, Macmillan, 1976.

——. *The Crew of the Merlin*. London, Constable Young Books, 1966.

——. *The Family Conspiracy*. London, Constable, 1962.

——. *Good Luck to the Rider*. Sydney, Angus and Robertson, 1953.

——. *Helping Horse*. London, Macmillan, 1974.

——. *Keep Calm*. London, Macmillan, 1978.

——. *Threat to the Barkers*. London, Constable Young Books, 1963.

——. *A Tide Flowing*. Sydney, Methuen, 1981.

——. *The Way Home*. London, Macmillan, 1973.

PITMAN, Emma. *Florence Godfrey's Faith: A Story of Australian Life*. London, Blackie, 1882.

[PORTER, Sarah]. *Alfred Dudley, or, The Australian Settlers*. London, Harvey and Darton, 1830.

POTTER, Dora Joan. *With Wendy at Winterton School*. London, Humphrey Milford, Oxford University Press, 1945.

PYKE, Lillian. *The Best School of All*. London, Ward Lock, 1921.

——. *The Lone Guide of Merfield*. London, Ward Lock, 1925.

——. *Max the Sport*. London, Ward Lock, 1916.

——. *A Prince at School*. London, Ward Lock, 1919.

——. *Sheila the Prefect*. London, Ward Lock, 1923.

——. *Three Bachelor Girls*. London, Ward Lock, 1926.

RAYMENT, Tarlton. *The Prince of the Totem: A Simple Black Tale for Clever*

White Children. Melbourne, Robertson and Mullens, 1933.

RENTOUL, Annie R. *The Little Green Road to Fairyland* by Annie R. Rentoul and Ida Rentoul Outhwaite. London, A. & C. Black, 1922.

RICHARDSON, Robert. *Black Harry, or, Lost in the Bush.* Edinburgh, William Oliphant, 1877.

——. *The Cold Shoulder, or, A Half-Year at Craiglea.* Edinburgh, William Oliphant, 1876.

——. *Our Junior Mathematical Master, and, A Perilous Errand.* Edinburgh, William Oliphant, 1876.

ROBERTS, Beth. *Manganinnie.* South Melbourne, Macmillan, 1979.

[ROWE, Richard]. *The Boy in the Bush.* London, Strahan, 1872 (first published 1869).

——. *Roughing It in Van Diemen's Land, Etc.* London, Strahan, 1880.

ST. JOHNSTON, Alfred. *In Quest of Gold, or, Under the Whanga Falls.* London, Cassell, 1885.

SARGENT, George. *Frank Layton: An Australian Story.* London, Religious Tract Society, n.d. (first published 1865).

SCOTT, Bill. *Boori.* Melbourne, Oxford University Press, 1978.

——. *Darkness Under the Hills.* Melbourne, Oxford University Press, 1980.

SHELLEY, Noreen. *Faces in a Looking-Glass.* London, Oxford University Press, 1974.

——. *Family at the Lookout.* London, Oxford University Press, 1972.

SOUTHALL, Ivan. *Ash Road.* Sydney, Angus and Robertson, 1965.

——. *Bread and Honey.* Sydney, Angus and Robertson, 1970.

——. *Finn's Folly.* Sydney, Angus and Robertson, 1969.

——. *Hills End.* Sydney, Angus and Robertson, 1962.

——. *Josh.* Sydney, Angus and Robertson, 1971.

——. *To the Wild Sky.* Sydney, Angus and Robertson, 1967.

——. *What About Tomorrow?* London, Angus and Robertson, 1977.

SPENCE, Eleanor. *A Candle for Saint Antony.* London, Oxford University Press, 1977.

——. *The Green Laurel.* London, Oxford University Press, 1963.

——. *Jamberoo Road.* London, Oxford University Press, 1969.

——. *Lillipilly Hill.* London, Oxford University Press, 1960.

——. *The Nothing-Place.* London, Oxford University Press, 1972.

——. *The October Child.* London, Oxford University Press, 1976.

——. *Patterson's Track.* Melbourne, Oxford University Press, 1958.

——. *The Seventh Pebble.* Melbourne, Oxford University Press, 1980.

——. *The Summer In Between.* London, Oxford University Press, 1959.

——. *The Switherby Pilgrims*. London, Oxford University Press, 1967.

——. *The Year of the Currawong*. London, Oxford University Press, 1965.

STEBBING, Grace. *Edward Bertram, or, The Emigrant Heir*. London, Marcus Ward, 1882.

STOW, Randolph. *Midnite: The Story of a Wild Colonial Boy*. Melbourne, F. W. Cheshire, 1967.

STREDDER, Eleanor. *Archie's Find: A Story of Australian Life*. London, Nelson, 1890.

[STRETTON, Hesba]. *Enoch Roden's Training*. London, Religious Tract Society, [1865].

SYRED, Celia. *Cocky's Castle*. Sydney, Angus and Robertson, 1966.

TALBOT, Ethel. *That Wild Australian School-girl*. London, Robert South, 1925.

[TANDY, Sophia]. *The Children in the Scrub: A Story of Tasmania*. London, Religious Tract Society, [1878].

THIELE, Colin. *Blue Fin*. Adelaide, Rigby, 1969.

——. *February Dragon*. Adelaide, Rigby, 1965.

——. *Storm Boy*. Adelaide, Rigby, 1963.

——. *The Sun on the Stubble*. Adelaide, Rigby, 1961.

——. *Uncle Gustav's Ghosts*. Adelaide, Rigby, 1974.

THOMPSON, C. K. *King of the Ranges: the Saga of a Grey Kangaroo*. Sydney, Dymocks Book Arcade, 1945.

——. *Monarch of the Western Skies: the Story of a Wedge-Tailed Eagle*. Sydney, Dymock's Book Arcade, 1946.

THOMPSON, Valerie. *Gold on the Wind*. Sydney, Collins, 1977.

——. *The Mountain Between*. Sydney, Collins, 1981.

——. *Rough Road South*. Sydney, Collins, 1975.

TIMMS, E. V. *The Valley of Adventure: A Story for Boys*. Sydney, Cornstalk Publishing Company, 1926.

TIMPERLEY, W. H. *Bush Luck: An Australian Story*. London, Religious Tract Society, n.d. (first published 1892).

TURNER, Ethel. *The Camp at Wandinong*. London, Ward Lock, 1898.

——. *Captain Cub*. London, Ward Lock, 1917.

——. *The Cub*. London, Ward Lock, 1915.

——. *The Family at Misrule*. London, Ward Lock & Bowden, 1895.

——. *Flower o' the Pine*. London, Hodder and Stoughton, 1914.

——. *Fugitives From Fortune*. London, Ward Lock, 1909.

——. *Jennifer, J*. London, Ward Lock, 1922.

——. *John of Daunt*. London, Ward Lock, 1916.

——. *Judy and Punch*. London, Ward Lock, 1928.

——. *King Anne*. London, Ward Lock, 1921.

——. *The Little Larrikin*. London, Ward Lock, 1896.

——. *Little Mother Meg*. London, Ward Lock, 1902.

——. *Mother's Little Girl*. London, Ward Lock, 1904.

——. *Nicola Silver*. London, Ward Lock, 1924.

——. *St. Tom and the Dragon*. London, Ward Lock, 1918.

——. *Seven Little Australians*. London, Ward Lock and Bowden, 1894.

——. *The Stolen Voyage*. London, Ward Lock, 1907.

——. *Three Little Maids*. London, Ward Lock, 1900.

——. *The Wonder-Child: An Australian Story*. London, Religious Tract Society, 1901.

TURNER, Lilian. *An Australian Lassie*. London, Ward Lock, 1903.

——. *Betty the Scribe*. London, Ward Lock, 1906.

——. *The Lights of Sydney, or, No Past is Dead*. London, Cassell, 1896.

——. *Paradise and the Perrys*. London, Ward Lock, 1908.

——. *The Perry Girls*. London, Ward Lock, 1909.

——. *Three New Chum Girls*. London, Ward Lock, 1910.

——. *War's Heart Throbs*. London, Ward Lock, 1915.

VILLIERS, Alan. *Whalers of the Midnight Sun: A Story of Modern Whaling in the Antarctic*. Sydney, Angus and Robertson, 1949 (first published 1934).

WALL, Dorothy. *Blinky Bill and Nutsy: Two Little Australians*. Sydney, Angus & Robertson, 1937.

——. *Blinky Bill Grows Up*. Sydney, Angus & Robertson, 1934.

——. *Blinky Bill: the Quaint Little Australian*. Sydney, Angus & Robertson, 1933.

WALPOLE, Andrew. *The Black Star: A School Story for Boys*. Sydney, Cornstalk Publishing Company, 1925.

WELDRICK, Valerie. *Time Sweep*. London, Hutchinson, 1976.

WESTBURY, Atha. *Australian Fairy Tales*. London, Ward Lock, 1897.

WHITFELD, J. M. *The Spirit of the Bush Fire and Other Australian Fairy Tales*. Sydney, Angus & Robertson, 1898.

WILSON, T. P. (pseud.). *Frank Oldfield, or, Lost and Found: A Tale*. London, Nelson and the United Kingdom Band of Hope Union, 1877.

WRIGHTSON, Patricia. *Behind the Wind*. Richmond, Victoria, Hutchinson, 1981.

——. *The Crooked Snake*. Sydney, Angus and Robertson, 1955.

——. *The Dark Bright Water*. Richmond South, Victoria, Hutchinson, 1978.

——. *Down to Earth*. Richmond, Victoria, Hutchinson of Australia, 1965.

——. *'I Own the Racecourse.'* London, Hutchinson, 1968.

——. *The Ice Is Coming.* Richmond South, Victoria, Hutchinson, 1977.

——. *The Nargun and the Stars.* Richmond, Victoria, Hutchinson, 1973.

——. *An Older Kind of Magic.* London, Hutchinson, 1972.

——. *The Rocks of Honey.* Sydney, Angus and Robertson, 1960.

Other Sources

Manuscripts

Angus and Robertson Papers (ML).

Bruce Papers (SLV), MS.9975.

Papers of Ethel Turner, 1888-1948 (ML), MS.667.

Ethel Turner Papers (NLA), MS.749.

Ethel Turner Diaries (ML), Microfilm FM 4/6539-6541.

Papers of Curlewis Family, 1881-1966 (ML), MS.2159.

Newspapers and Periodicals

Age (Melbourne).

Australian Boys' Paper (Melbourne).

Australian Town and Country Journal (Sydney).

Australian Woman's Mirror (Sydney).

Blackwood's Magazine (Edinburgh).

Boy's Own Paper (London).

Bulletin (Sydney).

Leader (Melbourne).

Parthenon (Sydney).

Windsor Magazine (London).

Books and Articles

ADAMS, J. D. 'Australian Children's Literature: a history to 1920'. *Victorian Historical Magazine* (Melbourne), 38, February 1967: pp. 6-28.

ALCOTT, Louisa May. *Little Women.* New York, Macmillan, 1962 (first published 1868).

ALDERMAN, Belle. 'Research in Children's Literature in Australia'. *Reading Time* (Canberra), April 1983: pp. 10-28.

ALLAN, Fran. 'The Role of Angus & Robertson in the Development of Australian Children's Literature'. Melbourne, Melbourne State College, 1977.

ANDERSON, Hugh (ed.). *The Singing Roads: a Guide to Australian Children's Authors and Illustrators.* 2nd ed. Surry Hills, N.S.W., Wentworth Press, 1966.

AUCHMUTY, Rosemary. 'The Schoolgirl Formula'. *Meanjin* (Melbourne) 36, 3, 1977: pp. 391-9.

Australia and Its Settlements. London, Religious Tract Society, [c. 1854].

Australian Dictionary of Biography. Melbourne University Press, 1966-83.

AVERY, Gillian. *Childhood's Pattern.* Leicester, Brockhampton Press, 1975.

——. *Nineteenth Century Children: Heroes and Heroines in English Children's Stories, 1780-1900.* London, Hodder & Stoughton, 1965.

BAGNOLD, Enid. *National Velvet.* London, Vanguard Library, 1953 (first published 1935).

BALLANTYNE, R. M. *The Coral Island.* New York, Garland, 1977 (first published 1858).

BARKER, A. W. (ed.). *Dear Robertson: Letters to an Australian Publisher.* Sydney, Angus & Robertson, 1982.

BLAINEY, Geoffrey. *Wesley College: the First Hundred Years* by G. Blainey, J. Morrissey and S. E. K. Hulme. Melbourne, Council of Wesley College with Robertson & Mullens, 1967.

BLOUNT, Margaret. *Animal Land: the Creatures of Children's Fiction.* London, Hutchinson, 1974.

BOLDREWOOD, Rolf (pseud.). *Robbery Under Arms.* London, Collins, 1954 (first published 1888).

BOYD, Martin. *The Cardboard Crown.* London, Cresset Press, 1952.

——. *The Montforts.* London, Constable, 1928.

BRATTON, J. S. *The Impact of Victorian Children's Fiction.* London, Croom Helm, 1981.

BRAZIL, Angela. *The Nicest Girl in the School.* London, Blackie, 1909.

BRINK, Carol Ryrie. *Caddie Woodlawn.* New York, Macmillan, 1950 (first published 1935).

BRUCE, Dorita Fairlie. *Dimsie Among the Prefects.* London, Oxford University Press, 1923.

——. *Dimsie Goes to School.* London, Oxford University Press (first published 1921).

BUCHAN, John. *The Thirty-Nine Steps.* Edinburgh, Blackwood, 1915.

——. *John Macnab.* London, Hodder & Stoughton, 1925.

BUICK, Barbara and WALKER, M. 'Books for Children' in Bennett, B. (ed.). *The Literature of Western Australia.* Nedlands, University of Western Australia Press, 1979.

BURNETT, Frances Hodgson. *Little Lord Fauntleroy.* London, Dent, 1962 (first published 1886).

——. *A Little Princess.* London, Warne, n.d. (first published 1888).

——. *The Secret Garden.* London, Heinemann, 1957 (first published 1911).

CADOGAN, Mary. *You're a Brick, Angela! A New Look at Girls' Fiction from 1839 to 1975* by Mary Cadogan and Patricia Craig. London, Gollancz, 1976.

CARROLL, Lewis (pseud.). *Alice's Adventures in Wonderland*. London, Bodley Head, 1974 (first published 1865).

CAWELTI, John. *Apostles of the Self-Made Man*. Chicago, University of Chicago Press, 1965.

CHESTERTON, G. K. *The Club of Queer Trades*. London, Harper,1905.

CLARKE, Marcus. *His Natural Life*. Harmondsworth, Middlesex, Penguin Books, 1970 (first published 1874).

——. *Marcus Clarke*. Edited by Michael Wilding. Brisbane, University of Queensland Press, 1976. (Portable Australian Authors).

COE, R. N. 'Portrait of the Artist as a Young Australian: Childhood, Literature and Myth'. *Southerly* (Sydney), June 1981, pp. 126-62.

The Colonial Child: Papers presented at the 8th Biennial Conference of the Royal Historical Society of Victoria, Melbourne, 12-13 October 1979. Edited by Guy Featherstone. Melbourne, Royal Historical Society of Victoria, 1981.

COOLIDGE, Susan (pseud.). *What Katy Did at School*. London, Collins, 1963 (first published 1873).

COOPER, Susan. *The Dark is Rising*. London, Chatto & Windus, 1973.

CROMPTON, Richmal. *Just–William*. London, Newnes, 1922.

CROUCH, Marcus. *The Nesbit Tradition: the Children's Novel 1945-1970*. London, Benn, 1972.

——. *Treasure Seekers and Borrowers: Children's Books in Britain, 1900-1960*. London, Library Association, 1962.

CUTT, M. N. *Ministering Angels: A Study of Nineteenth Century Evangelical Writing for Children*. Wormley, Five Owls Press, 1979.

DARK, Eleanor. *The Timeless Land*. London, Collins, 1949.

DARTON, F. J. Harvey. *Children's Books in England: Five Centuries of Social Life*. 2nd ed. Cambridge, Cambridge University Press, 1966.

DEFOE, Daniel. *The Life and Adventures of Robinson Crusoe*. Harmondsworth, Middlesex, Penguin Books, 1965 (first published 1719).

DENING, G. *Xavier: A Centenary Portrait*. Melbourne, Old Xavierians' Association, 1978.

DEVANEY, James. *The Vanished Tribes*. Sydney, Cornstalk Publishing Company, 1929.

DOUGLAS, B. A. 'A Bibliography of Early Australian Children's Books Held at the E.R.C., Melbourne State College' by B. A. Douglas and A. Hanzl. Melbourne State College, 1977.

DUGAN, Michael (comp.). *The Early Dreaming: Australian Children's Authors on Childhood*. Brisbane, Jacaranda, 1980.

DUTTON, G. *The Vital Decade: Ten Years of Australian Art and Letters* by G. Dutton and M. Harris. Melbourne, Sun Books, 1968.

DYSON, Edward. *The Golden Shanty: Short Stories.* Selected, with an introduction by Norman Lindsay. Sydney, Angus & Robertson, 1976 (first published 1963).

EGOFF, Sheila (ed.). *Only Connect: Readings on Children's Literature.* Edited by S. Egoff, G. T. Stubbs and L. F. Ashley. Toronto, Oxford University Press, 1969.

——. *The Republic of Childhood.* London, Oxford University Press, 1967.

——. *Thursday's Child: Trends and Patterns in Contemporary Children's Literature.* Chicago, American Library Association, 1981.

EYRE, Frank. *British Children's Books in the Twentieth Century.* London, Longmans, 1971. Revised edition of his *Twentieth Century Children's Books, 1900-1950.* London, Longmans, 1952.

——. *Oxford in Australia, 1890-1978.* Melbourne, Oxford University Press, 1978.

——. 'Oxford University Press and Children's Books'. *School Library Journal* (New York), October 1978: pp. 107-11.

FARJEON, Eleanor. *A Nursery in the Nineties.* London, Gollancz, 1935.

FARRAR, F. W. *Eric, or, Little by Little.* London, Ward Lock, 1910 (first published 1858).

FIELDING, Sarah. *The Governess.* London, Oxford University Press, 1968 (first published 1749).

FISHER, Margery. *Intent Upon Reading: A Critical Appraisal of Modern Fiction for Children.* 2nd ed. Leicester, Brockhampton Press, 1964.

FORBES, Esther. *Johnny Tremain.* Boston, Houghton Mifflin, 1943.

FRANKLIN, Miles. *My Brilliant Career.* Edinburgh, Blackwood, 1901.

FREEMAN, Gillian. *The Schoolgirl Ethic: the Life and Works of Angela Brazil.* London, Allen Lane, 1976.

GILDERDALE, Betty. *A Sea Change: 145 Years of New Zealand Junior Fiction.* Auckland, Longman Paul, 1982.

GOLDING, William. *Lord of the Flies.* London, Faber, 1954.

GRAHAME, K. *The Wind in the Willows.* London, Methuen, 1932 (first published 1908).

GREEN, R. L. *Tellers of Tales.* Rev. ed. London, Kaye & Ward, 1969.

GREEN, Samuel G. *The Story of the Religious Tract Society for One Hundred Years.* London, Religious Tract Society, 1899.

GUNN, Jeannie. *We of the Never-Never.* London, Hutchinson, 1908.

HABBERTON, John. *Helen's Babies.* London, Routledge, n.d.(first published 1876).

HANSEN, I. V. *Young People Reading: the Novel in Secondary Schools.* Melbourne

University Press, 1973.

HAVILAND, Virginia. *The Travelogue Story Book of the Nineteenth Century*. Boston, Horn Book, 1950.

HAZARD, Paul. *Books, Children and Men*. Translated by M. Mitchell. Boston, Horn Book, 1963 (first published 1944).

HEALY, J. J. *Literature and the Aborigine in Australia, 1770-1975*. St. Lucia, University of Queensland Press, 1978.

HENTY, G. A. *For Name and Fame*. London, Blackie, n.d. (first published 1886).

HOLLINDALE, Peter. *Choosing Books for Children*. London, Elek, 1974.

HUGHES, Felicity. 'The Bars on the Nursery Window: an Essay on Children's Literature and Literary Theory'. *Reading Time*. (Canberra), October 1980: pp. 4-11.

——. 'Value for Sixpence: an Essay on Fantasy and Criticism'. *Reading Time* (Canberra), Jan. 1981: pp. 16-21.

HUGHES, Thomas. *Tom Brown's School Days*. London, Dent, 1949 (first published 1857).

INGLIS, Fred. *The Promise of Happiness: Value and Meaning in Children's Fiction*. Cambridge University Press, 1981.

KELLY, R. Gordon. 'Children's Literature' in *Handbook of American Popular Culture*. Westport, Conn., Greenwood Press, 1978. Vol. 1, pp. 49-76.

——. *Mother Was a Lady: Self and Society in Selected American Children's Periodicals, 1865-1890*. Westport, Conn., Greenwood Press, 1974.

KIDDLE, Margaret. *Caroline Chisholm*. Melbourne University Press, 1950.

——. *Men of Yesterday: A Social History of the Western District of Victoria, 1834-1890*. Melbourne University Press, 1961.

KINGSFORD, M. R. *The Life, Work and Influence of William Giles Kingston*. Toronto, Ryerson Press, 1947.

KINGSLEY, H. *The Recollections of Geoffry Hamlyn*. London, Macmillan, 1859.

KINGSTON, W. H. G. *Emigrant Manuals*. London, Society for the Propagation of Christian Knowledge, 1851.

KIPLING, Rudyard. *Stalky & Co*. London, Macmillan, 1899.

LANSBURY, Coral. *Arcady in Australia: the Evocation of Australia in Nineteenth-Century English Literature*. Melbourne University Press, 1970.

LAWRENCE, D. H. *Kangaroo*. Harmondsworth, Middlesex, Penguin Books, 1950 (first published 1923).

LAWSON, Henry. *The Prose Works*. Sydney, Angus & Robertson, 1948.

——. *Collected Verse*. Edited by C. Roderick. Sydney, Angus & Robertson, 1967-69, 3 vols.

LESLIE, Shane. *The Oppidan*. London, Chatto & Windus, 1922.

LINDSAY, Norman. *Redheap*. London, Faber and Faber, 1930.

——. *'Saturdee'*. London, T. Werner Laurie, 1936.

McINNES, Graham. *The Road to Gundagai*. Melbourne, Sun Books, 1967 (first published 1965).

McVITTY, Walter. *Innocence and Experience: Essays on Contemporary Australian Children's Writers*. Melbourne, Nelson, 1981.

MARRYAT, Frederick. *The Children of the New Forest*. London, Dent, 1951 (first published 1847).

——. *Masterman Ready*. London, Dent, 1948 (first published 1841-42).

——. *Mr. Midshipman Easy*. London, A. & C. Black, 1930 (first published 1836).

MARTINEAU, Harriet. *The Crofton Boys*. London, Routledge, 1856 (first published 1841).

MASTERMAN, K. C. 'Nan Chauncy, 1900-1970', *Reading Time* (Sydney), July 1975, pp. 35-42.

MEADE, L. T. *A World of Girls: the Story of a School*. London, Cassell, n.d. (first published 1886).

MILLER, Edmund Morris. *Australian Literature from its Beginnings to 1935*. Melbourne University Press, 1940.

——. *Australian Literature: a Bibliography to 1938, extended to 1950* by F. T. Macartney. Sydney, Angus & Robertson, 1956.

MONTGOMERY, L. M. *Anne of Green Gables*. Sydney, Cornstalk Publishing Company, 1924 (first published 1908).

MUIR, Marcie. *Australian Children's Book Illustrators*. Melbourne, Sun Books, 1977.

——. *A Bibliography of Australian Children's Books*. London, André Deutsch, 1970-76, 2 vols.

——. *Charlotte Barton: Australia's First Children's Author*. Sydney, Wentworth Books, 1980.

——. *A History of Australian Childrens Book Illustration*. Melbourne, Oxford University Press, 1982.

NESBIT, E. *The Story of the Amulet*. Harmondsworth, Middlesex, Penguin Books, 1959 (first published 1906).

NIALL, Brenda. *Seven Little Billabongs: The World of Ethel Turner and Mary Grant Bruce*. Melbourne University Press, 1979.

The Open Hearted Audience. Edited by V. Haviland. Washington, D.C., Library of Congress, 1980.

PARKER, K. Langloh. *My Bush Book*. Edited by Marcie Muir. Adelaide, Rigby, 1982.

PEARCE, Philippa. *Tom's Midnight Garden*. London, Oxford University Press,

1958.

PENTON, Brian. *Landtakers: the Story of an Epoch*. Sydney, Endeavour Press, 1934.

PHELAN, Nancy. *A Kingdom by the Sea*. Sydney, Angus & Robertson, 1980 (first published 1969).

QUIGLEY, Isabel. *The Heirs of Tom Brown: The English School Story*. London, Chatto & Windus, 1982.

QUAYLE, Eric. *The Collector's Book of Boys' Stories*. London, Studio Vista, 1973.

——. *The Collector's Book of Children's Books*. London, Studio Vista, 1971.

RANSOME, Arthur. *Swallows and Amazons*. London, Jonathan Cape, 1930, and others by this author.

RAYMOND, Ernest. *Tell England: A Study in a Generation*. London, Cassell, 1953 (first published 1922).

REED, Talbot Baines. *The Fifth Form at St. Dominic's: A School Story*. London, Blackie, 1951 (first published 1887).

REES, David. *Marble in the Water: Essays on Contemporary Writers of Fiction for Children and Young Adults*. Boston, Horn Book, 1979.

REID, Ian. 'Sheep Without a Fold, Publishing and Fiction-Writers in the Thirties'. *Meanjin* (Melbourne), 33, June 1974, pp. 163-9.

RICHARDSON, Henry Handel (pseud.). *The Getting of Wisdom*. London, Heinemann, 1910.

RINGER, J. B. 'W. H. G. Kingston: A Borrower Afloat'. *Turnbull Library Record* (Wellington, N.Z.), 13, 1, May 1980, pp. 26-32.

——. *Young Emigrants: New Zealand Juvenile Fiction 1833-1919*. Hamilton, N.Z., 1980.

RUDD, Steele (pseud.). *On Our Selection*. Sydney, The Bulletin, 1899.

SAKI (pseud.). 'Sredni Vashtar' in *The Short Stories of Saki*. New York, Modern Library, 1958, pp. 151-5.

SALINGER, J. D. *The Catcher in the Rye*. Harmondsworth, Middlesex, Penguin Books in association with Hamish Hamilton, 1958 (first published 1951).

SALWAY, Lance (ed.). *A Peculiar Gift: Nineteenth Century Writings on Books for Children*. Harmondsworth, Middlesex, Kestrel Books, 1976.

SAXBY, H. M. *A History of Australian Children's Literature*. Sydney, Wentworth Books, 1969-71, 2 vols.

SHERWOOD, M. M. *The History of the Fairchild Family*. London, Hatchard, 1841-47, 3 vols.

SINCLAIR, Catherine. *Holiday House: A Book for the Young*. London, Hamish Hamilton, 1972 (first published 1839).

Society & Children's Literature: Papers Presented on Research, Social History, and

Children's Literature at a Symposium . . . 1976. Edited by James H. Fraser. Boston, David R. Godine in association with American Library Association, 1978.

SOUTHALL, Ivan. *A Journey of Discovery: On Writing for Children*. Harmondsworth, Middlesex, Kestrel Books, 1975.

SPENCE, Catherine Helen. *Clara Morison*. London, John W. Parker, 1854.

THOMPSON, Valerie. 'Feet on the Ground: the Yass-Port Phillip Road, 1838'. *The Push from the Bush* (Canberra) No. 3, December 1979, pp. 3-18.

Through Folklore to Literature: Papers Presented at the Australian National Section of I.B.B.Y. Conference on Children's Literature. Edited by M. Saxby. Sydney, I.B.B.Y. [International Board of Books for Young People] Australia Publications, 1979.

THWAITE, Mary F. *From Primer to Pleasure*. London, Library Association, 1963.

TOWNSEND, John Rowe. *A Sounding of Storytellers*. Harmondsworth, Middlesex, Kestrel Books, 1979.

A Track to Unknown Water: Proceedings of the Second Pacific Rim Conference on Children's Literature, Melbourne 1979. Edited by Stella Lees. Melbourne, Melbourne State College, 1980.

TRAVERS, P. L. *Mary Poppins*. London, Peter Davies, 1948 (first published 1934).

TREASE, Geoffrey. *Bows Against the Barons*. London, Martin Lawrence, 1934.

——. *Tales Out of School*. 2nd ed. London, Heinemann, 1964.

TUCKER, Nicholas. *The Child and the Book: a Psychological and Literary Exploration*. Cambridge University Press, 1981.

——. (ed.). *Suitable for Children: Controversies in Children's Literature*. London, Chatto & Windus for Sussex University Press, 1976.

TURNER, E. S. *Boys Will Be Boys*. New revised ed. London, Michael Joseph, 1957.

TURNER, Ethel. *The Diaries of Ethel Turner*. Compiled by Philippa Poole. Sydney, Ure Smith, 1979.

TWAIN, Mark (pseud.). *The Adventures of Huckleberry Finn*. London, Dent, 1955(first published 1884).

——. *Tom Sawyer*. London, Collins, 1957 (first published 1876).

——. *Tom Sawyer, Detective as Told to Huck Finn, and Other Tales*. London, Chatto & Windus, 1909 (first published 1896).

UTTLEY, Alison. *A Traveller in Time*. London, Faber, 1966 (first published 1939).

VACHELL, Horace Annesley. *The Hill: A Romance of Friendship*. London, John Murray n.d. (first published 1905).

VAIZEY, Mrs. George de Horne. *Pixie O'Shaughnessy*. London, Religious

Tract Society, 1900.

WALKER, Maxine. *Writers Alive: Current Australian Authors of Books for Children.* Perth, Westbooks, 1977.

WARNER, Phillip. *The Best of British Pluck: the 'Boy's Own Paper' Revisited.* London, Macdonald and Janes, 1977.

WEBSTER, Jean. *Daddy Long-legs.* London, Hodder and Stoughton, 1941 (first published 1912).

WHITE, Antonia. *Frost in May.* London, Virago, 1978 (first published 1933).

Who's Who of Children's Literature. Compiled and edited by Brian Doyle. London, Hugh Evelyn, 1968.

WIGHTON, Rosemary. *Early Australian Children's Literature.* Surrey Hills, Victoria, Casuarina Press, 1979 (first published 1963).

WILDER, Laura Ingalls. *Little House in the Big Woods.* New York, Harper & Row, 1953 (first published 1937).

WILLIAMSON, Henry. *Tarka the Otter.* London, Bodley Head, 1965 (first published 1927).

WODEHOUSE, P. G. *Mike and Psmith.* London, Jenkins, 1953 (first published 1909).

The World of the Public School. Introduced by George Macdonald Fraser. London, Weidenfeld & Nicolson, 1977.

YONGE, Charlotte M. *The Daisy Chain, or, Aspirations: A Family Chronicle.* London, Macmillan, 1888 (first published 1856).

Index

Compiled by Frances O'Neill

Where subject headings within the index have been divided according to period (e.g. 'religion in colonial period'), the time is that of the novel's publication, not its setting.